D0545958

International

THE LIBRARY

University of Ulster at Magee

Due Back (subject to recall)

- 6 MAY 2011		
2 5 OCT 2011		

Fines will apply to items returned after due date

1323U0011/0238/09/07

International Tax Handbook

2nd Edition

Published by
Tottel Publishing Ltd
Maxwelton House
41–43 Boltro Road
Haywards Heath
West Sussex
RH16 1BJ

ISBN 978 1 84766 294 1
© Nexia International 2009
This edition published 2009

British Library Cataloguing-in-Publication Data
A catalogue record for this book is available from the British Library

Typeset by Phoenix Photosetting, Chatham, Kent
Printed and bound in Great Britain by
Athenæum Press Limited, Gateshead, Tyne & Wear

Contents

Introduction

This book has been produced by Nexia International, a leading international network of independent accounting and consulting firms with 520 offices in over 100 countries. I would like to thank all the contributors for their invaluable assistance.

Each chapter provides an overview of the tax system in the relevant country and deals with information generally sought by businesses to understand the fiscal regime.

This book has been prepared in a tabular format to unify the content of each chapter and highlight the core tax aspects for each country. Each section is split into corporate, personal and indirect taxes which should provide the reader with an overview of the tax system in place in a specific country.

Every effort has been taken to ensure that the information provided in this book is accurate and up to date. However, it is only meant to provide a general overview of the prevailing tax system and should not be used as a substitute for professional tax advice.

Neither the author nor the publishers can accept any responsibility for any loss sustained by any person relying on the information provided in this book and failing to seek appropriate professional advice.

Therefore, I would like to stress the importance of obtaining local advice before any action is taken or decision is made. Any queries can be addressed to the local Nexia offices directly, using the contact information provided in the Nexia Contacts Chapter at the end of the book, or to the Nexia Secretariat.

Rajesh Sharma
(rajesh.sharma@smith.williamson.co.uk)

Editor
January 2009

Nexia International
Tel: +44 20 7487 4648
Fax: +44 20 7487 3484
E-mail: info@nexia.com
Web: www.nexia.com

Glossary

CGT	Capital Gains Tax
CT	Corporate Tax (tax on income of corporation)
IHT	Inheritance Tax
PE	Permanent establishment (PE) is a fixed place of business, such as a place of management, a branch, an office, a factory, a workshop, an installation or structure for the exploration of natural resources, any place of extraction of natural resources, a building site or construction or installation project, through which the business is carried on. An agent acting on behalf of the company may also constitute a PE if he has and habitually exercises the authority to do business on behalf of the company.
SME	Small and medium-sized enterprise
VAT	Value Added Tax

Argentina

(Graciela Valles, bg@bga.com.ar)

I MAIN LEGAL FORMS

Legal form Characteristics	Partnership and Limited Liability Partnership (LLP)	Ltd (private corporation) and Plc (public corporation)
Partners/shareholders • Number • Restrictions	• Minimum partners: two • LLP: maximum 50	• Minimum shareholders: two • No maximum limit
Directors	Partnerships are not treated as separate legal persons LLP: at least one manager must be appointed	Ltd minimum: single director with an alternate should be appointed. The majority of directors must be resident in Argentina Plc: directors, Statutory Auditors' Committee (SAC) and Shareholders' Surveillance Committee (SSC) are mandatory
Establishment	Partnership deed	Statutes approved by shareholders
Registration	Partnership, LLP and Ltd: with the Public Registry of Corporations Plc: with the Public Registry of Corporations and the National Securities Commission	
Minimum capital	Partnership: none LLP: ARS 12,000	Ltd: ARS 12,000 Plc: ARS 2,100,000
Liability	Partnerships: unlimited liability Limited to subscribed capital for LLP	Limited to subscribed shares
Governance	Partnership deed for Surveillance Committee	
Audit requirements	Annual audit report of financial statements is required	
Taxation	Companies are subject to corporation tax. LLPs are transparent for tax purposes	
Usage	Small businesses	Large capital businesses

II   CORPORATION TAX

Legal form / Description	Resident corporation	Permanent establishment (PE)
General description	Corporation tax	
Taxable entities	Resident companies are liable to corporation tax on their worldwide profits	Non-resident companies are liable to corporation tax only on the profits derived in Argentina
Taxable income	Worldwide profits	Profits derived by PE in Argentina
Calculation of taxable profits	Accounting profit is adjusted for various tax add-backs and allowances to arrive to profits chargeable to corporation tax	
Interest payments	Interest paid or accrued is deductible Thin capitalisation rules apply to related party loans	
Related party transactions	All related party transactions must take place on arm's length basis	
Tax year, return and payment	Tax year is normally the financial year of the company Taxpayer must prepare a return determining taxable income and assessing the tax One part of the return provides figures from the taxpayer's financial statements and must be signed by an independent accountant 10 monthly advance tax payments, based on the previous year's tax liability are due commencing on the 6th month of the financial year	
Capital gains	Capital gains and losses are assessed to corporation tax Losses arising on the sale of shares may only be offset against similar profits	
Losses	The losses can be carried forward for 5 years	
Tax group	None	
Tax rate	35%	

III TAXES FOR INDIVIDUALS

<table>
<tr><td colspan="2"></td><td colspan="5">**Residents**</td><td>**Non-residents**</td></tr>
<tr><td rowspan="8">Income Tax</td><td>General description</td><td colspan="6">Tax levied on the chargeable income of a chargeable person for a year of assessment</td></tr>
<tr><td>Taxable entities and taxable income</td><td colspan="5">Residents are taxed on their worldwide income</td><td>Non-residents are taxed on income arising in Argentina, through withholding</td></tr>
<tr><td>Types of taxable income</td><td colspan="6">• Property income (usually rent)
• Income from capital investment (interest, sale of goodwill, dividends, royalties, annuities)
• Income from business activities
• Employment from personal services or pensions</td></tr>
<tr><td>Calculation of income</td><td colspan="6">Tax is calculated on earned taxable income after deduction of necessary expenses to obtain and preserve the income
Personal allowances (basic, family, etc) are available</td></tr>
<tr><td>Tax year, tax assessment and tax payment</td><td colspan="6">• Tax year – calendar year
• Tax assessment – returns must be filed in April of the following year</td></tr>
<tr><td>Losses</td><td colspan="6">Tax losses can be carried forward for 5 years</td></tr>
<tr><td>Tax rates</td><td colspan="6">

Taxable income		**Basic**	**Plus**	**On the**
From ARP	**To ARP**	**tax ARP**	**%**	**excess of ARP**
0	10,000	0	9	0
10,001	20,000	900	14	10,000
20,001	30,000	2,300	19	20,000
30,001	60,000	4,200	23	30,000
60,001	90,000	11,100	27	60,000
90,001	120,000	19,200	31	90,000
120,001+	No limit	28,500	35	120,000

</td></tr>
<tr><td rowspan="2">Capital Gains Tax (CGT)</td><td>General description</td><td colspan="6">Tax on increase in the value of asset between acquisition and disposal, not chargeable to income or corporate tax</td></tr>
<tr><td>Taxable entities and chargeable assets</td><td colspan="6">As a general rule, capital gains are not taxable for individuals, although capital gains made in the course of business are assessed to income tax</td></tr>
<tr><td colspan="2"></td><td colspan="5">**Domiciled**</td><td>**Non-domiciled**</td></tr>
<tr><td rowspan="2">Inheritance Tax (IHT)</td><td>General description</td><td colspan="6">No inheritance tax – N/A</td></tr>
<tr><td>Taxable entities and chargeable assets</td><td colspan="6">There are no gift or inheritance taxes levied in Argentina</td></tr>
</table>

IV   WITHHOLDING TAXES

	Payments to non-residents[1]
Dividends	Nil[2]
Interest	Tax rate 35% on assumed taxable income of 43%
Royalties	Tax rate 35% on assumed taxable income of 60% (technical assistance) or 80% (licences)
On payments to artists and sportsmen	35% on assumed taxable income of 70%

1   Reduced rates of withholding tax may apply where there is an appropriate double tax treaty.
2   Excess of book profit dividends over tax profit are subject to full and final payment of 35% on such excess.

V   INDIRECT TAXES

		Residents	Non-residents
Value Added Tax (VAT)	General description	Tax on the supply of goods and services	
	Entities being obliged to levy VAT	Individuals, partnerships and corporations supplying goods and services in Argentina	
	Taxable activities	Supply and import of goods and services	
	Taxable activities – zero rated (examples)	N/A	
	Exemptions (examples)	• Exports of goods and services are tax exempt • Books, publishing, newspapers are exempt • Life insurance and annuities are exempt • Educational services provided by authorised institutions are exempt	
	Refund of VAT	Exporters' VAT on purchases is reimbursable	
	Tax liability	• VAT on supplies must be paid in the following month. VAT incurred by businesses can be offset against VAT invoiced to clients • Withholding schemes on VAT invoiced are applicable	
	Tax rates	• General tax rate: 21% • Gas, electricity and telecommunication are taxed at 27% • Certain farming products: 10.5% • Machinery and spare parts specifically designated: 10.5%	
	Administrative obligations	Recording of sales and purchases on special forms	
Stamp Duty Land Tax		Covered by Stamp Duty below	
Stamp Duty		• Provinces apply a stamp tax on contracts, promissory notes, banker's drafts, and certain other documents. The most common rate is 1% • In the city of Buenos Aires the stamp duty has been withdrawn except on the transfer or lease of real estate where the rate applicable varies in accordance to the value of the transaction (with a maximum rate of 2.5%)	

Australia

(Stephen Rogers, srogers@nexiacourt.com.au)

I MAIN LEGAL FORMS

Characteristics \ Legal form	Partner-ship	Limited partnership	Private company	Public company	Trust
Partners/ Shareholders	Two or more	At least one general partner, at least one limited partner	One or more	One or more	One or more trustees
Number	20	20	None	None	None
Restrictions	None	None	None	None	None
Directors	Management by partners		One or more	Three or more	One or more trustees
Foundation	Partnership deed		Constitution		Trust deed
Registration	None		ASIC	ASIC	None
Minimum capital	None	None	None	None	None
Liability	Unlimited to all partners	Unlimited for general partner, limited to capital for limited partner	Limited to capital for all shareholders	Generally limited to capital for all shareholders Companies limited by guarantee limited to members' respective contributions	Trust property
Governance	Partner meeting	Partner meeting	Director's meeting Shareholders' meeting		Trustees' meeting

Legal form / Characteristics	Partnership	Limited partnership	Private company	Public company	Trust
Audit requirements	None	None	None – if over any two of following must audit: • gross revenue $10m • gross assets $5m • 50 employees	Yes	None
Taxation	Pass-through entity	Corporate limited partnerships effectively treated as companies for tax purposes. Partners' drawings deemed to be dividends Foreign limited partnerships – such as a US LLC or UK LLP, can be treated as 'flow-throughs' in Australia in certain circumstances Venture capital limited partnerships treated as ordinary partnerships	Subject to company tax, but can pay franked dividends to shareholders	Subject to company tax, but can pay franked dividends to shareholders	Subject to trustee resolution, is a pass-through entity

II CORPORATION TAX

	Resident corporations	Non-resident corporations
General	30% federal tax	Australian permanent establishment (PE) and sale of Australian property
Other	No state income taxes or trade taxes	
Taxation in Australia	Incorporated in Australia, or management and control in Australia – worldwide income	Australian PE or management and control in Australia
Calculation of taxation income	Accounting profit X Plus/Minus Tax timing differences Y Plus/Minus Tax permanent differences $\underline{Z}$ Australian taxation income $\underline{T}$	
Interest payments	Thin capitalisation rules: De minimis exemption: <u>$250,000 or less</u> *Safe Harbour*: Interest bearing debt of 75% of average net value of assets of Australian entity, plus any surplus value in associated entities	
Related party transactions	Strict adherence to the arm's length principle Very detailed transfer pricing methodologies, procedures and requirements	
Tax year and tax payments	• Tax year = 1 July to 30 June • Annual federal tax return • Quarterly prepayments final payment or refund after tax assessment	
Capital gains	Taxable at regular company tax rate (30%) (no concessions as for individuals and trusts)	Since December 2006 capital gains are now limited to Australian land, shares in land-rich companies, sale of Australian branch assets and Australian mining/prospecting rights
Losses	• No carry back allowed • Must satisfy Continuity of Ownership (COT) (generally greater than 50% underlying individual ownership) • Concessions on COT test for public companies or • Same Business Test (SBT)	
Tax group – prerequisites	Tax consolidation rules for 100% wholly owned Australian entities – Head entity must be a company	Special rules for PEs and Australian tax consolidation
Company tax rate	30%	
Wealth tax	No wealth tax in Australia	

	Resident corporations	Non-resident corporations
Real Estate Taxes		
1. Stamp duty on transfer of real property	Yes – levied by Australian states – range of 1.25%–5.5% of value of real property	
2. Annual land tax levied by states on commercial and investment properties	Land tax levied by Australian states with tax-free thresholds ranging from $25,000–$599,000 and tax rates ranging from 0.02–2.5% per annum	

III   TAXES FOR INDIVIDUALS

	Residents	Non-residents
General	Australian resident – worldwide income	Australian source income
Calculation of income	Generally cash for salaried employees – accruals if running a business	
Tax year	• Tax year = 1 July to 30 June • Sole individual annual return • Quarterly prepayments	
Capital gains	• Starting point – same as other income • 50% reduction in gain if asset held for more than 12 months	Since December 2006 capital gains are now limited to Australian land, shares in land-rich companies, sale of Australian branch assets and Australian mining/prospecting rights
Losses	• No carry back • Unlimited time in which to utilise	
Tax rates as at 1 July 2008	*Income ($)* *Tax (%)* 0–6,000 Nil 6,001–34,000 15 34,001–80,000 30 80,001–180,000 40 180,001+ 45	*Income ($)* *Tax (%)* 0–34,000 29 34,001–80,000 30 80,001–180,000 40 180,001+ 45
Tax rates as at 1 July 2009	*Income ($)* *Tax (%)* 0–6,000 Nil 6,001–35,000 15 35,001–80,000 30 80,001–180,000 38 180,001+ 45	*Income ($)* *Tax (%)* 0–35,000 29 35,001–80,000 30 80,001–180,000 38 180,001+ 45
Other	No wealth tax and no inheritance tax in Australia (but there are CGT issues on the death of an individual). However, note also there are minimum superannuation requirements for Australian employees	

IV   WITHHOLDING TAXES

	Non-residents
Employment income	Same for employment in Australia
Dividends	• Nil if fully franked • 30% to non-treaty country • 5%–15% for treaty country and depending on number of shares held
Interest	Generally 10% for treaty and non-treaty
Royalties	• Between 5% and 15% for treaty countries • 15% for non-treaty countries
Payments to artists and sportsmen	• Company tax rate for payments to companies • Foreign resident marginal rates if paid to individuals • Need to also consider relevant Double Taxation Agreement (DTA) article (where appropriate)

V   INDIRECT TAXES

		Residents	Non-residents
Value Added Tax (VAT)	General description	Goods and services tax (GST) on the supply of goods and services	
	Entities being obliged to levy VAT	Federal tax levied by way of GST at all levels of the production/ service chain with right to tax credit	
	Taxable activities	All types of services and goods	
	Taxable activities – zero rated (examples)	A zero rate applies to the export of goods and services	
	Exemptions (examples)	None	
	Refund of VAT	By way of tax credit in the chain of entrepreneurial activity	
	Tax liability	Strict liability with entity rendering service or effecting sale	
	Tax rates	10%	
	Administrative obligations	Precise accounting and documentation required	
Stamp Duty Land Tax		Levied at state level	
Stamp Duty		Imposed on various transactions and conveyances at either a fixed rate or at ad valorem rates	

Austria

(Wolfgang Korp, wolfgang.korp@ketreuhand.at)

I MAIN LEGAL FORMS

Legal form / Characteristics	Partnership (OEG)	Limited Partnership (KG)	Private Corporation (GmbH)	Public Corporation (AG)
Partners/shareholders • Number • Restrictions	• Two or more • No restrictions		• One or more • No restrictions	
Directors	Management by partners		No restrictions	
Foundation	No formal requirements		Notarial deed	
Registration	Commercial Register			
Minimum capital	None	None	€35,000	€70,000
Liability	Unlimited for all partners	Unlimited for general partner, limited for limited partner	Limited for all shareholders	
Governance	• Partner • General meeting		• Managing director • Shareholders' meeting	• Managing director • Supervisory board • Shareholders' meeting
Audit requirements	Generally not		Yes, exemptions for small companies[1]	

---

1 Small companies are companies which do not exceed two of the following criteria: turnover of €9.68m, total assets of €4.84m, 50 employees on average per year.

Legal form / Characteristics	Partnership (OEG)	Limited Partnership (KG)	Private Corporation (GmbH)	Public Corporation (AG)
Taxation	• Partnership considered transparent/no taxation • Partners subject to income tax or corporate tax on their profit shares		• Subject to corporate tax at a rate of 25% • Dividends distributed to individuals subject to withholding tax at 25% giving correspondent tax credit to recipient at 25% of dividend (semi-income system) • Dividends distributed to corporations are tax exempt at level of recipient company (holding privilege) • Minimum taxation of €1,750 pa for GmbH and at €3,500 pa for AG (accountable on future profit, loss carry forward unlimited)	
Usage	Not popular for reason of unlimited liability	Popular as GmbH and Co KG,[2] especially for SMEs	Popular, especially for SMEs	Legal form for listed companies, banks and insurances; usual for others big in size and number of shareholders

---

2 A 'GmbH & Co KG' is a Limited Partnership with a GmbH as general partner; the limited partners may be individuals or corporations as well. A very common structure is the GmbH & Co KG with individuals as limited partners or even with only one limited partner being the only shareholder(s) of GmbH. A variation is the 'AG & Co KG'.

II CORPORATION TAX

Legal form / Description	Resident corporation	Permanent establishment (PE)
General description	Corporation tax	
Taxable entities	Resident companies are liable for corporate income tax on their worldwide income	Non-resident companies are liable for corporate income tax only on Austrian source income
Taxable income	Worldwide profits	Profits derived by PE in Austria
Calculation of taxable profits	Accounting profit is adjusted for various tax add-backs and allowances to arrive to profits chargeable to corporation tax (PCTCT)	
Interest payments	Deductible, no thin capitalisation rules	
Related party transactions	All related party transactions must take place on arm's length basis	
Tax year, return and payment	Calendar year, but the financial year of a company may be any fixed 12-month period Tax is payable in advance in instalments in the middle of each quarter and the residual tax is payable within one month of receipt of an assessment. Interest is added after October the following year	
Capital gains	Included in normal income	
Losses	Carried forward but maximum offset is 75% of the profits	
Tax group	Group taxation introduced by the Tax Reform Act 2005 results in the tax effect that profits or losses of subsidiaries are attributed to the controlling corporation. The only condition for group membership will be a direct or indirect majority investment into a corporation	
Tax rate	25%	

III   TAXES FOR INDIVIDUALS

<table>
<tr><th></th><th></th><th>Residents</th><th>Non-residents</th></tr>
<tr><td rowspan="8">Income Tax</td><td>General description</td><td colspan="2">Tax levied on the chargeable income of a chargeable person for a year of assessment</td></tr>
<tr><td>Taxable entities and taxable income</td><td>Residents are taxed on their worldwide income</td><td>Non-residents are taxed on income arising in Austria</td></tr>
<tr><td>Types of taxable income</td><td colspan="2">• Property income (usually rent)
• Income from capital investment (interest, sale of goodwill, dividends, royalties, annuities)
• Income from business activities
• Employment from personal services or pensions</td></tr>
<tr><td>Calculation of income</td><td colspan="2">Seven so-called schedules (agriculture, professional service, business, employment, rental, capital and 'other')</td></tr>
<tr><td>Tax year, tax assessment and tax payment</td><td colspan="2">• Tax year – rules regarding the tax year, due dates for filing tax returns, assessments and payments are substantially the same as those described for companies
• Tax assessment – residents need not file tax returns if their income consists solely of employment income or employment income plus other income of €730 or less</td></tr>
<tr><td>Losses</td><td colspan="2">Deductible against income from the same category. Excess amounts can be set off against other income in the year</td></tr>
<tr><td>Tax rates</td><td colspan="2">*Band of taxable income (€)*   *Rate of tax applicable to band (%)*
0–10,000   0
10,000–25,000   38.33
25,000–51,000   43.6
51,000+   50</td></tr>
<tr><td rowspan="6">Capital Gains Tax (CGT)</td></tr>
<tr><td>General description</td><td colspan="2">There is no extra CGT</td></tr>
<tr><td>Taxable entities and chargeable assets</td><td colspan="2">Capital gains of individuals and companies are part of their taxable income. Individual non-business capital gains are generally tax-free except from movable items held less than one year, real estate held for less than 10 years and shares if the portion exceeded 1% during the preceding 5 years</td></tr>
<tr><td>Calculation of gain</td><td colspan="2">Sales proceeds minus book value based on acquisition costs</td></tr>
<tr><td>Tax year, tax assessment and tax payment</td><td colspan="2">As for income tax, special rate for capital gains from shares</td></tr>
<tr><td>Losses</td><td colspan="2">• Corporation tax: unlimited carry forward
• Income tax, business income: unlimited carry forward
• Income tax, other income: no carry forward</td></tr>
<tr><td>Tax rates</td><td colspan="2">As above</td></tr>
</table>

		Domiciled	**Non-domiciled**
Inheritance Tax (IHT): cancelled with effect from 1 August 2008 as well as gift tax	General description	Concept of tax equally applying to donations	
	Taxable entities and chargeable assets	Individuals are liable for inheritance and gift tax on property acquired by reason of death or by way of gift. The tax applies to property located in Austria and abroad unless the beneficiary and the deceased individual are both non-resident	
	Calculation of charge	Rates vary according to relationship and value of heritage	
	Taxable events	Death – equal to donation	
	Allowances	Smaller amounts only	
	Tax rates	Rates of tax vary from 2%–60%, depending on the recipient's relationship to the donor or deceased and the value of the property transferred	

IV   WITHHOLDING TAXES

	Payments to non-residents[3]
Dividends	25%
Interest from banks	Nil
Royalties	20%

---

3   Reduced rates of withholding tax may apply where there is an appropriate double tax treaty.

V   INDIRECT TAXES

		Residents	Non-residents
Value Added Tax (VAT)	General description	Tax on the supply of goods and services (VAT)	
	Entities being obliged to levy VAT	Federal tax levied by way of a sales tax at all levels of the production/ service chain with right to tax credit	
	Taxable activities	All types of services	
	Taxable activities – zero rated (examples)	A zero rate applies to the export of goods and services	
	Exemptions (examples)	None, except private sale and smallest not registered for VAT	
	Refund of VAT	By way of tax credit in the chain of business activity	
	Tax liability	Strict liability with entity rendering service or effecting sale	
	Tax rates	Most goods and services in Austria are taxed at 20%, but certain essential goods and services are taxed at 10%	
	Administrative obligations	Precise accounting and documentation required	
Stamp Duty Land Tax		N/A	
Stamp Duty		Numerous cases of deeds and documents are charged with flat or sometimes proportionate duties (eg rental agreements according to duration)	

Bahrain

(Nabeel Al Saie – nabilsai@batelco.com.bh

I MAIN LEGAL FORMS

Legal form / Characteristics	Partnership, Limited Liability Partnership (WLL), Single Person Company (SPC)	BSC (Closed) and BSC (Public)
Partners/shareholders • Number • Restrictions	General partnership: minimum number – two WLL companies: partners should not exceed 50 SPC companies: fully owned by one person	BSC (Closed): number of persons not less than two BSC (Public): minimum number – seven
Directors	No minimum/maximum requirements	BSC (Public): minimum number of directors is five BSC (Closed): minimum number of directors is three
Establishment	In accordance with Bahrain Commercial Companies Law	
Registration	Registration through Bahrain Commercial Companies Law	
Minimum Capital	WLL: BD 20,000 SPC: BD 50,000	BSC (Public): BD 1m BSC (Closed): BD 250,000
Liability	WLL: only liable to the extent of their respective share in the capital Partnership: partners are jointly liable to the extent of all their property of the company's obligations	BSC (Public): liable for the company's debts and obligations only to the extent of the value of their share BSC (Closed): N/A
Governance	As per Memorandum and Articles	Board of Directors and ultimately the equity shareholders in General Meeting
Audit requirements	As per Memorandum and Articles – audit is mandatory	Independent audit report to the shareholders as per the regulations
Taxation	No tax	No tax

II CORPORATION TAX

Legal form / Description	Partnership, Limited Liability Partnership WLL, Single Person Company (SPC)	BSC (Closed) and BSC (Public)
General description	No tax	No tax
Taxable entities	N/A	N/A
Taxable income	N/A	N/A
Calculation of taxable profits	N/A	N/A
Interest payments	Interest is allowed on accrual basis	
Related party transactions	Transactions between related companies or persons are deemed to take place at market value	
Tax year, return and payment	N/A	N/A
Capital Gains	N/A	N/A
Losses	As per the Articles of Association	
Tax group	N/A	N/A
Tax rate	N/A	N/A

III TAXES FOR INDIVIDUALS

<table>
<tr><td colspan="2"></td><th>Residents</th><th>Non-residents</th></tr>
<tr><td rowspan="7">Income Tax</td><td>General description</td><td>N/A</td><td></td></tr>
<tr><td>Taxable entities and taxable income</td><td></td><td></td></tr>
<tr><td>Types of taxable income</td><td></td><td></td></tr>
<tr><td>Calculation of income</td><td></td><td></td></tr>
<tr><td>Tax year, tax assessment and tax payment</td><td></td><td></td></tr>
<tr><td>Losses</td><td></td><td></td></tr>
<tr><td>Tax rates</td><td></td><td></td></tr>
<tr><td colspan="2"></td><th>Residents</th><th>Non-residents</th></tr>
<tr><td rowspan="6">Capital Gains Tax (CGT)</td><td>General description</td><td>N/A</td><td></td></tr>
<tr><td>Taxable entities and chargeable assets</td><td></td><td></td></tr>
<tr><td>Calculation of gain</td><td></td><td></td></tr>
<tr><td>Tax year, tax assessment and tax payment</td><td></td><td></td></tr>
<tr><td>Losses</td><td></td><td></td></tr>
<tr><td>Tax rates</td><td></td><td></td></tr>
<tr><td colspan="2"></td><th>Domiciled</th><th>Non-domiciled</th></tr>
<tr><td rowspan="5">Inheritance Tax (IHT)</td><td>General description</td><td>N/A</td><td></td></tr>
<tr><td>Taxable entities and chargeable assets</td><td></td><td></td></tr>
<tr><td>Calculation of charge</td><td></td><td></td></tr>
<tr><td>Taxable events</td><td></td><td></td></tr>
<tr><td>Allowances</td><td></td><td></td></tr>
<tr><td>Tax rates</td><td></td><td></td></tr>
</table>

IV   WITHHOLDING TAXES

	Payments to residents	Payments to non-residents
Dividends	N/A	N/A
Interest	N/A	N/A
Royalties	N/A	N/A
On payments to artists and sportsmen	N/A	N/A

V   INDIRECT TAXES

		Residents	Non residents
Value Added Tax (VAT)	General description	N/A	
	Entities being obliged to levy VAT		
	Taxable activities		
	Taxable activities – zero rated (examples)		
	Exemptions (examples)		
	Refund of VAT		
	Tax liability		
	Tax rates		
	Administrative obligations		
Stamp Duty Land Tax		N/A	
Stamp Duty		N/A	

Belgium

(Edwin Vervoort, edwin.vervoort@vgd.eu)

I MAIN LEGAL FORMS

Legal form / Characteristics	Partnership	Ltd (private corporation) and Plc (public corporation)
Partners/shareholders • Number • Restrictions	This concept does not exist in Belgium Partnerships are not treated as separate taxable persons	Public limited liability company (NV): at least two shareholders Private limited liability company (BVBA): at least one shareholder (when this is a legal person, the company-subscriber of the whole capital of a BVBA is also jointly responsible for all engagements of the company, as long as the company-shareholder remains the only shareholder)
Directors	N/A	NV: three directors at least or two, in the cases where there are only two shareholders BVBA: at least one director
Establishment	N/A	Notarial deed
Registration	N/A	• Deposit on the registry of the commercial court • Publication in the Belgian Gazette • Inscription in the register of legal persons (Crossroads Bank for Enterprises)
Minimum capital	N/A	NV: €61,500, fully paid and subscribed BVBA: €18,550, fully subscribed €6,200 paid on minimum or €12,400 in the case of one shareholder
Liability	Unlimited	Limited liability The liability is limited to the shares of the shareholders

Legal form / Characteristics	Partnership	Ltd (private corporation) and Plc (public corporation)
Governance	No special rules apply	Board meetings Shareholders' meetings
Audit requirements	N/A	SMEs and large companies are subject to statutory audit
Taxation	Transparent for the purposes	Resident companies are subject to corporation tax on their profits derived anywhere in the world

II   CORPORATION TAX

Legal form / Description	Resident corporation	Permanent establishment (PE)
General description	Corporation tax	
Taxable entities	Resident companies are subject to corporate tax on their worldwide income	Companies with a Belgian PE are taxable on all income derived from such establishment, including foreign source income
Taxable income	Worldwide profits	All income derived from such establishment, including foreign source income
Calculation of taxable profits	Accounting profit is adjusted for various tax add-backs and allowances to arrive to profits chargeable to corporation tax (PCTCT)	
Interest payments	• Interest expenses are tax deductible expenses when these are at arm's length • Thin capitalisation restrictions apply to loan if granted by shareholders or directors; 1:1 debt to equity ratio • For loans granted by a company enjoying an advantageous tax regime the rate is 7:1 debt to equity ratio	
Related party transactions	All related party transactions must take place on arm's length basis and transactions between related parties must be at fair market value	
Tax year, return and payment	Usual tax year coincides with the calendar year, but the accounting year of a company can be fixed for any 12-month period The annual tax return cannot be filed later than 6 months after the end of the accounting period	
Capital gains	Capital gains are subject to the standard corporate income tax rate of 33.99% Capital gains on shares are exempted if certain conditions are met	
Losses	Tax losses can be carried forward indefinitely	
Tax group	Not available	
Tax rate	33.99%	

III TAXES FOR INDIVIDUALS

		Residents	Non-residents
Income Tax	General description	Tax levied on the chargeable income of a chargeable person for a year of assessment	
	Taxable entities and taxable income	Residents are taxed on their worldwide income with some relief for double taxation	Non-residents are taxed on income arising in Belgium
	Types of taxable income	• Property income (usually rent) • Income from capital investment (interest, sale of goodwill, dividends, royalties, annuities) • Income from business activities • Employment from personal services or pensions	
	Calculation of income	The taxable income equals the gross income minus business expenses and minus certain allowances	
	Tax year, tax assessment and tax payment	• Tax year – calendar year • Tax assessment – issued by the Belgian tax authorities by the end of June of the second year following the calendar year • When no form is received by 30 June of the year following the calendar year during which the income is earned, the taxpayer must ask the authorities to send a form	
	Losses	Tax losses of professional activities can be carried forward indefinitely	
	Tax rates	*Income (€)* *Tax rate(%)* 0–7,560 25 7,560–10,760 30 10,760–17,920 40 17,920–32,860 45 32,860+ 50	
Capital Gains Tax (CGT)	General description	In general no capital gains tax for individuals, subject to certain exemptions	

		Belgian domiciled	Non-Belgian domiciled
Inheritance Tax (IHT)	Taxable entities and chargeable assets	If a Belgian tax residency, Belgian inheritance taxes become due	N/A
	Calculation of charge	Based on value of estate, subject to exemptions	
	Taxable events	Any annuity received by an heir, from the estate of a Belgian tax resident	N/A
	Allowances	Varies from region to region	
	Tax rates	Tax rates vary between 3%–27% between parents and children but may reach 80% for non-related persons depending upon total value of assets and the kinship between the deceased and the beneficiary	N/A

IV WITHHOLDING TAXES

	Payments to residents	Payments to non-residents[1]
Dividends	15% or 25%	
Interest	15%	
Royalties	15%	
On payments to artists and sportsmen	19%	

1 Reduced rates of withholding tax may apply where there is an appropriate double tax treaty.

V   INDIRECT TAXES

		Residents	Non-residents
Value Added Tax (VAT)	General description	Tax on the supply of goods and services (VAT)	
	Entities being obliged to levy VAT	Nature of entity is of no relevance. The kind of transactions triggers the VAT status	
	Taxable activities	All goods and services excluding sales of (old) real property, education and cultural activities	
	Taxable activities – zero rated (examples)	Newspapers	
	Exemptions (examples)	• Sales of (old) real property • Education and healthcare • Cultural activities	
	Refund of VAT	Companies dealing in the export of goods and services may receive a reimbursement of VAT on exports on a monthly basis	
	Tax liability	Normally the supplier of goods and services is responsible for charging VAT	
	Tax rates	Standard rate = 21%	
Stamp Duty Land Tax		10% (Flemish Region) or 12.5% in the other regions of Belgium	
Stamp Duty		N/A	

Bolivia

(Willy Tudela, La Paz, willytudela@tztudela.com)

I MAIN LEGAL FORMS

Legal form / Characteristics	Partnership and Limited Liability Partnership (LLP)	Private corporation and Plc (public corporation)
Partners/shareholders • Number • Restrictions	• Minimum of two partners for LLPs and Partnerships • More for corporations	
Directors	Partnerships, LLPs: no restrictions	Minimum three directors
Establishment	Written agreement presented to a public notary which certifies its establishment	
Registration	Chamber of Commerce or Industry – National Tax Service	
Minimum capital	None	
Liability	• Up to the amount of their equity • Limited to capital participation	Up to the amount of their shares
Audit requirements	Financial statements certified by public accountant	
Taxation	Taxable on worldwide income. Partnerships are transparent	
Usage	No restriction	

II   CORPORATION TAX

Legal form / Description	Resident corporation	Permanent establishment (PE)
General description	Corporation tax	
Taxable entities	Taxable entities are both resident and non-resident, except those companies that have services partially provided in Bolivia	Tax is applicable also to non-resident companies doing business in Bolivia
Taxable income	Profits derived in Bolivia	
Calculation of taxable profits	Accounting profit is adjusted for various tax add-backs and allowances to arrive to profits chargeable to corporation tax (PCTCT)	
Interest payments	Interest paid to an official financial institution is accounted as a business cost, interest paid to third persons should be paid with a deduction of 13% VAT and transaction tax of 3%. Interest paid to related parties cannot exceed 30% of the interest paid to third parties	
Related party transactions	All related party transactions must take place on arm's length basis	
Tax year, return and payment	• Fiscal year • Manufacturing, oil and construction industries – 1 April to 31 March • Agricultural and agro-industrial companies – 1 July to 30 June • Mining industries – 1 October to 30 September • Trading, banking, insurance, general services and all other industries not specifically mentioned – 1 January to 31 December	
Capital gains	Taxed as business income	
Losses	Net total losses are accumulated and updated and can be carried forward for unlimited periods until fully utilised against profits	
Tax group	None	
Tax rate	25%	

III   TAXES FOR INDIVIDUALS

		Residents	Non-residents
Income Tax	General description	Tax levied on the chargeable income of residents' and non-residents' income from Bolivian sources	
	Taxable entities and taxable income	Residents are taxed on their territorial income	Non-residents are taxed on income received from Bolivian sources through withholding when payment is made
	Types of taxable income	• Property income (usually rent) • Income from capital investment (interest, sale of goodwill, dividends, royalties, annuities) • Income from business activities • Employment from personal services or pensions	
	Calculation of income	Residents are charged with 13% complementary VAT when receiving salaries and 13% VAT and 3% transaction tax when receiving other kinds of income. Non-residents are charged with a 12.5% income tax on income received	
	Tax year, tax assessment and tax payment	Complementary VAT taxpayers, performing dependent personal services, are subject to a monthly withholding which the employer must apply on the salary payroll	
	Losses	For individuals, if deductions are more than taxable income, the balance is carried forward (compensated) against the next month filed	
	Tax rates	13% income tax	
Capital Gains Tax (CGT)	Taxable entities and chargeable assets	There are no capital gains taxes levied on individuals in Bolivia	

		Bolivia domiciled	Non-Bolivia domiciled
Inheritance Tax (IHT)	General description	Cost of goods transferred by inheritance	
	Taxable entities and chargeable assets	Individuals are levied with an inheritance tax when receiving and declaring the following chargeable assets: real estate property, vehicles, investments and all other assets subject to public registration	
	Calculation of charge	Levied on property received and value of goods subjected to property tax (real estate and vehicles)	
	Taxable events	When a relative dies	
	Allowances	No allowances exist	
	Tax rates	1% inheritance tax 3% transaction tax	

IV   WITHHOLDING TAXES

	Payments to non-residents[1]
Dividends	12.5%
Interest	12.5%
Royalties	12.5%
On payments to artists and sportsmen	12.5%

---

1   Reduced rates of withholding tax may apply where there is an appropriate double tax treaty.

V   INDIRECT TAXES

		Residents	Non-residents
Value Added Tax (VAT)	General description	Tax on the supply of goods and services (VAT)	
	Entities being obliged to levy VAT	All entities selling goods and services are levied with VAT	
	Taxable activities	All goods and services; all phases of production and wholesale or retail selling of goods as well as services and leisure or entertainment activities	
	Taxable activities – zero rated (examples)	N/A	
	Exemptions (examples)	Sale of shares, debentures, securities	
	Refund of VAT	VAT included in export costs is refunded at invoice (of costs) levied with VAT presentation	
	Tax liability	Normally the supplier of goods and services is responsible for charging VAT and paying it	
	Tax rates	Standard rate = 13%	
	Administrative obligations	VAT must be paid during the next month (day 13 through to day 22) depending on the last number of its tax registration number	
Stamp Duty Land Tax		There is no Stamp Duty Land Tax in Bolivia	
Stamp Duty		There is no Stamp Duty in Bolivia	

Brazil

(Ricardo Rodil, rodil@nexia.com.br)

I   MAIN LEGAL FORMS

Legal form / Characteristics	Partnership and Limited Liability Partnership (LLP)	Ltd (private corporation) and Plc (public corporation)
Partners/shareholders • Number • Restrictions	• Two or more • No restrictions, except for certain activities, regarding foreign shareholders/partners	
Directors	Not to have been convicted because of commercial crimes (such as fraudulent bankruptcy)	
Establishment	Articles of Incorporation for LLP and by-laws	
Registration	Articles of Incorporation or by-laws in the Registrar of Commerce	
Minimum capital	None	
Liability	Limited to capital subscribed for	
Governance	No requirements	Representation of minority Listed companies, banks and regulated sector with some specific requirements
Audit requirements	Not mandatory, in general	Mandatory for listed companies, banks, regulated entities and 'accountable entities' regardless of legal form (total assets higher than R$240m or annual gross revenue higher than R$300m)
Taxation	Partnerships are transparent (flow-through entities)	Corporation tax

II   CORPORATION TAX

Legal form / Description	Resident corporation	Permanent establishment (PE)
General description	Corporate income tax	
Taxable entities	Companies resident in Brazil are taxed on their worldwide income	PEs located in Brazil are taxed on their Brazilian income
Taxable income	Worldwide profits	Profits derived by PE in Brazil
Calculation of taxable profits	Accounting profit is adjusted for various tax add-backs and allowances to arrive to profits chargeable to corporation tax (PCTCT) Smaller entities eligible for simplified forms of taxation	
Interest payments	Interest paid on loans and debts either to banks or to other entities is deductible as an operating expense	
Related party transactions	All related party transactions must take place on arm's length basis. Transfer pricing rules apply (similar to international)	
Tax year, return and payment	The tax year corresponds to the calendar year. As a general rule, companies close their financial year at 31 December in order to avoid administrative burden, but they may have a financial year over any 12-month period Payments are usually made during the year, as advances and, after the return is filed, as definite payments	
Capital gains	Capital gains and losses have no special treatment for corporate income tax purposes	
Losses	Carry forward for indefinite time; but offset limited to 30% of taxable income of each subsequent year	
Tax group	Not allowed	
Tax rate	15% on the first R$240,000 of taxable income with the excess subject to an additional 10%, plus a so-called 'social contribution' of 9% on taxable income, resulting in an effective rate of 34%	

III TAXES FOR INDIVIDUALS

		Residents	Non-residents
Income Tax	General description	Tax levied on the chargeable income of a chargeable person for a year of assessment	
	Taxable entities and taxable income	Residents are taxed on their worldwide income with some relief for double taxation	Non-residents are taxed on income arising in Brazil
	Types of taxable income	• Property income (usually rent) • Income from capital investment (interest, sale of goodwill, royalties, annuities) • Income from business activities (except for dividends) • Employment from personal services or pensions	
	Tax year, tax assessment and tax payment	Tax year – calendar year Tax assessment – up to 30 April following year Tax payment: 1–6 monthly instalments	
	Losses	Not allowed to be deducted or carried forward	
	Tax rates	*Calculation/payment on taxable income:* • up to R$1,372.81 – exempt • R$1,372.82–R$2,743.25, apply 15% and deduct R$205.92 • above R$2,743.26, apply 27.5% and deduct R$548.82 *Adjustment/annual basis on taxable income:* • up to R$16,473.72 – exempt • R$16,473.73–R$32,919.00, apply 15% and deduct R$2,471.04 • above R$32,919.00, apply 27.5% and deduct R$6,585.84	
Capital Gains Tax (CGT)	General description	Tax on increase in the value of asset between acquisition and disposal, not chargeable to income or corporate tax	
	Taxable entities and chargeable assets	An individual's capital gains are taxable, although capital losses are not deductible or in any way off-settable	
	Calculation of gain	Proceeds – cost = gain	
	Tax year, tax assessment and tax payment	Tax year – calendar year Tax assessment – up to 30 April following year Tax payment – 1–6 instalments; minimum value of individual instalment applies	
	Losses	Individual cannot deduct losses, as each transaction is considered regardless of other operations	
	Tax rates	15%, due on a monthly basis	
		Domiciled	**Non-domiciled**
Inheritance Tax (IHT)	Taxable entities and chargeable assets	Individuals that donate assets and heirs, regarding the assets received	
	Calculation of charge	4% on amount	
	Taxable events	Donations, legacies, inheritance	
	Allowances	Transactions up to approximately R$17,000 are exempt	
	Tax rates	4%	

IV   WITHHOLDING TAXES

	Payments to non-residents[1]
Dividends	Nil, except if remitted to tax havens[2]
Interest	15% on interest accrued or remitted[2]
Royalties	15%[2]
On payments to artists and sportsmen	25%

1   Reduced rates of withholding tax may apply where there is an appropriate double tax treaty.
2   Withholding taxes levied at 25% for payments to recipients in tax havens.

V INDIRECT TAXES

<table>
<tr><th></th><th></th><th>Residents</th><th>Non-residents</th></tr>
<tr><td rowspan="10">Value Added Tax (VAT)</td><td>General description</td><td colspan="2">Tax on the supply of goods and services (VAT)</td></tr>
<tr><td>Entities being obliged to levy VAT</td><td colspan="2">Companies that manufacture and/or sell products and goods within the country</td></tr>
<tr><td>Taxable activities</td><td colspan="2">Almost all domestic products as well as some services</td></tr>
<tr><td>Taxable activities – zero rated (examples)</td><td colspan="2">Some basic food items</td></tr>
<tr><td>Exemptions (examples)</td><td colspan="2">Exports</td></tr>
<tr><td>Refund of VAT</td><td colspan="2">Usually, credits are negotiated with suppliers</td></tr>
<tr><td>Tax liability</td><td colspan="2">Normally the supplier of goods and services is responsible for charging VAT. Some activities, such as breweries and carmakers, pay the amount for the whole chain when the product leaves the plant</td></tr>
<tr><td>Tax rates</td><td colspan="2">Taxable rates range from 7%–25% for tax administered at state level</td></tr>
<tr><td>Administrative obligations</td><td>Monthly return filing
Special records kept</td><td>N/A</td></tr>
<tr><td colspan="2">Stamp Duty Land Tax</td><td colspan="2">None</td></tr>
<tr><td colspan="2">Stamp Duty</td><td colspan="2">None</td></tr>
</table>

British Virgin Islands (BVI)

(Kenneth Morgan, kenneth.morgan@rawlinson-hunter.vg)

I MAIN LEGAL FORMS

Legal form / Characteristics	Partnership and Limited Liability Partnership (LLP)	Ltd (private corporation) and Plc (public corporation)
Partners/shareholders • Number • Restrictions	• Two or more including at least one general partner • No restrictions	• One or more • No restrictions
Directors	Management by general partner	At least one No BVI resident directors required
Establishment	Partnership agreement	Memorandum and Articles of Association
Registration	Yes but minimal information	Yes but minimal information
Minimum Capital	None	None
Liability	Limited for limited partners only Unlimited liability for other partners	Limited to share capital or contributed capital
Governance	General partner usually	Board of Directors and Shareholders' meetings
Audit requirements	Not required	Not required
Taxation	None	None Payroll tax only if BVI based employees, 2%–6%

II   CORPORATION TAX

Description \ Legal form	Resident corporation	Permanent establishment (PE)
General description	N/A	N/A
Taxable entities	N/A	N/A
Taxable income	N/A	N/A
Calculation of taxable profits	N/A	N/A
Interest payments	N/A	N/A
Related party transactions	N/A	N/A
Tax year, return and payment	N/A	N/A
Capital Gains	N/A	N/A
Losses	N/A	N/A
Tax group	N/A	N/A
Tax rate	N/A	N/A

III TAXES FOR INDIVIDUALS

		Residents	Non-residents
Income Tax	General description	Payroll taxes only on BVI resident employees – generally 8% of salary payable by employees after basic deductions	
	Taxable entities and taxable income	N/A	
	Types of taxable income	N/A	
	Calculation of Income	N/A	
	Tax year, tax assessment and tax payment	N/A	
	Losses	N/A	
	Tax Rates	N/A	

		Residents	Non-residents
Capital Gains Tax (CGT)	General description	No capital gains taxes	
	Taxable entities and chargeable assets	N/A	
	Calculation of gain		
	Tax year, tax assessment and tax payment	N/A	
	Losses	N/A	
	Tax rates	N/A	

		Domiciled	Non-domiciled
Inheritance Tax (IHT)	General description	No inheritance taxes	
	Taxable entities and chargeable assets	N/A	
	Calculation of charge	N/A	
	Taxable events	N/A	
	Allowances	N/A	
	Tax rates	N/A	

IV   WITHHOLDING TAXES

	Payments to residents	Payments to non-residents
Dividends	N/A	N/A
Interest	N/A	N/A
Royalties	N/A	N/A
On payments to artists and sportsmen	N/A	N/A

V   INDIRECT TAXES

		Residents	Non-residents
Value Added Tax (VAT)	General description	No VAT	
	Entities being obliged to levy VAT	N/A	
	Taxable activities	N/A	
	Taxable activities – zero rated (examples)	N/A	
	Exemptions (examples)	N/A	
	Refund of VAT	N/A	
	Tax liability	N/A	
	Tax rates	N/A	
	Administrative obligations	N/A	
Stamp Duty Land Tax		N/A	
Stamp Duty		N/A	

Bulgaria

(Ivaylo Pazvanski, vsi_ko@abv.bg)

I MAIN LEGAL FORMS

Legal form Characteristics	Partnership and Limited Liability Partnership (LLP)	Ltd (private corporation) and Plc (public corporation)
Partners/shareholders • Number • Restrictions	• Minimum: two • None	Can be set up by one or more persons, as well as a public corporation
Directors	A manager, a chairman	A limited liability company is managed by a manager – a public corporation by an executive director
Establishment	District Court	Company Register
Registration	Competent authority in both cases is the District Court, within the scope of which is included the seat of the newly established company. From 1 January 2008 the competent authority is going to be the Company Register	
Minimum capital	There is no such regulation	Minimum capital in case of a limited liability company – 5,000 BGN (€2,560) Minimum capital in case of a joint-stock company – 50,000 BGN (€25,565)
Liability	Partners liable for partnership debt. Unlimited liability for general partner	Limited to the amount of the capital
Governance	Managing bodies: supreme collective body (General Assembly of members of the association) and managing body (could be a Board of Managers, a chairman or a manager)	Ltd: a General Assembly of associates and a manager Plc: • in a single-stage managing system – a Board of Directors and a General Assembly of shareholders • in a two-stage managing system – a Board of Managers, a Supervisory Council and a General Assembly of shareholders

Legal form Characteristics	Partnership and Limited Liability Partnership (LLP)	Ltd (private corporation) and Plc (public corporation)
Audit requirements	Required for joint stock companies. Financial and insurance companies; otherwise no audit if assets are less than 1.5m BGN; turnover less than 2.5m BGN; employees less than 50	
Taxation	Resident entities are subject to corporation tax on worldwide profits	

II CORPORATION TAX

Legal form / Description	Resident corporation	Permanent establishment (PE)
General description	Corporation tax	
Taxable entities	Taxable entities are both resident and non-resident. Companies resident in Bulgaria are taxed on their worldwide income	PEs located in Bulgaria are taxed on their Bulgarian income
Taxable income	Worldwide profits	Profits derived by PE in Bulgaria
Calculation of taxable profits	Accounting profit is adjusted for various tax add-backs and allowances to arrive to profits chargeable to corporation tax (PCTCT)	
Interest payments	All expenses related to the business operations of companies are tax deductible Thin capitalisation rules apply when a company ends up with an accounting loss or when the debt to equity ratio exceeds 3:1	
Related party transactions	All related party transactions must take place on arm's length basis	
Tax year, return and payment	Tax year – calendar year Corporate income tax returns for a tax year must be filed by 31 March of the following year	
Capital gains	Capital gains are included in the taxable income of an enterprise	
Losses	Loss incurred by a company can be carried forward indefinitely as a deduction against future assessable income for 5 years after the year in which the loss was incurred	
Tax group	None	
Tax rate	10% with effect from 1 January 2007	

III   TAXES FOR INDIVIDUALS

		Residents	Non-residents
Income Tax	General description	Tax levied on the chargeable income of a chargeable person for a year of assessment	
	Taxable entities and taxable income	Residents are taxed on their worldwide income with some relief for double taxation	Non-residents are taxed on income arising in Bulgaria
	Types of taxable income	• Property income (usually rent) • Income from capital investment (interest, sale of goodwill, dividends, royalties, annuities) • Income from business activities • Employment from personal services or pensions • Imposed fines and forfeits	
	Calculation of income	Accounting profit is adjusted for various tax add-backs, allowances and exemptions to arrive at the taxable profit	
	Tax year, tax assessment and tax payment	Tax year – calendar year Tax assessment – all individuals liable to tax are required to file an annual tax return by 30 April of the year following the tax year	
	Losses	No specific rules	
	Tax rates	Flat rate of 10% since 1 January 2008	
Capital Gains Tax (CGT)	General description	No separate tax regarding capital gains	
	Taxable entities and chargeable assets	In general, capital gains are treated as normal income and charged at full rates	
	Calculation of gain	Profit from sales of fixed assets and other property is calculated on the difference between sales price and the cost of acquisition reduced by depreciation accrued and expenses incurred on selling that asset	
	Tax year, tax assessment and tax payment	Tax year – calendar year	
		Domiciled	**Non-domiciled**
Inheritance Tax (IHT)	Taxable entities and chargeable assets	Individuals, other than the surviving spouse and relatives in the direct line, inheriting property situated in Bulgaria are subject to inheritance tax. Bulgarian nationals are also subject to inheritance tax on property inherited abroad. The individual liable to the tax is the beneficiary	
	Calculation of charge	Tax levied on market value of assets, when the inheritance exceeds 250,000 BGN	
	Taxable events	Death	
	Tax rates	Tax rates are determined by the municipality the inherited property is located in, and the rate depends on the beneficiary. Namely: • between 0.7% and 1.4% when the beneficiary is a relative in the lateral line • between 5% and 10% when the beneficiary is a person other than mentioned above	

IV   WITHHOLDING TAXES

	Payments to non-residents[1]
Dividends	5%
Interest	10%
Royalties	10%
On payments to artists and sportsmen	10%

1   Reduced rates of withholding tax may apply where there is an appropriate double tax treaty.

V INDIRECT TAXES

<table>
<tr><td colspan="2"></td><th>Residents</th><th>Non-residents</th></tr>
<tr><td rowspan="9">Value Added Tax (VAT)</td><td>General description</td><td colspan="2">Tax on the supply of goods and services (VAT)</td></tr>
<tr><td>Entities being obliged to levy VAT</td><td colspan="2">In general, entities registered for VAT
There are some specific regulations regarding entities not registered for VAT being obliged to levy VAT</td></tr>
<tr><td>Taxable activities</td><td colspan="2">Every business activity, except the activities exempted from VAT under the VAT regulations</td></tr>
<tr><td>Taxable activities – zero rated (examples)</td><td colspan="2">• International transportation of goods and people
• Supplies relating to the international transportation</td></tr>
<tr><td>Exemptions – activities exempted from VAT (examples)</td><td colspan="2">Healthcare; sales of land and property; supplies connected with religion and culture</td></tr>
<tr><td>Refund of VAT</td><td colspan="2">Within 45 days from the date of VAT return submission</td></tr>
<tr><td>Tax liability</td><td colspan="2">By the 14th day of each month taxable persons must pay the liable VAT in accordance with submitted VAT return for the previous VAT period</td></tr>
<tr><td>Tax rates</td><td colspan="2">• Standard rate – 20%
• In specific cases – 7% and 0%</td></tr>
<tr><td>Administrative obligations</td><td colspan="2">Each month a VAT return must be completed relating to the applicable VAT period</td></tr>
<tr><td colspan="2">Stamp Duty Land Tax</td><td colspan="2">N/A</td></tr>
<tr><td colspan="2">Stamp Duty</td><td colspan="2">N/A</td></tr>
</table>

Cameroon

(CLS Audit Conseil, contact@clsauditconseil.com)

I MAIN LEGAL FORMS

Legal form / Characteristics	Partnership and Limited Liability Partnership (LLP)	Ltd (private corporation) and Plc (public corporation)
Partners/shareholders • Number • Restrictions	*Société en nom collectif (SNC):* • at least one partner *Société en Commandite Simple (SCS:)* • at least one partner *Société civile (SC):* • at least one partner	*Société à responsabilité limitée (SARL) or société à responsabilité limitée unipersonnelle (SARLU):* • between one or many shareholders *Société anonyme (SA):* • between one or many shareholders

Directors	*SNC:*
	• One or more managers
	SCS:
	• Unless otherwise stipulated in the company's articles, all the 'commandités' are managers
	• It is possible to choose one or more managers, who can be a partner or not
	SC:
	• One or more manager or partner
		SARL:
		• One or more manager or partner
		SA:
		• *Classic system* – 'conseil d'administration' (CA):
		  – between 3 and 12 members
		  – management of the company by the President of the CA or a 'general director'
		  – management of the company by an 'administrateur directeur général'[1]
		• *Dualistic system* – 'directeur général' and 'conseil d'administration':
		  – the 'directeur général' manages the company
		  – 'conseil d'administration': between 3 and 12 members (checks the 'directeur général')

---

1 Public limited liability companies with not more than three shareholders may not form a board of directors and may appoint a managing director who shall be responsible for administering and managing the company. In this case, the provisions of the first paragraph of Article 417 shall not apply

Legal form / Characteristics	Partnership and Limited Liability Partnership (LLP)	Ltd (private corporation) and Plc (public corporation)
Establishment	Partnership deed	By-laws of company
Registration	All entities to be registered at the Commercial Court and publication of by-laws	
Minimum capital	*SNC, SCS and SC:* • No minimum	*SARL:* • Minimum capital: F CFA 1m *SA:* • Minimum capital: F CFA 10m
Liability	*SNC:* • Jointly and unlimited liability of all debts *SCS:* • 'commandités': joint and unlimited liability of all debts • 'commanditaires': liability limited to their contribution *SC:* • Unlimited liability of all debts	*SARL, SA,* • Liability limited to contribution
Governance	Partnership deed	*SARL and SA:* • Defined by the commercial law
Audit requirements	*SNC, SC and SCS:* • No obligation for audit	*SARL:* • No obligation Except if the company exceeds one of the three following ceilings: • registered capital > F CFA 10m • annual turnover > F CFA 250m • employees > 50 *SA:* • The legal auditor has to certify the corporate accounts annually
Taxation	*SNC, SCS and SC* Each partner subject to personal income tax. From January 2009, taxes should be withheld by the entity	*SARL and SA* Corporate income tax
Usage	*SNC/SCS:* • Used for small businesses *SC:* • Used for patrimonial operations or civil/professional activity or real estate operations	*SARL:* • Start-ups and small or medium-sized companies *SA:* • Listed companies and medium-sized companies

II CORPORATION TAX

Legal form / Description	Resident corporation	Non-resident corporation
General description	Corporation tax	
Taxable entities	The company	Foreign entity
Taxable income	Territoriality principle: tax is only due on business income generated by enterprises operating in Cameroon	
Calculation of taxable profits	Taxable profits result from accountable benefits plus reinstatement less deduction	
Interest payments	Deductible unless paid to shareholders. Certain other restrictions apply	
Related party transactions	All related party transactions must take place on an arm's length basis	
Tax year, return and payment	• Calendar year, or if the taxpayer's financial year does not coincide, the financial year of 12 months closed during the relevant calendar year • Returns to be filed within 2½ months of financial year end • Advance payments required each month, each corporation submits a tax return to the tax administration for the payment in advance of a part of the corporation tax. The amount of this partial payment is equal to 1.1%, 1.65% applied to monthly turnover without VAT	
Capital gains and dividends	• Generally deemed as ordinary income and subject to standard corporate tax rate • Dividends: 10% exempt, 90% of dividends received plus tax credit are subject to corporate income tax • Capital gains: subject to corporate income tax • Capital gains of real estate company are subject to corporate income tax	
Losses	Carried forward for 4 years, it is extended to 5 years for firms with a special statute	
Tax rate	• Standard rate: 38.5% with a minimum of 1.1% of turnover without VAT • Reduced rate for firms with a special statute: 19.25%, 30%	

III   TAXES FOR INDIVIDUALS

		Residents	Non-residents
Income Tax	General description	Income tax	
	Taxable entities and taxable income	Worldwide	Cameroon source income only
	Types of taxable income	• Real estate income • Commercial and non-commercial income (BIC, BNC, BA …) • Salary • Investment income	
	Calculation of income	• Net salary: gross salary less rebate of 30% represents families charges and 500 000 for professional charges • Net real estate rental income • Net income from BIC, BC, BNC, BA.	Net global income
	Tax year, tax assessment and tax payment	• Generally the calendar year	
		• Individuals with business income may be assessed on the basis of an accounting period	
		• One instalment is required on 15 March	
	Losses	A loss in one category of professional income can not be offset against income of another category	
	Tax rates	• Dependent upon income • Progressive tax brackets from 10%–35%	
	Dividends	Taxation to the income progressive tax brackets or optional withholding tax of 16.5%, 15% if the beneficiary is French and 12% if a Tunisian	
Capital Gains Tax (CGT)	General description	Capital gains tax (the products of shares, bonds, income of indebtedness, deposits)	
	Taxable entities and chargeable assets	Disposal of business assets % immovable properties	
	Calculation of gain	*Shares:* proceeds less acquisition costs *Immovable property*: Difference between actual value and the value at the precedent transfer	
	Tax year, tax assessment and tax payment	*Shares:* with tax return *Immovable property:* within 1 month of disposal	
	Exceptions	• Capital gains tax under F CFA 500 000 • Interest of saving account • Interest of certificate of deposit	
	Tax rates	*Shares:* 16.5% *Immovable property:* 10%–35%	

		Residents	**Non-residents**
Inheritance Tax (IHT)	General description	Registration fees	
	Taxable entities and chargeable assets	Each beneficiary is subject to tax	
	Calculation of charge	Levied on the value of all transferred assets less related liabilities. In the case of gifts liabilities are usually not deductible	
	Taxable events	On death and all gifts made prior to death	
	Allowances	N/A	
	Tax rates	Dependent upon the proximity of the relationship between the donor and the recipient and upon the value of the elements transferred: from 2%–10%	

IV WITHHOLDING TAXES

	Payments to non-residents[2]
Dividends	12%, 15%, 16.5%
Interest	16.5%
Royalties	Depending on the treaty
On payments to artists and sportsmen	12%, 15%, 16.5%

2 Reduced rates of withholding tax may apply where there is an appropriate double tax treaty.

V INDIRECT TAXES

		Residents	Non-residents
Value Added Tax (VAT)	Entities being obliged to levy VAT	Persons making taxable supplies of goods and services in the course of a business	
	Taxable activities	Unless expressly exempt, all goods and services are taxable activities	
	Taxable activities – zero rated (examples)	Exports	
	Exemptions (examples)	• Former necessity product • Commission for health insurance	
	Refund of VAT	Quarter reimbursement if VAT refund is greater than F CFA 10m	
	Tax liability	Supplier or provider of services established in Cameroon	
	Tax rates	• 0% exports • 19.25% standard	
	Administrative obligations	VAT return	
Stamp Duty Land Tax		0.11% of the land value	
Stamp Duty		Paid for registration and administrative documents	

Canada

(Jonathan Bicher, bicher@nexiafriedman.ca)

I   MAIN LEGAL FORMS

Legal form / Characteristics	Partnership and Limited Liability Partnership (LLP)	Ltd (private corporation) and Plc (public corporation)
Partners/shareholders • Number • Restrictions	• Two or more • No restrictions but all partners must be Canadian to be a Canadian partnership	• One or more • No restrictions
Directors	Management by partners	Depending on jurisdiction, may need resident directors
Establishment	Partnership agreement (unregistered)	Articles of Incorporation (registered)
Registration	None	Federal or provincial authorities
Minimum capital	None	
Liability	Unlimited for all partners in a general partnership, unlimited for general partners and limited for limited partners in a limited partnership, limited to capital and files involved for LLP	Generally limited to share capital for all shareholders
Governance	• Partners • General meeting	• Board of Directors • Shareholders' meetings
Audit requirements	Not required	Not required for private companies, required for public companies
Taxation	• Not subject to income taxes (pass-through entity) • Partners subject to income tax or corporate tax on their profit share	• Subject to corporate tax and possibly capital tax • Dividends distributed to individuals subject to reduced income tax rate • Dividends distributed to Canadian corporations generally tax-free

II   CORPORATION TAX

Legal form / Description	Resident corporation	Permanent establishment (PE)
General description	Corporation tax	
Taxable entities	Companies incorporated in Canada and foreign companies with management and control located in Canada	PE located in Canada
Taxable income	Worldwide profits	Profits derived by PE in Canada
Calculation of taxable profits	Accounting profit is adjusted for various tax add-backs and allowances to arrive at taxable income	
Interest payments	Thin capitalisation rules on payments to non-arm's length non-residents: • maximum debt/equity ratio of Canadian subsidiaries is 2:1 • excess interest not deductible	
Related party transactions	All related party transactions must take place on arm's length basis	
Tax year, return and payment	• Tax year – business year (calendar or different) • Tax return has to be filed within 6 months after end of the financial year of the company. • Monthly prepayments, final payment generally 2 months after year end	
Capital gains	50% of all realised worldwide capital gains are taxable	50% of certain taxable Canadian properties are taxed on capital gains
Losses	• Business losses must be fully deducted against any income arising in the same year • Losses may be carried back for up to 3 years • Losses may be carried forward for up to 20 years	
Tax group	• Special rules allow groups of commonly controlled Canadian corporations to reorganise on a tax-free basis. This includes the movement of shares and assets and in some cases, capital losses and business losses • Certain reorganisations of company's own debt and share capital can also be done on a tax-free basis • However, consolidated tax returns are not permitted • Associated groups consider group tax attributes to determine limits on tax incentives	N/A
Tax rate	13.50%–50.67%	Non-resident controlled corporations not eligible for low rate on certain business income

III TAXES FOR INDIVIDUALS

		Residents	Non-residents
Income Tax	General description	Federal and provincial income tax on income for individuals	
	Taxable entities and taxable income	Resident individuals are subject to personal income tax on their worldwide income from all sources	Non-resident individuals are taxable generally on income from Canadian sources
	Types of taxable income	• Employment and business • Capital gains • Investment income (eg rental, dividends, interest) • Certain other income	• Employment and business • Capital gains on certain taxable Canadian property (see below) • Rental, if election made • Pension, if election made
	Calculation of income	Aggregate of incomes listed above minus certain tax deductions	
	Tax year, tax assessment and tax payment	• Tax year – calendar year • Self-assessment return is due for filing on 30 April following the end of the tax year • No joint tax return for spouses • Quarterly prepayments, final payment generally due 30 April of following year	• Normally, no tax assessment in case of withholding taxes • Can file Canadian tax returns in certain cases to claim back some withholding taxes • Canadian tax returns may be required if have employment or business income in Canada
	Losses	Non-capital losses can be carried back for 3 years and carried forward for 20 years	

	Tax rates	• Basic personal amount (tax-free earnings):
		  – Federal: $9,600;
		  – Provincial: $7,566–$16,161
		• Progressive tax rates
		• Highest marginal tax rates: 39%–48.2% (depending on province)
			Same as for residents except no personal amounts

Capital Gains Tax (CGT)	General description	Only 50% of realised capital gains are taxable	
	Taxable entities and chargeable assets	Capital gains on worldwide investments	Capital gains generally on Canadian real estate or shares of corporation deriving its value primarily from real estate in Canada and certain other situations
	Calculation of gain	• The excess of the disposal proceeds over the original cost, improvement costs and disposal expenses such as commission and fees • One half of a realised capital gain is taxable, the other half is tax-free	
	Tax year, tax assessment and tax payment	Same tax return as that for all other types of income	
	Losses	Capital losses can be carried back 3 years and forward indefinitely	
	Tax rates	50% of applicable income tax on personal tax rates	

		Domiciled	**Non-domiciled**
Inheritance Tax (IHT)	General description	No inheritance taxes in Canada	
	Tax rates	Canada has no inheritance duties, estate taxes, or gift taxes but there is a deemed disposition of assets at their fair market value upon death, and any gains or losses are realised	

IV WITHHOLDING TAXES

	Payments to non-residents[1]
Dividends	Up to 25%
Interest	Up to 25%
Royalties	Up to 25%
On payments to artists and sportsmen	Up to 24% if service performed in Canada

1 Reduced rates of withholding tax may apply where there is an appropriate double tax treaty.

V   INDIRECT TAXES

<table>
<tr><th></th><th></th><th>Residents</th><th>Non-residents</th></tr>
<tr><td rowspan="9">Value Added Tax (VAT)</td><td>General description</td><td colspan="2">Goods and services tax (GST) is a VAT, some provincial sales taxes (PSTs) are VATs whereas others are charged to the end consumers only</td></tr>
<tr><td>Entities being obliged to levy VAT</td><td colspan="2">Corporations, partnerships and individuals with more than $30,000 of taxable supplies</td></tr>
<tr><td>Taxable activities</td><td colspan="2">Goods and services, unless exempt or zero rated</td></tr>
<tr><td>Taxable activities – zero rated (examples)</td><td colspan="2">For GST, includes prescription drugs and biologicals, medical devices, basic groceries, agricultural and fishing, exports, certain travel and transportation</td></tr>
<tr><td>Exemptions (reduced rate examples)</td><td colspan="2">For GST, includes certain real properties, healthcare, education, legal aid, supplies by charities, financial services</td></tr>
<tr><td>Refund of VAT</td><td>Input tax credits if related to taxable or zero-rated supplies</td><td>If registered for GST, same rules as residents</td></tr>
<tr><td>Tax rates</td><td colspan="2">• GST at 5%
• PST 0%–10%</td></tr>
<tr><td>Administrative obligations</td><td>• Registration if more than $30,000 of taxable supplies ($50,000 for public sector bodies)
• Collecting sales tax
• Filing periodic sales tax returns and remitting balance due</td><td>• Same requirements for residents if non-resident is carrying on business in Canada
• Security may be required if no PE in Canada</td></tr>
<tr><td colspan="2">Stamp Duty Land Tax</td><td colspan="2">Levied by each province at varying rates</td></tr>
<tr><td colspan="2">Stamp Duty</td><td colspan="2">None</td></tr>
</table>

Channel Islands, Guernsey

(Mark Le Ray, mark.leray@saffery.gg)

I   MAIN LEGAL FORMS

Legal form / Characteristics	Partnership and Limited Liability Partnership (LLP)	Ltd (private corporation) and Plc (public corporation)
Partners/shareholders • Number • Restrictions	• Two or more • None	• Private company: one or more, but generally less than 30 • Public company: two or more
Directors	Management by partners	Management by directors
Establishment	Partnership Deed	Articles of Association
Registration	Registration with Registrar of Companies, Guernsey Financial Services Commission	Registration with Registrar of Companies, Guernsey Financial Services Commission
Minimum Capital	None	£1
Liability	• Partners liable either jointly or jointly and severally for debts • LLP: general partners; unlimited liability but liability of partners limited	Limited to capital
Governance	Partners	Directors' meetings, shareholders' meetings
Audit requirements	No audit requirements for partnership or LLP	Not required unless stated in articles
Taxation	Tax transparent partners assessed and share of profits	Resident companies are subject to income tax, usually at 0%, on their profits derived anywhere in the world

II CORPORATION TAX

Legal form / Description	Resident corporation	Permanent establishment (PE)
General description	Liability to Guernsey Income tax, usually at the standard rate of 0%	Liability to Guernsey Income tax, usually at the standard rate of 0%
Taxable entities	Resident companies are subject to income tax at the standard rate of 0% on their worldwide income Certain income is taxable above 0%, being: • certain banking activities (10%) • activities regulated by the Office of Utility Regulation (20%) • Guernsey property income (20%) Certain companies may still be exempt companies, with no liability to tax	Resident companies are subject to income tax at the standard rate of 0% on their worldwide income Certain income is taxable above 0%, being: • certain banking activities (10%) • activities regulated by the Office of Utility Regulation (20%) • Guernsey property income (20%) Certain companies may still be exempt companies, with no liability to tax
Taxable income	Worldwide profits	Worldwide profits, at 0%, if company is Guernsey resident
Calculation of taxable profits	Accounting profit is adjusted for various tax add-backs and allowances to arrive to profits chargeable to income tax	
Interest payments	Relevant interest payments allowed	
Related party transactions	All related party transactions must take place on arm's length basis and transactions between related parties must be at fair market value	
Tax year, return and payment	Tax year – calendar year Profits from trade are assessed on the accounting period ending in the year of assessment Tax is due, in equal instalments, at the end of June and December	
Capital Gains	Capital gains are not subject to tax	
Losses	Loss relief available	
Tax group	Group loss relief is available	
Tax rate	• Standard rate = 0% • See taxable entities for other rates	Exemption from income tax can still be granted in limited circumstances

III TAXES FOR INDIVIDUALS

		Residents	Non-residents
Income Tax	General description	Tax levied on the chargeable income of a chargeable person for a year of assessment	
	Taxable entities and taxable income	Residents are taxed on their worldwide income with some relief for double taxation	Generally not taxable apart from on certain income arising in Guernsey
	Types of taxable income	• Employment, bonuses, casual earnings • Business activities • State/occupational pensions • Property (usually rent) • Investment income (eg interest, dividends, bonds, government stock, settlements, royalties, annuities, deemed distributions)	
	Calculation of income	All income is taxable on a current year basis	
	Tax year, tax assessment and tax payment	Tax year – calendar year Tax assessment – individual returns for each taxpayer Income tax is finalised after the year end. Tax is collected throughout the year on employed persons Interim assessments may be issued with tax payable in June and December (ie payments on account)	
	Losses	Business losses may be offset against other income of the individual	
	Tax rates	20% income tax	
Capital Gains Tax (CGT)	General description	Tax on increase in the value of assets between acquisition and disposal, not chargeable to income tax	
	Taxable entities and chargeable assets	Capital gains are not subject to tax in Guernsey	
	Calculation of gain	N/A	
	Tax year, tax assessment and tax payment	N/A	
	Losses	N/A	
	Tax rates	N/A	
		Domiciled	**Non-domiciled**
Inheritance Tax (IHT)	General description		
	Taxable entities and chargeable assets	There is no estate or inheritance tax in Guernsey	
	Calculation of charge	N/A	
	Taxable events	N/A	
	Allowances	N/A	
	Tax rates	N/A	

IV   WITHHOLDING TAXES

	Payments to non-residents
Dividends	0%
Interest	0%
Royalties	0%
On payments to artists and sportsmen	First £2,000 = 0% Thereafter 20%

V INDIRECT TAXES

		Residents	Non-residents
Value Added Tax (VAT)	General description	Tax on the supply of goods and services	
	Entities being obliged to levy VAT	There is no VAT, or sales tax, in Guernsey	
	Taxable activities	N/A	
	Taxable activities – zero rated (examples)	N/A	
	Exemptions (examples)	N/A	
	Refund of VAT	N/A	N/A
	Tax liability	N/A	
	Tax rates	N/A	
	Administrative obligations	N/A	N/A
Stamp Duty Land Tax		There is no stamp duty land tax	
Stamp Duty		Stamp duty on some property transactions	

Channel Islands, Jersey

(Michael Weston, michael.weston@ifgint.com)

I MAIN LEGAL FORMS

Legal form / Characteristics	Partnership and Limited Liability Partnership (LLP)	Ltd (private corporation) and Plc (public corporation)
Partners/shareholders • Number • Restrictions	• Two or more • None	• Private company: one or more, but generally less than 30 • Public company: two or more
Directors	Management by partners	Management by directors
Establishment	Partnership deed	Articles of Association
Registration	Registration with Registrar of Companies, Jersey Financial Services Commission	
Minimum capital	None	£1
Liability	• Partners liable either jointly or jointly and severally for debts • LLP: general partners; unlimited liability but liability of partners limited	Limited to capital
Governance	Partners	Directors' meetings, shareholders' meetings
Audit requirements	No audit requirements for partnership or LLP	Not required unless stated in articles
Taxation	Tax transparent partners assessed and share of profits	Resident companies are subject to corporation tax on their profits derived anywhere in the world
Usage	• Partnerships: professional firms • LLPs – non-residents	• Small and medium-sized enterprises • Public companies used by larger entities generally seeking a listing on Stock Exchange or AIM

II   CORPORATION TAX

Legal form / Description	Resident corporation	Permanent establishment (PE)
General description	Corporation tax	
Taxable entities	Resident companies are subject to corporate tax on their worldwide income From 3 June 2008 Jersey resident companies are taxed at 0% or 10%. Instead Jersey resident shareholders of these companies are taxed on a deemed dividend basis. Non-resident shareholders are not taxed on cash dividends or interest paid by such companies	Exemption from income tax is granted to companies incorporated in other jurisdictions that are controlled in Jersey
Taxable income	Worldwide profits	All income derived from such establishment, including foreign source income
Calculation of taxable profits	Accounting profit is adjusted for various tax add-backs and allowances to arrive to profits chargeable to corporation tax (PCTCT)	
Interest payments	Qualified interest payments allowed	
Related party transactions	All related party transactions must take place on arm's length basis and transactions between related parties must be at fair market value	
Tax year, return and payment	• The year of assessment for income tax is the calendar year • Profits from trade are normally assessed on a preceding year basis • Taxpayers are issued with assessments in the year following the year of assessment and tax is payable the day following the issue of an assessment	
Capital gains	Capital gains are not subject to tax	
Losses	Loss relief available	
Tax group	Group relief for losses available for qualifying financial services companies. Companies taxed at 0% and which are part of a group allowed to pass on losses so as to offset the profits of another company in the group	
Tax rate[1]	From 3 June 2008 Jersey resident companies are taxed at either 0% or 10%	Exemption from income tax is granted to companies incorporated in other jurisdictions that are controlled in Jersey

---

1   There is a proposal to reduce the rate to 0% (except for financial service providers, taxable at 10%) with effect from 1 January 2009.

III TAXES FOR INDIVIDUALS

		Residents	Non-residents
Income Tax	General description	Tax levied on the chargeable income of a chargeable person for a year of assessment	
	Taxable entities and taxable income	Residents are taxed on their worldwide income with some relief for double taxation	Not taxable
	Types of taxable income	• Property income (usually rent) • Income from capital investment (interest, sale of goodwill, dividends, royalties, annuities) • Income from business activities • Employment from personal services or pensions	
	Calculation of income	• Property – current year basis • Trading – current year basis • Investment – current year basis • Employment – current year basis	
	Tax year, tax assessment and tax payment	• Tax year – calendar year. • Tax assessment – individual self-assessment returns for each taxpayer • Income tax is assessed about 11 months following the year of assessment • Employees pay income tax as a deduction from their earnings throughout the year under the Income Tax Instalment Scheme (ITIS). Any balance remaining when the assessment is issued then requires settlement	
	Losses	N/A	
	Tax rates	20% income tax Some personal allowances and interest payments relief are being phased out over the next 5 years	
Capital Gains Tax (CGT)	General description	Tax on increase in the value of asset between acquisition and disposal, not chargeable to income or corporate tax	
	Taxable entities and chargeable assets	Capital gains are not subject to tax	
		Domiciled	**Non-domiciled**
Inheritance Tax (IHT)	Taxable entities and chargeable assets	There is no estate or inheritance tax in Jersey	

IV   WITHHOLDING TAXES

	Payments to non-residents
Dividends	Nil
Interest	20%
Royalties	20%
On payments to artists and sportsmen	20%

V INDIRECT TAXES

		Residents	Non-residents
Goods and Services Tax (GST)	General description	Tax on the supply of goods and services (GST)	
	Entities being obliged to levy (GST)	From 1 May 2008 registered businesses required to apply GST at standard rate of 3% on consumption of imported and locally produced goods/services. They will be able to deduct from their quarterly payments of any tax they have collected the GST they have incurred. International Services Entities, which are mainly financial service entities, may apply for an alternative to the GST registration for businesses scheme. This alternative to GST registration primarily serves non-residents	
Land Transaction Tax		This tax, equivalent to stamp duty, collects tax on some property transactions not previously caught by the stamp duty legislation. This law awaits enactment but expected shortly	
Stamp Duty		Stamp duty on some property transactions	

Chile

(David Barros, david.barros@humphreys.cl)

I MAIN LEGAL FORMS

Legal form / Characteristics	Partnership and Limited Liability Partnership (LLP)	Ltd (private corporation) and Plc (public corporation)
Partners/shareholders • Number • Restrictions	• From 2–50 partners, who have property rights • Changes to the by-laws must be approved unanimously	• More than two stock holders. • Both kinds of companies are subject to the Corporations Act of 1981
Directors	N/A	Minimum: three directors
Registration	By-laws in public deed, registered and published Public Corporations must register with the Superintendence of Corporations and file periodic information	
Minimum capital	None	
Liability	Limited to rights ownership for LLPs General partnerships unlimited	Limited to capital ownership
Governance	Partners Legal representative	Assembly of Shareholders Board of Directors General manager
Audit requirements	None (IFRS not applicable; use of GAAPs instead)	Private corporations: None Public corporations: Yes (IFRS applicable from 2009, only to public corporations)
Taxation	Resident companies taxable on worldwide profits Partnerships are transparent	
Usage	Small businesses; family owned businesses; wholly owned subsidiaries	Joint ventures; medium-sized and large companies. By law, banks, insurance companies, pension funds managing companies, etc

II   CORPORATION TAX

Legal form / Description	Resident corporation	Permanent establishment (PE)
General description	Company or 'first category' tax	
Taxable entities	Basic entities are deemed to be resident, for tax purposes, if they are incorporated or indentured in the country	Income derived by PE in Chile
Taxable income	Chilean income on accrued basis and income from foreign sources received by Chilean residents (see double taxation treaties below)	
Calculation of taxable profits	All operating and non-operating income is treated as taxable income with relief for all operating and non-operating expenses incurred in producing this income	
Interest payments	Transfer pricing rules are in place that require funding arrangements to be at arm's length for interest payments to remain tax deductible	
Related party transactions	All related party transactions must take place on arm's length basis	
Tax year, return and payment	• Tax period normally coincides with calendar year • Annual tax return must be filed by the following 30 April • Business entities are required to make monthly provisional payments against their annual tax liabilities. The annual net balance of the tax liability accrued after deductions of provisional payments is due, or recoverable, with the filing of the return in April	
Capital gains	Capital gains are tax exempt if derived from transactions of first public offerings and listed corporations, with qualified market presence	
Losses	Losses may be carried forward indefinitely	
Tax group	None	
Tax rate	17%	
Double taxation treaties	See www.sii.cl/pagina/jurisprudencia/convenios.htm	
Free trade agreements	See www.aduana.cl/prontus_aduana_eng/site/edic/base/port/international_agree.html	

III TAXES FOR INDIVIDUALS

		Residents	Non-residents
Income Tax	Taxable entities and taxable income	Any individual becomes tax resident if he stays in the country for 6 months or more in one year, or more than 6 months in total in 2 consecutive years Any person resident or domiciled in Chile must pay tax on their worldwide income	Subject to tax only on income arising in Chile, during the first 3 years
	Types of taxable income	• Property income (usually rent) • Income from capital investment (interest, sale of goodwill, dividends, royalties, annuities) • Income from business activities • Employment from personal services or pensions	
	Taxable income	• Gross earnings less social security payments (with limits) • Individuals are also covered by the double taxation treaties	
	Tax year, tax assessment and tax payment	• Tax year – calendar year • Employees pay a withheld scaled tax rate monthly as sole requirement, without further filings • Persons receiving income from more than one source and independent service providers must file an annual tax return	
	Losses	No specific rules	
	Tax rates	Tax rate computed on a progressive marginal scale, exempt up to US$11,000 pa and increasing from 5% (up to US$25,000 pa) to 40% for income equivalent to US$125,000 or more per year	15%–30% on gross compensations, with no allowances or deductions, depending on type of activity
Capital Gains Tax (CGT)	General description	Investments in shares of listed companies that comply with stock exchange IPOs and general public offerings, are exempt from capital gains tax	

		Domiciled	Non-domiciled
Inheritance Tax (IHT)	General description	Tax is applied to assessed inheritable estate	
	Taxable entities and chargeable assets	All legal inheritors	
	Calculation of charge	The tax base includes the whole inventory of assets and liabilities in the estate: property, securities, funds in every form, vehicles, participations in businesses, etc, less debts, each one valued according to the specifications in the law. If the originator was married under a connubial society regime only 50% of the estate is subject to this procedure	
	Taxable events	Death	
	Allowances	Equivalent to US$42,000 per inheritor	
	Tax rates	Gifts and inheritances are subject to a progressive tax that goes up to 25% on the net amount, after deducting expenses and allowances	

IV   WITHHOLDING TAXES

	Payments to non-residents[1]
Dividends	35%. The 17% corporate income tax paid is credited to this tax
Interest	4% when paid to a bank, otherwise can go up to 35%
Royalties	30%
On payments to artists and sportsmen	20%
On payments to service providers who perform work of technical or engineering nature	15%

---

1   Reduced rates of withholding tax may apply where there is an appropriate double tax treaty.

V INDIRECT TAXES

		Residents	Non-residents
Value Added Tax (VAT)	Entities being obliged to levy VAT	• All entities that transfer title of a new good on a recurring basis • All entities that sell commercial services	
	Taxable activities	Supply of goods and services, imports of goods, etc	
	Taxable activities – zero rated (examples)	N/A	
	Exemptions (examples)	• Life assurance • Exports and insurance relating to exports • Property • Sale of used fixed assets • Personal services rendered by employees or by independent contractors	
	Refund of VAT	If in a given month credit exceeds debit, the difference may be carried forward and added to the credit of the next month	
	Tax liability	Normally the supplier of goods and services is responsible for charging VAT	
	Tax rates	19% flat rate	
	Administrative obligations	Tax payable monthly	
Land Tax		Land and buildings, including housing that exceeds a certain value are taxed at 2% each year on the taxable valuation of the property. This annual tax is paid in four quarterly instalments	
Stamp Duties		• Applicable to transactions related to credit operations • 0.1% per month with a maximum of 1.2%, calculated on the par value of the document, or 0.5% if the document is payable on sight, is applied to bills of exchange, promissory notes, import letters of credit, IOUs and in general to any document representative of a loan or credit operation (rates valid from 1 January 2009) • All taxes on cheques, ATM withdrawals, electronic money transfers, etc repealed as of 1 October 2008	

China

(Henry Tan, henrytan@nexiats.com.sg)

I MAIN LEGAL FORMS

Legal form / Characteristics	Partnership and Limited Liability Partnership (LLP)	Ltd (private corporation) and Plc (public corporation)
Partners/shareholders • Number • Restrictions	• Minimum: two persons • Unlimited liability	Ltd: 1–50 persons Plc: Minimum: two persons
Directors	No appointment of director is required	Ltd: no mandatory Board of Directors Board of Directors ranges from 3–13 persons Plc: must set up Board of Directors Number of directors: 5–19
Establishment	Required registered business name, registered address and partnership deed	Ltd: required registered business name, registered address and article and memorandum Plc: required registered business name, registered address Founders number: 2–200 Founders share: no less than 35%
Registration	All business to be registered at the Ministry of Industry and Commerce	
Minimum capital	No restriction	Ltd: private corporation not less than RMB100,000 Plc: not less than RMB5m
Liability	Unlimited liability for partners and general partners	Limited to share capital
Governance	By partners	Ltd: Board of Shareholders Plc: governance consists of: • Board of Shareholders • Board of Directors • Audit Committee
Audit requirements	Annual statutory audit required performed by certified public accountant (CPA)	Ltd: annual statutory audit required – performed by CPA Plc: annual statutory audit required – performed by CPA
Taxation	Enterprise income tax on worldwide profits Partnerships are transparent	
Usage	Rarely used	Commonly used for the larger/public businesses

II CORPORATION TAX

Legal form / Description	Non-resident enterprise	Resident enterprise
General description	Enterprise income tax	
Taxable entities	Corporations incorporated overseas but with substantial management and control located in China (also includes companies doing business in China but without management or control in China)	Enterprise that is formally registered as a company in China
Taxable income	Taxed on China-related income only	Worldwide profits derived by the entity in China
Calculation of taxable profits	Adjusted profits	
Interest payments	Thin capitalisation rules to be considered	
Related party transactions	All related party transactions must take place on arm's length basis	
Tax year, return and payment	• Tax period normally coincides with calendar year • Income tax on enterprises is based on an annual tax. Provisional income tax is collected in quarterly instalments and must be paid within 15 days after the end of each quarter	
Capital gains	No capital gains tax, although gain on the disposal of property may be subject to corporate income tax	
Losses	Trading losses may be carried forward for up to 5 years	
Tax group	None	
Tax rate	25%[1]	

---

1 Companies that can meet criteria as high technology, infrastructure, or environmentally based, or some agricultural companies may enjoy rates as low as 15%.

III   TAXES FOR INDIVIDUALS

<table>
<tr><th></th><th></th><th>Residents</th><th>Non-residents</th></tr>
<tr><td rowspan="8">Income Tax</td><td>General description</td><td colspan="2">Individual income tax</td></tr>
<tr><td>Taxable entities and taxable income</td><td>Individuals, trustees and estates that are permanently resident in China and have been resident for more than 5 years are liable to tax on their worldwide income</td><td>Taxation on income derived from Chinese sources</td></tr>
<tr><td>Types of taxable income</td><td colspan="2">• Wages, salaries and business income
• Compensation for personal services
• Royalties, interest, dividends and bonuses
• Income from lease of property
• Other income as specified by the Ministry of Finance</td></tr>
<tr><td>Calculation of income</td><td colspan="2">For wages and salaries; deducted fixed allowance and taxed at the appropriate rate</td></tr>
<tr><td>Tax year, tax assessment and tax payment</td><td colspan="2">• Tax year – calendar year
• An annual tax return must be filed within 3 months following the end of each year
• Monthly tax payments should be made to the state treasury based on the actual income within the first 7 days of the following month</td></tr>
<tr><td>Losses</td><td colspan="2">No specific rates</td></tr>
<tr><td>Tax rates</td><td colspan="2">

Grade	Monthly income payable (including tax) (for wages and salaries only)	Rate(%)	Quick calculation deduct
1	<500	5	0
2	500–2000	10	25
3	2,000–5,000	15	125
4	5,000–20,000	20	375
5	20,000–40,000	25	1,375
6	40,000–60,000	30	3,375
7	60,000–80,000	35	6,375
8	80,000–100,000	40	10,375
9	>100,000	45	15,375

</td></tr>
<tr><td rowspan="6">Capital Gains Tax (CGT)</td><td>General description</td><td colspan="2">Individual income tax</td></tr>
<tr><td>Taxable entities and chargeable assets</td><td colspan="2">Individuals, trustees and estates that are permanently resident in China and have been resident for more than one year are liable to tax on their worldwide income</td></tr>
<tr><td>Calculation of gain</td><td colspan="2">Selling price minus deductible expenses (including cost and other deductible expenses)</td></tr>
<tr><td>Tax year, tax assessment and tax payment</td><td colspan="2">Tax year – N/A
Capital gain is subject to tax on the payment made from buyer to seller</td></tr>
<tr><td>Losses</td><td colspan="2">N/A</td></tr>
<tr><td>Tax rates</td><td colspan="2">20%</td></tr>
</table>

		Domiciled	Non-domiciled
Inheritance Tax (IHT)	Taxable entities and chargeable assets	No inheritance tax	

IV WITHHOLDING TAXES

	Payments to non-residents[2]
Dividends	10%
Interest	20%
Royalties	20%
On payments to artists and sportsmen	20%

---

2 Reduced rates of withholding tax may apply where there is an appropriate double tax treaty.

V   INDIRECT TAXES

		Residents	Non-residents
Value Added Tax (VAT)	Entities being obliged to levy VAT	Enterprises, organisations or individuals who sell goods, provide process services, repair services or import goods	
	Taxable activities	Supply of goods and services, imports of goods, etc	
	Taxable activities – zero rated (examples)	Export goods	
	Exemptions (examples)	• Agricultural product sold by agricultural producers • Contraceptive drugs and devices • Antique books • Imported instruments and equipment used directly in scientific research, experiments and education	
	Refund of VAT	VAT paid on materials used for export products can be refunded	
	Tax liability	Normally the supplier of goods and services is responsible for charging VAT	
	Tax rates	• General taxpayer = 17% • Small scale taxpayer = 4% for commercial enterprises; 6% for production enterprises	
	Administrative obligations	N/A	
Stamp Duty Land Tax		Deed tax – deed tax is a tax of between 3%–5% on the total value of land use rights or building ownership rights transferred, imposed under provisional rules on deed tax and provisional rules on deed tax implementing rules. It is payable by the transferee	
Stamp Duty		• Transactions related to documents of contractual nature • Ranges between 0.005%–0.1%	

Colombia

(Roberto Montes Marin, montesyasociados@nexiamya.com.co)

I MAIN LEGAL FORMS

Legal form / Characteristics	Partnership and Limited Liability Partnership (LLP)	Ltd (private corporation) and Plc (public corporation)
Partners/shareholders • Number • Restrictions	Minimum of two partners to begin	Minimum of five shareholders to begin
Directors	As a minimum a general manager and Board of Directors	
Establishment	Written agreement presented to notary public which certifies legality	
Registration	• Chamber of Commerce • National Tax Administration	
Minimum capital	None	No less than authorised capital amount and not less than one-third of the shares to be paid up front
Liability	Unlimited liability	Up to the full amount of share capital
Governance	Optional external auditor (fiscal revisor)	External auditor (fiscal revisor only applies for Colombia)
Audit requirements	Financial statement must be certified by public accountant	Financial statement must be certified by public accountant and audited by fiscal revisor
Taxation	Corporate taxes on worldwide profits Partnerships are transparent (flow-through entities)	
Usage	No restrictions	

II   CORPORATION TAX

Legal form / Description	Resident corporation	Permanent establishment (PE)
General description	Corporate tax	
Taxable entities	Colombian companies, regardless of whether ownership is in the hands of non-Colombian residents, pay tax on income derived from all sources, with some activities and services performed outside Colombia being taxable	PE located in Colombia
Taxable income	Worldwide profits	Profits derived by PE in Colombia
Calculation of taxable profits	Accounting profit is adjusted for various tax add-backs and allowances to arrive to chargeable profits	
Interest payments	Interest paid to authorised local banks or other authorised financial institutions is deductible in full, if certified by the recipient	
Related party transactions	All related party transactions must take place on arm's length basis	
Tax year, return and payment	Tax period coincides with calendar year The return should be filed within 2 years after the financial year end Tax payable in two or five instalments depending on how the National Tax Administration has classified the taxpayer	
Capital gains	Capital gains are subject to corporation tax at normal rates	
Losses	Companies may offset current year losses against the income earned over the following 5 years	
Tax group	None	
Tax rate	33%	

III   TAXES FOR INDIVIDUALS

		Residents	**Non-residents**
Income Tax	Taxable entities and taxable income	Taxed on worldwide income	Taxed on Colombian source income
	Types of taxable income	• Property income (usually rent) • Income from capital investment (interest, sale of goodwill, dividends, royalties, annuities) • Income from business activities • Employment or pension income	
	Calculation of income	Gross income − Non taxable income = Net income − Cost − Expenses = Liquid rent − Tax-exempt income = Taxable liquid rent	
	Tax year, tax assessment and tax payment	Tax year – calendar year Self-assessment returns should be filed by August of the following year	
	Losses	No specific rules	
	Tax rates	Income tax based on a progressive rate schedule, with 33% being the highest marginal rate, applicable to earnings of approximately US$45,500 or more	
Capital Gains Tax (CGT)	General description	Not taxable	

		Domiciled	**Non-domiciled**
Inheritance Tax (IHT)	General description	No inheritance or gift taxes	

IV   WITHHOLDING TAXES

	Payments to non-residents
Dividends	33%
Interest	33%
Royalties	33%
On payments to artists and sportsmen	33%

V INDIRECT TAXES

		Residents	Non-residents
Value Added Tax (VAT)	Entities being obliged to levy VAT	All those companies and retailers who sell or import taxable goods and services	
	Taxable activities	Supply of goods and services, imports of goods, etc	
	Taxable activities – zero rated (examples)	• Some products of the basic family diet, like milk, meat, fish and eggs. • Sale and import of scientific and cultural books and magazines	
	Exemptions (examples)	• Export of moveable goods • Scientific and cultural books and magazines • Services rendered in Colombia and used exclusively abroad	
	Refund of VAT	For exempt goods	
	Tax liability	Normally the supplier of goods and services is responsible for charging VAT	
	Tax rates	• Standard rate = 16% • Differential rates of 0%, 8%, 10%, 20%, 25%, 35%, on various goods depending on circumstances described in the Tax Code	
	Administrative obligations	Charging, filing and payment of taxes	
Stamp Duty Land Tax		Determined by Municipal Government	
Stamp Duty		• Stamp tax charged on documents • General rate = 1.0%	

Costa Rica

(Mitry Breedy and Associates, mbreedy@nexiacostarica.com)

I   MAIN LEGAL FORMS

Characteristics \ Legal form	Partnership and Limited Liability Partnership (LLP)	Ltd (private corporation) and Plc (public corporation)
Partners/shareholders • Number • Restrictions	• Minimum: two persons • Unlimited liability	• Ltd: one • Plc: minimum of two persons
Directors	No appointment of director is required	No restrictions
Establishment	Required to register business name, address and partnership deed	Required to register business name and address
Registration	Chamber of Commerce and National Tax Registration at the Finance Ministry	Chamber of Commerce and National Tax Registration at the Finance Ministry
Minimum Capital	N/A	10,000 colons
Liability	Unlimited liability for general partner Unlimited liability for other partnerships	Up to full amount of their shares
Governance	Optional external auditor (fiscal revisor)	External auditor (fiscal revisor)
Audit requirements	N/A	No statutory audit requirements imposed upon private companies, only on public companies
Taxation	Transparent	Taxable only on Costa Rican income – not worldwide income

II   CORPORATION TAX

Legal form / Description	Resident corporation	Permanent establishment (PE)
General description	Corporation tax	
Taxable entities	Corporations incorporated in Costa Rica	
Taxable income	Costa Rican profits with considerations for double taxation treaties	
Calculation of taxable profits	All operating and non-operating income is treated as taxable income with relief for all operating and non-operating expenses incurred in producing this income	
Interest payments	Transfer pricing rules are in place that require funding arrangements to be arm's length for interest payments to remain tax deductible	
Related party transactions	All related party transactions must take place on arm's length basis	
Tax year, return and payment	Companies must use calendar or fiscal year Returns are filed on the 15th day of the 12th month of the year Payment is on or before the due date for tax return	
Capital Gains	Treated as income	
Losses	Industry or agriculture losses may be carried forward for the next 3 and 5 years respectively Others must be absorbed in the same year	
Tax group	All taxes are independent by each corporation	
Tax rate	Corporations	

Corporations

Income in colons (CRC)	Tax rate
0–38,891,000	10%
38,891,001–78,231,000	15%
78,231,001+	30%

III TAXES FOR INDIVIDUALS

		Residents	Non-residents
Income Tax	General description	Tax levied on the chargeable income as a chargeable person for a year or fiscal period	
	Taxable entities and taxable income	Residents are taxed under Costa Rican law	
	Types of taxable income	• Property income • Dividends • Professional fees • Commissions • Personal business	
	Calculation of income	Individuals *Income in colons (CRC)* *Tax rate* 0–2,599,000 exempt 2,599,001–3,880,000 10% 3,880,001–6,473,000 15% 6,473,001–12,972,000 20% 12,972,001+ 25%	
	Tax year, tax assessment and tax payment	30 September is the end of fiscal year starting on October of the previous year Taxes are filed on the 15th day of the 12th month of the year	
	Losses	Should be absorbed in the same fiscal year they occurred	
	Tax rates	*Income in colons (CRC)* *Tax rate* 0–2,599,000 exempt 2,599,001–3,880,000 10% 3,880,001–6,473,000 15% 6,473,001–12,972,000 20% 12,972,001+ 25%	
Capital Gains Tax (CGT)	General description	Gains realised from the difference between the acquisition and disposal price of an asset	
	Taxable entities and chargeable assets	Assessed as part of business income	
	Calculation of gain	Gross proceeds less adjusted tax basis and selling expenses equals to capital gain	
	Tax year, tax assessment and tax payment	Fiscal year ending on 30 September Payment 15 December of every year	
	Losses	All losses may be deducted from total income	
	Tax rates	*Income in colons (CRC)* *Tax rate* 0–2,599,000 exempt 2,599,001–3,880,000 10% 3,880,001–6,473,000 15% 6,473,001–12,972,000 20% 12,972,001+ 25%	

		Domiciled		Non-domiciled
Inheritance Tax (IHT)	General description	Tax on transfer of property		
	Taxable entities and chargeable assets	Costa Rican assets included		N/A
	Calculation of charge	*Colons (CRC)*	*Tax rate*	
		0–2,599,000	exempt	
		2,599,001–3,880,000	10%	
		3,880,001–6,473,000	15%	
		6,473,001–12,972,000	20%	
		12,972,001+	25%	
	Taxable events	All income		
	Tax rates	*Colons (CRC)*	*Tax rate*	
		0–2,599,000	exempt	
		2,599,001–3,880,000	10%	
		3,880,001–6,473,000	15%	
		6,473,001–12,972,000	20%	
		12,972,001+	25%	

IV   WITHHOLDING TAXES

	Payments to non-residents
Dividends	15% individual 0% corporations
Interest	0%
Royalties	0%
On payments to artists and sportsmen	15% individual 0% corporations

V   INDIRECT TAXES

		Residents	**Non-residents**
Value Added Tax (VAT)	General description	Tax on supply goods and services	
	Entities being obliged to levy VAT	Costa Rica does not impose VAT	
	Taxable activities	Assessed as part of business income	
	Taxable activities – zero rated (examples)	Free zone industrial activities	

Croatia

(Igor Dukić, Igor.dukic@zgombic.hr)

I   MAIN LEGAL FORMS

Legal form / Characteristics	Limited liability company	Joint stock company	General partnership	Limited partnership
Partners/ shareholders • Number • Restrictions	• One or more shareholders • No restrictions	• One or more shareholders • No restrictions	• Two or more partners • No restrictions	• Two or more partners • At least one general partner and one limited partner
Directors	Management by directors	Management by directors	Management by partners	Management by general partner
Establishment	Articles of Incorporation	Articles of Incorporation	Articles of Incorporation	Articles of Incorporation
Registration	Trade court register	Trade court register	Trade court register	Trade court register
Minimum capital	HRK 20,000 (approx €2,800)	HRK 200,000 (approx €28,000)	No subscribed capital unless prescribed by Articles of Incorporation	No subscribed capital
Liability	Limited	Limited	Unlimited	Unlimited for general partner, limited for limited partner
Governance	• Management board • Supervisory board (mandatory only in certain cases) • General assembly	• Management board • Supervisory board/Board of Directors • General assembly	Partners	General partner

109

Legal form / Characteristics	Limited liability company	Joint stock company	General partnership	Limited partnership
Audit requirements	Yes, if prior year income exceeded certain thresholds (or under special regulations)	Yes, if prior year income exceeded certain thresholds (or under special regulations, eg banks, insurance companies, etc)	No	Yes, if prior year income exceeded certain thresholds (or under special regulations)
Taxation	Corporate income tax	Corporate income tax	Corporate income tax	Corporate income tax

II CORPORATION TAX

Legal form / Description	Resident corporation	Permanent establishment (PE)
General description	National tax on income of corporations	
Taxable entities	• Company or another legal entity, resident of Croatia • Individual entrepreneurs (natural persons) may become voluntary or obligatory corporate income taxpayers	Permanent establishment of a non-resident enterprise
Taxable income	Worldwide income	Croatian sourced income
Calculation of taxable profits	Accounting profit – in line with IFRSs (large and listed companies) or Croatian FRSs (medium and small companies) +/– adjustments in line with the tax legislation = taxable profit	
Interest payments	Restrictions on tax deductibility of interest charged between related parties Thin capitalisation rules – interest on loans from (or guaranteed by) foreign shareholder holding at least 25% of shares or voting rights of the borrower is not deductible if the loan balance exceeds four times the lender's share in the equity of the borrower. Loans from financial institutions are not subject to thin capitalisation rules	Same rules are applied
Related party transactions	Should be made at arm's length. There are special documentation requirements for transactions between foreign related parties (ie transfer pricing documentation)	Same rules are applied
Tax year, return and payment	• Business year (calendar year or different business year if requested) • Monthly prepayments payable by the end of the month for the previous month. Calculated on the basis of prior year tax liability (1/12 per month) • Annual tax return must be filed 4 months after expiry of period in which tax is assessed – payment of final tax liability or tax refund	Same rules are applied
Capital gains	Taxable at regular corporate income tax rate (no special capital gains tax)	Same rules are applied

Legal form / Description	Resident corporation	Permanent establishment (PE)
Losses	• May be carried forward for 5 years • May not be carried back • In the process of mergers, acquisition or divisions tax losses may be transferred to legal successors	Same rules are applied
Tax group	Tax grouping is not allowed	N/A
Tax rate	20%	20%

III TAXES FOR INDIVIDUALS

<table>
<tr><th colspan="2"></th><th>Residents</th><th>Non-residents</th></tr>
<tr><td rowspan="10">Income Tax</td><td>General description</td><td colspan="2">Taxes on income of individuals</td></tr>
<tr><td>Taxable entities and taxable income</td><td>• Individuals (natural persons) incurring taxable income
• Residents – individuals with permanent or temporary residence in Croatia – taxable on worldwide income. Tax residency is determined in accordance with domestic regulations, or in accordance with double taxation treaty, where applicable</td><td>Non-residents – individuals without permanent or temporary residence in Croatia – taxable on Croatian sourced income</td></tr>
<tr><td rowspan="2">Types of taxable income</td><td colspan="2">• Employment income
• Self-employment income
• Income from capital (eg loan interest)
• Property and property rights income
• Income from life insurance savings
• Other income</td></tr>
<tr><td colspan="2">NOTE: Income from dividends is not taxable (unless from retained earnings from years 2001–04)</td></tr>
<tr><td>Calculation of income</td><td>• All types of income taxed on cash basis
• During the year – progressive tax rates (eg employment income) or flat tax rate (eg other income, income from capital)
• Application of personal allowances available in line with the personal income tax legislation. No personal allowance for certain types of income
• Annual tax return – report on all types of income, taxed at progressive tax rates, personal allowance applicable</td><td>• Same rules are applied
• Same rules are applied
• Only basic personal allowance
• No special rules (other than above mentioned)</td></tr>
<tr><td>Tax year, tax assessment and tax payment</td><td colspan="2">• Tax year – calendar year
• Taxes are paid together with the payment of income and (generally) declared on a monthly basis
• Final tax liability/refund – through annual tax return. Annual tax return should be filed by the end of February for the previous year
• No obligation to file annual tax return in certain cases</td></tr>
<tr><td>Losses</td><td colspan="2">Applicable only for self-employment income. Tax losses may be carried forward for the period of 5 years</td></tr>
<tr><td>Tax rates</td><td>• Employment income – tax prepayments paid at progressive tax rates: 15%, 25%, 35%, 45%
• Tax prepayments are paid at flat tax rates:
– income from capital – 15%/35% (depending on the type of income)
– property and property rights income – 15%/25%
– income from life insurance savings – 15%
– other income – 25%</td><td>Same rules are applied</td></tr>
</table>

		Residents	Non-residents
Capital Gains Tax (CGT)	General description	No special tax. Capital gain is taxed in line with corporate or personal income tax legislation Capital gain on sale of securities is not taxable for individuals provided that this is not their regular business	

		Domiciled	Non-domiciled
Inheritance and Gifts Tax (IGT)	General description	County (local) taxes	
	Taxable entities and chargeable assets	• Legal entity or individual that inherits or receives in form of a gift (without any compensation) assets in Croatia • Cash, monetary receivables, securities, movables (if market value is over HRK 50,000 (approx €7,000)). IGT is not paid if movables were subject to VAT. Real estate ownership transfer is taxed in line with the Real Estate Transfer Tax Act or the VAT Act	N/A
	Calculation of charge	Amount of cash or market value of monetary receivables, securities, movables reduced by debt and expenses in relation to the assets	N/A
	Exemptions	• Spouses, direct relatives, children, adoptees • Republic of Croatia, public institutions, religious communities, Red Cross, etc • Individuals and legal entities receiving gifts (as indemnity) from local or state government in relation to the War for Independence in Croatia • Legal entities and individuals receiving gifts in line with special regulations	N/A
	Tax rates	5%	N/A

IV WITHHOLDING TAXES

	Payments to non-residents
Dividends	No withholding tax
Interest	At a rate of 15%, may be lower or exempt in line with the double tax treaty, if applicable
Royalties	At a rate of 15% (25% if paid to individuals), may be lower or exempt in line with the double tax treaty, if applicable
Fees in relation to tax and business consultancy services, market research, auditor's fees	At a rate of 15%, may be exempt in line with the applicable double tax treaty

V INDIRECT TAXES

		Residents	Non-residents
Value Added Tax (VAT)	General description	National tax on supply of goods and services	
	Entities being obliged to levy VAT	• Entrepreneurs making taxable supplies • Domestic entrepreneur for certain services received from abroad • Importers • Exporters (only in certain cases)	
	Taxable activities	Supply of goods and services within Croatia, personal consumption, import of goods, receipt of services from abroad which are taxable in Croatia, export (in certain cases)	
	Taxable activities – zero rated (examples)	• Certain food • Books • Medicines, etc	
	Taxable activities – 10% (examples)	• Tourist accommodation services and related agency services • Daily and periodic newspapers and magazines	
	Exemptions (examples)	• Services of banks, insurance companies • Medical services • Rental of residential premises • Export, supplies to free trade zones, supplies to diplomatic missions, etc (with right to recover input VAT) • Goods in transit through Croatia • Temporary import of goods • Transfer of land – out of scope	
	Refund of VAT	Available	Not available to non-residents
	Tax liability	• By the end of the month for the previous tax period (month, quarter) • At the moment of filing the annual tax return	
	Tax rates	0%, 10%, 22%	
	Administrative obligations	• File monthly (or quarterly) tax returns – by the end of the period for the previous tax period • File annual tax return by the end of April for corporate income taxpayers/end of February for personal income taxpayers for the previous tax year	Non-residents may generally not register for VAT in Croatia. Croatian branches of foreign companies may/must register for VAT
Real estate transfer tax (RETT)		• RETT is paid on sales or transfers of ownership on buildings constructed before 31 December 1997 (prior to introduction of VAT) or if real estate is transferred by a person who is not a VAT taxpayer. Transfer of land is generally always subject to RETT (and never to VAT) • Taxpayer – the person or legal entity acquiring the real estate • The tax basis is the market value of the real estate at the time of acquisition. Tax rate is 5% • Contribution of real estate in a company's share capital is generally exempt from RETT • RETT is not paid on inheritance, donation or other form of acquisition without compensation between certain categories of persons (eg spouses) • First acquisition of ownership of a house or an apartment by which a Croatian national resolves his/her housing issue is also exempt from RETT under certain conditions	

VI   EXCISE TAXES

Types of excise taxes	Excise taxes may be levied on the following goods and services: alcoholic beverages, tobacco, oil products, soft drinks, beer, coffee, vehicles (cars, ships, boats and aircrafts), insurance premiums and luxury goods

Cyprus

(John Poyiadjis, np@nexia.com.cy)

I MAIN LEGAL FORMS

Characteristics / Legal form	Partnership – general and limited (no Limited Liability Partnerships exist in Cyprus)	Ltd (private corporation) and Plc (public corporation)
Partners/shareholders • Number • Restrictions	General partnership: not more than 20 partners Limited partnership: at least one general partner	Ltd: minimum one shareholder – not more than 50 shareholders Plc: minimum number of shareholders required to register the company is seven
Directors	Management by partners	Plc: minimum number of two directors on the Board of Directors required For private companies one director and one company secretary. Where there is only one director, the company secretary must be another individual or corporate entity unless the same person is also the shareholder of the company For private, no restrictions. Regulated by the Articles of Association. Alternate directors are permitted
Establishment	Partnership deed	Articles of Association
Registration	Registrar of Companies	
Minimum capital	None	Ltd: no minimum Plc: minimum €25,629
Liability	Unlimited	Capital subscribed
Governance	Partners	Board of Directors
Audit requirements	Audit required Partnerships with a turnover above €68,400 should prepare audited financial statements	Audit required Cyprus companies by law require an audit. Only under certain circumstances specified by the companies act consolidated financial statement will not be audited

Legal form / Characteristics	Partnership – general and limited (no Limited Liability Partnerships exist in Cyprus)	Ltd (private corporation) and Plc (public corporation)
Taxation	Partners taxed on worldwide income	Worldwide income
Usage	Professionals	SMEs, listed companies

II CORPORATION TAX

Legal form / Description	Resident corporation	Permanent establishment (PE)
General description	Corporation tax	
Taxable entities	Resident companies	PE located in Cyprus
Taxable income	Worldwide profits	Profits derived by PE in Cyprus
Calculation of taxable profits	For corporation tax purposes in order to derive to the taxable income you must take into account all tax allowable and disallowable expenditure. In addition to corporation tax in Cyprus also defence tax exists which companies are liable to	
Interest payments	Arm's length principle applies in order for interest payments to be tax deductible	
Related party transactions	Arm's length basis	
Tax year, return and payment	• Tax year – calendar year • Normally the financial year of a company is the same as the tax year • The due date for the temporary return is 1 August, but for the final return this is due 31 December following the year of assessment • Three instalment payments required with a balancing payment upon submission of the final return. The submission dates are 1 August, 30 September and 31 December	
Capital gains	20% on all gains arising out of the sale of immovable property in Cyprus or on the sale of shares of companies which own immovable property in Cyprus excluding shares listed in any recognised stock exchange	
Losses	May be carried forward and set off against profits indefinitely	
Tax group	Set off of group losses are allowed only with profits of the corresponding year of assessment. Both companies should be members of the same group for the whole year of assessment. Two companies shall be deemed to be members of a group if: • one is a 75% subsidiary of the other or • each one separately is a 75% subsidiary of a third company	N/A
Tax rate	10%	10%

III   TAXES FOR INDIVIDUALS

		Residents	Non-residents
Income Tax	General description	Tax levied on the chargeable income of a chargeable person for a year of assessment	
	Taxable entities and taxable income	Resident individual means an individual who stays in Cyprus for a period or periods exceeding in aggregate 183 days or more in the year of assessment Resident individuals are liable to income tax at 10% on income accruing in, derived from or received in Cyprus, as well as income accrued abroad	Non-residents only liable to income tax on income accrued in Cyprus
	Types of taxable income	• Rents and royalties in Cyprus and abroad • Income from business activities in Cyprus and abroad • Employment from personal services in Cyprus and abroad	
	Calculation of income	Gross income less allowances	
	Tax year, tax assessment and tax payment	• Tax year – calendar year • Individuals file self-assessment returns • Returns must be filed by 30 April of the following year	
	Losses	May be carried forward and set off against income from any source of the following years of assessment	
	Tax rates	Nil tax rate up until €19,500 *Income (€)* *Tax rate (%)* 0–19,500 0 19,500–28,000 20 28,000–36,300 25 Over 36,300 30	
Capital Gains Tax (CGT)	General description	Tax on increase in the value of asset between acquisition and disposal	
	Taxable entities and chargeable assets	Tax on all gains arising out of the sale of immovable property or shares in companies which own immovable property excluding shares listed in any recognised stock exchange	
	Calculation of gain	The net profit is calculated as the disposal proceeds less the greater of the cost or market value on 1 January 1980 adjusted for inflation. Inflation is calculated using the official retail price index	
	Tax year, tax assessment and tax payment	A chargeable person should submit a tax return (a declaration of disposal of property) in respect of each chargeable disposal within one month from the date of the disposal and pay any tax due per such return, and in any case before the transfer of the property in question at the Land Registration Office. This is a self-assessment system	
	Losses	Capital losses are set off against chargeable gains made on the same date. If there are no gains on the same date or if the gains are not enough to absorb the capital losses, any unrelieved loss is carried forward and is set off against a chargeable gain or gains made at a future disposal until the loss is relieved No carry back of losses	
	Tax rates	20% (there is an exemption of €17,086 on gains accruing from the disposal or disposals during the same year or any other year)	

		Cyprus domiciled	Non-Cyprus domiciled
Inheritance Tax (IHT)	General description	No inheritance tax in Cyprus	

IV   WITHHOLDING TAXES

	Payments to non-residents[1]
Dividends	None
Interest	None
Royalties	None
On payments to artists and sportsmen	10%

1   Reduced rates of withholding taxes may apply where there is an appropriate double tax treaty.

V   INDIRECT TAXES

		Residents	Non-residents
Value Added Tax (VAT)	General description	Tax on the supply of goods and services (VAT)	
	Entities being obliged to levy VAT	• Self-employed persons • Companies • Informal bodies of persons, such as joint ventures, deemed partnerships, associations • Partnerships • Clubs, charities, institutions, societies, trade unions	
	Taxable activities	VAT is applied on all imports and taxable supplies made in the republic by a taxable entity in the normal course of its business	
	Taxable activities – zero rated (examples)	This is a taxable supply but at zero rate. Examples of zero-rated supplies are exports, food, medicine, children's clothing and footwear	
	Exemptions (examples)	Post office services, hospital and medical care, dental services, social providence and insurance, education, sports, cultural services, insurance, financial services, lotteries	
	Refund of VAT	If there is a balance in favour of the taxpayer (a VAT credit), it is refundable by the VAT Commissioner. The VAT Commissioner may direct that the VAT credit be carried forward to a later VAT return, or postpone the refund in case a trader failed to submit a VAT return of any previous VAT period	
	Tax liability	Normally the supplier of goods and services is responsible for charging VAT	
	Tax rates	• Standard rate = 15% • Minimum rate (ie taxi fare, bus fare) = 8% • Minimum rate (ie newspapers) = 5% • Zero rate (ie food, medicine) = 0%	
	Administrative obligations	VAT returns must be completed and submitted to the VAT Commissioner together with any VAT payable due on the 10th of the month following each quarter which the company files its returns	
Stamp Duty Land Tax		The rate of the duty may depend on the value of the property specified in the document such as for conveyances or transfers on sale and leases, or a fixed duty may be payable such as for declarations of trust	
Stamp Duty		Stamp duty is levied on certain documents at various, generally low, rates	

Czech Republic

(Vladimir Kralicek, vladimirkralicek@auditplus.cz)

I MAIN LEGAL FORMS

Legal form / Characteristics	Partnership and Limited Liability Partnership (LLP)	Ltd (private corporation) and Plc (public corporation)
Partners/shareholders • Number • Restrictions	Partnership: at least two natural persons LLP: at least one unlimited partner and at least one limited partner	Ltd: at least one, maximum 50 partners Plc: at least one, if the shareholder is a corporation or at least two
Directors	Partnership: partners LLP: unlimited partner	Ltd: at least one executive Plc: Board of Directors – at least three, except when one shareholder owns 100%, then there must be at least one director
Establishment	Partnership agreement	Establishment contract (Plc) and Partnership agreement (Ltd), both notarised
Registration	The request for registration in the Commercial Register must be placed within 90 days from the establishment of company	
Minimum capital	Partnership: no requirements LLP: no requirements regarding the minimum capital, but the input (deposit) of the partner with limited liability must be at least CZK 5,000	Ltd: CZK 200,000 Plc: CZK 2m when established without public bid, CZK 20m with public bid
Liability	Partnership: unlimited liability of partners LLP: at least one partner with unlimited and at least one with limited liability who is liable up to the amount of unpaid capital	Corporation: limited up to the amount of assets Shareholders (Plc): no liability Partners (Ltd): limited up to the amount of unpaid capital
Governance	Not determined	Ltd: only when the partnership agreement determines Plc: at least three members, the number of members must be divisible by three

Legal form / Characteristics	Partnership and Limited Liability Partnership (LLP)	Ltd (private corporation) and Plc (public corporation)
Audit requirements	Audit is obligatory when units exceed or meet two of following criteria: • a balance sheet total of over CZK 40m • a net turnover of over CZK 80m • an (adjusted) average number of employees of over 50	Ltd: must reach at least two of the mentioned criteria Plc: must reach at least one of the mentioned criteria
Taxation	Corporations are taxable on worldwide profits	

II CORPORATION TAX

Legal form / Description	Resident corporation	Permanent establishment (PE)
General description	Tax on income of corporations	
Taxable entities	Corporations incorporated in Czech Republic and/or overseas companies with central management and control located in the Czech Republic	PE located in the Czech Republic
Taxable income	Income from worldwide sources	Income arising in the Czech Republic
Calculation of taxable profits	Taxable profit is based on accounting profit adjusted under the tax law	
Interest payments	Generally, interest payments are considered to be business expenses and are under certain conditions deductible; as of 1 January 2008 thin capitalisation rules are tightened and apply also to non-related parties	
Related party transactions	All related party transactions must take place on arm's length basis	
Tax year, return and payment	Tax year – calendar year or fiscal year A tax return must be filed within 3 months after the end of the tax year or within 6 months if a chartered tax adviser is acting on behalf of the company, or if mandatory statutory audit is performed	
Capital gains	Capital gains are subject to corporation tax at standard rates; dividends and profits from shareholding received by resident corporations from abroad are included in a separate income tax base	
Losses	Incurred losses until 31 December 2003 may be offset against the profits of the seven subsequent tax periods and incurred losses from 1 January 2004 five subsequent tax periods	
Tax group	None	
Tax rate	21%[1]	

---

1 Taxable period starting in 2009: 20%.
  Taxable period starting in 2010: 19%.

III   TAXES FOR INDIVIDUALS

		Residents	Non-residents
Income Tax	General description	Individuals' monetary and non-monetary income is subject to personal taxes	
	Taxable entities and taxable income	Resident individuals are taxed on their income from worldwide sources	Non-resident individuals are subject to income tax solely on income arising in the Czech Republic
	Types of taxable income	• Employment income • Income tax on entrepreneurs • Capital gains • Income from lease • Other income	
	Calculation of income	• Employment income • Business income – sole proprietor, share of income from a partnership • Capital income – dividends, interest and other income from bonds, securities, certificates of deposit, deposits in a bank, etc • Rental income	
	Tax year, tax assessment and tax payment	Tax year – calendar year. Tax assessment: individual self-assessment returns for each taxpayer Advanced payments based on tax paid in previous year Payroll deductions: monthly by the employer, tax deducted can be offset against the final income tax	
	Losses	Losses can be offset against income from other sources in the current year with the exception of employment income. Excess losses can be carried forward for 5 years	
	Tax rates	As of 1 January 2008 flat tax rate 15%	
Capital Gains Tax (CGT)	General description	• No special tax • Capital gains may be subject to income tax (see above)	

		Domiciled	Non-domiciled
Inheritance Tax (IHT)	General description	Applies to the acquisition of assets by inheritance	
	Taxable entities and chargeable assets	Taxable entities: legal entities and individuals except the so-called first group of relatives (parents, children and husband or wife) and as of 1 January 2008 also except the second group of relatives (siblings, nephews, nieces, aunts, uncles, husbands, husband's children, husband's parents, parent's husbands and cohabitating partners) Chargeable assets: realties, movable assets, cash, securities, receivables, rights in property and other assets	
	Calculation of charge	Percentage of a tax base	
	Taxable events	The probate in inheritance procedure	
	Allowances	• Proved decedent's debts passed to the heritor • Assets exempt from inheritance tax • Appropriate funeral cost • Notary's remuneration and cost certified by court • Inheritance charge paid to foreign country	
	Tax rates	Running progressive taxation	

IV   WITHHOLDING TAXES

	Payments to non-residents[2]
Dividends	15% or 0%[3]
Interest	15% or 0%[3]
Royalties	15%[4, 5]
On payments to artists and sportsmen	15%[4]

2   Reduced rates of withholding tax may apply where there is an appropriate tax treaty.
3   Exemptions apply on payments made by a subsidiary to parent company (under certain conditions).
4   Reduced to 12.5% as of 1 January 2009.
5   As of 1 January 2011 exemption applies on payments made to an EU-resident company by a Czech tax resident or Czech PE of an EU-resident company.

V   INDIRECT TAXES

<table>
<tr><th></th><th></th><th>Residents</th><th>Non-residents</th></tr>
<tr><td rowspan="9">Value Added Tax (VAT)</td><td>General description</td><td colspan="2">VAT is due on most supplies of goods and services</td></tr>
<tr><td>Entities being obliged to levy VAT</td><td colspan="2">Legal entities and individuals carrying out economic activities (production, trade, services, etc). Obliged are those with a turnover exceeding CZK 1m in the preceding 12 months</td></tr>
<tr><td>Taxable activities</td><td colspan="2">Supplies of goods and services, imports of goods, etc</td></tr>
<tr><td>Taxable activities – zero rated (examples)</td><td colspan="2">Export of goods and services, financial and insurance services, postal services, education, etc</td></tr>
<tr><td>Exemptions (examples)</td><td colspan="2">• Disposal of company or contribution of company or of its part, integral organisational branch of company
• Free supply of advertising articles which are marked by trademark or trade name or the name of advertised good or service, acquisition cost does not exceed CZK 500 apiece and is not the object of the consumption tax</td></tr>
<tr><td>Refund of VAT</td><td>Refund of VAT is possible on taxable supply made by the registered subject who settles this supply from resources of international help in accordance with international treaty which is part of Czech legislation</td><td>• Subject registered to VAT in the EU country or third county which did not make any taxable supply in the Czech Republic in the calendar year
• Persons enjoying privilege and immunity and related persons</td></tr>
<tr><td>Tax liability</td><td colspan="2">VAT is usually calculated and is paid over to the local tax authority quarterly on the difference between the VAT charged on sales and the VAT incurred on expenditure. If the turnover exceeds CZK 10m in the previous calendar year or in case of tax group, the VAT is paid over monthly</td></tr>
<tr><td>Tax rates</td><td colspan="2">• Standard rate = 19% (most of goods and services)
• Reduced rate = 9% (specified goods and services, eg food, books, health and social care)
• Zero rate = 0% (export of goods and services)</td></tr>
<tr><td>Administrative obligations</td><td>Any business making taxable supplies may register for VAT voluntary. However, registration is compulsory if taxable income exceeds the registration limit, currently CZK 1m per annum</td><td>Subjects registered to VAT in the EU country or third country and having PE in the Czech Republic, use the same rules as the Czech subjects. Subjects registered to VAT in the EU country or third country and having no PE in the Czech Republic, are liable to VAT as from the day of making certain types of taxable supplies</td></tr>
<tr><td colspan="2">Stamp Duty Land Tax (Real Estate Transfer Tax)</td><td colspan="2">The rate is 3% of the higher of the sale price and the value of the property. The real estate transfer tax is payable by the seller of immovable property and is deductible for income tax purposes</td></tr>
<tr><td colspan="2">Stamp Duty</td><td colspan="2">N/A</td></tr>
</table>

Denmark

(Iver Haugsted, ih@ck.dk)

I   MAIN LEGAL FORMS

Legal form Characteristics	Partnership and Limited Liability Partnership (LLP)	Ltd (private corporation) ApS and Plc (public corporation) A/S
Partners/ shareholders • Number • Restrictions	• One or more • None	• One or more • None
Directors	No minimum	No minimum
Establishment	Deeds	• Deeds • Registration
Registration	Registration takes place at the Danish Commerce and Companies Agency (Erhvervs- og Selskabsstyrelsen). Only companies with limited liability must register	
Minimum capital	N/A	• DKK 125,000 for ApS • DKK 500,000 for A/S
Liability	• Unlimited for partnership • Limited to capital for LLP	Limited to share capital
Governance	Deeds	Corporate law
Audit requirements	None	Yes (micro-entities are exempt)
Taxation	Partnerships are transparent, ie individual partners are assessed on their share of profits	Resident companies are subject to corporation tax on their profits derived in Denmark
Usage	No general restrictions exist, ie any business activity conducted by the entity	

II   CORPORATION TAX

Legal form / Description	Resident corporation	Permanent establishment (PE)
General description	Corporation tax, 25%	
Taxable entities	Corporations incorporated in Denmark and/or overseas companies with central management and control located in Denmark	PE located in Denmark
Taxable income	Worldwide profits	Profits derived by PE in Denmark
Calculation of taxable profits	Accounting profit is adjusted for various tax add-backs and allowances to arrive to profits chargeable to corporation tax	
Interest payments	Deductible. Limitation on interest charges of approx. DKK 20m on group level	
Related party transactions	All related party transactions must take place on arm's length basis	
Tax year, return and payment	• Company can choose any period as its financial year as long as it runs to the end of the month • Company must file its tax return no later than 6 months after the end of the financial year. If the financial year ends between 1 February and 31 March, the tax return must be filed by 1 August in the same calendar year. Preliminary tax is payable in two equal instalments on 20 March and 20 November	A PE may use the same period as foreign corporation, or calendar year is used
Capital gains	Certain types of realised capital gains are included in the ordinary taxable income	
Losses	Tax losses may be carried forward indefinitely and offset against future taxable profits. No carry back is permitted	
Tax group	Danish Group entities must be jointly taxed. A subsidiary[1] in Denmark or a PE in Denmark must be included in the joint taxation regime All subsidiaries or PEs – including non-resident companies may also apply for international joint taxation regime where all group entities (resident and non-resident) are included in a Danish tax consolidation scheme. The decision is binding for a period of 10 years	A PE is taxed on its Danish income. However, the PE must be included in the Danish joint taxation regime provided there are other group entities that are registered in Denmark
Tax rate	25%	

1   A majority of the voting rights.

III TAXES FOR INDIVIDUALS

<table>
<tr><td colspan="2"></td><th>Residents</th><th>Non-residents</th></tr>
<tr><td rowspan="8" style="writing-mode:vertical-lr">Income Tax</td><td>General description</td><td colspan="2">Tax levied on the chargeable income of a chargeable person for a year of assessment</td></tr>
<tr><td>Taxable entities and taxable income</td><td>Residents are taxed on their worldwide income, with some relief for double taxation</td><td>Non-residents are taxed on income from personal services performed in Denmark for Danish employers or on income from Danish immovable property or as self-employed with a PE in Denmark on all income derived from Danish sources</td></tr>
<tr><td>Types of taxable income</td><td colspan="2">• Employment income
• Income from capital investment (interest, sale of goodwill, dividends, royalties, annuities, etc), property income
• Income from business activities
• Pensions</td></tr>
<tr><td>Calculation of income</td><td colspan="2">In general, taxable income is calculated as gross income less deductible costs</td></tr>
<tr><td>Tax year, tax assessment and tax payment</td><td colspan="2">• Tax year – calendar year
• Each individual has to complete a self-assessment (tax return) for each year
• Returns must be filed by 1 May in the year following the taxable period (or 1 July for individuals engaged in business activities)
• Payment of preliminary tax on an accrual basis, ie deductions from employment income (at source)</td></tr>
<tr><td>Losses</td><td colspan="2">Losses can be carried forward indefinitely and off-set against future income</td></tr>
<tr><td>Tax rates</td><td>• Local tax approx 26% (2009) (average rate)
• State tax of 5.04% (2009)
• State tax of 6% on personal income positive capital income if these two amounts exceed DKK 347,200 (2009)
• State tax of 15% on personal income, positive capital income and lump sum payments to a pension scheme with a deduction of DKK 347,200 (2009)
• Labour market contribution 8% of the total income. This labour market contribution is deductible when calculating income tax</td><td>In principle, the tax calculation is similar to residents' assessment</td></tr>
</table>

		Residents	Non-residents
Capital Gains Tax (CGT)	General description	Tax on increase in the value of asset between acquisition and disposal	
	Taxable entities and chargeable assets	• Shares • Investments • Immovable property (private homes and holiday homes may be exempt under certain conditions)	Immovable property located in Denmark (private homes and holiday homes may be exempt under certain conditions)
	Calculation of gain	The difference between disposal price reduced by incidental expenses and the acquisition cost including incidental expenses and capital refurbishment costs, etc	
	Tax year, tax assessment and tax payment	• Gains are included each year in the self-assessment return • Returns must be filed by 1 May in the year following the taxable period (or 1 July for individuals engaged in business activities)	
	Losses	Losses are normally deductible and may be carried forward indefinitely Some can only be offset against gains arising on assets of a similar type. An example is losses on immovable property	
	Tax rates	Normal income tax rate, but without the labour market contribution	

		DK domiciled	Non-DK domiciled
Inheritance Tax (IHT)	General description	Inheritance tax comprises an estate duty on the net value of the estate of a deceased person	
	Taxable entities and chargeable assets	The worldwide net estate is subject to tax in Denmark	Only immovable property in Denmark and assets of PE in Denmark are subject to Danish tax
	Calculation of charge	Net assets (market value)	
	Taxable events	• Death • Gift	
	Allowances	Transfers at death to surviving spouse are exempt from inheritance tax	
	Tax rates	• Flat rate of 15% on the net value of the estate exceeding DKK 264,100 (2009) • 36.25% for beneficiaries other than close relatives	

IV   WITHHOLDING TAXES

	Payments to non-residents[2]
Dividends	28%
Interest	N/A
Royalties	25%
On payments to artists and sportsmen	N/A

2   Other rates of withholding tax may apply where there is an appropriate double tax treaty.

V   INDIRECT TAXES

		Residents	Non-residents
Value Added Tax (VAT)	General description	Tax on the supply of goods and services	
	Entities being obliged to levy VAT	Suppliers of goods and services with annual turnover of more than DKK 50,000	
	Taxable activities	All goods and services excluding sales of real property, personal transport, education and cultural activities	
	Taxable activities – zero rated (examples)	Goods and services supplied to registered businesses within the EU	
	Exemptions (examples)	• Sales of real property • Financial services • Personal transport • Education • Cultural activities	
	Refund of VAT	Yes Companies dealing in the export of goods and services may receive a reimbursement of VAT on exports on a monthly or weekly basis and export companies may receive the reimbursement in advance	Foreign companies with taxable activities in Denmark may receive a reimbursement of VAT similar to Danish companies
	Tax liability	Normally the supplier of goods and services is responsible for charging VAT	
	Tax rates	Standard rate of 25%	
	Administrative obligations	Filing of returns	
Stamp Duty Land Tax		DKK 1,400 + 0.6% (transfer of immovable property)	
Stamp Duty		DKK 1,400 + 1.5% (loans against immovable property, mortgage loans)	

Dominican Republic

(Manuel Guerrero, mguerrero@franciscoyasociados.com)

I MAIN LEGAL FORMS

Characteristics \ Legal form	Partnership and Limited Liability Partnership (LLP)	Ltd (private corporation) and Plc (public corporation)
Partners/shareholders • Number • Restrictions	• Seven partners • Limitations based on participation in shares	• Seven shareholders • Limitations based on participation in shares
Directors	Unlimited	Unlimited
Establishment	Register the trade name in Onapi, Mercantile Registry and the DGII (each institution has a process to follow)	
Registration	• Chamber of Commerce • Trading Registry	
Minimum capital	RD$1,000	
Liability	For partnerships unlimited For LLP limitations based on participation.	Unlimited
Governance	Secretary of Finance	
Audit requirements	Societies with a partners equity above RD$50,000	Societies with a shareholders equity above RD$50,000
Taxation	5% based on the partners equity	5% based on the shareholders equity

II CORPORATION TAX

Legal Form / Description	Resident corporation	Permanent establishment (PE)
General description	Tax is charged on the taxable profits of the company	
Taxable entities	All organisations except for the non-governmental organisations (NGOs)	
Taxable income	Revenues less expenses	
Calculation of taxable profits	Earnings per books plus (or less) permanent or temporary differences	
Interest payments	25% There are no restrictions on interest deductibility	
Related party transactions	Must be done on arm's length basis	
Tax year, return and payment	• Four periods in a fiscal year. (March, June, September and December) • Can be paid up to 120 days after closing fiscal year • Tax returns are contemplated by the law	
Capital gains	All types are taxable	
Losses	Usable up to 3 years after emerging on the basis of the percentage established by law	
Tax group	Groups are taxed together and individually and can be compensated forward	
Tax rate	• Income Tax = 25% over the profit • VAT = 16% • Selective consumption tax = variable	

III   TAXES FOR INDIVIDUALS

		Residents	Non-residents
Income Tax	General description	All income generated in the Dominican Republic by the individual is taxed; for non-residents, an exception for the first 82 days of stay	
	Taxable entities and taxable income	The law stipulates that all entities are collectors for retaining the tax	
	Types of taxable income	• Salaries • Commissions • Any amount received in cash or as a good	
	Calculation of income	Based on the total income earned, with an exemption of RD$26,500 monthly	
	Tax year, tax assessment and tax payment	• Deductions are monthly with an annual closure in February each year • The tax is due annually for non-employed individuals and on a monthly basis for employed individuals	
	Losses	Can be carried forward	
	Tax rates	• Income up to RD$316,017 – exempt • Income from RD$316,017.01 to RD$474,024.00 – 15% • Income from RD$474,024.01 to RD$658,367.00 – RD$23,701.00 plus 20% on surplus over RD$474,024.01 • Income over RD$658,367.01 – RD$60,570.00 plus 25% on surplus over RD$658,367.01	
Capital Gains Tax (CGT)	General description	25% of the gain resulting	
	Taxable entities and chargeable assets	• Fixed Assets • Investment in shares	
	Calculation of gain	Calculated based on the difference between the cost of the asset indexed for inflation and the selling price	
	Tax year, tax assessment and tax payment	Deductions are monthly with an annual closure in February each year	
	Losses	Can be carried forward and applied only against capital gains	
	Tax rates	25%	

		Domiciled	Non-domiciled
Inheritance Tax (IHT)	General description	Paid on the amount of net inheritance assets adjusted for inflation	
	Taxable entities and chargeable assets	All the net assets	
	Calculation of charge	Total assets, less total liabilities	
	Taxable events	Death	
	Allowances	N/A	
	Tax rates	3%	

IV   WITHHOLDING TAXES

	Payments to non-residents
Dividends	25% of the amount declared as dividend
Interest	25%
Royalties	25%
On payments to artists and sportsmen	Artist depends on the market value Section III Taxes for Individuals – non-residents

V   INDIRECT TAXES

		Residents	Non-residents
Value Added Tax (VAT)	General description	Tax on the supply of goods and services	
	Entities being obliged to levy VAT	All companies considering the exemptions specified by law	
	Taxable activities	The sale or transfer of goods or services	
	Taxable activities – zero rated (examples)	N/A	
	Exemptions (examples)	Education services, zone, health services, etc	
	Refund of VAT	The law provides	
	Tax liability	The law stipulates that all entities are collectors for retaining the tax	
	Tax rates	16%	
	Administrative obligations	Payments in the next 20 days of following month	
Stamp Duty Land Tax		N/A	
Stamp Duty		• Law 243 for liquors and similar products • Laws 84–71 for cigars and similar products	

Egypt

(Adel Saad & Co, as@adelsaadandco.com)

I MAIN LEGAL FORMS

Legal form / Characteristics	Partnership and Limited Liability Partnership (LLP)	Ltd (private corporation) and Plc (public corporation)
Partners/shareholders • Number • Restrictions	Partnership: Unlimited number of partners LLP: One general partner, unlimited number of limited partners	Ltd: At least two shareholders (partners) Joint Stock Co: At least three shareholders
Directors	Partnership: At least one partner LLP: At least one general partner	Ltd: One or more managing director(s) Joint Stock Co: Board of directors of at least three persons (including the chairman)
Establishment	Partnership deed	Legalised, approved contract by the investment authority
Registration	• Commercial register • Tax department	• Authority of Investment • Commercial register • Tax department
Minimum capital	Partnership: 5,000 EG P LLP: 5,000 EG P	Ltd: 50,000 EG P Joint Stock Co: 250,000 EG P
Liability	• General partner liability is unlimited • Limited partner liability is limited to the extent of his share	Shareholders liability is limited to the extent of their shares
Governance	• Commercial register • Tax department	• Authority of Investment • Commercial register • Tax department
Audit requirements	• Not generally required • For companies with a revenue higher than 2m EG P the tax department require that the FS must be audited by a chartered accountant	Yes
Taxation	Corporate income tax (no tax on partners share)	Corporate income tax

II   CORPORATION TAX

Legal form / Description	Resident corporation	Permanent establishment (PE)
General description	In June 2005, the Egyptian Ministry of Finance issued a new tax law. The new law has mainly changed and reformed the following: • Decreased the tax rates to encourage investment • Simplified the rules and procedures • Changed the tax return inspection system. Currently tax departments inspect tax returns, taxpayer's accounts on a random basis, once every 3–5 years. Previously, inspection was on a yearly basis	
Taxable entities	Joint Stock Co (corporation), Ltd, Partnership, LLP: • Tax shall apply to entities residing in Egypt, with respect to all profits realised in Egypt or abroad • Tax shall apply to non-resident entities with respect to the profits realised in Egypt	
Taxable income	Profits of a business activity shall be determined based on the revenues resulting from all the business operations, including capital gains , and after deducting all allowable costs Taxable profit is determined based on net profit as per the income statement prepared according to the Egyptian Accounting Standards, adjusted by taxable bases	
Calculation of taxable profits	The taxable profit is calculated based on net income adjusted by (for example): • taxable depreciation bases • taxable bases for capital gain and losses • deductible donations limited to 10% from annual net profit • reserves and provisions as per FS are not tax deductible • bad debts and interest paid shall be in accordance to tax bases and law provisions • losses can be carried forward for 5 years	
Interest payments	Debt to equity ratio of 4:1. Any excess amounts of interest are not deductible	
Related party transactions	Arm's length rates apply	
Tax year, return and payment	Tax year: 31 December Return and payment: 30 April	
Capital gains	Treated as ordinary income	
Losses	Carried forward for 5 years	
Tax group	N/A	
Tax rate	20%	

III TAXES FOR INDIVIDUALS

<table>
<tr><td colspan="2"></td><th>Residents</th><th>Non-residents</th></tr>
<tr><td rowspan="9">Income Tax</td><td>General description</td><td colspan="2">An annual tax shall be imposed on the total net income of resident and non-resident Egyptian persons in respect to their revenues earned in Egypt.

Resident individuals consist of Egyptians and non-Egyptians having a permanent resident in Egypt, who reside more than 183 days within 12 months</td></tr>
<tr><td>Taxable entities and taxable income</td><td colspan="2">Sole practitioner</td></tr>
<tr><td>Types of taxable income</td><td colspan="2">• Employment revenues (individuals with employment revenues do not need to submit a tax return. Tax is deducted and remitted by employer)
• Commercial or manufacturing business
• Professional income (activity)
• Real estate income (activity)
• Profits of a business activity shall be determined based on the revenues resulting from all the business operations, including capital gains, and after deducting all allowable costs</td></tr>
<tr><td rowspan="2">Calculation of income</td><td>*Employee:*
The following deductions are allowed on the gross salary, in order to calculate the payroll taxable income:

• employee social insurance share deducted according to social insurance laws; employee subscription in private insurance/pension funds
• life and health insurance premiums paid by the employee in his favour, for his/her spouse or minor children
• employee's profit sharing</td><td>No allowed deduction</td></tr>
<tr><td colspan="2">*Sole practitioner:*
The taxable profit is calculated based on net income adjusted by (for example):

• taxable depreciation bases
• taxable bases for capital gain and losses
• deductible donations limited to 10% from annual net profit
• reserves and provisions as per FS are not tax deductible
• losses can be carried forward for 5 years</td></tr>
<tr><td>Tax year, tax assessment and tax payment</td><td colspan="2">*Employee:*
Employer submits a tax declaration on a quarterly basis, remits the tax deducted from his employee on a monthly basis.

Sole practitioner:
Tax year: 31 December
Return and payment: 31 March</td></tr>
<tr><td>Losses</td><td colspan="2">*Sole practitioner:*
Carried forward for 5 years</td></tr>
</table>

		Residents		Non-residents
Income Tax	Tax rates	*Sole practitioner:*		10%
		Tax Bracket in EG P	%	
		0–5,000	0	
		5,001–20,000	10	
		20,001–40,000	15	
		40,001+	20	
		Employee:		
		Tax Bracket in EG P	%	
		0–9,000	0	
		9,001–20,000	10	
		20,001–40,000	15	
		40,001+	20	
Capital Gains Tax (CGT)	General description	N/A		
	Taxable entities and chargeable assets			
	Calculation of gain			
	Tax year, tax assessment and tax payment			
	Losses			
	Tax rates			
		Domiciled		**Non-domiciled**
Inheritance Tax (IHT)	General description	N/A		
	Taxable entities and chargeable assets			
	Calculation of charge			
	Taxable events			
	Allowances			
	Tax rates			

IV WITHHOLDING TAXES

	Payments to non-residents
Dividends	Exempt
Interest	• Interest received on deposits, saving accounts from banks registered in Egypt are exempt • Interest received from other sources are taxable at 20%
Royalties	20%
On payments to artists and sportsmen	20%

V   INDIRECT TAXES

		Residents	Non-residents
Value Added Tax (VAT)	General description	Tax on the supply of goods and services	
	Entities being obliged to levy VAT	• Manufacturing entities with turnover higher than 54,000 EG P • Commercial, trading entities with turnover higher than 150,000 EG P	
	Taxable activities	All activities except: agricultural, professional	
	Taxable activities – zero rated (examples)	All exporting activities	
	Exemptions (examples)	• All activities with some important governmental sector (ministry of defence, interior ministry, petroleum sector) • All activities within the free zone areas	
	Refund of VAT	Yes	
	Tax liability	Goods and services provided in Egypt	
	Tax rates	The general tax rate is 10% Some exceptions exist such as: • 5% for food products • From 15% to 45% for vehicles	
	Administrative obligations	N/A	
Stamp Duty Land Tax		Property tax is 10%	
Stamp Duty		• Stamp duty per signed document 0.40 EG P • Newspaper advertisement stamp duty is 15% • Stamp duty on other advertisements is calculated based on length/ space of the advertisement	

Estonia

(Evald Veldemann, evald.veldemann@elss.ee)

I   MAIN LEGAL FORMS

Legal form / Characteristics	Partnership and Limited Partnership (LP)	Ltd (private corporation) and Plc (public corporation)
Partners/shareholders • Number • Restrictions	Two or more persons	One or more shareholders
Directors	Management by partners	At least one director
Establishment	Partnership Deed	Memorandum of Association
Registration	Notarised agreements filed on the commercial register	
Minimum capital	No formal requirements	Ltd: EEK 40,000 (€2,557) Plc: EEK 400,000 (€25,566)
Liability	Unlimited liability for general partner, limited liability for limited partner	Limited to capital
Governance	Partners	Annual general meeting Ltd: meeting of shareholders, management board, a private limited company shall have a supervisory board if the share capital is greater than EEK 400,000 (€25,566) and the management board of the private limited company has less than three members, or if prescribed by the Articles of Association of the private limited company Plc: general meeting, supervisory board, management board

Legal form / Characteristics	Partnership and Limited Partnership (LP)	Ltd (private corporation) and Plc (public corporation)
Audit requirements	Partnership and LP: if a general partner is not an individual, a copy of the signed annual report and some other documents shall be submitted to the Commercial Register, if auditing is compulsory. In addition to the other cases provided by law, the annual report of an accounting entity shall be audited if at the balance sheet date of the accounting year the accounting entity exceeds the limits of at least two of the three following criteria: • sales revenue (net turnover), in the case of a company, or income, in the case of other accounting entities: EEK 10m (€639,117) • balance sheet total: EEK 5m (€319,558) • number of employees: 10	A private limited company shall have an auditor if the share capital of the private limited company is greater than EEK 400,000 (€25,566) or if prescribed by law or the articles of association Plc companies must have an auditor In addition to the other cases provided by law, the annual report of an accounting entity shall be audited if at the balance sheet date of the accounting year the accounting entity exceeds the limits of at least two of the three following criteria: • sales revenue (net turnover), in the case of a company, or income, in the case of other accounting entities: EEK 10m (€639,117) • balance sheet total: EEK 5m (€319,558) • number of employees: 10
Taxation	Transparent	Corporate taxes on worldwide income
Usage	Rare	Common

II CORPORATION TAX (ETTEVÕTE TULUMAKS, KASUMIMAKS)

Description \ Legal form	Resident corporation	Permanent establishment (PE)
General description	Distribution tax on distributed profits. Amounts that could be considered hidden profit distributions are also taxed Also income tax is charged on amounts that have arisen from the reduction in the share capital of a corporation, payments made to a person in the case of return of the holding and the liquidation proceeds	Non-residents subject to tax on Estonian business source income, which will be exported
Taxable entities	Corporations with seat and/or place of management and control in Estonia	Foreign corporations with PE in Estonia
Taxable income	Worldwide profits	Estonian source income
Calculation of taxable profits	Distributed profit of the period	Distributed profit of the PE
Interest payments	Deductible subject to thin capitalisation rules	
Related party transactions	Arm's length prices should be applied	
Tax year, return and payment	• The taxable period is the calendar year or the financial year in the case of those it does not coincide with • Advance payments are required to be paid twice a year: on 10 March and 10 October. The size of an advance payment is calculated on the basis of total amount of income tax calculated during the previous 3 years • The tax return is required to be submitted and the final tax to be paid no later than 1 July of the following year. In the case of overpaid tax, the overpaid amounts shall be refunded within 30 days after submitting the tax return	
Capital gains	Subject to regular corporation tax	
Losses	No relief	
Tax group	No group taxation	
Tax rate	21% (2008); 20% (2009); 19% (2010); 18% (after 2011) on distributed profit	

III TAXES FOR INDIVIDUALS

		Residents	Non-residents
Income Tax	General description	Federal tax on income of individuals	
	Taxable entities and taxable income	A natural person is a resident if their place of residence is in Estonia or if they stay in Estonia for at least 183 days over the course of 12 consecutive calendar months. All income is taxable, whether derived in Estonia or outside Estonia	A non-resident shall pay income tax only on income derived from Estonian sources
	Types of taxable income	Income tax is charged on income derived by a resident natural person during a period of taxation from all sources of income in Estonia and outside Estonia	
	Calculation of income	• Trade income: accrual basis • Small businesses: cash basis • Rural income: special method • Other types of income: cash basis	
	Tax year, tax assessment and tax payment	The tax year is the calendar year and declaration of income must be presented on 31 March of the next calendar year	Taxes are mainly collected through withholding of tax
	Losses	Business-related loss may be carried forward for 7 years	
	Tax rates	21% (2008); 20% (2009); 19% (2010); 18% (after 2011)	
Capital Gains Tax (CGT)	General description	There is no special capital gains taxation Capital gains are taxed alongside taxable income	
	Taxable entities and chargeable assets	Disposal of securities	Disposal of shares in Estonian companies and of shares in companies, where assets are constituted more than 50% from irrecoverable property located in Estonia
	Calculation of gain	Difference between selling price and acquisition costs	
	Tax year, tax assessment and tax payment	Declaration is the same as for other incomes	
	Losses	If the amount of loss earned by a transfer of securities exceeds the amount of gains earned by the same transfers during the same period of taxation, then the amount by which the loss exceeds the gains may be deducted from the gains of subsequent periods without a time limit	Losses not deductible
	Tax rates	21% (2008); 20% (2009); 19% (2010); 18% (after 2011) on gains	
		Estonia domiciled	**Non-Estonia domiciled**
Inheritance Tax (IHT)	General description	No inheritance tax is levied	

IV WITHHOLDING TAXES

	Payments to non-residents[1]
Dividends	No withholding tax
Interest	Tax is not charged
Royalties	Tax is not charged
On payments to artists and sportsmen	15%

---

1 Reduced rates of withholding tax should be applied where there is an appropriate double tax treaty.

V   INDIRECT TAXES

		Residents	Non-residents
Value Added Tax (VAT) (käibemaks)	General description	Tax on the supply of goods and services, imports and others	
	Entities being obliged to levy VAT	• Those with taxable turnover exceeding EEK 250,000 (€15,980) in a calendar year • Entities who import from the EU	
	Taxable activities	• The supply of goods and services in Estonia • Importation of goods to Estonia • Obtaining goods from EU • Acquiring goods or services from a non-resident taxpayer, who is not registered as an Estonian taxpayer (if the location of creation of turnover is in Estonia)	
	Taxable activities – zero rated (examples)	• Exports • Intra-Community supply of goods • Services, where the place of service is not Estonia	
	Exemptions (examples)	The following are tax-free: • medical services • certain educational services • insurance services	
	Refund of VAT	The excess amounts paid will be refunded within 30 days starting from the day the application is received	
	Tax liability	Taxable period is calendar month. Submission declaration and date for paying VAT to the tax administrator is 20th day of the following month	
	Tax rates	Standard rate of 18%, 5% or 0% for certain other activities Note that probably from 2009 onwards the preferential tax rate 5% will be increased to 9%, also the list of those certain other activities will be shortened	
	Administrative obligations	• Service has to be issued within 7 days • Special requirements for details of invoices • In some cases invoice can be issued by the acquirers of goods or the recipients of services	
Stamp Duty Land Tax		The subject of land tax is land, of which the owner pays tax on the assumption of the taxable price of the land (which differs regionally)	
Stamp Duty		Practically all juridical actions, examination applications and issuing documents where the second party is a governmental authority, state authority, court, etc are taxed with stamp duty. Each operation has its own rate of stamp duty. It can be defined as a concrete sum or as a certain percentage of the sum of transaction	

Finland

(Karri Nieminen, karri.nieminen@fiscales.fi)

I MAIN LEGAL FORMS

Legal form / Characteristics	Partnership and Limited Partnership (LP)	Ltd (private corporation) and Plc (public corporation)
Partners/shareholders • Number • Restrictions	Partnership: minimum two partners – general partners LP: at least one general partner and one limited partner	Ltd: minimum one shareholder Plc: minimum one shareholder
Directors	Management by partners	Ltd: minimum one director and one deputy Plc: minimum three directors
Establishment	Deed	Notarial deed
Registration	Trade register; registration usually takes less than a month	
Minimum capital	Partnership: no minimum capital LP: at least one limited partner with financial input	Ltd: €2,500 Plc: €80,000
Liability	Unlimited for general partner Limited for limited partner	Limited
Governance	No formal requirements	Shareholder and director meetings
Audit requirements	Audit mandatory if two out of three conditions are satisfied for consecutive years: • turnover of at least €200,000 • balance sheet of at least €100,000 • employs at least three people The new Auditing Act came into operation on 1 July 2007. It contains implementing provisions concerning audit requirements	
Taxation	All income is assessed on individual partners; part of the income is taxed as capital income depending on the net assets of the partnership and the rest is taxed at progressive rates	Subject to corporation tax, 2009: 26% flat
Usage	Uncommon due to unlimited liability and higher rates of tax	More common, especially with higher incomes

II   CORPORATION TAX

Legal form / Description	Resident corporation	Permanent establishment (PE)
General description	Corporation tax	
Taxable entities	Corporations incorporated in Finland	PE located in Finland
Taxable income	Worldwide profits	All income attributable to PE, whether derived from Finland or abroad
Calculation of taxable profits	Accounting profit is adjusted for various tax add-backs and allowances to arrive to chargeable profits	
Interest payments	Interest paid on borrowed capital is deductible. Dividend paid on equity capital is not deductible. There are no specific rules concerning thin capitalisation other than transfer pricing rules	
Related party transactions	All related party transactions must take place on arm's length basis Transfer pricing rules in effect from 1 January 2007 onwards which are in line with EU regulations	
Tax year, return and payment	• The financial year of a company may be any 12-month period • Companies must file the tax return no later than 4 months after the end of their financial year • Companies are required to settle tax on account during the course of the year	
Capital gains	Capital gains and losses are usually assessed as part of company's profits subject to corporation tax Sale of shares in associated companies can, under certain conditions, be tax-free	
Losses	Losses can be carried forward and set off against profits of the subsequent 10 years. Losses are utilised on a first-in, first-out basis. Capital losses may have a set-off period of 3–5 years	
Tax group	There is no group taxation in Finland. All group companies are taxed separately	There is no group taxation in Finland. All group companies are taxed separately. Moreover, some kind of group taxation may be achieved by tax-deductible contributions which are taxed at the other company
Tax rate	2009: 26%	

III TAXES FOR INDIVIDUALS

<table>
<tr><td rowspan="11">Income Tax</td><td></td><td>Residents</td><td>Non-residents</td></tr>
<tr><td>General description</td><td colspan="2">Tax levied on the chargeable income of a chargeable person for a year of assessment</td></tr>
<tr><td>Taxable entities and taxable income</td><td>Residents are taxed on their worldwide income with some relief for double taxation</td><td>Non-residents are taxed on income derived in Finland including investments. There is an expatriate regime for a flat tax of 35% for a period of 48 months</td></tr>
<tr><td>Types of taxable income</td><td colspan="2">Capital income:
• property income
• income from capital investment (interest, sale of goodwill, dividends (partly), royalties, annuities)
• income from business activities (partly)

Earned income:
• income from business activities (partly)
• dividends (partly)
• employment income including benefits in kind stock options</td></tr>
<tr><td>Calculation of income</td><td colspan="2">Dividends to residents:

From listed companies 30% of dividend income is exempt and 70% is taxed as capital income. Dividends from non-quoted shares are divided into capital income and earned income. 9% of shares' mathematical (corrected net asset) or market value (foreign shares) at the end of the fiscal year preceding the tax year is regarded as capital income, which is tax exempt up to €90,000 per year per individual. If the amount of 9% exceeds €90,000, 30% is tax exempt and 70% is taxed as capital income with tax rate of 28%. The rest of dividend (the amount over 9%) is taxed at 70% as earned income with progressive tax rate and 30% is tax exempt</td></tr>
<tr><td>Tax year, tax assessment and tax payment</td><td colspan="2">• Tax year – calendar year
• Individual self-assessment returns should be completed and filed by mid May
• Tax is deducted at source on employment income</td></tr>
<tr><td>Losses</td><td colspan="2">Losses can be deducted from other income. Some restrictions</td></tr>
<tr><td>Tax rate</td><td colspan="2">(€)   *Rate*
13,100–21,700   7% + €8[1]
21,700–35,300   18% + €610
35,300–64,500   22% + €3,058
64,500+   30.5% + €9,482

In addition there is a municipality tax, sickness insurance and church tax. The highest marginal tax rate can go up to around 51%

These are tax rates for 2009

Flat rate tax for capital income is 28%</td></tr>
</table>

---

1 This represents the amount of tax that has to be paid at the lower end of the bracket, ie a tax of €8 has to be paid on €12,600. Tax at a rate of 8.5% will be levied on amounts in excess of €12,600 on top of the €8.

		Residents	**Non-residents**
Capital Gains Tax (CGT)	General description	Tax on increase in the value of asset between acquisition and disposal, chargeable to income or corporate tax	
	Taxable entities and chargeable assets	Capital gain arising on the sale of a private residence is exempt if the person has lived in this property for at least 2 years during the period of ownership. Sale of business can also be tax exempt if sold under strict conditions to members of immediate family	
	Calculation of gain	Capital gain is calculated by deducting the acquisition and sale costs from the disposal proceeds A minimum deduction of 20% of the sale price is applied. If the asset has been owned for at least 10 years, the minimum deduction is 40%	
	Tax year, tax assessment and tax payment	• Tax year – calendar year • Tax return has to be filed at the latest in early May (dates vary). Tax can be paid interest-free up until the end of January and must be paid at the latest by December of the following year and February the year after (eg tax for 2008 will have to be paid at the latest by December 2009 (first half) and February 2010 (second half))	
	Losses	Losses can be deducted from gains arising in the same year or the following 3 years. No possibility of carry back	
	Tax rates	28%	
		Domiciled	**Non-domiciled**
Inheritance Tax (IHT)	General description	Chargeable on estates and beneficiaries resident in Finland. Transfer of a business or a farm to a descendant is partially exempt from taxes	
	Taxable entities and chargeable assets	All assets	
	Calculation of charge	Calculation based on the market value of the assets	
	Taxable events	Death	
	Allowances	• Allowance for household belongings of €4,000 • Spouse allowance of €60,000 • Minor allowance of €40,000 • Payments of up to €35,000 per recipient from life insurance policies are exempt	
	Tax rates	There are two different classes of recipients for inheritance tax purposes A spouse, children and parents of the deceased and spouse's children belong to the first class. The remaining belong to the second class • The tax rates in first class are as follows: *(€)* *Rate* 20,000–40,000 7% + €100 40,000–60,000 10% + €1,500 60,000+ 13% + €3,500 • The tax rates in second class are as follows: *(€)* *Rate* 20,000–40,000 20% + €100 40,000–60,000 26% + €4,100 60,000+ 32% + €9,300	

IV WITHHOLDING TAXES

	Payments to non-residents[2]
Dividends	28%
Interest	28%
Royalties	28%
On payments to artists and sportsmen	15%

---

2 Reduced rates of withholding tax may apply where there is an appropriate double tax treaty.

V   INDIRECT TAXES

<table>
<tr><th></th><th></th><th>Residents</th><th>Non-residents</th></tr>
<tr><td rowspan="10">Value Added Tax (VAT)</td><td>General description</td><td colspan="2">Tax on the supply of goods and services</td></tr>
<tr><td>Entities being obliged to levy VAT</td><td colspan="2">Minimum turnover €8,500 (obligatory); if turnover is less than €8,500 entity is allowed to register</td></tr>
<tr><td>Taxable activities</td><td colspan="2">Broad-based tax on most goods and services</td></tr>
<tr><td>Taxable activities – zero rated (examples)</td><td colspan="2">• Subscribed newspapers and magazines
• Sale of gold to the Bank of Finland
• Goods and services sold in connection with the sale of a business</td></tr>
<tr><td>Exemptions (examples)</td><td colspan="2">• Healthcare, certain education, sale of properties (usually)
• Certain financial services, gold bullions, insurance services</td></tr>
<tr><td>Refund of VAT</td><td colspan="2">Yes (if overpaid or if taxpayer is in export business and makes VAT purchases in Finland)</td></tr>
<tr><td>Tax liability</td><td colspan="2">Normally the supplier of goods and services is responsible for charging VAT</td></tr>
<tr><td>Tax rates</td><td colspan="2">• Standard rate = 22%
• Reduced tax rates for certain commodities and services are 17%, 8% and 0%</td></tr>
<tr><td>Administrative obligations</td><td colspan="2">Monthly tax returns</td></tr>
<tr><td colspan="2">Stamp Duty Land Tax</td><td colspan="2">4%</td></tr>
<tr><td colspan="2">Stamp Duty</td><td colspan="2">1.6%</td></tr>
</table>

France

(Yves Sevestre, y.sevestre@cabinet-sevestre.com)

I MAIN LEGAL FORMS

Legal form / Characteristics	Partnership and Limited Liability Partnership (LLP)	Ltd (private corporation) and Plc (public corporation)
Partners/shareholders • Number • Restrictions	*Société en nom collectif (SNC):* • at least two partners *Société en Commandite Simple (SCS:)* • at least two partners *Société civile (SC):* • at least two partners	*Société à responsabilité limitée (SARL) or entreprise unipersonnelle à responsabilité limitée (EURL):* • between one and 100 *Société anonyme (SA):* • at least seven shareholders *Société par actions simplifiée (SAS):* • at least one partner

Directors	*SNC:*
	One or more manager registered at the Commercial Court
	SCS:
	Unless otherwise stipulated in the company's articles, all the 'commandités' are managers
	It is possible to choose one or more managers, who can be a partner or not
	SC:
	One or more manager or partner
		SARL:
		One or more manager or partner
		SA:
		• *Classic system* – 'conseil d'administration' (CA):
		  – between 3 and 18 members
		  – management of the company by the President of the CA or a general director
		• *Dualistic system* – 'directoire' and 'conseil de surveillance':
		  – 'directoire': maximum five members
		  – the 'directoire' manages the company
		  – 'conseil de surveillance': between 3 and 18 members (checks the directoire)
		SAS:
		One President

Establishment	Partnership deed	By-laws of company
Registration	All entities to be registered at the Commercial Court and publication of by-laws	

Legal form / Characteristics	Partnership and Limited Liability Partnership (LLP)	Ltd (private corporation) and Plc (public corporation)
Minimum capital	*SNC:* No minimum *SCS:* No minimum	*SARL:* Minimum capital: €1 *SA:* Minimum capital: • €37,000 • €225,000 for listed public companies *SAS:* Minimum capital: €1
Liability	*SNC:* Jointly and unlimited liability of all debts *SCS:* • 'commandités': joint and unlimited liability of all debts • 'commanditaires': liability limited to their contribution *SC:* Unlimited liability of all debts	*SARL, SA, SAS:* Liability limited to contribution
Governance	Partners	*SARL and SA:* Defined by the commercial law *SAS:* Freedom of governance, defined in the by-laws
Audit requirements	*SNC and SCS:* No obligation for audit Except if the company exceeds two of the three following: • balance sheet > €1.55m • turnover > €3.1m • employees > 50 *SC:* No obligation for audit	*SARL:* No obligation Except if the company exceeds two of the three following ceilings: • balance sheet > €1.55m • turnover > €3.1m • employees > 50 *SA:* The legal auditor has to certify the corporate accounts annually *SAS:* From January 2009, obligation for audit only: • if the company exceeds the following ceiling: – balance sheet > €1m – turnover > €2m – employees > 20 • if the company belongs to the group SAS which already has legal auditor and which has no obligation for audit has to wait until the end of the legal auditor mandate before stopping the obligation of audit

Legal form / Characteristics	Partnership and Limited Liability Partnership (LLP)	Ltd (private corporation) and Plc (public corporation)
Taxation	*SNC* Each partner subject to personal income tax. Share of profits included in corporate return (except election for corporate income tax) *SCS* Each partner subject to personal income tax. Share of profits included in corporate return (except election for corporate income tax) *SC* Each partner subject to personal income tax	*SARL* Corporate income tax, unless elected to be assessed for personal income tax *SA and SAS* Corporate income tax
Usage	*SNC/SCS:* Used for small businesses *SC:* Used for patrimonial operations or civil/professional activity or real estate operations	*SARL:* Start-ups and small or medium-sized companies *SA:* Listed companies *SAS:* As SARLs and not SAs

II CORPORATION TAX

Legal form / Description	Resident corporation	Permanent establishment (PE)
General description	Corporation tax	
Taxable entities	The company	Foreign entity
Taxable income	Territoriality principle: tax is only due on business income generated by enterprises operating in France	Territoriality principle: tax is only due on business income generated by the French PE
Calculation of taxable profits	• Net taxable benefits less tax losses: carry forward • Losses can be carried back over 3 years • Accruals method of accounting	• Net taxable benefits less tax losses: carry forward • Possibility to claim for a carry back at a reduced rate • Accounting method of accrual
Interest payments	Deductible unless paid to shareholders. Certain other restrictions apply	
Related party transactions	All related party transactions must take place on an arm's length basis	
Tax year, return and payment	• Calendar year, or if the taxpayer's financial year does not coincide, the financial year of 12 months closed during the relevant calendar year • Returns to be filed within 3 months of financial year end • Advance payments required each quarter	
Capital gains and dividends	• Generally deemed as ordinary income and subject to standard corporate tax rate • Long-term gains taxed at a reduced rate • Dividends: 95% exempt, 5% of dividends received plus tax credit are subject to corporate income tax • Capital gains: 95% exempt, 5% subject to corporate income tax • Capital gains of real estate company at reduced rate of $33\frac{1}{3}\%$	
Losses	Carried forward indefinitely or option for carry back	
Tax group	A group of companies can opt for a consolidated tax regime. The income and losses of resident companies within a 95% group may be aggregated and dealt with in the hands of the parent corporation	Possibility of a consolidated tax regime: the foreign PE can be the head of the group or can be a tax member
Tax rate	• Standard rate: $33\frac{1}{3}\%$ • Small and medium-sized enterprises: 15% on first €38,120 of profits, standard thereafter	

III TAXES FOR INDIVIDUALS

<table>
<tr><td colspan="2"></td><th>Residents</th><th>Non-residents</th></tr>
<tr><td rowspan="8">Income Tax</td><td>General description</td><td>Income tax</td><td></td></tr>
<tr><td>Taxable entities and taxable income</td><td>Worldwide</td><td>French source income only if no permanent dwelling held in France</td></tr>
<tr><td>Types of taxable income</td><td>• Employment and business income
• Capital gains
• Income from immovable property
• Investment income</td><td>• Real estate income
• Certain income subject to tax at source</td></tr>
<tr><td>Calculation of income</td><td>• Net salary: gross salary less compulsory social charges and less rebate of 10% on salaries or effective expenses
• Net capital gains: gross capital gains less acquisition costs
• Net real estate rental income</td><td>Net real estate income</td></tr>
<tr><td>Tax year, tax assessment and tax payment</td><td>• Generally the calendar year
• Individuals with business income may be assessed on the basis of an accounting period
• Income tax computed on the income of the preceding year
• Two instalments are required on 15 February and 15 May
• Final liability due on 15 September</td><td>• Filing date for EU residents: 30 June
• Other residents: 31 July</td></tr>
<tr><td>Losses</td><td>A loss in one category of professional income can be offset against income of another category. Excess losses that cannot be offset against the income of a given year may be carried forward for 6 years</td><td></td></tr>
<tr><td>Tax rates</td><td>• Dependent upon family situation (ie marital status and number of children)
• Progressive tax brackets from 5%–40%
• Tax shield: all taxes paid cannot be higher than 50% of all incomes</td><td></td></tr>
<tr><td>Dividends</td><td>• Taxation to the income progressive tax brackets or optional withholding tax of 18%
• Mandatory social charges are paid at the standard taxation rate of 12.1% within the first 15 days of the month, which follows the payment of dividends, whatever the taxation regime of dividends</td><td></td></tr>
</table>

		Residents	**Non-residents**
Capital Gains Tax (CGT)	General description	Capital gains tax	
	Taxable entities and chargeable assets	• Disposal of business assets • Immovable properties	
	Calculation of gain	*Shares:* proceeds less acquisition costs Rebate of $^1/_3$ per year as from the fifth year of ownership by individuals *Capital gains of immovable property:* net gains less a rebate of 10% per year as from the fifth year of ownership	*Capital gains of immovable property:* net gains less a rebate of 10% per year as from the fifth year of ownership
	Tax year, tax assessment and tax payment	*Shares:* with tax return *Immovable property:* within 2 months of disposal	*Immovable property:* on disposal
	Tax rates	*Shares:* rate of 18% + 12.1% (social security) = 30.1% *Immovable property, furniture and racehorses:* rate of 16% + 12.1% (social security) = 28.1%	

		France domiciled	**Non-France domiciled**
Inheritance Tax (IHT)	General description	Registration fees	
	Taxable entities and chargeable assets	Each beneficiary is a taxable person	Taxation on French assets
	Calculation of charge	Levied on the value of all transferred assets less related liabilities. In the case of gifts liabilities are usually not deductible	
	Taxable events	On death and all gifts made prior to death	
	Allowances	No inheritance tax between spouses and persons liable to PACS (Pacte civile de solidarité, which is a civil contract binding non-married partners) €150,000 direct line for each parent to each child; €150,000 for brothers and sisters	
	Tax rates	Dependent upon the proximity of the relationship between the donor and the recipient and upon the value of the elements transferred: from 20%–60%.	
Wealth tax		On the net assets of worldwide basis more than €770,000	On the immovable property evaluated more than €770,000

IV WITHHOLDING TAXES: DEPENDING ON THE TAX TREATY

	Payments to non-residents[1]
Dividends	18%
Interest	16%
Royalties	33$\frac{1}{3}$% subject to treaty or Royalty Directive
On payments to artists and sportsmen	15%

1 Reduced rates of withholding tax may apply where there is an appropriate double tax treaty or the EU Parent Subsidiary Directive.

V   INDIRECT TAXES

		Residents	Non-residents
Value Added Tax (VAT)	Entities being obliged to levy VAT	Persons making taxable supplies of goods and services in the course of a business	
	Taxable activities	Unless expressly exempt, all goods and services are taxable activities	
	Taxable activities – zero rated (examples)	Exports	
	Exemptions (examples)	• Financing and banking • Insurance • Commission • Interest	
	Refund of VAT	• Annual reimbursement if VAT refund is greater than €150 • Possible quarterly reimbursement if conditions are fulfilled	
	Tax liability	Supplier or provider of services established in France	Regime of reverse charge system: payment of the VAT by the French client for a supplier or a provider of service not established in France
	Tax rates	• 2.1% on press and medicines • 5.5% on water, food and other essentials • 19.6% standard	
	Administrative obligations	VAT registration	
Stamp Duty Land Tax		None but registration duty of 5.10%	
Stamp Duty		None	

Germany

(Heinrich Watermeyer, Bonn, heinrich.watermeyer@dhpg.de)

I MAIN LEGAL FORMS

Legal form / Characteristics	Partnership (OHG)	Limited Partnership (KG)	Private Corporation (GmbH)	Public Corporation (AG)
Partners/shareholders • Number • Restrictions	• Two or more • No restrictions		• One or more • No restrictions	
Directors	Management by partners		No restrictions	
Establishment	No formal requirements		Notarial deed	
Registration	Commercial Register			
Minimum capital	None	Some €500	€25,000	€50,000
Liability	Unlimited for all partners	Unlimited for general partner, limited for limited partner	Limited for all shareholders	Limited for all shareholders
Governance	• Partner • General meeting		• Managing director • Shareholders' meeting	• Managing director • Supervisory board • Shareholders' meeting
Audit requirements	Only when all general partners are corporations, especially in the case of GmbH (AG) & Co KG,[1] but not for small companies[2]		Yes, but not for small companies[2]	

---

1 A 'GmbH & Co KG' is a Limited Partnership, where the general partner is a GmbH; the limited partners may be individuals or corporations as well. A very common structure is the GmbH & Co KG with individuals as limited partners or even with only one limited partner being the only shareholder of GmbH. A variation is the 'AG & Co KG'.
2 Small companies are companies which do not exceed two of the following criteria: (i) turnover of €8.03m, (ii) total assets of €4.015m, (iii) 50 employees.

Legal form / Characteristics	Partnership (OHG)	Limited Partnership (KG)	Private Corporation (GmbH)	Public Corporation (AG)
Taxation	• Subject to trade tax, but not subject to income tax or corporate tax (pass-through entity) • Partners subject to income tax or corporate tax on their profit shares		• Subject to trade tax as well as subject to corporate tax • Dividends distributed to individuals subject to income tax on 60% of dividends as of 2009 (part-income-system) • Dividends distributed to corporations 95% tax-free	
Usage	Not popular	Popular as GmbH and Co KG, especially for SMEs	Popular, especially for SMEs	Legal form for listed companies; for others not so popular

II   TAXES FOR CORPORATIONS

Taxes on Income

	Resident corporations		Special rules for non-resident corporations
	Corporate tax	Trade tax	
General description	Federal tax on income of corporations	Municipal tax on business income	No special rules
Taxable entities and taxable income	Corporations with seat and/or place of management and control in Germany: worldwide income	Business income of PEs located in Germany	Corporations with German income (especially from German PE)
Calculation of income	Profit of commercial accounts $+/-$ results deriving from different rules for tax balance sheet[3] $+/-$ other differences[4] $=$ income for corporate tax purposes	Income for corporate tax purposes $+/-$ adjustments[5] $=$ income for trade tax purposes	Normally no special rules
Interest payments	Restrictions by so-called 'Zinsschranke'. Generally, only 30% of tax EBITDA (Earnings before interest, taxes, depreciation and amortisation) is deductible if interest payments minus interest earnings exceed €1m. Certain exceptions apply	So-called 'Zinsschranke' as in case of corporate tax applicable. If no restrictions by 'Zinsschranke', only 75% interest on all kind of debts financing deductible	Normally no special rules
Related party restrictions	To be at arm's length; special documentation requirements for cross-border transactions		No special rules
Tax year and tax payment	• Tax year – business year (calendar year or different business year) • Tax return • Quarterly prepayments, final payment or refund after tax assessment		Normally no special rules
Capital gains	• Taxable at regular rates (no special capital gains tax) • Capital gains on disposal of shares normally 95% tax-free		Normally no special rules

3   Examples: certain provisions.
4   Examples: 95% exemption for dividends and capital gains, no deductibility of losses deriving from the sale of shares. Gifts and entertaining expenses are only partly deductible.
5   Examples: part of interest, rental, lease, licence and fee payments.
6   For an intermediate period latest up to 2013 old rules additionally applicable: carry forward lost, if transfer of more than 50% of shares plus harmful transfer of assets to company.

	Resident corporations		Special rules for non-resident corporations
	Corporate tax	**Trade tax**	

Taxes on Income — Losses	• One year carry back (maximum €511,500)
	• Carry forward may be offset against profits up to €1m, exceeding amount by 60%
	• Carry forward lost in case of direct or indirect share transfer:
	  – of more than 25% during a 5-year period – lost quotally
	  – of more than 50% during a 5-year period – lost completely
		• No carry back
		• Carry forward may be offset against profits up to €1m, exceeding amount by 60%
			Normally no special rules

Tax group • Prerequisites • Consequences	• More than 50% shareholding of business company in corporation plus profit and loss absorption agreement • Consolidation of profits and/or losses		No cross-border tax consolidation

Tax rate	15% + 5.5% × 15% solidarity surcharge = 15.83%
	
	Overall tax rate 2008
	  – trade tax (levy rate = 400%) − 14.00
	  – corporate tax/solidarity surcharge − 15.83
	                                     = 29.83
		Normally 14%–19%, depending on levy rate of municipality	Normally no special rules
			
			Normally no special rules

Solidarity surcharge	Federal tax of 5.5% of corporate tax (included above)		No special rules
Wealth tax	No wealth tax is levied		
Real estate tax	• Local tax, paid by the owner of real estate • Approximately 1% per year of value of real estate as per 1964, final tax burden depending on levy rate of respective municipality		

III TAXES FOR INDIVIDUALS

Individuals pay trade tax on their business income. The rules are nearly the same as for corporations (see II above).

		Residents	**Non-residents**
Income Tax	General description	Federal tax on income of individuals	
	Taxable entities and taxable income	Individuals with residence or habitual abode in Germany: worldwide income	Individuals with neither residence nor habitual abode in Germany: domestic income (eg from real estate or PE located in Germany)
	Types of taxable income	• Trade income • Professional income • Rural income • Employment income • Capital income • Rental income • Certain other income	
	Calculation of income	• Trade income: accrual basis; small businesses: cash basis • Rural income: special method • Other types of income: cash basis	
	Tax year, tax assessment and tax payment	• Tax year – calendar year (business year for business income) • Tax return; joint tax return for spouses possible • Quarterly prepayments, final payment or refund after tax assessment	• Normally no tax assessment in case of withholding taxes (eg on dividends, on employment income) • No joint tax return for spouses (exceptions for EU-nationals)
	Capital gains	• No special capital gains tax • Selling business assets: taxable at regular rates; capital gains on shares 60% tax-free (part-income system) • Selling private assets: tax-free, unless held for less than one year (except shares) or 10 years (real estate) • If shareholding in a corporate entity by individual (eg stock corporation, limited liable corporation) amounts to at least 1% during any point of time of 5 years before the disposal: 60% tax-free (part-income-system) • Other securities: capital gain is subject to a flat tax of 25% plus solidarity surcharge of 5.5% leading to 26.38% as of 2009	• Real estate, PE: assets must be located in Germany • Shares: if seat and/or place of management of control is in Germany
	Losses	• See I above, corporate tax • In case of joint assessment of spouses: loss carry forward may be offset against profits up to €2m, exceeding amount by 60%	• No joint assessment of spouses

		Residents	**Non-residents**
Income Tax	Tax rates	• Personal allowance (tax-free earnings): €7,664 (€15,328 for spouses) • Progressive tax rate • Highest marginal tax rate for business, rural and professional income: 42% + 5.5% × 42% solidarity surcharge = 44% for income exceeding €52,152 (€104,254 for spouses) • Highest marginal tax rate for income exceeding €250,000 (€500,000 for spouses): 45% + 5.5% × 45% = 48%[7]	• No joint assessment of spouses • No personal allowance (tax-free earnings)
Solidarity surcharge		Federal tax of 5.5% of income tax	
Capital Gains Tax	General description	• No special tax • Capital gains may be subject to income tax (see above)	
Inheritance Tax and Gift Tax[8]	General description	Federal tax for recipients of inheritances and lifetime gratis conveyances	
	Taxable events	Inheritances or lifetime gifts of net assets located worldwide	Inheritances or lifetime gifts of assets located in Germany (real estate, PE, shares in German corporations with minimum quota of 1%)
	Valuation	• Normally market value • Special valuations for real estate, businesses and non-quoted shares	
	Allowances	• €500,000 for spouse • €400,000 per child • Minor amounts for others	• €1,100 in any case
	Tax rates	7%–30% for children and spouses (higher rates for others)	
Wealth tax		No wealth tax is levied	
Real estate tax		See II above	
Church tax		• For members of catholic or protestant church • 8%–9% of income tax, deductible for income tax purposes	

---

7 From 2008 onwards.
8 Major changes are under discussion that are likely to come into place in 2009.

IV   WITHHOLDING TAXES

	Payments to non-residents
On employment income (wage tax)	Only wage tax bracket for singles (exceptions for EU-residents)
On dividends	• 15% + 5.5% solidarity surcharge of 15% = 15.83% in case of a foreign corporate entity (s 44, para 9, Income Tax Act) as of 2009 • Possibly rate reduced by Tax Treaty or Parent Subsidiary Directive within the EU
On interest paid by banks	N/A
On royalties	15% + 5.5% solidarity surcharge of 15% = 15.83%, often reduced by Tax Treaty or Interest and Royalty Directive within the EU
On payments to artists and sportsmen	15% + 5.5% solidarity surcharge of 15% = 15.83%, often reduced by Tax Treaty

V INDIRECT TAXES

		Residents	Non-residents
Value Added Tax (VAT)	General description	Tax on the supply of goods and services, imports and others	
	Entities being obliged to levy VAT	• Any individual, partnership, corporation or other body, which carries out economic activities • On request no VAT, if turnover does not exceed €17,500 in the proceeding year and €50,000 in the current year • Fiscal unity, if entrepreneur owns more than 50% of shares in subsidiary and if certain other conditions are met	
	Taxable activities	Supply of goods and services, import of goods, intra-Community acquisition of goods, use of goods and services by entrepreneur or staff Place of delivery or rendering of service must be in Germany	
	Exemptions (examples)	• Lease of premises (in certain cases allowed to opt for VAT) • Bank and insurance services • Exports and supply of services in EU member state • Certain hospital and medical care services	
	Refund of VAT	VAT on supplies and services paid by an entrepreneur is deductible as input tax, if supply or service was for taxable supplies and services of his enterprise No credit for input tax paid on tax-exempt supplies and services (main exceptions: input tax for exports and delivery of goods within the EU)	Special refund system for non-resident enterprises with no taxable supplies in Germany
	Tax liability	• Normally supplier of goods and services • Reverse charge for certain supplies of goods and services (eg real estate)	
	Tax rates	• Regular rate = 19% • Reduced rate = 7% (food, books, certain medical and cultural goods, etc)	
	Administrative obligations	• Formal requirements concerning business records and invoices • Monthly tax self-assessments plus annual tax return (smaller companies quarterly or no self-assessments) • VAT identification number	• Registration for VAT purposes, if rendering of supplies and services in Germany • Fiscal representation possible but not obligatory
Real estate transfer tax		• Transfer of real estate located in Germany; transfers of shares in corporations as well as participations in partnerships owning real estate, if at least 95% of shares are transferred • Regular tax rate = 3.5%, ie effective tax rate may vary from state to state	

Ghana

(K. Manu-Debrah, Debrah@Nexiadebrah.com)

I MAIN LEGAL FORMS

Legal form / Characteristics	Partnership[1] and Limited Liability Partnership (LLP)	Ltd (private corporation) and Plc (public corporation)
Partners/shareholders • Number • Restrictions	• A minimum of two and maximum of 20 partners • None except that the partnership must be used for legal purposes No LLP permitted under Ghana law[1]	• A minimum of one shareholder for Ltd and Plc • Maximum of 50 shareholders for Ltd • No restriction for Plc
Directors	N/A	A minimum of two directors for Ltd and Plc
Establishment	Partnership agreement or deed	Company Regulations (ie Memorandum or Articles of Association)
Registration	The Registrar General of Ghana is responsible for the registration of all partnerships and companies	
Minimum capital	None required by law	GH¢ 500
Liability	Liabilities of the partnership are unlimited and every partner is jointly and severally responsible for them	Liability limited to the value of any unpaid liability on issued shares
Governance	The Board (or Council) of Partners	The Board of Directors
Audit requirements	Audit not required by law	Audited accounts due by law not later than 6 months after every accounting year
Taxation	Partners as individuals are liable for incomes accruing to each from their share of partnership profits	Profit and dividend taxes are applicable at the corporate level

1 Under Ghanaian law, partnership firms are registered under the Incorporated Private Partnership Act 1962 (Act 152). The law considers partnership firms as a separate legal personality distinct from its owners. A change in the composition of partners does not therefore lead to the automatic dissolution of the firm as is the case in some jurisdictions. Notwithstanding this, each and every partner of the firm is jointly and severally responsible for the liabilities of the firm.

II   CORPORATION TAX

Legal form / Description	Resident corporation	Permanent establishment (PE)
General description	Corporate income tax	
Taxable entities	A resident corporation or company is one incorporated in and under the laws of the Republic of Ghana, or having its management and control exercised from within Ghana at any time during the year of assessment	A PE located in Ghana includes a business carried on through an agent or any such representative of independent status acting in the ordinary course of business in Ghana, or a business having installed substantial equipment or machinery, or having business operations in Ghana requiring more than 90 days to complete
Taxable income	The full amount of income from business, employment or investment accruing in, derived from or brought into Ghana within a basis period	
Calculation of taxable profits	All incomes/revenues accruing to the business less deductions allowable by law	
Interest payments	Payment of interest to both resident and non-residents attracts 8% withholding tax on the gross amount	
Related party transactions	Provided the transactions are at full arm's length and not a scheme to avoid or evade tax, they are permissible. Otherwise the commissioner may adjust the chargeable income of both parties to prevent a reduction in tax payable	
Tax year, return and payment	The fiscal year in Ghana is January to December. Companies are expected to file their tax returns by the end of the fourth month after the end of their financial year, or by the 30 April each year, whichever is earlier	
	The filing requirements include a full set of audited financial statements together with the necessary forms disclosing relevant details about the earnings of the company for the tax year involved. Non-compliance attracts pecuniary and sometimes punitive penalty	
	A non-resident company with an established place of business in Ghana is also expected to file its returns in this manner	
	Tax payments are made on an advance quarterly instalment basis within the year based on a provisional assessment sent by the commissioner at the commencement of the year of assessment. A final assessment is prepared after the filing of the audited accounts with the Internal Revenue Service and the difference either paid or refunded	
Capital gains	Capital gains is the appreciation in the capital value of a chargeable asset between the date of its acquisation and the date of its disposal. Capital gain is taxed at 5%	
Losses	Businesses engaged in farming, agro processing, mining, timber, tourism, and software development are generally permitted by law to carry over tax losses to future periods	
Tax group	N/A	
Tax rate	• General corporate tax rate is 25% • Companies listed on the Ghana Stock Exchange pay tax at 22%	

III   TAXES FOR INDIVIDUALS

<table>
<tr><th></th><th></th><th>Residents</th><th>Non-residents</th></tr>
<tr><td rowspan="7">Income Tax</td><td>General description</td><td colspan="2">Unless specifically exempt by international protocol or the constitution of the Republic of Ghana, personal income tax is levied on the chargeable income of every chargeable person residing in Ghana in a year of assessment</td></tr>
<tr><td>Taxable entities and taxable income</td><td>Income derived from business, employment, or investments accruing from, brought into, or received in Ghana</td><td>Income derived from business, employment, or investments accruing in, derived from Ghana (does not include exempt income)</td></tr>
<tr><td>Types of taxable income</td><td colspan="2">• Employment income
• Income from business activities
• Income from investments (interest, dividends, rent and royalties)</td></tr>
<tr><td>Calculation of income</td><td colspan="2">All gains and receipts less standard deductions and personal reliefs applicable under the law</td></tr>
<tr><td>Tax year, tax assessment and tax payment</td><td colspan="2">• Year of assessment is the calendar year from 1 January to 31 December
• A return of income must be filed no later than 4 months after the end of a basis period. For employment income a fixed monthly Pay As You Earn (PAYE) regime is in place</td></tr>
<tr><td>Losses</td><td colspan="2">N/A</td></tr>
<tr><td>Tax rates</td><td>*Income (Monthly)*　　　　*Rate (%)*

First GH¢ 20　　　　　Free
Next GH¢ 20　　　　　　5
Next GH¢ 100　　　　　10
Next GH¢ 600　　　　　17.5
Exceeding GH¢ 800　　25.0</td><td>Flat rate of 15%</td></tr>
<tr><td rowspan="6">Capital Gains Tax (CGT)</td><td>General description</td><td colspan="2">Capital gains tax is the taxation on the appreciation in the capital value of a chargeable asset between the date of its acquisition and the date of its disposal</td></tr>
<tr><td rowspan="2">Taxable entities and chargeable assets</td><td colspan="2">Taxable entities: individuals and companies</td></tr>
<tr><td colspan="2">Chargeable assets: land and buildings in Ghana, businesses and business assets including goodwill, shares in companies, etc. Income derived from the realisation of assets brought into or received in Ghana</td></tr>
<tr><td>Calculation of gain</td><td colspan="2">Gains and losses are calculated by deducting the net book value of the assets disposed of from the sales proceeds realised at the date of disposal</td></tr>
<tr><td>Tax year, tax assessment and tax payment</td><td colspan="2">Capital gains tax is due 30 days after the realisation of a chargeable asset. The earner of capital gain must furnish the commissioner with the returns of the transaction</td></tr>
<tr><td>Losses</td><td colspan="2">No relief granted</td></tr>
<tr><td></td><td>Tax rates</td><td colspan="2">5% on the capital gain</td></tr>
<tr><td></td><td></td><th>Domiciled</th><th>Non-domiciled</th></tr>
<tr><td>Inheritance Tax (IHT)</td><td>General description</td><td colspan="2">Inheritance tax is not applicable in Ghana. However, a regime of gift tax is in operation in Ghana under which the value of gifts given beyond a certain limit is subject to gift tax at the rate of 5%. Exchange of gift between spouses, father and child or mother and child and vice versa is exempt from gift tax</td></tr>
</table>

IV   WITHHOLDING TAXES

	Payments to non-residents
Dividends	8%
Interest	8%
Royalties	10%
On payments to artists and sportsmen	15% Subject to applicable international protocols

V INDIRECT TAXES

		Residents	Non-residents
Value Added Tax (VAT)	General description	VAT is imposed on every supply of goods and services and the supply of any imported service, other than exempt goods and services	
	Entities being obliged to levy VAT	All registered businesses	
	Taxable activities	Any activity that terminates in the exchange of goods and services for valuable consideration and profit in the course of, or as part of, any business activity including without limitation the following: • processing of data or supply of information or similar service • delivery of accounting, legal, or other professional services given in an advisory capacity but excluding banking and insurance • leasing or letting of goods on hire	
	Taxable activities – zero rated (examples)	• Exports of taxable goods and services • Exports of goods shipped as stores on aircraft and vessels leaving the territories of Ghana	
	Exemptions (examples)	Goods or services with exempt status include imports of commodities such as musical instruments, agricultural inputs like fertilisers, books, medical/surgical instruments and cellular (mobile) phones etc	
	Refund of VAT	Subject to certain conditions, VAT refunds may be paid by the commissioner of VAT upon receipt of an application from a VATable entity within 30 days of the refund claim arising	
	Tax liability	The tax liability is the excess of output VAT over input VAT in any reporting period (ie a 30-day period)	
	Tax rates	VAT rate is 12.5% and a National Health Insurance Levy of 2.5% making a total of 15%	
	Administrative obligations	Returns should be filed on or before the last working day of the month following the month of transaction	
Stamp Duty Land Tax		N/A	
Stamp Duty		It is levied at 0.5% of the face value of the transaction and payable on items such as stated capital on the incorporation of a company, as well as on the transfer of landed property	

Gibraltar

(Moe Cohen, mcohen@benadycohen.com)

I MAIN LEGAL FORMS

Legal form / Characteristics	Partnership and Limited Partnership (LP)	Ltd (private corporation) and Plc (public corporation)	Protected Cell Companies (PCC)	Experienced Investor Funds (EIF)
Partners/shareholders • Number • Restrictions	• Two or more • Only LPs are restricted to no more than 20 partners	• 1 or more • Private corporations restricted to no more than 50 shareholders		• One or more • None
Directors	Management by partners or general partner for an LP	Management by directors		
Establishment	Partnership deed	Articles of Association	Articles of Association for insurance companies and collective investment schemes; consent and approval is required from the Financial Services Commission	
Registration	Gibraltar Companies House (and the Financial Services Commission for PCCs and EIFs)			
Minimum capital	None	None except £20,500 for Plcs A European Public Liability Company (EPLC or Societas Europaea SE) requires issued share capital of €120,000		
Liability	Unlimited but limited partners of LP are limited to capital	Limited to capital	Limited to the net assets of the cell and any non-cellular assets	Limited to capital
Governance	Partners, general meeting	Managing director/Board of Directors, secretary, shareholders' meeting		

Legal form / Characteristics	Partnership and Limited Partnership (LP)	Ltd (private corporation) and Plc (public corporation)	Protected Cell Companies (PCC)	Experienced Investor Funds (EIF)
Audit requirements	None	No audit required unless it is subject to taxation, regulated and medium sized	Required	
Taxation	Partners are subject to Gibraltar income tax on their share of the profits Non-Gibraltarian resident partners are only taxed on Gibraltarian sourced income	Only corporation tax is charged and only on Gibraltar sourced income Investment income is exempt		Tax transparent
Uses	Varied including professional and financial organisations	Small and medium-sized enterprises. Plc used for larger companies EPLCs allow EU companies to merge into one entity while avoiding legal and practical constraints	Insurance companies and collective investment schemes	

II   CORPORATION TAX

Legal form / Description	Resident corporation	Permanent establishment (PE)
General description	Gibraltar companies are subject to corporation tax only. See withholding tax below	
Taxable entities	• Companies are subject to corporation tax only on Gibraltar sourced income • Investment income is exempt	
Taxable income	Profits from Gibraltar activities after deduction of all expenses which are wholly and exclusively incurred in the production of income	
Calculation of taxable profits	Accounting profit is adjusted for various tax add-backs and allowances to arrive at profits chargeable to income tax	
Interest payments	Interest expenses for trading companies are fully tax deductible assuming they are at arm's length	
Related party transactions	All related party transactions must take place on arm's length basis	
Tax year, return and payment	• The tax year or the year of assessment for corporation tax purposes runs from 1 July to the following 30 June • A tax return should be completed and submitted by 30 September following the end of the previous year of assessment	
Capital gains	There is no capital gains tax	
Losses	Trading losses of a company may be offset against any other income in the tax year of the loss or carried forward and offset against future income of the same trade	
Tax rate	• The standard rate of corporation tax is 27%. Government is committed to reducing this to 10% by 2010 • A small companies tax rate of 20% is available for profits not exceeding £35,000 with marginal relief available	
Gaming tax	Levied at 1% of the relevant income on online gaming activities. Capped at £425,000 and a minimum of £85,000	

III   TAXES FOR INDIVIDUALS

<table>
<tr><td></td><td></td><td colspan="2" align="center">Residents</td><td align="center">Non-residents</td></tr>
<tr><td rowspan="8">Income Tax</td><td>General description</td><td colspan="3">Tax levied on the chargeable income of a chargeable person for a year of assessment</td></tr>
<tr><td>Taxable income</td><td colspan="2">Gibraltar residents are taxed on their worldwide income with relief for double taxation

There are special categories of individuals who have the tax capped, eg Category 2 (High Net Worth Individuals) pay a maximum tax of £23,000 and a minimum of £18,000 on worldwide income and similarly High Executives Possessing Specialist Skills (HEPPS) who are capped at £28,000</td><td>Permitted individuals (non-residents who work in Gibraltar) are liable to taxation on their Gibraltar income only</td></tr>
<tr><td>Types of taxable income</td><td colspan="3">• Property income
• Savings and investment income are not taxable
• Income from business activities
• Employment from personal services or pensions
• Income from trusts and estates</td></tr>
<tr><td>Calculation of income</td><td colspan="3">Generally that received in the year</td></tr>
<tr><td>Tax year, tax assessment and tax payment</td><td colspan="3">• Tax year – runs from 1 July to the following 30 June
• Tax assessment – individual returns and assessments for each taxpayer
• Returns must be filed by 30 September following the year of assessment
• Wages and salaries paid to employees are subject to tax deduction at source</td></tr>
<tr><td>Losses</td><td colspan="3">Losses created by trading activities can be offset against other income or carried forward against future profits</td></tr>
<tr><td>Tax rates</td><td colspan="2">Income is either taxed using the Allowance Based System or the Gross Income Based Method

Allowance Based System
• 17% on first £4,000 (reduced rate)
• 30% on next £12,000 (standard rate)
• 40% thereafter (higher rate)

Personal allowances are a minimum of £3,500 and include mortgage interest, life insurance, etc

Gross Income Based Method
• 20% on first £25,000
• 30% on next £75,000
• 38% thereafter

No personal allowances</td><td>Non-residents are taxed under the Allowance Based System applicable to residents, but may not receive any personal allowances and do not enjoy the reduced rate tax band</td></tr>
<tr><td rowspan="2">Capital Gains Tax (CGT)</td><td>General description</td><td colspan="3">There is no capital gains tax, estate duty tax or wealth or other capital taxes</td></tr>
<tr><td></td><td colspan="2" align="center">Domiciled</td><td align="center">Non-domiciled</td></tr>
<tr><td>Inheritance Tax (IHT)</td><td>General description</td><td colspan="3">There is no inheritance tax in Gibraltar</td></tr>
</table>

IV WITHHOLDING TAXES

	Payments to residents	Payments to non-residents
Dividends	None	
Interest	If situs of the loan is outside Gibraltar no withholding tax	
Royalties	None	

V INDIRECT TAXES

		Residents	Non-residents
Value Added Tax (VAT)	General description	No VAT in Gibraltar	
Stamp Duty Land Tax		Range between nil (for purchases up to £160,000) to 2.5% (for purchases in excess of £350,000)	
Stamp Duty		• Only payable on real estate (see above) and capital transactions • Capital transactions are payable at a fixed rate of £10 • Mortgages are subject to stamp duty at 0.13% (on mortgages not exceeding £200,000) or 0.2% (on mortgages exceeding £200,000)	

Greece

(Eleni Kaprani, estatus@eurostatus-nexia.gr)

I MAIN LEGAL FORMS

Legal form / Characteristics	General Partnership (OE) and Limited Liability Partnership (EE)	Limited Liability Partnership (EPE)	Limited by Shares Liability Company (AE)
Partners/shareholders • Number • Restrictions	• Two or more • None	• One or more • None	• One or more • None
Directors	Management by one or more partners or appointed administrator(s)	Management by one or more administrator(s)	Management by a board of directors consisting of a minimum of three persons Corporate governance law is applicable for listed companies
Establishment	Established by a private document, registered with the local Court of First Instance	Established by a Notary that contains the Memorandum of Incorporation and the Articles of Association. These are registered with the local Court of First Instance. A summary of the Articles of Association is published in the *Government Gazette*. Any amendments of the Articles of Association, including the transfer of portions must be made by a Notary	Established by a Notary that contains a Memorandum of Incorporation and the Articles of Association. These must be approved by a permit granted by the local department of the Companies Registry with the Ministry of Commerce. The permit and summary of the Articles of Association are published in the *Government Gazette*

Legal form / Characteristics	General Partnership (OE) and Limited Liability Partnership (EE)	Limited Liability Partnership (EPE)	Limited by Shares Liability Company (AE)
Registration	Registered with the local Court of First Instance		Registered with Companies Registry with the Ministry of Commerce
Minimum capital	None	€4,500 divided into share portions	€60,000 divided into shares
Liability	• For OE unlimited for all partners • For EE unlimited for at least one partner	Limited to subscribed capital	Limited to share capital
Governance	Civil law partners	Company Law 3190/55, administrator, partners' meeting. Decisions in partners' meetings require both majority in capital and majority in number of shareholders	Company Law 2190/20, Managing Director, Board of Directors, shareholders' meeting
Audit requirements	None	No audit is required unless the criteria mentioned for AE apply	The requirements for audit by certified auditors are if two out of three criteria are met: • turnover more than €5m • assets more than €2.5m • more than 50 employees If these requirements are not exceeded: audited by accountants
Taxation	50% of the profits are taxed at the corporate level and the other 50% are taxed at a personal level with the tax rates applicable for individuals	Resident companies are subject to corporation tax on their profits derived anywhere in the world	
Usage	Small businesses	Medium-sized enterprises	Medium and large companies

II   CORPORATION TAX

Legal form / Description	Resident corporation	Permanent establishment (PE)
General description	Corporation tax	
Taxable entities	Corporations, limited liability companies, state and municipal enterprises, cooperatives	PE located in Greece on all Greek-sourced income
Taxable income	Worldwide profits	Profits derived by PE in Greece
Calculation of taxable profits	Accounting profit is adjusted for various tax add-backs and allowances to arrive to profits chargeable to corporation tax (PCTCT)	
Interest payments	Interest expenses related to business income or to investments are tax deductible	
Related party transactions	All related party transactions must take place on arm's length basis	
Tax year, return and payment	Companies must file a tax return starting within 3–5 months from their year end	
Capital gains	Capital gains are treated as ordinary business profits and are taxed accordingly	
Losses	Current year trading losses can be offset against other current year profits After a current period claim, a further claim can be made to carry forward the trading losses and offset them against profits of the next 5 year	All rules mentioned for the Greek resident corporation will also apply to PE but only to the profits and losses of the Greek trade
Tax group	None	
Tax rate	For OE and EE 20%, for EPE and AE 25%	25%

III TAXES FOR INDIVIDUALS

		Residents	Non-residents
Income Tax	General description	Tax levied on the chargeable income of a chargeable person for a year of assessment.	
	Taxable entities and taxable income	Residents are taxed on their worldwide income with some relief for double taxation, or for taxes paid for their income abroad	Non-residents are taxed on income arising in Greece
	Types of taxable income	• Property income (usually rent) • Income from capital investment (interest, sale of goodwill, dividends, royalties, annuities) • Income from business activities • Employment from personal services or pensions • Royalties from Greece	
	Calculation of income	• Individuals may also be taxed according to deemed or notional income arising mainly from the use or acquisition of certain assets such as motor cars, private boats and houses • The net taxable income is determined after the deduction of certain allowances and expenses from the taxpayer's total income which include medical expenses, social security, rent, donations, interest on housing loans and private insurance subject to an upper limit • The tax is calculated based on a tax scale which is amended regularly • Employees are taxed on the Pay as You Earn (PAYE) system. PAYE withholding tax is calculated based on the applicable tax scale prevailing for the year. PAYE tax is withheld from the employee and it is the employer's obligation to pay it to the Tax Office every 2 months. Any penalties for late payment or non-payment of PAYE tax are imposed on the company	
	Tax year, tax assessment and tax payment	• Tax year – calendar year • Tax assessment – individual self-assessment returns for each taxpayer • Individuals are assessed on income earned on different dates, according to the type of income, starting from January to December following the year of the corresponding income earned	
	Losses	For companies losses are carried forward for 5 years to be offset against profits	
	Tax rates	*Rate* *Taxable income (€)* *Employees and pensioners* 0% 0–12,000 25% 12,001–30,000 35% 30,001–75,000 40% 75,000+ *Professionals* 10% 0–10,500 15% 10,501–12,000 25% 12,001–30,000 35% 30,001–75,000 40% 75,000+ *Various exemptions apply*	

		Residents	Non-residents
Capital Gains Tax (CGT)	General description	Tax on increase in the value of asset between acquisition and disposal, not chargeable to income or corporate tax	
	Taxable entities and chargeable assets	Any person resident in Greece Applicable only for real estate located in Greece. Sale of participation in companies worldwide is taxable in Greece	Any person holding real estate property or participation in local companies. If double tax treaties exist, exemption can be granted for sale of participation in local companies
	Calculation of gain	For real estate acquired after 1 January 2006, the difference between disposal proceeds and acquisition cost. For real estate acquired before 1 January 2006, no capital gains tax. In this case the buyer pays a transfer tax of 7%–11%. Shares are taxable at 5% For transfer of companies, gain is calculated based on a formula depending on profits, equity and real estate assets of an enterprise. For investments in companies registered abroad on the proceeds as shown on the relevant contract	
	Tax year, tax assessment and tax payment	Tax is payable in general before sale For sale of foreign enterprises, tax is payable within one month from the relevant contract, regardless of whether proceeds have been collected	
	Losses	No losses are recognised	
	Tax rates	On property, rates vary depending on the years the asset is held • 20% less than 5 years • 10% between 5–15 years • 5% between 15–25 years • 0% if held more than 25 years For transfer of AE the tax is 5%, with lower rates applicable for transfers between family members. For any other enterprise the tax is 20%	
		Domiciled	Non-domiciled
Inheritance Tax (IHT)	General description	Tax charged on a chargeable transfer of value made by a lifetime gift or estate on death	
	Taxable entities and chargeable assets	• The *movable and immovable estate* of the deceased or the donor is subject to taxation in Greece *if the assets are situated in Greece*, regardless of the nationality or residence of the deceased or the donor and the heirs or the beneficiaries • The *movable estate* (ie tangible and intangible assets other than real estate property such as cash, bank deposits, stocks, bonds, etc) of Greek tax residents situated abroad is subject to taxation in Greece • *Real estate situated abroad* is not taxed in Greece • The *movable estate of a foreign tax resident*, individual or legal entity situated abroad, which is donated to a Greek tax resident, is subject to taxation in Greece • Any *annuity* received by a heir, *from the estate of a Greek tax resident* is not subject to income tax, but is subject to inheritance tax at the time of the inheritance • The tax is calculated based on a tax scale, which is different, almost every year depending on the total value of the assets and the kinship between the deceased or the donor and the heir or the beneficiary. From the tax due in Greece, any relevant tax paid abroad, for the taxable assets, is deducted subject to certain conditions	

		Domiciled	**Non-domiciled**
Inheritance Tax (IHT)		• If assets are situated in Greece, they are subject to taxation regardless of nationality of the deceased or beneficiaries • The movable estate of Greek tax residents situated abroad is subject to taxation in Greece	
	Calculation of charge	Value of estate less allowances	
	Taxable events	Gifts (money or assets) during life, inheritance	
	Tax rates	Tax rates vary between 0% and 40% depending upon total value of assets and the kinship between the deceased and the beneficiary	

IV WITHHOLDING TAXES

	Payments to non-residents[1]
Dividends	10%
Interest	15%
Royalties	20%
Fees to professionals, artists, freelancers	20%

1 Reduced rates of withholding tax may apply where there is an appropriate double tax treaty.

V INDIRECT TAXES

		Residents	Non-residents
Value Added Tax (VAT)	General description	Tax on the supply of goods and services (VAT)	
	Entities being obliged to levy VAT	Any individual, partnership, corporation or other body, which carries out taxable activities	
	Taxable activities	All goods and services excluding sales of real property built before 1 January 2006, medical, educational, banking, insurance and legal services	
	Taxable activities – zero rated (examples)	Export of goods and supply of certain services with another EU member state, or abroad	
	Exemptions (examples)	Indirect tax levied on transactions which are not subject to VAT. The rate varies from 1.2%–3.6% according to the type of transactions	
	Refund of VAT	• VAT paid on supplies and services is deductible as input tax, if incurred in the course or furtherance of the business and for the purpose of making taxable supplies (including zero-rated supplies) • There is no credit for input tax incurred which relates to the provision of exempt supplies • Where mixed supplies occur (taxable and exempt supplies), subject to de minimis provisions, input tax must be apportioned and recovered according to a partial exemption method	• EC 8th Directive refund system for non-resident businesses established within the EU, providing its business is not otherwise required to be registered in Greece • Strict time-limits apply to claims
	Tax liability	Normally the supplier of goods and services is responsible for charging VAT	
	Tax rates	• Standard rate = 19% • Reduced rate of 9% for basic consumer goods • Reduced rate of 4.5% for books newspapers, magazines and theatre tickets • Special reduced rates for certain Greek islands 3%–13%	
	Administrative obligations	• Formal requirements concerning business records and invoices • Monthly self-assessment VAT return plus monthly payment of any VAT liability to Greek Tax Authorities • Certain arrangements may need to be disclosed • VAT identification number must be shown on all invoices issued • EU Invoicing Directive must be adhered to	• Registration for VAT purposes, if making supplies of goods and services in Greece • Appointment of fiscal tax representative possible but not obligatory
Stamp Duty Land Tax		For sales of property acquired after 1 January 2006, 1% paid by buyer	
Stamp Duty		• Levied on transactions, which are not subject to VAT, such as loans, credit facilities, rents, shareholders' deposits other than for capital increase or shareholders' withdrawals other than dividends, etc • The rate varies from 1.2%–3.6% according to the type of transaction	

Guatemala

(Jorge Garcia, jgarcia@wgarciayasociados.com)

I MAIN LEGAL FORMS

Legal form / Characteristics	Partnership and Limited Liability Partnership (LLP)	Ltd (private corporation) and Plc (public corporation)
Partners/shareholders • Number • Restrictions	• Minimum of two partners or shareholders • Shareholders are not anonymous	• Minimum of two partners or shareholders • Shareholders are not anonymous
Directors	President, Vice-president, and Secretary	
Establishment	By a public contract signed by the founders in front of a lawyer	
Registration	The registration has to be done at the 'Registro Mercantil' and SAT	
Minimum Capital	5,000 Quetzales	
Liability	The liability is just on the capital that each shareholder contributed	
Governance	It can be by one of two ways: • unique administrator • Administration Board	
Audit requirements	• A financial audit per fiscal year • An inventory audit per fiscal year	
Taxation	There is a choice between two regimes: • 5% on gross income • 31% on net profit	

II   CORPORATION TAX

Legal form / Description	Resident corporation	Permanent establishment (PE)
General description	Corporations, are companies that are not significantly dissimilar to LLCs in Guatemala in the way they operate and pay taxes, the only difference is that some corporations can have anonymous shareholders	
Taxable entities	Taxable entities are for-profit entities. Included are LLCs, Sociedades anónimas and Sociedades civiles	
Taxable income	Income derived from activities carried out in Guatemala and/or carried out with Guatemalan capital	
Calculation of taxable profits	Gross income minus cost of goods sold and operating expenses equals net income before taxes Profits are taxed at 31%	
Interest payments	Intercompany loans: The lending entity must submit a public contract between the two parties, specifying the loan amount, the due date and the interest rate. The lending party will be subject to a 10% tax on financial products Late payment interest due to the government, is assessed at the average of the current interest rate that the central bank has on that date	
Related party transactions	In Guatemala there is no restriction on transactions with related parties. If there is a profit between related parties it will be taxed as a normal transaction. If there is a loss between related parties, all involved parties must present a sworn statement to the government, stating that the losses are real and they will be subject to a government audit. The penalty for reporting fraudulent losses is 6 years of incarceration	
Tax year, return and payment	The tax year is from January to December The tax return and payment have to be submitted by 31 March	
Capital gains	Capital gains are subject to 10%	
Losses	If a company reports losses for 2 consecutive years, that company will be audited by the government If the losses are more than the capital of the company, there is a technical bankruptcy	
Tax group	None	
Tax rate	• Tax on Revenues: 31% on profits • IETAAP (temporary tax): 2.5% on gross income • VAT: 12% • Fiscal stamps: 3% • Capital gains: 10%	

III TAXES FOR INDIVIDUALS

		Residents	Non-residents
Income Tax	General description	There are two types of individuals, the individual that has his own company, and the individual that is an employee of a company. The first one, the one that we will focus on, is an 'individual company' just like a corporation, but instead of having a board of administration or a number of shareholders, this individual company is run by one person (but pays taxes as a corporation)	
	Taxable entities and taxable income	• All individual companies are subject to taxes • All the income that individuals generate is subject to taxation	
	Types of taxable income	Every profit or value added activity in every individual company in Guatemala or business operating with Guatemalan capital	
	Calculation of income	Income is the sum of all the sales that a company has in a period, a fiscal period that is from January to December	
	Tax year, tax assessment and tax payment	The tax year is from January to December The tax return and payment have to be submitted by 31 March	
	Losses	If an individual company reports losses for 2 consecutive years, that company will be audited by the government If the losses are more than the capital of the company, there is a technical bankruptcy	
	Tax rates	• Tax on revenues: 31% on profits • IETAAP: 2.5% on gross incomes • VAT: 12% • Fiscal stamps: 3% • Capital gains: 10%	
Capital Gains Tax (CGT)	General description	Capital gain is the difference between the sales price of an asset and its cost	
	Taxable entities and chargeable assets	Every company, corporation, individual or non-resident is subject to pay taxes on capital gains, and all assets are subject to this tax	
	Calculation of gain	The capital gain (or profit) results from the difference between the sales price and the cost of the asset	
	Tax year, Tax assessment and tax payment	The tax year is from January to December The tax return and payment have to be submitted by 31 March	
	Losses	If instead of having a capital gain there is a loss, there is no tax to be paid, but you can be subject to an audit from the government	
	Tax rates	The tax rate on capital gains is 10%	
		Domiciled	**Non-domiciled**
Inheritance Tax (IHT)	General description	The inheritance tax is applied to all succession activities from a person to another or from a company to another company	
	Taxable entities and chargeable assets	Every company or individual person that inherits a sum of money or assets	
	Calculation of charge	31% is applied to the value of the assets that will be inherited	
	Taxable events	Transfers of possessions from an entity to another are subject to pay the inheritance tax	
	Allowances	None	None
	Tax rates	31%	31%

IV WITHHOLDING TAXES

	Payments to non-residents
Dividends	3%
Interest	10% IPF
Royalties	5%
On payments to artists and sportsmen	31%

V   INDIRECT TAXES

		Residents	Non-residents
Value Added Tax (VAT)	General description	Tax on the supply of goods and services	
	Entities being obliged to levy VAT	All entities, besides government entities	
	Taxable activities	All activities carried out inside the country of Guatemala	
	Taxable activities – zero rated (examples)	• Exportation of services and goods • When a national company sells a product or provides a service to a non-resident company, and the goods or services are going to be used outside Guatemala	
	Refund of VAT	The refund of VAT can be requested from the government after 2 years of consecutive credit of VAT, and the company will be audited by the government to verify the requested VAT refund	No refund
	Tax liability	The supplier of the goods and services is responsible for charging VAT	
	Tax rates	12%	
	Administrative obligations	This tax has to be remitted every month	
Stamp Duty Land Tax		The stamp duty depends on the goods sold since there is a different rate for each product	
Stamp Duty		The stamp duty or customs tax is applied to all foreign goods that enter Guatemala	

Hong Kong

(Brenda Chan, bk@charles-marfan.com)

I   MAIN LEGAL FORMS

Legal form / Characteristics	Partnership and Limited Liability Partnership (LLP)	Ltd (private corporation) and Plc (public corporation)
Partners/shareholders • Number • Restrictions	Partnership: at least two and cannot be more than 20 partners Limited partnership: at least two and shall not consist of more than 20 persons and must consist of at least one general partner and one limited partner Restrictions: none	Ltd: at least one and not more than 50 shareholders Plc: one or more
Directors	Management by partners	Ltd: at least one director Plc: at least two directors
Establishment	By partnership agreement	Set up under the Companies Ordinance
Registration	Partnership: not necessary to be registered with the Hong Kong Companies Registry Limited Partnership, Ltd, Plc: registered with the Hong Kong Companies Registry	
Minimum capital	N/A	• None (for practical purposes this is not usually less than HK$1,000 or the equivalent in a foreign currency) • A minimum of one share can be issued to each shareholder

Legal form / Characteristics	Partnership and Limited Liability Partnership (LLP)	Ltd (private corporation) and Plc (public corporation)
Liability	Partnership: • jointly and severally liable for all debts and obligations Limited Partnership: • general partners shall be liable for all debts and obligations • limited partners shall be liable for debts and obligations within the amount they have agreed to contribute	Limited to share capital subscribed
Governance	Governed by the partners	Governed by the Board of Directors • secretary • shareholders' meeting • annual general meeting
Audit requirements	None	Annually
Taxation	Subject to profits tax on their profits arising in and derived from Hong Kong. Partnerships are transparent for tax purposes	
Usage	Professional practices	All other businesses

II CORPORATION TAX

Legal form / Description	Resident corporation	Permanent establishment (PE)
General description	Profits tax	
Taxable entities	Companies and partnerships	PE located in Hong Kong
Taxable income	Profit arising in or derived from Hong Kong	Profits derived by PE in Hong Kong
Calculation of taxable profits	Accounting profit is adjusted for various tax add-backs and allowances to arrive at profits chargeable to profits corporation tax	
Interest payments	Interest expenses are tax deductible if related to the generation of taxable profits	
Related party transactions	All related party transactions must take place on an arm's length basis	
Tax year, return and payment	Tax returns are issued in April each year and are required to be filed within one month	
	However, by special concession the following extensions for filing are usually granted:	
	Year-end	*Filing date*
	1 April to 30 November	30 April of the following year
	1 December to 31 December	15 August of the following year
	1 January to 31 March	15 November of the same year
Capital gains	Not taxable	
Losses	Net operating tax losses may be carried forward and set off against future taxable profits	
Tax group	None	
Tax rate	• 16.5% for limited companies • 15% for partnerships	

III TAXES FOR INDIVIDUALS

		Residents	Non-residents
Income Tax	General description	Tax levied on the chargeable income of a chargeable person for a year of assessment	
	Taxable entities and taxable income	Resident individuals are taxed on income arising in and derived from Hong Kong	Non-resident individuals are taxable on income derived in Hong Kong
	Types of taxable income	• Property income (usually rent) • Income from business activities • Employment income from personal services or pensions	
	Calculation of income	• Property income less 20% allowance for repairs and outgoings • Income from business activities is adjusted for various add-backs and allowances to arrive at profits chargeable to tax • Employment income or pensions on gross basis	
	Tax year, tax assessment and tax payment	Tax year – ends on 31 March each year Tax assessment – individual self-assessment returns for each taxpayer Return forms are issued on 1 April each year and must be submitted within one month	
	Losses	Losses may be carried forward and set off against future income on the election of personal assessment (combining all heads of income for assessment)	
	Tax rates	*Band* *(HK$)* First 40,000 Next 40,000 Next 40,000 On the remainder Standard rate	*Rate* *(%)* 2 7 12 17 15
Capital Gains Tax (CGT)	General description	Not taxable	

		Domiciled	Non-domiciled
Inheritance Tax (IHT)	General description	No inheritance tax	

IV   WITHHOLDING TAXES

	Payments to non-residents[1]
Dividends	No withholding taxes
Interest	No withholding taxes
Royalties	30%
On payments to artists and sportsmen	10.67%–11.67%

1   Reduced rates of withholding tax may apply where there is an appropriate double tax treaty.

V   INDIRECT TAXES

		Residents	Non-residents
Value Added Tax (VAT)	General description	Tax on the supply of goods and services (VAT)	
	Entities being obliged to levy VAT	There is no VAT or sales tax, with the exception of a first registration tax on automobiles	
Stamp Duty Land Tax		• On transfer of immovable property in Hong Kong • On property value less than HK$2m: $100 • For properties of value over HK$2m: range from 0.005%–3.75% based on the value of the properties	
Stamp Duty		On transfer of Hong Kong stock: 0.1% of the amount of the consideration	

Hungary

(Jozsef Lang, jozsef.lang@abt.hu)

I MAIN LEGAL FORMS

Legal form / Characteristics	Unlimited Partnership (ULP) and Limited Partnership (LP)	Limited Liability Company (Ltd) and Company Limited by Shares (Plc, including Closed Company Limited by Shares and Public Company Limited by Shares)
Partners/shareholders • Number • Restrictions	ULP: the number of partners is not restricted Two or more persons[1] LP: general partner – limited partner The number of partners is not restricted, but at least one limited and one general partner is required Restriction – an individual who has unlimited liability in another business cannot be an unlimited partner	Ltd:[2] the number of partners is not restricted One or more persons Plc: the number of partners is not restricted One or more persons Closed Company Limited by Shares: its shares are not put into public circulation Public Company Limited by Shares: its shares are put into public circulation
Directors	ULP: each member is entitled to manage independently LP: (one of the) general partner(s)	Ltd: managing director(s) Plc: Board of Directors
Establishment	ULP: by agreement and acceptance of the Memorandum of Association LP: by agreement and acceptance of the Memorandum of Association	Ltd: by agreement and acceptance of the Memorandum of Association Plc: by agreement and acceptance of the Articles of Association and by issuing shares
Registration	Registration at the Company Registrar (filing the Memorandum of Association and some other prescribed documents to the Court of Registry)	

---

1 Individual or corporate body.
2 Regarding the possible business forms in Hungary, the so-called 'Kft' might be met by the limited liability company. The foreign business forms of public limited company might be similar to the Hungarian so-called 'Rt'. An 'Rt' might be established in Hungary either in a form of closed company limited by shares ('ZRt') or in a firm of public company limited by shares ('NyRt').

Legal form / Characteristics	Unlimited Partnership (ULP) and Limited Partnership (LP)	Limited Liability Company (Ltd) and Company Limited by Shares (Plc, including Closed Company Limited by Shares and Public Company Limited by Shares)
Minimum capital	ULP: no minimum capital LP: no minimum capital	Ltd: minimum of HUF 500,000 (€2,000) Closed Company Limited by Shares: minimum of HUF 5m (€20,000) Public Company Limited by Shares: minimum of HUF 20m (€80,000)
Liability	ULP: unlimited up to assets of the partnership; members – unlimited and jointly LP: unlimited up to assets of the LP; members – unlimited for the general partner(s), limited for the external (limited) partner(s)[3]	Ltd: unlimited up to assets of the Ltd company; members – limited up to their capital contribution, plus up to the extra contribution, if there is any Plc: unlimited up to assets of the Plc; members – limited up to the face value or issue value of their shares
Audit requirements	Auditing of books is compulsory for all undertakings keeping double-entry books, if: • annual net sales exceed HUF 1,000m on average for the 2 financial years preceding the financial year under review, and/or • the average number of employees of the 2 financial years preceding the financial year under review exceeds 50 persons	
Taxation	Partnerships are transparent. Corporations are taxable on worldwide profits	
Usage	Partnership: limited use LP: LP is the second most common business form	Most companies operate in the business form of Ltd The companies with more significant economic role and businesses with higher need of capital investment generally operate in the form of Plc

---

3   The limited partner might remain to be liable for the liability of the LP within 5 years following the termination of his former status of general partner.

II CORPORATION TAX

Legal form / Description	Resident corporation	Permanent establishment (PE)
General description	Corporation tax on profits	
Taxable entities	Created under Hungarian law or with their place of management in Hungary	PE of foreign enterprises doing taxable activity in Hungary
Taxable income	Worldwide income: unlimited liability	Hungarian source income: limited liability
Calculation of taxable profits	Accounting profits adjusted for prescribed items 'Expected minimum profit' – should the profit before tax and the tax base for corporate income tax be less than the so-called 'expected minimum profit', then the corporate income tax (16%) is to be paid after the later, eg even in case of loss it can happen that a corporation is obliged to pay corporate income tax! The tax base of this is 2% of the total income (revenue, other income, income from financial and extraordinary transactions) decreased by the cost of goods sold and services intermediated	
Interest payments	Deductible as a business cost. Subject to thin capitalisation rules (1:3)	
Related party transactions	Transactions must be conducted on an arm's length basis at all times. If not, adjustment is a must for calculation of taxable profit in the case of the PE's taxable profit being lower due to the applied prices than would be on an arm's length basis	
Tax year, return and payment	Usually the calendar year, unless the taxpayer decides otherwise Advance payments must be made on a monthly or quarterly basis Returns must be filed by 31 May of the year succeeding the tax year	
Capital gains	Capital gains are taxed as business profit	
Losses	Losses may be carried forward at the taxpayers' election indefinitely. Under certain circumstances permission must be required from the tax authority to carry forward losses in the fourth and subsequent years	
Tax group	Not available	
Tax rate	Normal tax rate: 16% Solidarity surplus charge: 4% Beneficial rate of 10% might be applicable up to a profit of HUF 50m provided that the requirements are fulfilled	

III TAXES FOR INDIVIDUALS

		Residents	Non-residents
Income Tax	General description	Federal tax on income of individuals	
	Taxable entities and taxable income	Those with a habitual residence in Hungary. Tax levied on the worldwide income of the individual	Neither domiciled in Hungary nor with a habitual residence in Hungary. Hungarian source income subject to tax
	Types of taxable income	• Income from employment • Entrepreneurial income • Capital gains on movable and immovable property • Benefits in kind • Income from capital	Same types, taxation treaties between the countries are applicable Non-residents are taxable only after income derives from Hungary
	Calculation of income	• Employment income: full amount of revenue taxable as income • Entrepreneurial income: by calculation of the entrepreneurial profit (revenue minus costs) or in a lump sum method • Capital gains on movable and immovable property: by calculation of the selling price minus the amount of purchase price and some costs that belonged to the acquisition. • Capital gains tax on immovable property: see separate section • Benefits in kind: market value of them • Income from capital: depending on the sort of income derived from capital (transfer of securities, interest, security lending, dividend, Stock Exchange transactions)	
	Tax year, tax assessment and tax payment	The tax year is the calendar year Tax is collected by way of self-assessment Income tax returns must be filed by 20 May of the following year, entrepreneurs have until 15 February Advance payments are required	
	Losses	Losses may be carried forward indefinitely. Express permission required from the tax authorities to carry forward losses after the third year	
	Tax rates	18% on first HUF 1.7m. 36% on any excess Solidarity surplus charge of 4% is payable for the part of the income that exceeds the yearly limit of the annual limit for individual pension contribution (THUF 7,137 in 2008) 'Quasi third rate'	Same, according to mutual agreements between the countries

		Residents	Non-residents
Capital Gains Tax (CGT)	General description	Capital gains levied on immovable property and rights thereon	
	Taxable entities and chargeable assets	Individuals The net value of property transfer or of establishing and transferring rights thereon	Individuals, if the property is situated in Hungary
	Calculation of gain	Income shall be calculated regarding the income minus the amount of purchase price and some declared costs that belong to the acquisition of the immovable property, eg stamp duty, as well as the amount of improvement investments under certain conditions	
	Tax year, tax assessment and tax payment	Tax year – calendar year Calculation of gain yearly – in the year of gaining income from the capital Tax payable on the deadline for submitting tax return	
	Losses	Not taxable under personal income tax, nor might be carried forward	
	Tax rates	Standard 25%. After the property has been owned for certain amount of years the taxable base may be reduced: • with 10% of the calculated amount in the 2nd year following the year of acquisition • with 40% of the calculated amount in the 3rd year following the year of acquisition • with 70% of the calculated amount in the 4th year following the year of acquisition This new method will result in exemption on income from property selling after 5 years	
		Domiciled	**Non-domiciled**
Inheritance Tax (IHT)	General description	IHT is levied on property passing on the basis of an inheritance, a legacy or will, an acquisition of a legal share of an inheritance and a donation in the event of death	
	Taxable entities and chargeable assets	Individuals The net value of the inheritance constitutes the taxable base	There is no inheritance tax but there is an inheritance fee if the property is from Hungary
	Calculation of charge	Net value of inheritance subject to some allowances	
	Taxable events	Inheritance upon the death of the person leaving the property	
	Allowances (examples)	• Inheritance of savings deposits, movable inheritance up to a market value of THUF 300 per heir • Inheritance of usufruct or use of residential property by the surviving spouse • Inheritance, if the deceased is a minor and his estate is inherited by his parents	The allowances are the same as for domiciled persons and the rate of the fee is also the same
	Tax rates	Depending on the proximity of the recipient to the deceased donor and the value of the estate In case of inheritance of immovable property, reduced rates apply	

IV   WITHHOLDING TAXES

	Payments to non-residents[4]
Dividends	• No tax on dividends to corporates • In case of dividend on individuals: 5–15% of withholding tax might be levied • In case of dividend from security listed on any regulated market of any EEA member state 10% of withholding tax is levied
Interest	• Interest to corporates: 5%–10% of withholding tax • Interest to individual tax on interest is only levied to bank investments (deposit, securities, etc)
Royalties	In case of royalty to corporates: 5%–10%.
On payments to artists and sportsmen	Nil

---

4   Subject to double taxation treaty.

V INDIRECT TAXES

		Residents[5]	Non-residents
Value Added Tax (VAT)	General description	Tax on the supply of goods and services, imports and others	
	Entities being obliged to levy VAT	All natural persons and legal entities that supply goods or services on a regular basis (taxable persons) Non-taxable persons: in some cases, eg intra-Community acquisition of new means of transport	
	Taxable activities	Supply of goods and services within the territory of Hungary, intra-Community acquisitions, importation of goods, etc	
	Taxable activities – zero rated (examples)	Export, transactions that are regarded in the same way as export and international transport	
	Exemptions (examples)	Financial services, healthcare, social services, education, leasing or letting immovable properties (option is possible), etc	
	Refund of VAT	After meeting some requirements – possession of invoice issued for the taxpayer. The invoice meets all legal requirements Some other pre-conditions must also be met for refunding	In line with the 8th and 13th VAT Directives Possession of invoice issued for the taxpayer and meeting the entire legal requirement are also necessary
	Tax liability	Tax assessment, tax payment, submitting tax return	
	Tax rates	Standard rate of 20%; 5% is applied to textbooks and particularly medical supplies	
	Administrative obligations	Filing tax return on a monthly, quarterly or annual basis, depending on the VAT performance of the VAT subject to strict invoicing rules	Filing the application, the invoices, bank account statements, contracts, etc until 30 June of the subsequent year
Stamp Duty Land Tax		Residual estate: 2% up to THUF 4,000; 6% over THUF 4,000 Immovable property other than residual estate: 10% Calculation on the basis of market value	
Stamp Duty		Gift: 10%, in case of residual estate, reduced rates apply Transfer tax for movable property, certain rights: 10% Procedural duty (court, public/central administration)	

5   In view of this VAT schedule residents are domestic VAT taxpayers, as well as foreigners registered in Hungary for VAT purposes.

India

(Krupal Kanakia, krupal@chaturvedi-and-shah.com)

I   MAIN LEGAL FORMS

Legal form / Characteristics	Partnership and Limited Liability Partnership (LLP)	Ltd (private corporation) and Plc (public corporation)
Partners/shareholders • Number • Restrictions	Partnership: Minimum – two partners Maximum – 20 partners LLP (enacted January 2009)	Ltd: Minimum – two Maximum – 50 Plc: Minimum – seven No maximum limit
Directors	Management by partners	Ltd: Minimum – two Plc: Minimum – three
Establishment	Partnership deed	Memorandum and Articles of Association
Registration	Registrar of Firms Firms are required to obtain a Permanent Account Number (PAN) for filing of Return of Income, etc Further, registration is also required for various indirect taxes as may be applicable to the entity	Registrar of Companies Companies are required to obtain a PAN for filing of Return of Income, etc Further, registration is also required for various indirect taxes as may be applicable to the entity
Minimum capital	No minimum capital	Ltd: Rs 1m Plc: Rs 5m
Liability	Unlimited	Limited to capital
Governance	Partners	Board of Directors
Audit requirements	Optional. However, under Indian tax laws if a firm has turnover exceeding Rs 4m, then it is required to get its accounts audited in the manner prescribed under the Indian Income Tax Act 1961	Mandatory
Taxation	Partners assessed or share of profits	Corporation tax on adjusted profits
Usage	All types of business/industry	All types of business/industry

II   CORPORATION TAX

Legal form / Description	Resident corporation	Permanent establishment (PE)
General description	Corporation tax	
Taxable entities	Resident companies	PE located in India
Taxable income	Worldwide profits	Profits derived by PE in India
Calculation of taxable profits	Accounting profit is adjusted for various tax add-backs and allowances to arrive to profits chargeable to corporation tax (PCTCT)	
Interest payments	This is normally allowed on an accruals basis. Interest payable outside India is only deductible if withholding tax has been paid to the Government. However, interest paid to associate concerns should be on arm's length basis	
Related party transactions	Arm's length basis	
Tax year, return and payment	Tax year/assessment year means a period of 12 months commencing on 1 April every year and ending with 31 March of the next year	
	Companies must file the tax return on or before 30 September following the end of that financial year	
	The estimated tax liability for the year is to be paid in four instalments as given below:	
	Due date of instalment Up to 15 June of relevant financial year	*% of advance tax to be paid* Not less than 15%
	Up to 15 September of relevant financial year	Not less than 45%, as reduced by the amount, if any, paid in earlier instalment
	Up to 15 December of relevant financial year	Not less than 75%, as reduced by the amount, if any, paid in earlier instalment
	Up to 15 March of relevant financial year	The whole amount of advance tax as reduced by the amount/ amounts, if any, paid in the earlier instalments
Capital gains	10%–30% depending on nature of capital gain	
	Taxable amount: consideration received less disposal costs and acquisition cost	
Losses[1]	Net operating tax losses may be carried forward for 8 years and set off against taxable profits	
Tax group	None	
Tax rate[2]	33.99%	42.23%

---

1   There are special rules allowing the company to utilise other losses such as capital losses.
2   With effect from 1 April 2008, financial year 2008–09.

III   TAXES FOR INDIVIDUALS

<table>
<tr><td rowspan="12">Income Tax</td><td></td><td>Residents</td><td>Non-residents</td></tr>
<tr><td>General description</td><td colspan="2">Tax levied on the chargeable income of a chargeable person for a year of assessment</td></tr>
<tr><td>Taxable entities and taxable income</td><td>Residents are taxed on their worldwide income</td><td>Non-residents are taxed on income derived in India</td></tr>
<tr><td>Types of taxable income</td><td colspan="2"><ul><li>Employment from personal services or pensions</li><li>Property income</li><li>Income from business activities</li><li>Income arising from transfer of a capital asset</li><li>Income from capital investment</li><li>Cash gifts received in excess of Rs 50,000, except from family</li></ul></td></tr>
<tr><td>Calculation of income</td><td colspan="2"><ul><li>There are various provisions under the Income Tax Act 1961 which would determine the taxable income. Calculation of income would depend upon the head under which a particular income falls. Under India's Income Tax Act 1961, the following are the heads of income:<ul><li>– Income under the head 'Salaries'</li><li>– Income under the head 'House Property'</li><li>– Income under the head 'Profession or Business'</li><li>– Income under the head 'Capital Gains' (income arising from transfer of capital asset)</li><li>– Income under the head 'Income from Other Sources (Residuary section)'</li></ul></li><li>The maximum rate applicable to individuals under the Indian Tax Law is 33.99%</li></ul></td></tr>
<tr><td rowspan="6">Tax year, tax assessment and tax payment</td><td colspan="2">Tax year – financial year ending 31 March</td></tr>
<tr><td colspan="2">Tax assessment – criteria for assessment is fixed each year for which the Government of India issues separate guidelines</td></tr>
<tr><td colspan="2">The filing date of return of income for individuals is on or before 31 July of the assessment year</td></tr>
<tr><td colspan="2">A working partner of a firm whose accounts are required to be audited under the Income Tax Act or under any other law for the time being have to file their return on or before 30 September of the assessment year</td></tr>
<tr><td colspan="2">Advance tax liability</td></tr>
<tr><td colspan="2">The estimated tax liability for the year is to be paid in three instalments as given below:

Due date of instalment   % of advance tax to be paid
Up to 15 September of relevant financial year   Not less than 30% of advance tax
Up to 15 December of relevant financial year   Not less than 60%, as reduced by the amount, if any, paid in earlier instalment
Up to 15 March of relevant financial year   The whole amount of advance tax as reduced by the amount(s), if any, paid in the earlier instalments</td></tr>
<tr><td>Losses</td><td colspan="2">Business losses are fully deductible from any other income for the same year, and thereafter only against business income within the subsequent 8 years</td></tr>
</table>

		Residents				Non-residents
Income Tax	Tax rates	*Band* *(Rs)* 0–150,000 150,001–300,000 300,001–500,000 500,001 +	*Rate* *(%)* Nil 10 20 30	*Tax on Band* *(Rs)* Nil 15,000 40,000	*Cumulative tax* *(Rs)* 15,000 55,000 55,000 plus 30% of the amount by which income exceeds Rs 500,000	
		Plus, Education Cess @ 2% for primary education and 1% on secondary and higher education Where the income of any individual exceeds Rs 10m, surcharge @ 10% will also apply				
Capital Gains Tax (CGT)	General description	Tax on increase in the value of asset between acquisition and disposal				
	Taxable entities and chargeable assets	CGT is applicable to all persons who transfer a capital asset. Capital asset has been defined as property of any kind held whether or not connected with business/profession but does not include the following: • stock in trade • personal effects • agricultural land • Gold Bonds • Special Bearer Bonds • Gold Deposit Bonds (subject to the certain conditions)				
	Calculation of gain	Capital gains are computed by deducting from the full value of the consideration received or accruing as a result of the transfer of the capital asset the following amounts, namely: • expenditure incurred wholly and exclusively in connection with such transfer • the cost of acquisition of the asset and the cost of any improvement thereto				
	Tax year, tax assessment and tax payment	Tax year – financial year ending 31 March No separate CGT return is to be filed. A consolidated tax return is to be filed as explained earlier in II and III, depending on the type of the assessee Tax on capital gains has to be paid as per the time span mentioned in II and III depending upon the type of assessee (refer to tax payments' column of II and III)				
	Losses	• Long-term capital loss can be set off against long-term capital gain if any, in the same assessment year. The balance shall be carried forward to the following assessment year and can be set off only against long-term capital gains • Short-term capital loss can be set off against any income under the head Capital Gains (Short-Term Capital Gain as well as Long-Term Capital Gain) in the same assessment year and the remainder if any shall be carried forward to the following assessment year and can be set off against income under the head Capital Gains • Such losses can be carried forward for not more than 8 subsequent assessment years				
	Tax rates	10%–30% depending upon nature of capital gain				

		Domiciled	Non-domiciled
Inheritance Tax (IHT)	General description	In common parlance inheritance tax in India is understood as wealth tax. The levy of wealth tax aims to achieve the objective of ensuring that persons who possess huge wealth contribute a certain sum to the exchequer	
	Taxable entities and chargeable assets	Individual and companies Wealth tax is charged on specific assets only The broad list of chargeable assets, subject to specific exclusion/exemptions is as follows: • any building or land apportionment thereto • motor cars other than those used in hiring business or used as stock in trade • jewellery or any other precious metal • yachts, boats, aircrafts other than used for commercial purposes • urban land • cash in hand in excess of Rs 50,000 for individuals and unrecorded amounts in the case of companies	N/A
	Calculation of charge	Wealth tax is incurred on net wealth exceeding Rs 1.5m @ 1%. Net wealth is defined as gross wealth (value of all specified assets) less debts owed in relation to the said assets	
	Taxable events	As above	
	Allowances	Depending upon the nature of the assets and its usage, various allowances have been provided	
	Tax rates	1%	

IV   WITHHOLDING TAXES

	Payments to non-residents[3]
Dividends	Nil. Dividends are subjected to dividend distribution tax
Interest	Not exceeding 22.66% The rate as prescribed by the Income Tax Act is 22.66%. However, some double taxation agreements allow the interest to be taxed at lower rates of 10% or 15%
Royalties	Not exceeding 11.33%
On payments to artists and sportsmen	Not exceeding 11.33% The rate as prescribed by the Income Tax Act is 11.33%

---

3   Reduced rates of withholding tax may apply where there is an appropriate double tax treaty.

V INDIRECT TAXES

		Residents	Non-residents
Value Added Tax (VAT)[4]	General description	VAT is a multi-point sales tax with set off for the tax paid on purchases. It implies: • nil effective tax burden of purchases • no double taxation of the same base • tax does not become cost of doing business • no need for additional working capital to finance tax cost	
Stamp Duty Land Tax		N/A	
Stamp Duty		N/A	

---

4 Value Added Tax (VAT) being a state subject, different states have their own rules and regulations. Only two states have introduced the legislation.
   A service tax of 12.36% applies to various services whether provided in or outside India.

Iran

(Shirin Moshirfatemi, info@behradmoshar.com)

I   MAIN LEGAL FORMS

Legal form / Characteristics	Partnership and Limited Liability Partnership (LLP)*	Ltd (private corporation) and Plc (public corporation)
Partners/shareholders • Number • Restrictions	Minimum two persons No restrictions	Ltd: Minimum three Plc: Minimum five No restrictions
Directors	Minimum one person	Ltd: Minimum three Plc: Minimum five
Establishment	Partnership deed	Articles of incorporation
Registration	Commercial Registrar	
Minimum capital	N/A	Ltd: Rls 1m Plc: Rls 5m
Liability	Unlimited/Joint and several	Limited to nominal value of share
Governance	N/A	Shareholders AGM/Board of Directors
Audit requirements	Minimum turnover Rls 8bn or assets Rls 16bn	Ltd: Yes[1] Plc: Yes
Taxation	Resident partnerships are subject to income tax on their profits derived anywhere in the world Partnerships are taxed on the basis of overall partnership and not individual partners	Resident companies are subject to corporation tax on their profits derived anywhere in the world

---

*   'LLP' is not defined in the Iranian Commercial Code. Partnership is defined in the Commercial Code. Charities and certain firms (such as accountancy firms) are governed by special regulations.
1   Yes for companies with more than Rls 8bn turnover or assets of Rls 16bn.

II   CORPORATION TAX

Legal form / Description	Resident corporation	Permanent establishment (PE)
General description	Corporation tax	
Taxable entities	Taxable entities are both resident and non-resident. Companies resident in Iran are taxed on their worldwide income. Taxes paid to foreign governments are deducted from total tax payable	PEs located in Iran are taxed on their Iranian income
Taxable income	Worldwide profits	Profits derived by PE in Iran
Calculation of taxable profits	Adjusted accounting profits for the period	
Interest payments	Interest received from bank deposits is exempt from tax. Interest payments to authorised banks and financial institutions are deductible. No thin capitalisation rules	
Related party transactions	All related party transactions must take place on arm's length basis	
Tax year, return and payment	The fiscal year is the same as financial year Tax returns together with payment for tax due must be submitted within 4 months after year-end Some taxes are deducted at source and treated as prepayment	
Capital gains	Capital gains are taxed as part of taxable income	
Losses	Capital losses could also be included in the overall computation of tax for companies. Losses can be carried forward indefinitely	
Tax group	None	
Tax rate	25%	25% (Plc quoted) 22.5% (Plc other) 25%

III   TAXES FOR INDIVIDUALS

		Residents	Non-residents
Income Tax	General description	Tax levied on the chargeable income of a chargeable person for a year of assessment	
	Taxable entities and taxable income	Residents are taxed on their worldwide income with some relief for double taxation	Non-residents are taxed on income arising in Iran. Deemed salary schedule is used by tax authorities for foreign individuals employed in/managing a company
	Types of taxable income	• Property income (usually rent) • Income from capital investment (sale of goodwill, property/shares and securities) • Income from business activities • Employment from personal services	
	Calculation of income	• On rent income, if residential property, if property is below certain size, no tax is due. If property is for office/trading usage, taxable income would be after deduction of 25%. Capital gains tax is deducted at source for goodwill/property/shares and securities based on rates stipulated in the Tax Code • Income from business activities – total income after deduction of allowable expenses based on books (regulations of corporations apply) • Income is based on employment in Iran in cash or in kind after deduction of exemptions, if any	
	Tax year, tax assessment and tax payment	Tax year is based on lunar year (21 March to 20 March of following year) Tax deducted at source and paid over within a month	
	Losses	No provision	
	Tax rates	• For employees working in the governmental sector, a flat rate of 10% is applied after exemption • For others, after deducting exemption as follows: *(Rls)* *Rate* 0–42m 10% 42m–100m 20% 100m–250m 25% 250m–1bn 30% More than 1bn 35%	
Capital Gains Tax (CGT)	General description	No special set of laws for CGT	

		Residents	**Non-residents**
Inheritance Tax (IHT)	General description	Deceased and heir both resident	Properties in Iran
	Taxable entities and chargeable assets	Heirs are divided into three groups: • group 1 – parents, spouse, children and grandchildren • group 2 – grandparents, sisters, brothers and their children • group 3 – aunt, uncle and their children	Treated as group 2
	Calculation of charge	Value after exemptions	
	Taxable events	Death	
	Allowances	Exemptions for group 1 of Rls 30m (or Rls 50m for those aged under 20 or disabled)	None
	Tax rates	From 5%–65% based on the type of group and values	

IV WITHHOLDING TAXES

	Payments to non-residents
Dividends	None
Interest	Based on new regulations (May 2007) withholding tax calculated on arbitrary basis, ie interest is multiplied by a predefined rate (based on a table), to arrive at taxable item, and the resulting figure is multiplied by tax rate (25%) to calculate the tax due
Fees to individuals and services business and contractors	5%

V   INDIRECT TAXES

		Residents	**Non-residents**
Value Added Tax (VAT)	General description	From 22 September 2008 the law came into force. The general rate is 3% for all supply and import and export of goods and services in Iran apart from those exempted (eg some basic items of food). At this stage of the implementation of the law, all residents who are economically active and have had annual turnover of above Rls 3bn, or have imports or exports, or are not part of trade unions are required to register in the VAT system. Those registered would have to collect 3% VAT from their customers, and would be able to deduct their input tax from their output tax in preparation of a VAT return, which is submitted every 3 months. Exports are zero rated. Ultimately, VAT is borne by the individual consumers and those not registered within the VAT system	
Stamp Duty Land Tax		None	
Stamp Duty		Various stamp duties as follows: • Cheques issued by banks – Rls 200 per cheque • Bills of exchange/draft, etc – 0.003% of the value of the documents • Shipping negotiable documents – Rls 5,000 (air/sea) – Rls 1,000 (land) • Various other miscellaneous cases • Increase in capital – 0.002% of the value of increase in capital of companies	

Ireland

(Brian Egan, began@ofc.ie)

I MAIN LEGAL FORMS

Legal form / Characteristics	Partnership and Limited Liability Partnership (LLP)	Ltd (private corporation) and Plc (public corporation)
Partners/shareholders • Number • Restrictions	General Partnership: look-through entity. Governed by 1890 Partnership Act General Partnership: maximum of 20 persons (exception in the case of professional partnerships) No concept of LLPs	Private Limited Company: shareholders cannot exceed 99 Public Company: minimum of seven shareholders
Directors	N/A	Two directors and one company secretary. At least one Irish resident director necessary or company must pay a bond of €25,394.76
Establishment	Partnership deed	Articles of Association
Registration	Filed with Registrar of Companies	
Minimum capital	N/A	For a Plc €38,092 of share capital must be issued of which 25% must be paid up One share per shareholder for a Ltd company
Liability	Joint and several liability no limitations	Limited to capital subscribed
Audit requirements	N/A	Mandatory except for smaller private companies
Taxation	Transparent assessed on partners	Taxable on worldwide profits

II   CORPORATION TAX

Legal form / Description	Resident corporation	Permanent establishment (PE)
General description	Corporation tax	
Taxable entities	Incorporated in Ireland	Companies operating a branch or agency in Ireland
Taxable profits	Total worldwide profits (income and gains)	• Trading income arising directly or indirectly through a branch or agency in the state; and • any income or chargeable gains from property owned or used by, or held by or for, a branch or agency
Calculation of taxable profits	• Income is calculated under various schedules and cases and taxed thereon • Company chargeable gains (other than development land gains) are generally subject to corporation tax • Company chargeable gains on development land and shares deriving their value from development land are subject to capital gains tax	
Interest payments	• Interest on borrowings used for trade purposes is generally tax deductible on an accruals basis • Interest on borrowings used for non-trade purposes, such as acquisition of shares in another company, is deductible on a paid basis, subject to certain conditions • No thin capitalisation restrictions other than payments to a non-Irish resident 75% affiliate outside the EU that may be reclassified as dividends/distributions in certain limited cases	
Related party transactions	Transactions may be subject to the application of the 'market value' rules, although no other formal policy rules	
Tax year, return and payment	The tax year is the accounting year Corporation tax returns are due for submission to the Irish Revenue on the 21st day of the ninth month following the end of the accounting period to which it relates	
Taxation of capital gains	Chargeable gains are subject to either corporation tax at an effective rate of 22% or capital gains tax at a rate of 22%	
Taxation of income	Trading income is subject to the standard rate of corporation tax at 12.5% Passive income is taxed at 25%	
Losses[1]	• Trading losses may be set off against trading profits of the company in the same accounting period or preceding accounting period (of equal length) or alternatively can be carried forward indefinitely for use in the same trade • Trading losses can also be set against other income and gains of the current and preceding year on a 'value basis'. This means that the amount of the loss which is needed to shelter other income will depend on the tax rate which would have been applicable to that other income in the absence of loss relief	
Tax group	Each company in a group is taxed separately. Group relief may be claimed on a current period basis. A group consists of a parent company and all of its 75% subsidiaries. All group members must be resident in an EU member state or EEA member state	

---

1   There are special rules allowing the company to utilise other losses such as capital losses and loan relationship deficits.

III TAXES FOR INDIVIDUALS

<table>
<tr><td colspan="2"></td><th>Residents</th><th>Non-residents</th></tr>
<tr><td rowspan="16">Income Tax</td><td>General description</td><td colspan="2">Income tax and capital gains tax</td></tr>
<tr><td>Important definitions relevant to the scope of Irish taxation for individuals</td><td colspan="2"><ul><li>An individual is *resident* if he is present in Ireland at any time or several times in the tax year for a period in the whole amounting to 183 days or more; *or*</li><li>At any time or several times in the tax year and the preceding tax year for a period in the whole amounting to 280 days or more (no account is taken for a period in the whole amounting to 30 days or less in one of these years)</li><li>An individual is *ordinarily resident* in Ireland for a tax year if he has been resident for each of the 3 consecutive tax years preceding that year</li><li>*Domicile* is a legal concept and generally a person is domiciled in the country of which he is a national and in which he spends his life</li></ul></td></tr>
<tr><td></td><th>Individual resident, ordinarily resident and domiciled</th><th>Individual not resident but ordinarily resident and domiciled</th></tr>
<tr><td>Taxation of income</td><td>Liable to Irish income tax on his worldwide income</td><td>Liable to Irish income tax on worldwide income with the exception of income from:<ul><li>a trade or profession no part of which is carried on in Ireland</li><li>an office or employment all of the duties of which are performed outside Ireland</li><li>other sources of foreign income not exceeding €3,810</li></ul></td></tr>
<tr><td>Types of taxable income</td><td><ul><li>Rental income and land in Ireland</li><li>Trading profits</li><li>Employment and pension income</li><li>Distributions from companies</li></ul></td><td><ul><li>Rental income and land in Ireland</li><li>Trading profits</li><li>Employment and pension income</li><li>Distributions from companies</li></ul></td></tr>
<tr><td>Calculation of income</td><td colspan="2">Income is calculated under various schedules and cases and taxed thereon</td></tr>
</table>

		Individual resident, ordinarily resident and domiciled	**Individual not resident but ordinarily resident and domiciled**
Income Tax	Tax year, tax assessment and tax payment	• The tax year is the calendar year • Income tax on employment income is taxed at source and collected through the operation of PAYE • Generally, where an individual has income other than employment income subject to PAYE, he will be taxed under the self-assessment system, under which the taxpayer is obliged to submit a tax return to the Irish Revenue by 31 October in the year that follows the tax year of assessment • Under self assessment, preliminary income tax is paid on 31 October in the current year of assessment and the balance is payable on 31 October following the year of assessment (ie the date on which the return is filed) • Taxpayers can opt to file tax returns electronically	• Income tax on employment income is taxed at source and collected through the operation of PAYE • Generally, where an individual has income other than employment income subject to PAYE, he will be taxed under the self-assessment system, under which the taxpayer is obliged to submit a tax return to the Irish Revenue by 31 October in the year that follows the tax year of assessment • Under self assessment, preliminary income tax is paid on 31 October in the current year of assessment and the balance is payable on 31 October following the year of assessment (ie the date on which the return is filed) • Taxpayers can opt to file tax returns electronically
	Losses	Generally losses may be carried forward indefinitely for utilisation against profits arising from the same source Carry back of trade losses for 3 years is provided where there is a permanent discontinuance of that trade, to which the loss relates	
	Tax rates	• The standard rate of income tax is 20% • The marginal rate of income tax is 41% • Budget 2009 announced the introduction of a 1% levy on gross income up to €100,100. A 2% levy will apply to income in excess of this amount • Standard rate bands and tax credits are determined with reference to status factors such as single, married, one or both spouses working, etc	

		Irish resident/ordinarily resident and domiciled	**Non-resident**
Capital Gains Tax (CGT)		Liable to CGT on gains accruing on the disposal of worldwide assets	Liable to CGT on the disposal of 'specified assets' (eg land, buildings, minerals) in the state
	Taxation of chargeable capital	• Computed in accordance with the CGT rules • Budget 2009 announced changes to the payment dates for capital gains tax. The tax year is now to be split into an 'initial period' running from 1 January to 30 November and a 'later period' running for one month to 31 December • CGT for the initial period ending 30 November is due for payment in the following mid-December • CGT for the later period ended 31 December is due for payment on 31 October following the year of assessment • Details of chargeable gains for a tax year are due for submission to the Irish Revenue on 31 October following the year of assessment	
	Losses	Generally losses can be set off against gains realised in the same year or carried forward for utilisation in subsequent years	
	Tax rates	The standard rate of CGT is 22% Capital gains arising on the disposal of certain offshore funds are taxed at 40%	
Inheritance Tax (IHT)	The territorial scope of Irish Capital Acquisitions Tax	Levied on the recipients of gifts or inheritances Generally, Irish capital acquisitions tax will arise on gifts or inheritances taken where: • the disposer is resident or ordinarily resident in the state; • the donee is resident or ordinarily resident in the state; • so much of the property of which the gift as is situated in the state	
	Calculation of charge	Computed in accordance with the Capital Acquisition Tax Rules	
	Tax-free group thresholds	• Threshold (A) €521,208 – where the donee is a child or in some cases a parent of the disponer • Threshold (B) €52,121– where the donee is a lineal ancestor or descendant (eg brother, sister, or a child of a brother or sister) • Threshold (C) €26,060 – other	
	Tax rates	Tax at 20%. Subject to potential change to 22% in Finance Bill 2009	

IV   WITHHOLDING TAXES

	Payments to non-residents[2]
Dividends	20%
Interest	20%
Royalties	20%

---

2   Reduced rates of withholding tax may apply where there is an appropriate double tax treaty or the application of the EU Savings Directive.

V   INDIRECT TAXES

		Residents	**Non-residents**
Value Added Tax (VAT)	Charge to VAT	• On any person who makes taxable supplies of goods and services within the state in the course or furtherance of business in excess of the thresholds in any continuous period of 12 months. (Registration threshold of €37,500 for services and €75,000 for goods) • On a person whose intra-Community acquisitions of goods exceed €41,000 in any continuous period of 12 months • Goods imported into the state from outside the EU • A person who is not established in the state who supplies goods or services in the state	
	Tax rates	• Zero rate • 4.8% rate • 13.5% rate • 21.5% rate (effective 1 December 2008) • Exempt	
	Examples of zero-rated taxable activities	Most food and drink of a kind for human consumption, most clothing for children under 11 years of age, certain medical equipment and appliances	
	Examples of 4.8% rated taxable activities	Certain farmers	
	Examples of 13.5% activities	Immovable goods, services consisting of the development of immovable goods, hotel and holiday accommodation	
	Examples of 21.5% activities	All other goods and services not specifically legislated to be taxed under any other rate	
	Examples of exempt activities	Certain lettings of immovable property, medical, dental and optical services, insurance services, banking and stock exchange activities	
	Examples of administrative obligations	Registration for VAT Bi-monthly VAT returns	
Stamp Duty		See below	

(1) Rates of stamp duty for residential property effective from 5 November 2007

Value (€)	Owner occupiers and investors From 05/11/07	First-time buyers who are owner-occupiers
First 127,000	Nil	Exempt
Next 875,000	7%	Exempt
Excess over 1m	9%	Exempt

(2) Non-residential property (effective from 15 October 2008)

Value (€)	Rate
Up to 10,000	Exempt
10,001–20,000	1%
20,001–30,000	2%
30,001–40,000	3%
40,001–70,000	4%
70,001–80,000	5%
Over 80,000	6%

Isle of Man

(Craig Brown, craig.brown@abacusiom.com)

I   MAIN LEGAL FORMS

Legal form / Characteristics	Partnership and Limited Partnership (LP) (No LLPs exist in the Isle of Man (IOM))	Ltd (private corporation) and Plc (public corporation)
Partners/shareholders • Number • Restrictions	• Two or more • None	• One or more • None
Directors	Management by partners or general partner within an LP	Management by directors
Establishment	Partnership deed	Articles of Association
Registration	IOM registry	
Minimum capital	None	1931 company – £1 for Ltd and £2 for Plc 2006 company – no minimum
Liability	Unlimited but limited partners of LP may be limited to capital	Limited to capital
Governance	Partners, general meeting	Managing director/Board of Directors, secretary, registered agent, shareholders' meeting
Audit requirements	None	*1931 company:* No audit requirement for Ltd providing it meets two of the following conditions: • turnover does not exceed £5.6m • total assets do not exceed £2.8m • no more than 50 employees Audit is required for Plc *2006 company:* No audit requirement
Taxation	Partners are subject to IOM income tax on their share of the profits. Non-IOM resident partners are only taxed on IOM source income	Resident companies are subject to income tax on their profits derived anywhere in the world
Usage	Varied including professional and financial organisations	Small and medium-sized enterprises Plc used for larger companies seeking listing on AIM, etc

II   CORPORATION TAX

Legal form / Description	Resident corporation	Permanent establishment (PE)
General description	Corporation tax	
Taxable entities	Companies resident in the IOM are subject to Manx income tax on their worldwide income	Companies incorporated and controlled outside of IOM, engaged in business within the IOM through a branch are liable to Manx non-resident income tax at 0% or 10% on the profit arising from the business of the branch
Taxable income	Worldwide profits	Profits derived by PE in IOM
Calculation of taxable profits	Accounting profit is adjusted for various tax add-backs and allowances to arrive at profits chargeable to income tax	
Interest payments	Interest expenses for trading companies are fully tax deductible. However, the company must take into account the arm's length principle	
Related party transactions	All related party transactions must take place on arm's length basis	
Tax year, return and payment	Tax returns are due in respect of an accounting period and submission of the return is required within 12 months and 1 day of the end of the accounting period	
Capital gains	There is no capital gains tax	
Losses	Trading losses of a company may be offset against any other income in the same accounting period or carried forward and offset against future income of the same trade.	
Tax group	A group comprises a parent company and its 75% subsidiaries	Not applicable for non-resident companies
Tax rate	The standard rate of tax is 0%. The higher rate of 10% is chargeable for certain banking activities and income derived from IOM land and property	

III TAXES FOR INDIVIDUALS

<table>
<tr><th></th><th></th><th>Residents</th><th>Non-residents</th></tr>
<tr><td rowspan="8">Income Tax</td><td>General description</td><td colspan="2">Tax levied on the chargeable income of a chargeable person for a year of assessment</td></tr>
<tr><td>Taxable entities and taxable income</td><td>Residents are taxed on their worldwide income with relief for double taxation</td><td>Non-residents are taxed on income arising in IOM</td></tr>
<tr><td>Types of taxable income</td><td colspan="2"><ul><li>Property income</li><li>Savings and investment income but not bank interest for non-residents</li><li>Income from business activities</li><li>Employment from personal services or pensions</li><li>Income from trusts and estates but not non-IOM source for non-residents</li></ul></td></tr>
<tr><td>Calculation of income</td><td colspan="2">Generally that received in the year</td></tr>
<tr><td>Tax year, tax assessment and tax payment</td><td colspan="2"><ul><li>Tax year – runs from 6 April to the following 5 April</li><li>Tax assessment – individual returns and assessments for each taxpayer</li><li>Returns must be filed by 6 October following the year of assessment</li><li>Wages and salaries paid to employees are subject to tax deduction at source</li></ul></td></tr>
<tr><td>Losses</td><td colspan="2">Losses created by trading activities can be offset against other income or carried forward against future profits</td></tr>
<tr><td>Tax rates</td><td>Income is subject to Manx income tax at the standard rate of 10% on the first £10,500 of taxable income and thereafter at the higher rate of 18%

Personal allowance – £9,200</td><td>Non-residents are subject to income tax at a rate of 18%

Personal allowance – £2,120</td></tr>
<tr><td rowspan="2">Capital Gains Tax (CGT)</td><td>General description</td><td colspan="2">Tax on increase in the value of asset between acquisition and disposal, not chargeable to income or corporate tax</td></tr>
<tr><td>Taxable entities and chargeable assets</td><td colspan="2">There is no CGT in the IOM</td></tr>
<tr><td rowspan="2">Inheritance Tax (IHT)</td><td></td><td>IOM domiciled</td><td>Non-IOM domiciled</td></tr>
<tr><td>Taxable entities and chargeable assets</td><td colspan="2">There is no IHT in the IOM</td></tr>
</table>

IV   WITHHOLDING TAXES

	Payments to non-residents
Dividends	Nil
Interest	Nil. It may, however, be subject to tax at source under the EU Savings Directive rules
Royalties	Nil
On payments to artists and sportsmen	Nil

V INDIRECT TAXES

		Residents	Non-residents
Value Added Tax (VAT)	General description	Tax on the supply of goods and services	
	Entities being obliged to levy VAT	Generally any individual, partnership, corporation or other body which carries out taxable activities in the IOM or UK, subject to a turnover limit of £67,000, although other criteria also exists	
	Taxable activities	VAT is charged on the purchase and sale of goods and services VAT sales are either exempt, zero-rated or standard-rated	
	Taxable activities – zero rated (examples)	Export of goods and supply of services with another EU member state	
	Exemptions (examples)	Banking and insurance services	
	Refund of VAT	If appropriate it may be obtained on submission of the VAT return	
	Tax liability	Normally the supplier of goods and services is responsible for charging VAT	
	Tax rates	• Standard rate = 17.5% • Reduced rate = 5% (certain residential work) • Zero rate = 0%	
Stamp Duty Land Tax		There are no stamp duties in the IOM	
Stamp Duty		There are no stamp duties in the IOM	

Israel

(Guy Faigenboim, guy@slcpa.co.il)

I MAIN LEGAL FORMS

Legal form / Characteristics	Partnership and Limited Liability Partnership (LLP)	Ltd (private corporation) and Plc (public corporation)
Partners/shareholders • Number • Restrictions	No LLPs in Israel No minimum for partnerships None	Ltd: no minimum Plc: two directors minimum
Directors	N/A	No minimum except for listed companies
Establishment	Partnership deed	Articles of Incorporation
Registration	Registrar of Companies	
Minimum capital	None	None
Liability	Joint and several liability	Limited to share capital
Governance	Partners	Management Board
Audit requirements	None	Mandatory
Taxation	Transparent. Partners assessed on share of profits	Corporation tax on worldwide profits

II   CORPORATION TAX

Legal form / Description	Resident corporation	Permanent establishment (PE)
General description	Corporation tax	
Taxable entities	Incorporated in Israel	Income derived in Israel
Taxable income	Worldwide profits	Income derived in Israel
Calculation of taxable profits	Levied on gross income less certain allowable deductions	
Interest payments	Deductible subject to thin capitalisation rules	
Related party transactions	Related party transactions should take place at arm's length rates	
Tax year, return and payment	Tax year – calendar year Tax returns are due within 5–12 months after the year-end Estimated tax liability must be paid in either 10 or 12 instalments based on a percentage of the company's turnover	
Capital gains	Taxed as part of business profits	
Losses	Can be carried forward indefinitely subject to anti-avoidance rules	
Tax group	None	
Tax rate	2008: 27% 2009: 26% From 2010: 25%	2008: 27% 2009: 26% From 2010: 25%

III TAXES FOR INDIVIDUALS

		Residents	Non-residents
Income Tax	General description	Income tax	
	Types of taxable income	• Regular income • Capital gains • Interest • Royalties • Rent	Only taxed on Israeli source income
	Calculation of income	Levied on gross income less certain allowable deductions	
	Tax year, tax assessment and tax payment	Tax year – calendar year Tax returns are due within 5–12 months after the year-end Estimated tax liability must be paid in either 10 or 12 instalments based on a percentage of the company's turnover PAYE scheme for employees	
	Losses	May be offset against other profits (in general against the same kind of profit) and/or carried forward indefinitely	

	Tax rates	• Regular income:
		  2008: 10%–47%
		  2009: 10%–46%
		  From 2010: 10%–44%
		• Capital gain: 20/25%
		• Interest: 15/20% the same as the rates for regular income
		• Royalties: the same as the rates for regular income
		• Rent: the same as the rates for regular income	

Capital Gains Tax (CGT)	General description	Capital gains/real estate tax	
	Calculation of gain	Levied on gross income less certain allowable deductions	
	Tax year, tax assessment and tax payment	The tax year is the calendar year Estimated tax liability must be paid within 30 days after the sale	
	Losses	May be offset against other gain and/or carried forward indefinitely	
	Tax rates	15%, 20% and 25%	
		Domiciled	**Non-domiciled**
Inheritance Tax (IHT)	General description	Neither estate nor gift tax are imposed in Israel	

IV   WITHHOLDING TAXES

	Payments to non-residents[1]
Dividends	25%
Interest	25%
Royalties	25%
On payments to artists and sportsmen	25%

1   Reduced rates of withholding tax may apply where there is an appropriate double tax treaty.

V   INDIRECT TAXES

		Residents	Non-residents
Value Added Tax (VAT)	Entities being obliged to levy VAT	• Corporation • Licensed dealer	
	Taxable activities	• Sale of goods • Services	
	Taxable activities – zero rated (examples)	Unprocessed fruit and vegetables, exports provided to tourists and certain other income from foreign sources	
	Exemptions (examples)	Certain structural alterations	
	Refund of VAT	Monthly basis	
	Tax liability	Businesses selling goods and services	
	Tax rates	Uniform rate of 15.5%	
	Administrative obligations	• Monthly report • Monthly payment	
Stamp Duty Land Tax		No stamp taxes	
Stamp Duty			

Italy

(Salvatore Tarsia, s.tarsia@tcfct.it)

I   MAIN LEGAL FORMS

Legal form / Characteristics	Partnership and Limited Liability Partnership (LLP)	Ltd (private corporation) and Plc (public corporation)
Partners/shareholders • Number • Restrictions	No limitations No concept of LLPs	
Directors	One or more (joint or severally)	One or more (sole director or Board of Directors)
Establishment	Public deed	
Registration	Commercial Register	
Minimum capital	N/A	Ltd: €10,000 Plc: (limited by shares) €120,000
Liability	Joint and several liability for partners	Limited to capital
Governance	By partners	Sole director or Board of Directors
Audit requirements	No	Public companies only
Taxation	Tax transparent	Resident companies are subject to corporation tax on their profits derived anywhere in the world Tax transparent taxation rule is applicable only per option

II   CORPORATION TAX

Legal form / Description	Resident corporation	Permanent establishment (PE)
General description	Joint Stock Companies are subject to IRES (Corporate Income Tax)	PE of Foreign Companies are subject to IRES (Corporate Income Tax)
Taxable entities	Taxable entities are both resident and non-resident. Italian resident companies are taxed on their worldwide income	PEs located in Italy are taxed on their worldwide incomes if realised through the PE
Taxable income	Worldwide profits	Worldwide profits realised through the PE
Calculation of taxable profits	Accounting profit is adjusted for various tax add-backs and allowances to obtain the taxable profit	
Interest payments	Interest expenses are deductible according to the following tests: • Test 1: There is no restriction if the positive interest exceeds the negative interest • Test 2: The excess interest expenses not deducted according to test 1 can be deducted up to an amount equal to 30% of EBITDA (earnings before interest, taxes, depreciation and amortisation); the excess will be available for carry forward to future years	
Related party transactions	All related party transactions must take place at arm's length basis	
Tax year, return and payment	The tax year corresponds to the company's financial year The tax return must be filed within 7 months after the year-end Businesses are always required to file the tax return	
Capital gains	Capital gains on the disposal of shares are tax exempt for 95% subject to four conditions (PEX). If the conditions are not met, capital gains are fully taxable as corporate income	
Losses	Tax losses incurred in the first 3 financial years can be carried forward without time limit (the activity of the company must be new and not conferred or merged by an existing company) Tax losses incurred in the following years can be carried forward for 5 years	
Tax group	Domestic tax group Worldwide tax group	
Tax rate	27.50%[1,2]	

---

1   Resident companies are also subject to IRAP (4.25%) whose taxable basis is usually higher than corporate income taxable basis, because employees costs, financial costs and financial revenues are not relevant.
2   Companies operating in energetic sector, such as hydrocarbon exploration, generation and trade of electricity, refinery and trade of petroleum and its derivates, etc, are liable to an additional CIT of 5.5%.

III   TAXES FOR INDIVIDUALS

<table>
<tr><th></th><th></th><th>Residents</th><th>Non-residents</th></tr>
<tr><td rowspan="9">Income Tax</td><td>General description</td><td colspan="2">Tax levied on the chargeable income of a chargeable person for a year of assessment</td></tr>
<tr><td>Taxable entities and taxable income</td><td>Residents are taxed on their worldwide income with some relief for double taxation</td><td>Non-residents are taxed on incomes arising in Italy</td></tr>
<tr><td>Types of taxable income</td><td colspan="2"><ul><li>Property income (usually rent)</li><li>Income from capital investment (interest, sale of goodwill, dividends, royalties, annuities)</li><li>Employment income</li><li>Self-employment income</li><li>Business activities income</li><li>Other income</li></ul></td></tr>
<tr><td>Calculation of income</td><td colspan="2">The taxable basis is the sum of all kinds of income. The tax rate on individual income (IRE) is progressive</td></tr>
<tr><td>Tax year, tax assessment and tax payment</td><td colspan="2">Tax year – is always calendar year

Tax assessment – individuals are not required to file a tax return where they:<ul><li>do not receive any income</li><li>receive only exempt income</li><li>receive income solely from employment or pensions</li></ul>Business entities are always required to file the tax return

Tax returns must be filed by 31 July of the following year</td></tr>
<tr><td>Losses</td><td colspan="2">Tax losses deriving from a business activity (enterprise owned by an individual) or self-employed activity, or partnership, can be offset with other incomes, and are no longer carried forward in future years</td></tr>
<tr><td>Tax rates</td><td colspan="2"><table><tr><td>*Band (€)*</td><td>%</td></tr><tr><td>0–15,000</td><td>23</td></tr><tr><td>15,001–28,000</td><td>27</td></tr><tr><td>28,001–55,000</td><td>38</td></tr><tr><td>55,001–75,000</td><td>41</td></tr><tr><td>75,001 +</td><td>43</td></tr></table></td></tr>
<tr><td rowspan="6">Capital Gains Tax (CGT)</td><td>General description</td><td colspan="2">Capital gain as difference between sale and purchase price is a taxable income</td></tr>
<tr><td>Taxable entities and chargeable assets</td><td colspan="2">Capital gains are included in the income of a taxpayer in the year in which they are cashed. Capital gains on disposals of real estate owned for more than 5 years are tax exempt. If sold within 5 years a 20% final withholding tax is applied</td></tr>
<tr><td>Calculation of gain</td><td colspan="2">Selling price less purchase price</td></tr>
<tr><td>Tax year, tax assessment and tax payment</td><td colspan="2">Income tax rules apply</td></tr>
<tr><td>Losses</td><td colspan="2">The losses on disposal of participation can be carried forward for 4 years and utilised to offset with increases of the same nature</td></tr>
<tr><td>Tax rates</td><td colspan="2"><ul><li>20% on capital gain on real estate disposal if sold within 5 years</li><li>12.5% on capital gain on participation disposal, for not qualified participation</li><li>The capital gain on qualified participation disposal is exempt for the 60% and it is an Other Income taxed at progressive rate as indicated above</li></ul></td></tr>
</table>

		Residents	Non-residents
Inheritance Tax (IHT)	General description	Inheritance and donation tax is ruled again starting from 3 October 2006 Donation tax is ruled again starting from 29 November 2006	
	Taxable entities and chargeable assets	• Inheritance tax: the deceased is resident in Italy • Donation tax: the donator is resident in Italy • Inheritance tax: the deceased's estate • Donation tax: all assets donated	Only assets existent in Italy
	Calculation of charge	See below under tax rates	
	Taxable events	Death Donation	
	Allowances	N/A	
	Tax rates	Inheritance – donation to: • spouse/lineal relatives: 4%. Tax-free franchise €1m per each beneficiary • brothers and sisters: 6%. Tax-free franchise €100,000 per each beneficiary • other relatives until fourth degree: 6% • lineal congeners: 6% • collateral congeners until third degree: 6% • other: 8% Further tax on real estate: • *Inheritance*: 3% on the value of the real estate inherited, or €336 if it is the first house for the beneficiary • *Donation*: 3% on the value of the real estate donated, or €336 if it is the first house for the beneficiary	

IV WITHHOLDING TAXES

	Payments to non-residents[3]
Dividends	Dividends paid by an Italian company: • to non-resident individual 27% *final* withholding tax subject to double tax treaty relief • *no* withholding tax under the EU Parent-Subsidiary Directive
Interest	• No withholding tax on interest paid to EU resident companies if EU Directive 2003/49/EEC is applicable • Interest on loan paid to foreign companies is subject to a 12.5% withholding tax subject to double tax treaty relief • Interest on loan paid to companies not resident in white list countries is subject to 27% final withholding tax
Royalties	30% withholding tax subject to double tax treaty relief
On payments to artists and sportsmen	30% withholding tax

3 Reduced rates of withholding tax may apply where there is an appropriate double tax treaty.

V   INDIRECT TAXES

		Residents	Non-residents
Value Added Tax (VAT)	General description	Tax on the supply of goods and services (VAT)	
	Entities being obliged to levy VAT	All subjects (individual or companies) that perform a business activity or self-employed activity in Italy	
	Taxable activities	The sale of goods and services	
	Taxable activities – zero rated (examples)	• Export of goods and services • Certain transportation services	
	Exemptions (examples)	The most important are the following activities: financial; banking; insurance; medical; rent/sale of buildings (if the lessee/buyer is a VAT subject)	
	Refund of VAT	Is allowed if some conditions are met	
	Tax liability	Normally the supplier of goods and services is responsible for charging VAT	
	Tax rates	Ordinary rate is 20%, there are also reduced rates of 10% and 4% in particular cases	
	Administrative obligations	Record of all VAT books, registration of invoices issued, payment of VAT, filing of annual VAT returns, filing of Intrastat (only for intra-EU transactions)	If the non-resident has no VAT direct registration (applicable only for EU companies) or VAT representative, NO administrative obligations are required
Property tax		Properties are subject to ICI calculated on the value of the property (property tax). The value is not the market value	
Stamp Duty Registration Tax		Stamp duty and registration tax is levied on deeds, documents and registers	

Japan

(Naoko Enomoto, n-enomoto@gyosei-grp.or.jp)

I MAIN LEGAL FORMS

Legal form / Characteristics	Partnership and Limited Liability Partnership (LLP)	Ltd (private corporation) and Plc (public corporation)
Partners/shareholders • Number • Restrictions	Partnership company: at least one LLP: at least two None	At least one None
Directors	N/A	Ltd: at least one Plc: at least two
Establishment	Partnership company: corporation law LLP: partnership agreement law	Corporation law
Registration	At the local legal bureau	At the local legal bureau
Minimum capital	Partnership company: N/A LLP: JPY 2	JPY 1
Liability	Partnership company: unlimited liability LLP: limited to investment	Limited to investment
Governance	Partnership company: the articles of an association LLP: partnership agreement	Prescribed in corporation law
Audit requirements	None	Paid-in capital of JPY 500m or more, or liabilities of JPY 20,000m or more
Taxation	Partnership company: corporation tax, consumption tax, local taxes LLP: each partner is subject to tax	• Corporation tax • Consumption tax • Local taxes

II CORPORATION TAX

Legal form / Description	Resident corporation	Permanent establishment (PE)
General description	Corporation tax	
Taxable entities	Incorporated under the laws of Japan	Entities with a branch or fixed place of business in Japan, or carrying on business in Japan through dependent agents
Taxable income	Worldwide	Income derived from Japanese source
Calculation of taxable profits	Corporation tax is levied on the net income of each accounting period, adjusted in accordance with the requirements of general tax laws	
Interest payments	All interest incurred is deductible; subject to thin capitalisation rules	
Related party transactions	Must be carried out at arm's length	
Tax year, return and payment	Tax year is any chosen 12-month period	Tax year is any chosen 12-month period according to the head office
	Taxes must be filed and paid within 2 months of the financial year end	Taxes must be filed and paid within 2 months of the financial year end
Capital gains	Included in the corporate tax	
Losses	Losses may be carried forward for 7 years provided the company is registered under the 'blue' tax return scheme	
Tax group	Fiscal unity with the applied 100% own relationship companies only	N/A

Tax rate	• National tax: corporations with capital stock of over JPY 100m – 30%
	• Corporations with less that JPY 100m capital stock but income of JPY 8m or less – 22%
	• Surcharge tax for group-owned company – 10%–20% on undistributed income (if the share capital stock is over JPY 100m after 1 April 2007)
	• Local tax determined within bands:
	  – Prefectural inhabitants tax 5%–6% plus fixed pro-rata basis
	  – Municipal inhabitants tax 12.3%–14.7% plus fixed pro-rata basis
	• Enterprise tax 5%–9.6% (or capital stock tax if capital stock of over JPY 100m)	

III TAXES FOR INDIVIDUALS

		Residents	**Non-residents**
Income Tax	Taxable entities and taxable income	Individuals are resident if they have a Japanese domicile or have resided continuously in Japan for a year or more. Resident is classified as permanent resident (residing over 5 years) or non-permanent resident. A permanent resident is taxed on the worldwide income. A non-permanent resident is subject to tax on Japanese source income and remittance into Japan	Income tax on Japanese source income
	Types of taxable income	• Business income • Employment (salary) income • Retirement income • Property rent income • Capital gain (see below) • Dividend income • Interest income • Other income	• Japanese source income
	Calculation of income	Taxable income minus deductible expenses	
	Tax year, tax assessment and tax payment	Tax period is the calendar year Income tax returns should be filed for the period between 16 February and 15 March in the following fiscal year. For employees with a salary of less than JPY 20m, annual adjustment should be made by the employer and there is no need to file the tax returns	
	Losses	Losses can be offset in a specific order, ie first against recurring income and then against income of a temporary nature (except certain capital gains)	
	Tax rates	Progressive rates to 40%, plus local inhabitant tax	
Capital Gains Tax (CGT)	Taxable entities and chargeable assets	Property and stock security	
	Calculation of gain	Treatment differs depending on whether the gain arises from the sale of land and buildings or the sale of securities or other assets and when those are acquired The basic formula is the amount sold minus the amount purchased Special deductions may be available	
	Tax year, tax assessment and tax payment	Calendar year	
	Losses	Offset against other source income in the tax year Loss on disposal of stock security of listed companies and resident property can be carried forward 3 years	
	Tax rates	Rates vary between 14%–26% (including local tax) depending on asset involved	

		Domiciled	Non-domiciled
Inheritance Tax (IHT)	Taxable entities and chargeable assets	IHT is levied on the individual in receipt of the assets. Taxpayers who have an address in Japan, or taxpayers domiciled in Japan, who reside 5 years or less in Japan must pay tax on all assets regardless of their location	Non-domiciled residents will only pay tax on the assets located in Japan
	Calculation of charge	Tax levied by aggregating all properties inherited plus any gifts to heirs within 3 years of death	
	Taxable events	Inheritance or bequest	
	Allowances	Basic exemption of JPY 50m plus JPY 10m for each statutory heir	
	Tax rates	Increasing bands 10% on first JPY 10m to 50% on any amount in excess of JPY 30m	

IV WITHHOLDING TAXES

	Payments to non-residents[1]
Dividends	7% on dividend from listed companies; otherwise 20%
Interest	15%
Royalties	20%
On payments to professionals, artists and sportsmen, etc	20%

---

1 Reduced rates of withholding tax may apply where there is an appropriate double tax treaty.

V   INDIRECT TAXES

		Residents	Non-residents
Value Added Tax (VAT)	General description	Consumption tax	
	Entities being obliged to levy VAT	Entrepreneurs who supply goods or services in Japan; taxable income over JPY 10m in the 2 previous years, or new company with the share capital of over JPY 10m, or voluntary declaration; all for import consumption tax	
	Taxable activities	• Goods and services consumed in Japan • The importation of goods	
	Taxable activities – zero rated (examples)	• Transfer of land • Education services • Transfer of monetary assets/currency • Loan interest and insurance premium	
	Exemptions (examples)	Export transaction	
	Refund of VAT	Available	
	Tax liability	Output tax minus input tax	
	Tax rates	5% of sales value (including local consumption tax of 1%)	
	Administrative obligations	• File the tax returns within 2 months • Consumption tax should be managed in accounting books ('bookkeeping method')	
Stamp Duty Land Tax		JPY 15,000–540,000	
Stamp Duty		Promissory notes, consignment agreement, etc	

Kenya

(Charles Gitau, csg@carrsg.com)

I MAIN LEGAL FORMS

Legal form / Characteristics	Partnership and Limited Liability Partnership (LLP)	Ltd (private corporation) and Plc (public corporation)
Partners/shareholders • Number • Restrictions	• Maximum of 20 • No restrictions No concept of LLPs	Ltd: minimum two Plc: minimum seven
Directors	Partners	Ltd: one Plc: three Have full control in management of company
Establishment	Partnership deed	Memorandum and Articles of Association
Registration	Register of Companies, Registrar of Business Names for Partnerships	
Minimum capital	None	Kshs 2,000
Liability	Unlimited	Limited to share capital
Governance	Partnership deed	Board of Directors, Articles of Association
Audit requirements	None	Statutory audits
Taxation	Partners liable individually on their share of partnership profit	Corporation tax on profits at the prevailing rate, currently 30%
Usage	Professional services and small and medium-sized enterprises (SMEs)	For any form of business except some professional services, eg accountants, lawyers

II   CORPORATION TAX

Legal form / Description	Resident corporation	Permanent establishment (PE)
General description	Corporation tax	
Taxable entities	Incorporated under Kenyan law. Management and control exercised in Kenya	PEs
Taxable income	Worldwide	Income derived in Kenya only
Calculation of taxable profits	Business profit adjusted to allow for capital deductions, disallowable non-business expenses and to exclude non-chargeable income	
Interest payments	Deductible, subject to thin capitalisation rules	
Related party transactions	Arm's length principle	
Tax year, return and payment	Tax year may be either a calendar year or the financial year of the company	
	Self-assessment tax returns should be filed within 6 months of the end of the year of assessment	
	Tax is payable in instalments if certain thresholds are exceeded	
Capital gains	None	
Losses	Tax losses are carried forward for offset against future profits from the same source of income	
Tax group	None	
Tax rate	30%	37.5%

III TAXES FOR INDIVIDUALS

		Residents	Non-residents
Income Tax	Taxable entities and taxable income	• Individuals that have a permanent home in Kenya and have been present in Kenya for any period of time during the year of income • Individuals that have been present in Kenya for a period of at least 183 days during the year of income • Individuals that have been present in Kenya during the year of income and each of the 2 preceding years of income for periods averaging 122 days or more in each income year	Income derived in Kenya only
	Types of taxable income	• Employment income • Business income • Rent income • Interest income • Farming income • Insurance commission income • Other income	
	Calculation of income	Based on all sources of income adjusted to allow for personal relief and other qualifying relief	
	Tax year, tax assessment and tax payment	Tax year – calendar year Returns should be filed within 6 months of the end of the year of assessment Tax paid monthly on PAYE basis	
	Tax rates	Progressive rates from 10–30%	
Capital Gains Tax (CGT)	General description	No capital taxes	
		Kenya domiciled	
Inheritance Tax (IHT)	General description	No estate taxes	
Turnover Tax	Rate of 3% of income	For taxable persons with business income of up to Kshs 5m	

IV   WITHHOLDING TAXES

	Payments to non-residents[1]
Dividends	10%
Interest	15%
Royalties	20%
On payments to artists and sportsmen	20%

---

1   Reduced rates of withholding tax may apply where there is an appropriate double tax treaty.

V   INDIRECT TAXES

		Residents	Non-residents
Value Added Tax (VAT)	Entities being obliged to levy VAT	Registration threshold is turnover of Kshs 5m with effect from 1 January 2007. The threshold does not apply to providers of certain designated services or goods who are required to register irrespective of their turnover	
	Taxable activities	VAT is levied on the supply of goods and services in the course of furtherance to business	
	Taxable activities – zero rated (examples)	• Export of goods or services outside Kenya • Supply of goods or services to an export processing zone enterprise • Supply of coffee and tea to coffee and tea auction centres in Kenya	
	Exemptions (examples)	• Financial services subject to certain exclusions • Insurance and reinsurance services • Agricultural, animal husbandry and horticultural services	
	Refund of VAT	To submit claim, must be registered for VAT and have installed an Electronic Tax Register (ETR)	Applies to companies whose management and control is exercised from outside Kenya. To submit claim, must be registered for VAT and have installed an ETR
	Tax liability	Based on VAT returns	
	Tax rates	• Standard rate of 16% • Other rates – 14% and zero rated	
	Administrative obligations	VAT remitted by 20th day after month end	
Stamp Duty Land Tax		4%	
Stamp Duty		1%	

Korea

(Hyun-Soo Kwon, cpakwon@chollian.net)

I MAIN LEGAL FORMS

Legal form / Characteristics	Partnership and Limited Liability Partnership (LLP)	Ltd (private corporation) and Plc (public corporation)
Partners/shareholders • Number • Restrictions	Partnership: • two or more • no partner shall, without the consent of all other partners, transfer all or part of his/her shares in the company to another person Limited Partnership Company: • two or more • no partner with unlimited liability can transfer shares without the consent of all the partners. A partner with limited liability may transfer to another person the whole or part of his/her shares with the consent of all the partners with unlimited liability	Limited Liability Company: • between 2 and 50 • a member may transfer the whole or part of his/her shares to any other person only if a resolution of a general members' meeting is adopted by the affirmative votes of a majority of all the members and of the three-quarters of the total votes Stock Company: • one or more • shares shall be transferable to other persons provided that the Articles of Incorporation may subject the transfer of shares to the requirement of approval of the Board of Directors
Directors	Partnership Company: each of partners shall represent the company Limited Partnership Company: one or more of the partners with unlimited liability shall represent the company	Limited Liability Company: directors shall be elected at a general members' meeting Stock Company: minimum requirement of one director and one statutory auditor
Establishment	The company's Articles of Incorporation should be notarised	Stock Company: at least three promoters shall be required for the incorporation
Registration	A company's incorporation is registered with the appropriate district court controlling the area of head office	

Legal form / Characteristics	Partnership and Limited Liability Partnership (LLP)	Ltd (private corporation) and Plc (public corporation)
Minimum capital	Partnership: no minimum capital Limited Partnership Company: no minimum capital	Limited Liability Company: Won 10m Stock Company: Won 50m
Liability	Partnership: joint, several and unlimited liability Limited Partnership Company: general partner with unlimited liability and limited partners with limited liability	Limited Liability Company: limited to the amount of his/her contributions to the company Stock company: limited to the subscription amount of shares
Governance	Partnership Company: each partner has the right and duty to manage the affairs of the company Limited Partnership: every partner with unlimited liability shall have the right and duty to manage the affairs of the company	Limited Liability Company: management of the company's business shall be determined by a majority vote of the directors Stock Company: a Board of Directors, with its resolution, shall make decisions on management of affairs, appointment or dismissal of managers and establishment, transfer or abolition of branch offices
Audit requirements	N/A	Limited Liability Company : N/A Stock Company : A company over Won 7bn of total assets
Taxation	Resident companies are subject to corporation tax on their profits derived anywhere in the world Partnerships are transparent for tax purposes	
Usage	Partnership Company (Hapmyung-hoesa) Limited Partnership Company (Hapja-hoesa)	Limited Liability Company (Yuhan-hoesa) Stock Company (Chusik-hoesa)

II   CORPORATION TAX

Legal form / Description	Resident corporation	Permanent establishment (PE)
General description	Corporation tax	
Taxable entities	Companies are liable to corporate tax on their worldwide income	PE located in Korea on all Korea sourced income
Taxable income	Worldwide profits	Profits derived by PE in Korea
		No corporation tax is levied on the liquidation income of PE
Calculation of taxable profits	Accounting profit is adjusted for various tax add-backs and allowances to arrive to profits chargeable to corporation tax (PCTCT)	
Interest payments	In principle, all interest payments on loan and other debts of a company are considered to be business expenses and therefore deductible	
Related party transactions	All related party transactions must take place on arm's length basis	
Tax year, return and payment	A corporation may determine its fiscal year and where a corporation fails to determine its fiscal year, the fiscal year shall be 1 January to 31 December each year	
	A corporation tax return must be filed and corporation tax must be paid within 3 months from the last day of its fiscal year	
Capital gains	Normal corporate tax is charged on capital gains from the disposal of land and buildings, but special surtax on the gains is abolished as from 1 January 2002	
Losses[1]	Tax losses can be carried forward for 5 years	
Tax group	None	
Tax rate	From 2005: • Taxable income not exceeding Won 100m – 13% of taxable income • Taxable income exceeding Won 100m – Won 13m plus 25% of the amount in excess of Won 100m	

---

1   There are special rules allowing the company to utilise other losses such as capital losses and loan relationship deficits.

III   TAXES FOR INDIVIDUALS

		Residents	Non-residents
Income Tax	General description	Tax levied on the chargeable income of a chargeable person for a year of assessment	
	Taxable entities and taxable income	Residents are taxed on their worldwide income	Non-residents are taxed on income arising in Korea
	Types of taxable income	• Global income – interest, dividends, real estate rental income, business income, wage and salary income, temporary property income, pension income and other income • Scheduler income – retirement income, timber income and capital gains	• Korean source income • Scheduler income (both with or without PE) – retirement income, timber income and capital gains
	Calculation of income	• Global income is aggregated and taxed progressively • A combined income of dividend and interest exceeding Won 40m is subject to global taxation • Scheduler income is taxed separately at varying tax rates	
	Tax year, tax assessment and tax payment	Tax year – taxes are assessed for the calendar year Tax assessment – a resident who receives global income, retirement income, capital gains or timber income in a tax year is required to file a return for each category of income by the end of May of the following year Tax payment – a resident whose taxable amount exceeds Won 10m may pay tax accrued in instalments within 45 days from the closing date of the payment period	
	Losses	A deduction for losses from the previous 5 years in case of business profit, rents from real estate and timber income	
	Tax rates	*Income band (Won)* *Tax rate (%)* *Tax on band (Won)* *Cumulative tax (Won)* 12m or less 8 960,000 960,000 12m–46m 17 5,780,000 6,740,000 46m–88m 26 10,920,000 17,660,000 Over 88m 35	
Capital Gains Tax (CGT)	General description	Tax on increase in the value of asset between acquisition and disposal, not chargeable to income or corporate tax	
	Taxable entities and chargeable assets	• Income arising from the transfer of land or buildings • Income arising from the transfer of rights related to real estate • Income arising from transfer of shares in an non-listed company	• Gains derived from the transfer of land and buildings located in Korea • Gains arising from the transfer of investments in a domestic corporation or other securities issued by a domestic corporation or the domestic business place of a foreign corporation. However, gains arising from the transfer by a non-resident of domestically listed shares or corporate shares registered with the KOSDAQ

		Residents	**Non-residents**
Capital Gains Tax (CGT)			(Korean Securities Dealers Automated Quotations) shall not be taxed, subject to the reciprocity principal
	Calculation of gain	• Gain on transfer = selling price – necessary expenses • Amount of capital gain = gain on transfer – special deduction for long-term possession of land and buildings – capital gains deduction • Necessary expenses include acquisition costs, costs of instalments or improvements, and other capital expenditure	
	Tax year, tax assessment and tax payment	A resident who transfers assets subject to the capital gains is required to file a return and pay the tax due on the capital gains within 2 months from the month of transfer If the tax return including the payment is properly made, 10% of tax credit is allowed from the tax due	
	Losses	No specific rules	
	Tax rates	• Capital gains from transfers of land, buildings, and rights to real estate are taxed at a rate of 8%–35% • Capital gains arising from transfers of shares in a non-listed company are taxed at a rate of 20%	

		Domiciled	**Non-domiciled**
Inheritance Tax (IHT)	General description	A person or a company that acquires property through inheritance or bequest is liable to the IHT An inheritor that is a for-profit company is exempt from the IHT	
	Taxable entities and chargeable assets	Levied after deducting certain amounts from the total value of the assets acquired on death and assets gifted to an inheritor within the preceding 10 years	
	Calculation of charge	In principle, inherited properties are evaluated by the market price prevailing at the time of inheritance A 10% credit is granted to those taxpayers who submit their tax returns on time	
	Taxable events	IHT covers all property bequeathed by a resident and all property in Korea bequeathed by a non-resident	
	Allowances	• Public imposts, funeral expenses between Won 5m and Won 10m, debts left by the bequeathed of the inheritance • Basic deduction: Won 200m • Deduction for spouse: from Won 500m to Won 3bn • Other deductions	
	Tax rates	Rates of inheritance tax increase in bands from 10% on the first Won 100m of the statutory inheritance to 50% on the excess above Won 3,000m	

IV WITHHOLDING TAXES

	Payments to non-residents[2]
Dividends	25%
Interest	25%
Royalties	25%
On payments to artists and sportsmen	20%

V   INDIRECT TAXES

		Residents	Non-residents
Value Added Tax (VAT)	General description	Tax on the supply of goods and services (VAT)	
	Entities being obliged to levy VAT	Taxpayers include individuals, corporations, national and local governments, association of local authorities, any bodies of persons, and unincorporated foundations of any other organisations are generally subject to VAT	
	Taxable activities	• The supply of goods and services • The importation of goods	
	Taxable activities – zero rated (examples)	A zero rate applies to the supply of goods for export, services furnished from outside the Republic of Korea, international transportation services by ships or aircraft and foreign currency earnings derived from goods or services supplied to a non-resident or foreign corporation with no permanent establishment in Korea	
	Exemptions (examples)	The supply of the following goods or services is subject to exemption and input tax incurred thereon is not refundable: basic life necessities and services, social welfare services, goods or services related to culture, personal services similar to labour, goods or services supplied by the government, local authorities and duty-exempt goods	
	Refund of VAT	VAT is computed by deducting the input tax amount from the output tax amount chargeable on the goods or services supplied by the taxpayer. The input tax which exceeds the output tax is refundable	
	Tax liability	A trader is required to file a return on the tax base and tax amount payable or refundable within 25 days (50 days in case of foreign corporations) from the date of termination of each preliminary return period and from each taxable period	
	Tax rates	Standard rate = 10%	
Stamp Duty Land Tax		Aggregate land tax is levied on a person who actually owns taxable land (de facto taxpayer) as of the base date of assessment rate	
Stamp Duty		Stamp tax is levied on a person who prepares a document certifying establishment, transfer, or change of rights to property rate	

2   Reduced rates of withholding tax may apply where there is an appropriate double tax treaty.

Lebanon

(Usamah Tabbarah & Company, raouche@utcnexia.com)

I   MAIN LEGAL FORMS

Legal form / Characteristics	Partnership and Limited Liability Partnership (LLP)	Ltd (private corporation) and Plc (public corporation)
Partners/Shareholders • Number • Restrictions	There are three categories of partnerships: *General Partnership*: minimum number of partners – two *Partnership in Commendam*: minimum number of partners – two *Co-Partnership (Société en Participation)*: a co-partnership is known only to the parties concerned and, because it is secret, cannot be registered. Minimum number of partners – two. Each party is responsible for their own liabilities. Despite their secrecy, the partnership agreements are enforceable at law in cases of dispute	There are five categories of corporations: *Joint Stock Company (Société Anonyme Libanaise – SAL)*: minimum of three shareholders *Limited Liability Company (Société à Responsabilité Limitée – SARL)*: minimum number of three partners and maximum of 20 partners except in the case of inheritance where the number of partners may extend to a maximum of 30. The name of the company must be followed by the phrase 'limited liability company' and the amount of its capital must be placed on all printed matter. Banking, insurance and air transport activities are forbidden from registering as SARL companies *Corporation in Commendam*: a limited partnership company with no specific capital requirements. The general partner is liable for the debts of the partnership. The limited 'silent' partners are liable to the extent of their capital *Holding Company*: registered in the form of Joint Stock Companies. The word 'holding' must clearly appear in the company's name. A holding company is limited to buying shares in an existing Lebanese or foreign joint stock or limited liability company, or to holding intellectual property rights *Offshore Company*: Offshore corporate entities are structured as joint stock companies, and are limited to conduct activities outside Lebanon only

Legal form / Characteristics	Partnership and Limited Liability Partnership (LLP)	Ltd (private corporation) and Plc (public corporation)
Directors	Appointment of manager stipulated	*Joint Stock Company*: Directors: minimum three, maximum 12 Majority of board members must be Lebanese citizens. The board elects one of its members to serve as Chairman. The Chairman cannot be the director of more than six Lebanese companies. If he is over 70, that number is reduced to two. If the chairman is a foreign resident, he must have a work permit. Board members are chosen from those shareholders who hold a 'guarantee share', the exact size of which is stipulated in the Articles. Though a director can hold more than the laid-down guarantee share, he must quit the Board if the holding goes below the guarantee level *Holding Company*: at least two Lebanese citizens must be on the Board of Directors *Offshore Company:* members of the Board of Directors may all be non-Lebanese citizens
Registration		*General Partnership*: commercial in nature, must be registered with the Commercial Register *Every Joint Stock Company:* incorporated in Lebanon must have its registered office in the country. Founders are required to publish information, regarding the setup of the business, in the *Official Gazette*, one daily newspaper, and one economic publication All Lebanese corporations are considered members of the Beirut Stock Exchange, even if the corporation is not actually listed in the Beirut Stock Exchange *Limited Liability Company*: the Articles of Incorporation must be notarised or signed before the Clerk of the Commercial Register where it files its application *Holding Company:* required to be listed at the Commercial Register according to the rules of the Commercial Law *Offshore Company:* required to be registered at the Commercial Register
Minimum Capital	Partnerships: none	*Joint Stock Company (Société Anonyme Libanaise – SAL)*: minimum capital Lebanese Pounds (L£) 30m (US$20,000), with one-fourth paid-up at the time of registration. Capital can consist of cash or be in kind *Limited Liability Company (Société à Responsabilité Limitée – SARL)*: minimum capital of at least L£5m (US$3,300), wholly paid-up at the time of registration. A lawyer must be retained and an auditor appointed regardless of the capital investment

Legal form / Characteristics	Partnership and Limited Liability Partnership (LLP)	Ltd (private corporation) and Plc (public corporation)
		Offshore Company: added to the incorporation documents is a bank guarantee for L£100,000 (US$66.67) automatically renewable as a security against payment of annual taxes. The capital may be denominated in a foreign currency on condition that its accounts are maintained in that same foreign currency
Liability	Unlimited liability	Limited to the extent of the share capital
Governance	General partners per Articles of Partnership and/or Memorandum of Association	Board of Directors and ultimately the equity shareholders in a General Assembly Meeting
Audit requirements	No requirement unless stipulated in Deed of Partnership	*Joint Stock Company*: two auditors are designated – one is responsible to the General Assembly and the other to the Commercial Registrar *Holding Company*: only one auditor is mandatory *Offshore Company:* must appoint for a 3-year term at least one Lebanese auditor who resides in Lebanon
Taxation	Transparent	Taxable on worldwide profits *Offshore companies*: exempted from taxation on all revenues generated outside Lebanon. Shares and shareholders are exempted from taxation in connection with the transfer/ inheritance of shares and also such related fees of any kind. However, an annual levy of L£1m is payable by Offshore companies

II CORPORATION TAX

Legal form / Description	Resident corporation	Permanent establishment (PE)
General description	Corporation tax	
Taxable entities	Companies resident in Lebanon are taxed on their worldwide income	PEs located in Lebanon are taxed on profits derived in Lebanon
Taxable income	Income realised in Lebanon	
Calculation of taxable profits	Accounting profit is adjusted for various tax add-backs and allowances to arrive at the profits assessable to corporation tax	
Interest payments	Interest charges are fully deductible	
Related party transactions	All related party transaction must take place on arm's length basis	
Tax year, return and payment	Companies are required to file their tax returns by 31 May following the tax year	
	Partnerships and individuals must file their returns by 31 March following the 31 December year-end	
Capital gains	Capital gains are taxed separately at 10%	
Losses	Losses can be carried forward for a maximum period of 3 years	
Tax group	None	
Tax rate	Corporate tax rate 15%	

III TAXES FOR INDIVIDUALS

		Residents	**Non-residents**
Income Tax	General description	Tax levied on the assessable income of a chargeable person for a year of assessment	
	Taxable entities and taxable income	All individuals are taxed, based on profits from industrial, commercial and non-commercial trade. No income is exempt from tax except by explicit provision in legislation	On all sources of income arising within Lebanon
	Types of taxable income	• Lebanese tax law differentiates between taxation on (a) profits derived from industrial, commercial, and non-commercial professions; (b) salaries, wages and retirement pensions; and (c) income from movable assets • Property income (usually rent) • Income from capital investment (interest, sale of goodwill, dividends, royalties, annuities) • Income from business activities • Employment from personal services or pensions	
	Calculation of income	Tax liability is assessed on actual income after deduction of the tax-free allowance of L£7.5m for an unmarried taxpayer. For married taxpayers, this allowance increases by a further L£2.5m, and for each dependent child an extra allowance of L£500,000 is given up to a maximum of five children	
	Tax year, tax assessment and tax payment	Partnerships and individuals must file their tax returns by 31 March following the 31 December year-end Individuals are not required to file a tax return where they: • do not receive any income • receive only exempt income • receive income solely from employment or pensions	
	Losses	Set off against taxable income	
	Tax rates: salaries	*Band (L£)* *Rate (%)* 0–6,000,000 2 6,000,001–15,000,000 4 15,000,001–30,000,000 7 30,000,001–60,000,000 11 60,000,001–120,000,000 15 120,000,001 + 20	
	Taxable entities and chargeable assets	The Lebanese Income Tax Law stipulates that capital gains realised, on disposal, trade-off, and revaluation of capital assets are subject to taxation at the rate of 10% when these transactions are conducted for commercial purposes. This implies that personal capital gains are exempt from such taxation	
	Calculation of gain	The gain is calculated on the basis of the sale value realisation or the value resulting from re-valuation less the actual historical cost adjusted as permitted	
	Tax year, tax assessment and tax payment	Year of assessment for small taxpayers is the end of January, for partnerships and individuals is the end of March, for corporate entities is the end of May Value Added Tax and tax on salaries are payable quarterly 15 days after the relevant quarter-end	
	Losses	Capital losses incurred in one year can be deducted from the taxable income of the same year	
	Tax rates	10%	

		Domiciled	Non-domiciled
Inheritance Tax (IHT)	General description	Inheritance taxes are levied at progressive rates depending on the degree of kinship between the deceased and the heir. The lowest rates apply to the deceased's children, higher rates apply to parents and other close relatives, and the highest rates apply to distant relatives and other persons not related to the deceased	
	Taxable entities and chargeable assets	The estate through the Executor of the Wills Value of Inheritance less permitted *Offshore Companies*: Shares and shareholders are exempt from taxation in connection with the transfer/inheritance of shares and also such related fees of any kind	
	Calculation of charge	The inheritance tax is levied on each heir's net inheritance. The taxable inheritance is the gross estate less expired or irrecoverable debts, debts of the deceased, debts related to the estate, and burial expenses	
	Taxable events	Transfer/transmission of ownership to beneficiary	
	Allowances	Each heir may be entitled to a tax-exempt amount, depending on the heir's relationship to the deceased *Relationship* *Exemption amount* Child, spouse or parent L£40m (US$25,988) Other descendants L£16m (US$10,395) Other persons L£8m (US$5,198)	
	Tax rates	*Tax rate* Up to L£30m (US$19,491) 3%–16% L£30m–L£60m (US$38,982) 5%–21% L£60m–L£100m (US$64,970) 7%–27% L£100m + (US$64,970+) 10%–33%	

IV WITHHOLDING TAXES

	Payments to non-residents[1]
Dividends	Dividends or distributed profits of Lebanese shareholding companies are subject to a withholding tax of 10%
Interest	On deposits the effective rate is 15% for corporations and taxpayers and 5% for individuals not registered for tax
Royalties	Royalties are generally allowed as a deductible expense. A withholding tax at 15% is charged on 50% of the royalty payable
On payments to artists and sportsmen. Remuneration paid to foreign individuals, companies and institutions	Payments in Lebanon for services to individuals, companies or institutions that have no business offices in Lebanon, and any profits, receipts or proceeds realised in Lebanon by these individuals, companies and institutions are subject to withholding tax at 15% of 50% of such income

1   Reduced rates of withholding tax may apply where there is an appropriate double tax treaty.

V INDIRECT TAXES

<table>
<tr><th></th><th></th><th>Residents</th><th>Non-residents</th></tr>
<tr><td rowspan="11">Value Added Tax (VAT)</td><td>General description</td><td colspan="2">Tax on the supply of goods and services (IVA)</td></tr>
<tr><td>Entities being obliged to levy VAT</td><td colspan="2">VAT was introduced, for the first time in Lebanon, with effect from 1 February 2002. Registration for VAT purposes is compulsory for businesses with turnover, as follows:

• For the year from 1 February 2002 to 31 March 2003, L£500m or more
• From 1 April 2003 to 31 December 2003, L£300m or more, per year
• From 1 January 2004 to 31 December 2004, L£225m or more, per year
• From 1 January 2005 and thereafter, L£150m or more, per year

Registration for VAT purposes is voluntary where the turnover is less than that specified for compulsory registration</td></tr>
<tr><td>Taxable activities</td><td colspan="2">All goods and services</td></tr>
<tr><td>Taxable activities – zero rated (examples)</td><td colspan="2">Schools, hospitals, medicines, and other exempt essential items, such as certain foods</td></tr>
<tr><td>Exemptions (examples)</td><td colspan="2">Schools, hospitals, medicines, and other exempt essential items, such as certain foods</td></tr>
<tr><td>Refund of VAT</td><td colspan="2">A formal application must be submitted with the quarterly VAT declaration claiming credit for the refund of VAT or a set-off against the current liability</td></tr>
<tr><td>Tax liability</td><td colspan="2">Normally the supplier of goods and services is responsible for charging VAT</td></tr>
<tr><td>Tax rates</td><td colspan="2">Taxable rate of 10%</td></tr>
<tr><td>Administrative obligations</td><td colspan="2">Registered entity for VAT</td></tr>
<tr><td colspan="2">Stamp Duty Land Tax</td><td colspan="2">L£74,000 (Flat taxes)
+   5% of property value (transfer tax)
+   5% of the sum of transfer tax and flat taxes (municipal tax)
+   L£5,000 (stamp duty on new deed)
+   0.3% of property value (stamp duty)
+   0.1% of property value (bar association tax)</td></tr>
<tr><td colspan="2">Stamp Duty</td><td colspan="2">A stamp duty of 0.3% is levied on the amounts mentioned in various documents – such as issues of share capital, corporate bonds, commercial bills and contracts</td></tr>
</table>

Liechtenstein

(Janine Fischbacher, Janine.fischbacher@revitrust.li)

I   MAIN LEGAL FORMS

Legal form / Essentials	Company limited by Shares (Aktiengesellschaft, AG)	Foundation (Stiftung)	Establishment (Anstalt)	Trust	Trust reg (Treuunternehmen)
Structure	Corporation One-man-company possible	Independent assets devoted to a particular use	Unique legal form, intermediate between corporation and foundation (Continental European concept)	Independent assets placed at the disposal of a trustee, which is to be used in accordance with the provisions of the trust instrument	Intermediate between corporation and foundation (Anglo-Saxon Concept)
Legal entity	Yes	Yes	Yes	No	Yes
Mandatory bodies	• General Assembly • Board of Directors • Audit Board	• Board of Foundation	• Founder (bearer of the founder's rights) • Board of Directors • Audit Board (if purpose is commercial)	• Trustee(s)	• Settlor (bearer of the settlor's rights) • Board of Trustees • Audit Board (if purpose is commercial)
Basic capital	CHF 50,000	CHF 30,000	CHF 30,000	No amount defined (trust fund must be sufficiently resourced, at minimum CHF 10,000)	CHF 30,000
Usage	All commercial purposes, eg trading, production and financial business, but also non-commercial purposes	• Asset management • Organisation of family assets • Allocation to beneficiaries of a defined group • Holding function • Including non-commercial activities and purposes (unsuitable for commercial purposes)	• Universal use • All commercial purposes • Also suitable assets management tool	• Asset management • Organisation of family assets • Allocation to beneficiaries of a defined group • Holding function • Including non-commercial activities and purposes (unsuitable for commercial purposes)	• Universal use, advantageous in Anglo-Saxon countries • All commercial purposes • Also suitable as asset management tool

Legal form / Essentials	Company limited by Shares (Aktiengesellschaft, AG)	Foundation (Stiftung)	Establishment (Anstalt)	Trust	Trust reg (Treuunternehmen)
Registration	Public Register, obligatory and constitutive	• In practice foundations are 'deposited' with the Public Register with no right of inspection for third parties (family foundations and foundations with designated or definable beneficiaries) • In the other cases: obligatory and constitutive • registration is also permitted for foundations which may be deposited	Public Register, obligatory and constitutive	Registration or deposit in the Public Register obligatory, but not constitutive	Public Register, obligatory and constitutive
Beneficiaries	Shareholders (as dividends and liquidation proceeds)	Beneficiaries in accordance with the provisions of the by-laws	Beneficiaries in accordance with the provisions of the by-laws It is presumed by law that the settlor and/or his legal successors are the beneficiaries, unless other provision is made	Beneficiaries in accordance with the trust instrument, in particular regulations, or records of intent or letters of wishes	Beneficiaries in accordance with the provisions of the by-laws It is presumed by law that the settlor and/or his legal successors are the beneficiaries, unless other provision is made
Legal basis	Art 261 et seq Company Act (PGR), large number of mandatory legal provisions	Art 552 et seq PGR, hardly any mandatory legal provisions	Art 534 et seq PGR, hardly any mandatory legal provisions	Art 932a PGR, large number of mandatory legal provisions	Art 897 et seq PGR, comprehensive legal regulation, hardly any mandatory legal provisions

Legal form / Essentials	Company limited by Shares (Aktiengesellschaft, AG)	Foundation (Stiftung)	Establishment (Anstalt)	Trust	Trust reg (Treuunternehmen)
Tax on distributions (non-residents)	4% coupon tax (tax deducted at source) on distributions and liquidation surplus	No Liechtenstein Taxes for non-residents	No Liechtenstein Taxes	No Liechtenstein Taxes	No Liechtenstein Taxes
Capital tax (for domiciliary and Holding Companies)	1% (minimum tax CHF 1,000)	1% (minimum tax CHF 1,000)	• Generally: – 1% (minimum tax CHF 1,000) • Reduced rate: – for capital exceeding CHF 2m including reserves, capital tax is reduced to 0.75%, and for capital exceeding CHF 10m including reserves to 0.5%	1% (minimum tax CHF 1,000)	1% (minimum tax CHF 1,000)
Tax on profits (for domiciliary and holding companies)	None	None	None	None	None
Taxes for companies operating in Liechtenstein	• Capital tax: 2% • Tax on profits: 7.5%–20%	N/A	• Capital tax: 2% • Tax on profits: 7.5%–20%	• Capital tax: 2% • Tax on profits: 7.5%–20%	N/A
Usage	Suitable for all commercial transactions, with a well-understood legal form	A suitable instrument for asset investment and holding functions with few formalities	Flexible but in other jurisdictions unknown legal form, suitable for all purposes	Flexible legal form, suitable for all purposes, but unknown in other jurisdictions	A suitable instrument for asset investment and holding functions with few formalities, suitable for clients in Common Law jurisdictions in particular

Note: The Liechtenstein Tax Legislation is under revision but will probably not be altered before January 2009. The above information will basically be unchanged.

II CORPORATION TAX

Legal form / Description	Resident corporation	Permanent Establishment (PE)
General description	No taxation in Liechtenstein	

III   TAXES FOR INDIVIDUALS

		Residents	Non-residents
Income Tax	General description	Tax levied on the chargeable person for a year of assessment	
	Taxable entities and taxable income	Worldwide income	Income arising in Liechtenstein
	Types of taxable income	All earnings excluding benefits of taxed property	
	Calculation of income	Gross income less allowances	
	Tax year, tax assessment and tax payment	Annual returns filed by end of April. Tax is payable within 30 days of the assessment	
	Losses	N/A	
	Tax Rates	3.24%–17.01%	
Property Tax	General description	Tax levied on the chargeable person for a year of assessment	
	Taxable entities and chargeable assets	Residents and non-residents with property in Liechtenstein	
	Calculation of gain	Net rental income for the period	
	Types of taxable property	All personal and real property	
	Losses	N/A	
	Tax rates	1.62%–8.51%	
		Domiciled	**Non-domiciled**
Inheritance Tax (IHT)	General description	Assets acquired due to death. Assets are considered acquired in Liechtenstein if the assets constitute real property in Liechtenstein or movable assets left by a deceased whose temporary or permanent residence was in Liechtenstein at the time of death	
	Taxable entities and chargeable assets	Inheritance tax liability rests with the successor. Inheritance tax on movable assets is also levied if only the recipient (successor, devisee) is resident in Liechtenstein and the recipient cannot demonstrate that a similar tax on the inheritance is levied abroad	
	Calculation of charge	The tax rates depend on the family relationship between the deceased and the recipient; surcharges are added based on the amount of the inheritance. For example, the inheritance tax is between 0.5% and 0.75% for spouses and children and between 18% and 27% for non-related persons	
	Taxable events	Death and transfer of estate	
	Allowances	N/A	
	Tax rates	0.5% to 0.75% for spouses and children 18% to 27% for non-related persons	

IV WITHHOLDING TAXES

	Payments to non-residents
Dividends	None
Interest	None
Royalties	None
On payments to artists and sportsmen	None

V   INDIRECT TAXES

		Residents	Non-residents
Value Added Tax (VAT)	General description	Liechtenstein is part of the Swiss VAT system	
	Entities being obliged to levy VAT	VAT is imposed on supplies of goods for payment within the country, on services rendered for payment within the country, and on personal use and procurement of goods and services for payment from abroad	
	Taxable activities	VAT applies if commercial or professional self-employment generates earnings and the total annual taxable turnover of domestic deliveries, services, and private consumption exceeds CHF 75,000	
	Taxable activities – zero rated (examples)	N/A	
	Exemptions (examples)	N/A	
	Refund of VAT	The deduction of previously paid VAT therefore reduces the tax due to the Liechtenstein Fiscal Authority. Strongly export-oriented businesses may even generate a credit with the Liechtenstein Fiscal Authority, since the law exempts foreign transactions from tax	
	Tax liability	N/A	
	Tax rates	In general VAT is levied at 7.6% of the turnover value. Some few privileged goods and services are charged at the reduced rate of 2.4% and 3.6% The tax charged to a taxpayer by other taxpayers for supplies and services, the tax declared by him for purchasing services from abroad, and the tax paid by him to the customs authorities on the import of goods can be deducted as input tax in his tax statement	
	Administrative obligations	N/A	N/A
Stamp Duty Land Tax		The Swiss legislation on Stamp Tax is applicable in Liechtenstein. Swiss Tax Authorities are responsible for levying the Stamp Tax in Liechtenstein	
Stamp Duty			

Luxembourg

(VGD Experts-comptables Sàrl, vgd.luxembourg@vgd.eu)

I MAIN LEGAL FORMS

Legal form / Characteristics	Partnership and Limited Liability Partnership (LLP)	Ltd (private corporation) and Plc (public corporation)
Partners/shareholders • Number • Restrictions	*General partnership – Société en nom collectif (SNC)*: all partners have to be traders *Limited partnership – Société en commandite simple (SCS)*: two kinds of associates: one or more managing partners (associé(s) commandité(s)) and one or more capital partners (associé(s) commanditaire(s)) *Partnership limited by shares – Société en commandite par actions (SCA)*: two kinds of associates: one or more managing partners (associé(s) commandité(s)) and one or more capital partners (associé(s) commanditaire(s)) *Cooperative Society – Société Coopérative (SC)*: at least seven people	*Public limited liability company – Société Anonyme (SA)*: one shareholder (associé unique) or more *Private limited liability company – Société à responsabilité limitée (Sàrl)*: one shareholder (société unipersonnelle) or more (maximum 40)
Directors	*SNC*: one or more managing directors (gérant) appointed by the partners *SCS*: the managing director (gérant) is (one of) the founding managing partner(s), appointed in the Articles of Incorporation *SCA*: the managing director (gérant) is (one of) the founding managing partner(s), appointed in the Articles of Incorporation *SC*: one or more managers	*SA*: the board of directors consists of three directors at least or one in cases where there is only one shareholder *Sàrl*: one managing director at least

Legal form / Characteristics	Partnership and Limited Liability Partnership (LLP)	Ltd (private corporation) and Plc (public corporation)
Establishment	*SNC*: can be established by private agreement; a notarial deed is not required *SCS*: can be established by private agreement; a notarial deed is not required *SCA*: notarial deed *SC*: can be established by private agreement; a notarial deed is not required	Notarial deed
Registration	*SNC*: Registration and Deposit in the 'Registre de Commerce et des Sociétés' (RCS) for publication in the Mémorial by excerpt *SCS*: Registration and Deposit in the 'Registre de Commerce et des Sociétés' (RCS) for publication in the Mémorial by excerpt *SCA*: Registration and Deposit in the 'Registre de Commerce et des Sociétés' (RCS) for publication in the Mémorial *SC*: Registration and Deposit in the 'Registre de Commerce et des Sociétés' (RCS) for publication in the Mémorial	• Registration • Deposit in the 'Registre de Commerce et des Sociétés' (RCS) • Publication in the Mémorial
Minimum capital	*SNC*: no minimal capital required *SCS*: no minimal capital required *SCA*: €30,986.69 *SC*: variable capital, freely determined	*SA*: €30,986.69 *Sàrl*: €12,394.68
Liability	*SNC*: the partners have a joint and unlimited liability *SCS*: the managing partners have a joint and unlimited liability; the capital partners only liable for their contribution *SCA*: the managing partners have a joint liability; the capital partners only liable for their contribution (shareholders) *SC*: freely determined by the Articles of Incorporation	Limited liability; the liability is limited to the subscribed capital

Legal form / Characteristics	Partnership and Limited Liability Partnership (LLP)	Ltd (private corporation) and Plc (public corporation)
Governance	*SNC*: each director can perform alone *SCS*: joint governance by director and managing partners – right of veto of the managing director – shareholders' meeting (Assemblée Générale) *SCA*: joint governance by director and managing partners – right of veto of the managing director – shareholders' meeting (Assemblée Générale) *SC*: determined by the Articles of Incorporation – shareholders' meeting (Assemblée Générale)	*SA*: Board of Directors (Conseil d'Administration) – day-to-day management to the managing director (Administrateur Délégué) – Executive Committee (Directoire) – Audit Committee (Conseil de Surveillance) – shareholders' meeting (Assemblée Générale) *Sàrl*: each director can perform alone – shareholders' meeting (Assemblée Générale)
Audit requirements	*SNC*: N/A *SCS*: N/A *SCA*: at least three auditors *SC*: one or more auditor	*SA*: internal audit by one or more auditors (commissaire) – or external audit by auditor (réviseur d'entreprises) when: • turnover: €3,125m • balance sheet total: €6.25m • employed staff: 50 *Sàrl*: internal audit by one or more auditors if more than 25 shareholders – external audit as SA above
Taxation	*SNC*: personal income tax *SCS*: personal income tax *SCA*: corporate income tax *SC*: corporate income tax	• The SA and the Sàrl are both subject to corporate income tax on their profits and to fortune tax on their net fortune • Favourable tax regime for SOPARFI (Sociétés de Participations Financières) • Revenue of intellectual properties, 80% of income is tax-free. • SPF tax of 0.25% on net fortune with specific exemptions

II   CORPORATION TAX

Legal form / Description	Resident corporation	Permanent establishment (PE)
General description	Corporate taxes	
Taxable entities	Resident companies are subject to corporate tax on their worldwide income	Non-resident companies having a PE in Luxembourg pay income tax on their income originating in Luxembourg
Taxable income	Worldwide profits	All incomes derived from such establishment, including foreign source income
Calculation of taxable profits	'Income' for the purposes of the IRC is calculated by comparing the net worth (net balance sheet assets) of the taxable entity at the beginning and end of the period concerned. The 'fiscal' balance sheet used for calculating IRC is based on the commercial balance sheet, but some types of income and expense are treated differently for fiscal purposes	The income taxes are calculated on: • income attributable to the PE • dividends, interests, royalties and capital gains • income from immovable property in Luxembourg • interest on loans secured by immovable property in Luxembourg
Interest payments	Interest paid in relation to the business of the company or PE is fully deductible subject to thin capitalisation restrictions	
Related party transactions	All related party transaction must take place on arm's length basis and transactions between related parties must be at fair market value	
Tax year, return and payment	The tax year is the calendar year. The companies may have different accounting periods in which case the tax year is the year ending in the calendar in question	The tax year is the calendar year. The PE may have different accounting periods in which case the tax year is the year ending in the calendar in question
Capital Gains	Capital gains derived from the sale of shareholdings in other companies are excluded from taxation if the company gives the Luxembourg tax authorities an undertaking that it intends to hold the shares for at least 12 months and if they represent at least a 10% shareholding (or if less, whose acquisition cost was at least €6m)	
Losses	Losses arising during the year can be deducted from operating profits. Any unused balance of losses can be carried forward indefinitely	
Tax group	N/A	

Tax rate	• Corporate income tax:
	  – 20% for income lower than €10,000
	  – €2,000 + 26% of the income included between €10,000 and €15,000
	  – 22% of the income beyond €15,000
	  There is a 4% employment fund surcharge calculated on the income tax
	• Municipal business tax:
	  A charge of about 7.5% in respect of municipal services is calculated on the income after a reduction of €17,500. This latter component can vary according to location: in Luxembourg City it fell to 6.75% in 2006 and so decreased the tax rate from 30.38% to 29.63%
	• Net worth tax:
	  An annual net worth tax is calculated at 0.5% of the unitary value of the company as at 1 January each year	

III TAXES FOR INDIVIDUALS

		Residents	**Non-residents**
Income Tax	General description	Tax levied on the chargeable income of a chargeable person for a year of assessment	
	Taxable entities and taxable income	Residents are taxed on their worldwide income with some relief for double taxation	Non-residents are taxed on income arising in Luxembourg
	Types of taxable income	• Employment income • Business income • Income from professions • Capital gains • Others	
	Calculation of income	Taxable income is calculated by reference to specified categories, according to different rules, though losses made in one category may be offset against the income from another	
	Tax year, tax assessment and tax payment	The tax year is the calendar year Returns should be filed within 3 months of the end of the year. Postponement of filing is possible Quarterly prepayments, final payment or refund after tax assessment	
	Losses	Losses from a business or profession can be carried forward without limit. The offset of other losses is restricted	
	Tax rates	Income tax rates are progressive. They vary from 0%–38%. A 2.5% surcharge for unemployment fund applies so that the marginal income tax rate amounts to 38.95% The Luxembourg income tax liability is based on the individual's personal situation (eg family status). Three tax classes have been defined: • Class 1 • Class 1a • Class 2	
Capital Gains Tax (CGT)	General description	Profits realised on the disposal of movable and immovable property There is no special tax and it to be declared in the normal tax declaration	
	Taxable entities and chargeable assets	All assets acquired on a speculative basis	
	Calculation of gain	The difference between the sale price less the acquisition costs (these are adjusted to take account of inflation)	
	Tax year, Tax assessment and Tax payment	The tax year is the calendar year To be declared in the normal tax declaration	
	Losses	N/A Offset against taxable income	

	Tax rates	• The capital gains on real estate:
		   – the capital gain on the sale of taxpayers' main residence is tax exempt
		• The capital gain on other real estate property:
		   – is subject to progressive income tax rates if disposal takes place within 2 years of acquisition	

		Residents	**Non-residents**
Capital Gains Tax (CGT)		– is subject to a reduced tax rate if disposal takes place more than 2 years after acquisition: the reduced tax rate will not exceed 19.475% and a tax deduction of up to €50,000 (doubled for married taxpayers and civil partners). This said tax reduction may also be increased by €75,000 for inherited property (heir of line) – under specific conditions, taxation of capital gains from the disposal of property can be deferred to the extent that is used to fund the acquisition of a new property located in Luxembourg, which the owner intends to put up for rent. • The capital gains on shares: – the capital gain realised by an individual on the sale of a shareholding of more than 10% held for more than 6 months will be taxed under the same regime as capital gains arising from the sale of real estate more than 2 years after purchase • For the others, taxed at normal tax rate	

		Domiciled	**Non-domiciled**
Inheritance Tax (IHT)	General description	Death and succession duties	
	Taxable entities and chargeable assets	The worldwide property of an individual domiciled in Luxembourg at the time of his death is subject to estate duty excepted on the property located abroad	The heirs of non-resident individuals pay tax only on property located in Luxembourg
	Calculation of charge	Various rates depending on relationship to deceased	
	Taxable events	Death	
	Tax rates	Rates vary according to the nature of the relationship with the beneficiary and the value of the estate: • Individuals residents heirs: – direct descendants: nil – spouse with children: nil – spouse without children: 5% – brothers and sisters: 6% – others: 10%–15% • Individuals non-residents heirs: – direct descendants: 10%–12% – spouse with children: 10%–15% – spouse without children: 10%–15% – brothers and sisters: 10%–16% – others: 10%–15%	

IV WITHHOLDING TAXES

	Payments to non-residents
Dividends	Dividends are paid after a withholding tax of 20% for non-residents
	Some double tax treaties allow for the reduction of withholding tax
	Under the Parent-Subsidiary Directive, there is no withholding tax on dividends paid to companies resident in other EU countries under some conditions
Interest	Nil
Royalties	No withholding taxes
On payments to artists and sportsmen	No withholding taxes

V   INDIRECT TAXES

		Residents	Non-residents
Value Added Tax (VAT)	General description	Tax on the supply of goods and services (VAT)	
	Entities being obliged to levy VAT	Nature of entity is of no relevance. The kind of transactions triggers the VAT status	
	Taxable activities	All goods and services excluding in particular cases the supply and leasing of immovable property (option for VAT is possible on demand)	
	Taxable activities – zero rated (examples)	• Gold • Export	
	Exemptions (examples)	• Insurances • Hospitals • Education • Cultural activities (associations)	
	Refund of VAT	Company can demand a refund on the tax declaration but tax authorities reimburse only after control	Foreign companies may receive a reimbursement of VAT on exports of goods and services on a quarterly or an annual basis
	Tax liability	The supplier of goods and services is generally liable for the payment of VAT to the tax authorities	
	Tax rates	• Standard rate: 15% • Intermediate rate: 12% • Reduced rate: 6% • Super reduced rate: 3%	
	Administrative obligations	Monthly, quarterly or annual declaration to the tax authorities	Any business making taxable supplies or services has to register for VAT
Stamp Duty Land Tax		Levied by each town at varying rates	
Stamp Duty		On certain legal contracts	

Malaysia

(K J Singam, kjsingam@ssypartners.com)

I MAIN LEGAL FORMS

Legal form / Characteristics	Partnership and Limited Liability Partnership (LLP)	Sdn Bhd (private company) and Berhad (public company)
Partners/shareholders • Number • Restrictions	Minimum: two Maximum: not more than 20 (except lawyers, doctors and accountants)	Minimum: two Maximum: • public – no limit • private – 50
Directors	Every partnership shall have at least two partners, each of whom has his principal or only place of residence within Malaysia	Every company shall have at least two directors, each of whom has his principal or only place of residence within Malaysia
Establishment	Partnership deed	Memorandum and Articles of Incorporation
Registration	Registered under Companies Commission of Malaysia	
Minimum capital	N/A	Minimum two ordinary shares of RM1 each
Liability	Collectively responsible for all debts of firm Partners liability to pay the firm's debt is unlimited	Limited to the share capital invested by the shareholders in the company
Governance	Partnership Act 1961	Companies Act 1965 (Act 125)
Audit requirements	No audited accounts required	Every auditor of a company shall report to the members on the accounts required to be laid before the company in general meeting and on the company's accounting and other records relating to those accounts. If it is a holding company for which consolidated accounts are prepared, he shall also report to the members on the consolidated accounts
Taxation	Transparent	Resident companies are subject to corporation tax on their profits derived on a territorial basis

II CORPORATION TAX

Legal form / Description	Resident corporation[1]	Permanent establishment (PE)
General description	Income tax	
Taxable entities	Resident companies are liable to income tax on income accruing in or derived from Malaysia	PE located in Malaysia is liable to income tax on income accruing in or derived from Malaysia
Taxable income	Profits or gains derived in Malaysia	
Calculation of taxable profits	Accounting profit before tax is adjusted for various tax add-backs and allowances to arrive at profit chargeable to corporation tax (PCTCT)	
Interest payments	Interest incurred *wholly* in the production of gross income is allowable as a deduction for tax purposes	
Related party transactions	All related party transactions must take place on an arm's length basis	
Tax year of assessment, return and payment	The tax basis year of assessment corresponds to the calendar year but a company may adopt any accounting period as its basis period which ends in the basis year of assessment for a year of assessment All companies must complete and submit their tax returns within 7 months from the end of their accounting year	
Capital gains	Any gain on the disposal of real property or shares in a real property company (RPC) is exempt from real property gains tax as from 1 April 2007	
Losses	Current year business losses are allowed to be deducted against other sources of income during the same year of assessment Unabsorbed losses are allowed to be carried forward to be set off against future business income	
Tax rate	Year of assessment 2008 and onwards – 26% Companies with a share capital of RM2.5m or less – tax at 20% on chargeable income for the first RM500,000 and thereafter at 26%	

Note: An RPC is a company holding real property or shares in another RPC of which the defined value of the company is not less than 75% of the value of the company's total tangible assets.

---

1 A company (or a body of persons) carrying on a business is resident in Malaysia if, at any time in the basis year of assessment, the management and control of its business is exercised in Malaysia.

III TAXES FOR INDIVIDUALS

<table>
<tr><td rowspan="10">Income Tax</td><td></td><td colspan="2" align="center">Residents</td><td align="center">Non-residents</td></tr>
<tr><td>General description</td><td colspan="3">Tax levied on the chargeable income of a chargeable person for a year of assessment</td></tr>
<tr><td>Taxable entities and taxable income</td><td colspan="2">Residents are taxed on their territorial income with some relief for double taxation</td><td>Non-residents are taxed on income arising in Malaysia. No entitlement to reliefs</td></tr>
<tr><td>Types of taxable income</td><td colspan="3">• Property income (usually rent)
• Income from capital investment (interest, dividends, royalties, annuities)
• Income from business activities
• Employment from personal services or pensions</td></tr>
<tr><td>Calculation of income</td><td colspan="3">Accounting profit is adjusted for various tax add-backs and allowances to arrive at profits chargeable to tax</td></tr>
<tr><td>Tax year, tax assessment and tax payment</td><td colspan="3">Tax year – calendar year

Tax assessment – tax returns are normally issued to taxpayers in late February or March of each calendar year. Taxpayers must complete and submit the returns by 30 April (for a person not carrying on a business) and 30 June (for a person carrying on a business, ie sole proprietor, club, association and Hindu Joint family)

By 30 June of the following year for a person carrying on a business, ie sole proprietor, club, association and Hindu Joint family</td></tr>
<tr><td>Losses</td><td colspan="3">Business losses can be utilised against other sources of income in the basis year and any unutilised business losses can be offset against income from business sources in subsequent years. Losses can be carried forward indefinitely until permanent cessation of the business</td></tr>
<tr><td>Tax rates</td><td colspan="2">Scale rate as follows:</td><td rowspan="2">28% flat rate</td></tr>
<tr><td></td><td colspan="2">

Chargeable income	Tax rate (%)	Tax payable (RM)
First 2,500	0	0
Next 2,500	1	25
On 5,000		25
Next 15,000	3	450
On 20,000		475
Next 15,000	7	1,050
On 35,000		1,525
Next 15,000	13	1,950
On 50,000		3,475
Next 20,000	19	3,800
On 70,000		7,275
Next 30,000	24	7,200
On 100,000		14,475
Next 150,000	27	40,500
On 250,000		54,975
Exceeding 250,000	28	

</td></tr>
</table>

		Residents	**Non-residents**
Capital Gains Tax (CGT)	General description	Malaysia does not generally tax capital gains. Gains from the disposal of real property or shares in real property companies were previously subject to real property gains tax. This tax was repealed with effect from 1 April 2007	
		Domiciled	**Non-domiciled**
Inheritance Tax (IHT)	General description	No inheritance taxes	

IV WITHHOLDING TAXES[2]

	Payments to non-residents[3]
Dividends	Nil
Interest	15%
Royalties	10%
Contract payments	10% of the service portion of the contract
	3% of the service portion of the contract in respect of the employee's tax
Special classes of income	10%
On payments to public entertainers (eg artists and sportsmen)	15%

---

2 Payments for services which were performed by the non-resident offshore will not be subject to withholding tax provisions.

3 Reduced rates of withholding tax may apply where there is an appropriate double tax agreement.

V   INDIRECT TAXES

		Residents	**Non-residents**
General description		Types of indirect taxes in the country are: • Customs duties • Excise duties • Service tax • Sales tax	
Customs duties • Import duties • Export duties		Levied on goods imported into or exported from Malaysia Certain types of goods are exempted from customs duties under specific exemption orders • Import duties rates are either specific or ad valorem from 2%–300% • Export duties rates are either specific or on cost plus concept	
Excise duties		Imposed on certain locally manufactured goods (eg beer, stout, other intoxicating liquors, cigarettes, motor vehicles and playing cards) Rates are either specific or ad valorem	
Service tax		Consumption tax levied and charged on any taxable services provided by any taxable person Rate is 5% of the price, charge or premium of the taxable service	
Sales tax		Single stage tax imposed on all goods manufactured in or imported into Malaysia unless specifically exempted Rates are ad valorem from 5%–10%	
Value Added Tax (VAT)	General description	Tax on the supply of goods and services (VAT)	
	Entities being obliged to levy VAT	There is no VAT in Malaysia The Inland Revenue Board is planning to introduce a Goods and Service Tax (GST) to replace the sales and service tax but it has not been implemented to date	
Stamp Duty Land Tax		N/A	
Stamp Duty		Chargeable on certain instruments and documents Rate of duty varies (fixed or ad valorem) according to the nature of the instrument/documents and transacted values according to the First Schedule of the Stamp Act 1949	

Malta

(Karl Cini, Brian Tonna & Co, karl@briantonna.com)

I   MAIN LEGAL FORMS

Legal form / Characteristics	Partnership and Limited Liability Partnership (LLP)	Ltd (private corporation) and Plc (public corporation)
Partners/shareholders • Number • Restrictions	Two types of partnerships are possible, namely: • *En nom collectif:* unlimited partnership, where all partners' liability is unlimited, joint and several • *En commandite:* limited partnership, where at least one partner's liability has to be unlimited	Ltd: • minimum: one shareholder (as long as the sole shareholder and sole director are not themselves corporate entities, and the objects clause restricted to one main activity) • maximum: 50 shareholders Plc: • minimum: two shareholders • maximum: no limit
Directors	Management by partners	Minimum: one director Maximum: no limit
Establishment	Deed of partnership	Memorandum and Articles of Association
Registration	Filing of deed of partnership at the Registry of Companies	Filing of Memorandum and Articles at the Registry of Companies
Minimum Capital	*En nom collectif:* none *En commandite:* its capital may or may not be divided into shares. No minimum	Ltd: €1,164.69 with at least 20% thereof paid up upon subscription Plc: €46,587.47 with at least 25% thereof paid upon subscription
Liability	*En nom collectif:* unlimited *En commandite:* unlimited and joint and several liability of one or more general partners and liability limited to the amount, if any, unpaid on the contribution of one or more limited partners	Limited the portion, if any, still unpaid of the subscribed share capital
Governance	Partners	Board of Directors
Audit requirements	None	Audit required
Taxation	Transparent	Worldwide basis

II   CORPORATION TAX

Legal form / Description	Resident corporation	Permanent establishment (PE)
General description	Income tax	
Taxable entities	Resident companies	PE located in Malta
Taxable income	• Worldwide profits for resident companies incorporated and managed and controlled in Malta • Source basis for resident companies not incorporated and managed and controlled in Malta • Source and remittance (except foreign capital gains) basis for resident companies not incorporated but managed and controlled in Malta	Profits allocated to the PE in Malta
Calculation of taxable profits	Accounting profits as adjusted for various disallowable expenses and tax allowances	
Interest payments	Interest on any borrowed money is an allowable deduction if it is paid on capital employed in acquiring income	
Related party transactions	Arm's length basis	
Tax year, return and payment	Fiscal year is the calendar year	
	Malta operates a self-assessment system. Tax is payable at the time that the self assessment is filed. For companies the tax return date is 9 months after the financial year end, but not earlier than 31 March of each year	
	Companies and self-employed persons pay tax under the provisional tax system (PT). PT payments are due every 3 months Where the tax liability is not fully covered by the PT the balance must be paid at the time that the relative tax return is filed	
	Special rules apply to tax due by companies on foreign income	
Capital gains	Capital gains are added to the income of the recipient and chargeable to tax accordingly in Malta. The only capital gains that are subject to tax are those made on transfer of: • immovable property • securities and shares (but excluding those quoted on the Malta Stock Exchange) • beneficial interest in a Trust • business, goodwill, trademarks, trade names, patents and copyrights	
	Capital gains realised on the transfer of shares by non-residents are exempt from Malta income tax (with the exception of shares in companies, the assets of which consist wholly or principally of immovable property situated in Malta)	
Losses	Trading losses can be carried forward and set off against any type of income	
	Capital losses can be carried forward but may only be set off against capital gains	

Legal form / Description	Resident corporation	Permanent establishment (PE)
Tax group	A company may surrender its losses in favour of any group company subject to certain conditions. For this purpose two companies are considered to form part of a group if the shares of one company are at least 51% owned by the other, or both of them are 51% subsidiaries of a third company	N/A
Tax rate	35%[1]	

---

1 Various credits are available for participating holdings, trading income derived from passive assets in addition to credits for foreign losses suffered on the income.

III TAXES FOR INDIVIDUALS

<table>
<tr><td rowspan="10">Income Tax</td><td></td><td colspan="3">Residents</td><td>Non-residents</td></tr>
<tr><td>General description</td><td colspan="4">Tax levied on the chargeable income of a chargeable person for a year of assessment. A person's liability to tax in Malta hinges on the twin concepts of residence and domicile</td></tr>
<tr><td>Taxable entities and taxable income</td><td colspan="3">Persons that are both ordinarily resident and domiciled in Malta are subject to income tax on their worldwide income and certain capital gains</td><td>Taxable on any income and certain capital gains arising in Malta and on income arising outside Malta that is remitted in Malta</td></tr>
<tr><td>Types of taxable income</td><td colspan="4">• Gains or profits from trade, profession or vocation
• Employment income including certain fringe benefits
• Investment income
• Rent, royalties, premiums and any other profit arising from property
• Other gains or profits not taxed elsewhere</td></tr>
<tr><td>Calculation of income</td><td colspan="4">Income is generally taken to be the gross amount received less any allowances and generally on an accruals basis. Fringe benefits are calculated according to the value of the benefit based on calculations as prescribed by the Inland Revenue Department</td></tr>
<tr><td>Tax year, tax assessment and tax payment</td><td colspan="4">• Tax year – calendar year
• Tax assessment – individual self assessment
• Tax payment – by 30 June of the following year (also filing date)</td></tr>
<tr><td>Losses</td><td colspan="4">Trading losses can be carried forward and set off against any type of income

Capital losses can be carried forward but may only be set off against capital gains</td></tr>
</table>

Tax rates	**Single rates**			**Single and married**	
	Chargeable income (€)	*Rate (%)*	*Deduct (€)*	*Chargeable income (€)*	*Rate (%)*
	0–8,150	0	0.00	0–700	0
	8,151–14,000	0.15	1,222.50	701–3,100	20
	14,001–19,000	0.25	2,622.50	3,101–7,800	30
	19,001+	0.35	4,522.50	7,801+	35

	Married rates		
	Chargeable income (€)	*Rate (%)*	*Deduct (€)*
	0–11,400	0	0.00
	11,401–20,500	0.15	1,710.00
	20,501–28,000	0.25	3,760.00
	28,001+	0.35	6,560.00

Resident Scheme Certificate Holders
A flat rate of 15% on all income received in, or remitted to, Malta from either local or foreign sources. This is subject to a minimum tax payment of €4,192 per annum

		Residents	Non-residents
Capital Gains Tax (CGT)	General description	Taken to be gains made on the disposal of certain assets	
	Taxable entities and chargeable assets	Any person resident in Malta in the year during which the gain arises is taxable Chargeable assets being: • immovable property • securities and shares (but excluding those quoted on the Malta Stock Exchange) • beneficial interest in a Trust • business, goodwill, trademarks, trade names, patents and copyrights	
	Calculation of gain	Gain is based on the disposal proceeds less cost of acquisition and other allowable expenditure. Inflation allowance and maintenance allowance are allowed in certain instances involving the transfer or deemed transfer of immovable property. For certain transfers of immovable property tax is charged at 12% of the transfer value on a final withholding basis. Certain exemptions apply	
	Tax year, tax assessment and tax payment	Capital gains are recorded in the tax return of the individual. The tax year is hence a calendar year For the majority of transfers a provisional tax payment of 7% of the transfer value is payable upon transfer, with the resultant tax due, if any, to be paid by 30 June of the following year For transfers of immovable property based on the 12% Final Property Transfer Tax system, the 12% is payable upon transfer	
	Losses	Capital losses are set off against any capital gains made during that year Unutilised capital losses can be carried forward indefinitely to be set off against future capital gains	
	Tax rates	Capital gains, with the exception of transfers of immovable property based on the 12% Final Property Transfer Tax system, are recorded in the individual's tax return for that year and added to the other income. The applicable tax rate will then apply on the total income	
		Domiciled	**Non-domiciled**
Inheritance Tax (IHT)	General description	There is no inheritance or gift tax in Malta. The transmission of property and company shares is however, subject to tax under the Duty on Documents and Transfers Act, tax is due by heirs upon inheritance of real estate and shares. Duty will be due at the rate of €5 per €100 or part thereof in the case of real estate and €2 per €100 or part thereof in the case of shares	

IV   WITHHOLDING TAXES

	Payments to non-residents
Dividends	None
Interest	None
Royalties	None
On payments to artists and sportsmen	10% (applicable to foreign entertainers performing in Malta)

V INDIRECT TAXES

		Residents	Non-residents
Value Added Tax (VAT)	General description	Tax on the supply of goods and services (VAT)	
	Entities being obliged to levy VAT	Registration is compulsory for suppliers of goods with annual turnover over €28,000 and suppliers of services over €18,700. Entities include individuals, partnerships, corporation or other bodies. Following distance selling rules, foreign EU-based suppliers exceeding the current threshold of €35,000 sales made in Malta over a period of a year need to register in Malta	
	Taxable activities	All supplies of goods and services that take place in Malta, intra-Community acquisitions and imports	
	Taxable activities – zero rated (examples)	Zero rating applies to exports and intra-Community supplies, international transport, domestic passenger transport, food, pharmaceuticals and the supply and repair of ships and aircraft	
	Exemptions (examples)	Exemptions include the sale and leasing of immovable property, banking and insurance services, health, education and broadcasting	
	Refund of VAT	• VAT paid on supplies and services is deductible as input tax, if incurred in the course or furtherance of the business and for the purpose of making taxable supplies (including zero-rated supplies) • There is no credit for input tax incurred which relates to the provision of exempt supplies • Where mixed supplies occur (taxable and exempt), input tax must be apportioned and recovered according to a partial attribution method stipulated in the law	• EC 8th Directive refund system applies for non-resident businesses established within the EU, as long as its businesses do not require a registration in Malta • EC 13th Directive refund system for non-resident businesses established outside the EU, as long as its businesses do not require a registration in Malta • Such claims are required to be made to the Maltese VAT department within strict time limits
	Tax liability	• Normally the supplier of goods and services is responsible for charging VAT • Reverse charge system applies for certain types of goods and services (eg accountancy and consultancy services received from businesses established in EU but outside Malta)	
	Tax rates	• Standard rate = 18% • A reduced 5% rate applies to the supply of holiday accommodation, electricity, printed matter and confectionery • Zero rated = 0%	
	Administrative obligations	• Formal requirements concerning business records and invoices • Quarterly self-assessment VAT return. Returns are to be submitted one and a half months following the end of the quarter together with the payment of any VAT liability to the Commissioner of VAT (special arrangements allow for monthly returns to be filed)	• Registration for VAT purposes if making supplies of goods and services in Malta

		Residents	Non-residents
Value Added Tax (VAT)		• VAT invoices required to contain some basic data amongst which being the respective VAT identification number	
Stamp Duty Land Tax		Chargeable on the transfer, whether inter vivos or by way of inheritance, of immovable property	
		The rate is of €5 per €100 or part thereof	
		Exemptions include transfers of property between group companies, partitioning of property by joint owners and transfers between spouses (amongst others)	
Stamp Duty		Stamp duty is also chargeable on the transfer, whether inter vivos or by way of inheritance, of securities. The tax in this case is of €2 per €100 or part thereof but is increased to €5 per €100 or part thereof in the case of shares in property companies	
		Duty at various rates is also chargeable on emphyteutical grants, auction sales, credit cards and insurance policies (with the exemption of policies relating to health, marine, aviation, export finance and re-insurance)	

Mauritius

(Ouma Shankar, nexiamtius@intnet.mu)

I MAIN LEGAL FORMS

Legal form Characteristics	Partnership and Limited Liability Partnership (LLP)	Ltd (private corporation) and Plc (public corporation)
Partners/shareholders • Number • Restrictions	• Two or more partners • No limited liability partnership	• Minimum one • Private company: maximum 25 shareholders
Directors	All partners unless stated otherwise in the partnership deed	Minimum one director
Establishment	Partnership deed	Constitution of the Company
Registration	Must be registered with the Registrar of Companies	
Minimum capital	No minimum capital	
Liability	Unlimited liability	Limited by shares or by guarantee or both shares and guarantee
Governance	The Code de Commerce (Amendment) Act, Act 21 of 1985	Companies Act 2001
Audit requirements	No audit required	Financial statements must be audited unless it is a small private company whose annual turnover is less than MUR 30m
Taxation	Transparent, but the individual partners are directly liable for their respective share of income	Flat rate of 15%
Usage	Any business	

II CORPORATION TAX

Legal form / Description	Resident corporation	Permanent establishment (PE)
General description	Corporation tax	Corporate tax
Taxable entities	Companies, trusts and trustees of unit trust schemes	Branch or agent of foreign company and non-resident société
Taxable income	Worldwide income	Income arising or deemed to arise in Mauritius
Calculation of taxable profits	Profit as adjusted for tax purposes	
Interest payments	Deductible, no thin capitalisation rules	
Related party transactions	Transactions not carried out at arm's length may be subject to tax adjustments	
Tax year, return and payment	Annual return to be filed not later than 6 months from the end of the month in which its accounting period ends	
	Besides the annual return, companies are required to file quarterly Advance Payment System (APS) Statements as from 1 July 2008 for companies having a turnover exceeding Rs100m and as from 1 July 2009 for all other companies	
Capital gains	No CGT in Mauritius	
Losses	May be carried forward and set off against its income derived in the following 5 income years	
Tax group	None	
Tax rate	15%	

III TAXES FOR INDIVIDUALS

		Residents	Non-residents
Income Tax	General description	Income tax	
	Taxable entities and taxable income	Any individual present in Mauritius for a period of 183 days or more in an income year or for an aggregated period of 270 days or more in the current income year and the 2 preceding income years	Income derived from sources in Mauritius
	Types of taxable income	Income related to employment and income derived from trade, business, profession and rent	
	Calculation of income	Chargeable income is the amount remaining after deducting from the net income, the income exemption threshold to which the individual is entitled	
	Tax year, tax assessment and tax payment	Tax year runs to 30 June and tax returns should be filed by the end of September PAYE system is in operation, and is based on a cumulative basis Current Payment System (CPS) concerns self-employed persons with income derived from trade, business, professional and rent. The individual must submit the statement of income on a quarterly basis and at the same time pay the tax	
	Losses	May be carried forward to offset against future business income only	
	Tax rates	15%	
Capital Gains Tax (CGT)	General description	No capital gains tax in Mauritius	
		Mauritius domiciled	**Non-Mauritius domiciled**
Inheritance Tax (IHT)	General description	No gift or inheritance taxes in Mauritius	

IV   WITHHOLDING TAXES

Nature of payment	Payments to non-residents[1]
Dividends	No withholding tax
Interest	15%
Rent	5%
Royalties	10%
Services provided by architects, engineers, land surveyors, project managers in construction industry, property valuers and quantity surveyors	3%
Payments to contractors or subcontractors	0.75%

---

1   No withholding tax for exempt companies.

V INDIRECT TAXES

		Residents	Non-residents
Value Added Tax (VAT)	Entities being obliged to levy VAT	• Any business person with a turnover of taxable supplies of more than MUR 2m must register with VAT Department, Mauritius Revenue Authority • Persons engaged in certain businesses or professions may also be required to register, irrespective of their turnover	
	Taxable activities	Goods and services produced or improved locally	
	Taxable activities – zero rated (examples)	Exports and other items as specified in the VAT Act	
	Exemptions (examples)	Certain essential goods and services	
	Refund of VAT	On capital goods in excess of MUR 100,000 and input tax relating to zero-rated supplies	
	Tax liability	Liable to pay tax for a period prior to registration if the person ought to have been registered	
	Tax rates	Standard rate of 15%	
	Administrative obligations	A return together with payment of tax to be submitted monthly, unless the annual turnover is less than MUR 10m, in which case the return is submitted quarterly	
Registration duties on immovable properties		5% on value of immovable property transferred payable by purchaser	
Registration duty on loans		Duties of fixed amounts are levied upon registration of a loan agreement	
Land Transfer Tax		Land transfer tax payable by the seller at the rate of 5% if the property transferred has been acquired more than 5 years from date of transfer. If transfer made within 5 years the rate is 10%	

Mexico

(Hector Garcia, hgarcia@gossler.com.mx)

I   MAIN LEGAL FORMS

Legal form / Characteristics	Partnership and Limited Liability Partnership (LLP)	Ltd (private corporation) and Plc (public corporation)
Partners/shareholders • Number • Restrictions	• Two minimum • 50 maximum	• Two minimum • No limit
Directors	Might be sole director or a board	
Establishment	A notary public makes the deed and it has to be registered in the public registry of property and commerce	
Registration	Registration before tax authorities, social security authorities and state payroll tax	
Minimum capital	3,000 pesos	50,000 pesos
Liability	The legal representative (with power of attorney) and in some cases the partners up to the amount of their contribution	
Governance	Not mandatory	Board of Administration (Board of Directors)
Audit requirements	Required if turnover exceeds 27m pesos	
Taxation	Resident companies are subject to corporation tax on their profits derived anywhere in the world Partnerships are transparent	
Usage	For some countries, the Mexican LLC (Limited Liability Company) might be utilised as a pass-through vehicle Publicly held companies cannot use this type of entity	Mandatory for publicly held companies
Official name	Sociedad de Responsabilidad Limitada (SRL)	Sociedad Anónima (SA) which might be of fixed or variable equity (SA de CV)

II   CORPORATION TAX

Legal form / Description	Resident corporation	Permanent establishment (PE)
General description	Corporate income tax	Branch income tax
Taxable entities	Corporations incorporated in Mexico and/or overseas companies with central management and control located in Mexico	PE located in Mexico
Taxable income	Worldwide profits	Profits derived by PE in Mexico
Calculation of taxable profits	Accounting profit is adjusted for various tax add-backs and allowances to arrive to profits chargeable to corporation tax (PCTCT)	
Interest payments	Interest payments are tax deductible, and the comparisons with inflation rates generate gains or losses, which are taxable or tax deductible	
	Thin capitalisation rule is 3:1 and in case the liability exceeds the 3:1 ratio the interests paid in excess are non-deductible	
	Thin capitalisation rule applies only to interest paid to residents abroad	
Related party transactions	All related party transactions must take place on an arm's length basis and companies are obligated to substantiate such a basis preparing a formal transfer pricing study	
Tax year, return and payment	The tax year is the calendar year and tax is paid monthly or quarterly in advance depending on the level of revenue	
	The tax return must be filed within 3 months after the end of the tax year	
Capital gains	Capital gains are subject to income tax at the same rate of corporations (28%). In some cases, capital gains are subject to withholding tax on gross proceeds	
Losses	Net operating tax losses may be carried forward for 10 years and set off against taxable profits	
Tax group	A group is formed by a holding company with at least one subsidiary. The group can consolidate the results of each individual subsidiary and up to 100% of the losses from subsidiaries can be offset against the profits of others	
Tax rate	28%	
Alternative Minimum Tax	Effective 1 January 2008, a new alternative minimum tax came into force. The new tax is called 'Impuesto Empresarial a Tasa Única (IETU)' (Single Rate Business Tax) and will substitute the 'Tax on Assets'	
	The tax base is computed on a cash-flow basis in connection with income actually collected less deductions actually paid, except salaries and wages, interests and royalties paid to related parties	
	The flat tax rate is 17.5% although a transitory provision allows the taxpayers to apply 16.5% for 2008, 17% for 2009 and as of 2010 the rate will be 17.5%	
	As an alternative minimum tax, the IETU tax will only be paid if it exceeds the income tax payable of any specific year	

III TAXES FOR INDIVIDUALS

		Residents	Non-residents
Income Tax	General description	Tax levied on the chargeable income of a chargeable person for a year of assessment	
	Taxable entities and taxable income	Residents are taxed on their worldwide income	Non-residents are taxable if they are based in Mexico for business purposes, and are taxed on all income arising from Mexican sources
	Types of taxable income	• Property income (usually rent) • Income from capital investment (interest, sale of goodwill, dividends, royalties, annuities) • Income from business activities • Employment from personal services or pensions	
	Calculation of income	• Taxable income is generally computed by reducing the cost of goods or the cost of acquisition of the goods to be sold • Rent income is entitled to a 35% blind deduction (optional) • Salary income is computed by applying a progressive table which starts from 0% and goes up to 28% income tax	
	Tax year, tax assessment and tax payment	Tax usually is withheld by the payer and is payable in the following month of the date of payment A calendar year January to December or any period of time until December The employer is obliged to compute the annual tax and optionally the individual may do the calculation himself if there is any deduction that helps Annual tax for individuals is due before the end of April the following year	
	Losses	In some very specific cases such as losses from the sale of assets and from business activities	
	Tax rates	0–28%	0–40%
Capital Gains Tax (CGT)	General description	Tax on increase in the value of asset between acquisition and disposal, not chargeable to income or corporate tax	
	Taxable entities and chargeable assets	Capital gains tax is actually computed and added to the corporate/individual taxable income Except for real estate	Only assets located in the Mexican territory
	Calculation of gain	Liability is calculated by deducting historical cost adjusted to current value, accounting for inflation between the date of acquisition and the date of disposal	
	Tax year, tax assessment and tax payment	The tax year is the calendar year and tax is paid monthly or quarterly in advance The tax return must be filed within 4 months after the end of the tax year	
	Losses	Tax losses may be carried forward for 10 years and set off against future taxable profits	
	Tax rates	0–28%	

		Domiciled	Non-domiciled
Inheritance Tax (IHT)	General description	There is no IHT in Mexico	
Single Rate Business Tax (IETU)	General description	The tax was enacted as a replacement of the tax on asset and it works as an alternative minimum tax, so it is only paid to the extent it exceeds the income tax	
	Taxable entities and taxable income	The tax base is computed on a cash-flow basis in connection with income actually collected less deductions actually paid, except salaries and wages, interests and royalties paid to related parties	
	Tax year, tax assessment and tax payment	The tax year is the calendar year and the tax is paid monthly (in advance)	
		The tax return must be filed within 4 months after the end of the tax year	
	Losses	Tax losses may be carried forward for 10 years and may be used to offset future taxable profits of the IETU tax	
	Tax Rate	• 16.5% for 2008 • 17% for 2009 • 17.5% starting in 2010	

IV WITHHOLDING TAXES

	Payments to non-residents[1]
Dividends	Nil
Interest	From 4.9%–40%
Royalties	From 5%–40%
On payments to artists and sportsmen	From 25%–40%

1 Reduced rates of withholding tax may apply where there is an appropriate double tax treaty.

V   INDIRECT TAXES

		Residents	Non-residents
Value Added Tax (VAT)	General description	Impuesto al Valor Agregado (VAT) Tax on the supply of goods and services	
	Entities being obliged to levy VAT	All entities or individuals (either residents or not) performing activities into the Mexican territory are obliged to levy VAT	
	Taxable activities	• Transfer of goods • Rendering services • Property income (rent) • Importation of goods	
	Taxable activities – zero rated (examples)	• Food • Primary activities (agriculture, fishing, catering) • Exports	
	Exemptions (examples)	• Medicines • Books • Interest from financial institutions • Services rendered or goods transferred by not-for-profit organisations	
	Refund of VAT	Refunds paid within a period of 40 working days	Not allowed under general rules
	Tax liability	The supplier of the goods and services is responsible for charging VAT	
	Tax rates	• Standard rate = 15% • Rate along the border = 10% • Rate on exports and food = 0% • The tax is computed on a cash-flow basis	
	Administrative obligations	• Apply for registration • File monthly returns • Withhold VAT in case of payments made to individuals • File annual information returns • Issue specially stamped invoices	
Stamp Duty Land Tax		Owners of land and buildings pay tax to local councils, who apply rules to each city	
Stamp Duty		N/A	

Morocco

(Mohamed Ouedghiri, fidunex@menara.ma)

I MAIN LEGAL FORMS

Legal form / Characteristics	Partnership and Limited Liability Partnership (LLP)	Ltd (private corporation) and Plc (public corporation)
Partners/shareholders • Number • Restrictions	Partnership: minimum of two LLP: between one and 50	Minimum of five shareholders
Directors	Managers (one or more) named by partners	Directors (one or more) named by the board. Those directors could be subjected to the president of the board (CEO) or a physical person named as general manager
Establishment	On the whole, two steps: • status and others documents must be signed by associates • deposit and advertising formalities	
Registration	Formalities of registration are done at the court and/or administrations where the permanent establishment is legally domiciled	
Minimum capital	Partnership: no minimum capital LLP: 10,000 MAD	Private company: 300,000 MAD Listed company: 3,000,000 MAD
Liability	Partnership: unlimited LLP: limited	Limited
Governance	Managers/partners' general meeting	Board of Directors/shareholders' general meetings
Audit requirements	Audit required if sales are higher than 50m MAD	Statutory audit is always required
Taxation	Partnership: submitted to income tax except option for corporation tax LLP: submitted to corporation tax	Resident companies are subject to corporation tax on the profits derived from activities in Morocco (including income and capital gains) and overseas profits attributed under the double tax treaty provisions

II   CORPORATION TAX

Legal form / Description	Resident corporation	Permanent establishment (PE)
General description	Corporation tax	
Taxable entities	Companies incorporated in Morocco	PE located in Morocco
Taxable income	Profits on business activities carried out in Morocco and overseas income attributed under the double tax treaty provisions	Profits derived by PE in Morocco
Calculation of taxable profits	Accounting profit is adjusted for various tax add-backs and allowances to arrive to profits chargeable to corporation tax (PCTCT)	
Interest payments	Interest payments are deductible, unless paid to shareholders, in which case: • not deductible if the capital is not fully paid up • deductible only on the amount of the loan not exceeding the company's nominal capital and • the rate of interest is limited to the yearly average rate on treasury bonds	
Related party transactions	All related party transactions must take place on arm's length basis	
Tax year, return and payment	Company may choose its accounting year-end date Tax return must be filed within 3 months after the end of the accounting year Tax is payable in quarterly instalments based on prior year profits Balance of tax is payable on the tax return filing date	
Capital gains	• Capital gains are subject to corporation tax at normal rates. A deduction (25%–50%) is allowed in accordance with special rules • Capital gains on quoted transferable securities realised by non-resident companies are tax-free	
Losses	• Net operating tax losses may be carried forward for 4 years and set off against future taxable profits • The loss arising from depreciation can be carried forward indefinitely	
Tax group	None	
Tax rate	A rate of 30% is applicable to all profits. For insurance, banking and leasing companies the rate is 37%	

III   TAXES FOR INDIVIDUALS

		Residents	Non-residents
Income Tax	General description	Tax levied on the chargeable income of a chargeable person for the year of assessment	
	Taxable entities and taxable income	Residents are taxed on their worldwide income	Non-residents are taxable on all income arising in Morocco unless excluded under a double tax treaty
	Types of taxable income	• Professional income (from business activities) • Farming income • Wages and similar income • Real estate income and capital gains • Income and profits derived from securities	
	Calculation of income	Total taxable income is the aggregate of various descriptive categories. The net income of each of these categories is separately assessed according to its own rules	
	Tax year, tax assessment and tax payment	Fiscal year is the calendar year PAYE or assessed by authorities after filing the return Instalments are assessed annually on prior year income tax	
	Losses	Losses can only be offset against income arising from the same source	
	Tax rates	Rates between 0%–42% are applied to total taxable income on increasing basis	
Capital Gains Tax (CGT)	General description	Tax on increase in the value of assets between acquisition and disposal, not chargeable to income tax	
	Taxable entities and chargeable assets	Capital gains are normally assessed as income: • movable property sold by individuals is subject to a final tax fixed in special rules • fixed assets sold by individuals are subject to a final tax of 20% of the gain subject to a minimum liability of 3% of gross proceeds	• Capital gains on quoted transferable securities realised by non-resident are subject to income tax • Fixed assets sold by non-resident are subject to a final tax of 20% of the gain subject to a minimum liability of 3% of gross proceeds
	Calculation of gain	See above	
	Tax year, tax assessment and tax payment	Regarding real estate assets, a statement has to be made within 60 days of the transfer, together with payment of the tax As to movable capital, the taxpayer has to make an annual statement of the profits and losses registered during the previous year at the latest on 31 March of the current year. Notice to pay the tax will be sent by the Tax Administration which is responsible for calculating the due tax	
	Losses	In the case of real estate assets a loss is allowed. A minimum tax of 3% is due to be paid on the basis of the selling price Regarding movable capital, there is a possibility of compensating losses and profits by carrying forward the net loss of one year over the 4 following years	
	Tax rates	See above	

IV   WITHHOLDING TAXES

	Payments to non-residents[1]
Dividends	10%
Interest	10%
Royalties	10%
On payments to artists and sportsmen	10%

---

1   Reduced rates of withholding tax may apply where there is an appropriate double tax treaty.

V   INDIRECT TAXES

		Residents	Non-residents
Value Added Tax (VAT)	General description	Tax on the supply of goods and services (VAT)	
	Entities being obliged to levy VAT	Taxable businesses	
	Taxable activities	Supply of goods and services	
	Taxable activities – zero rated (examples)	Exports, equipment acquired by new companies, equipment for special activities	
	Exemptions (examples)	Exports, equipment acquired by new companies, equipment for special activities	
	Refund of VAT	For export activities	For passengers
	Tax liability	It is up to the firm providing the goods or service to recover the VAT amount charged to the client and transfer it to the Treasury	
	Tax rates	Standard rate of 20% but lower rates of 14%, 10% and 7%	
	Administrative obligations	Filing return	Filing return
Stamp Duty Land Tax		None	
Stamp Duty		None	

Namibia

(Richard Theron, rtheron@grandnam.net)

I   MAIN LEGAL FORMS

Legal form / Characteristics	Partnership and Limited Liability Partnership (LLP)	Ltd (private corporation) and Plc (public corporation)
Partners/shareholders • Number • Restrictions	Partnership: maximum 20 LLP: maximum 50 Only natural persons	Private: minimum one and maximum 50 Public: minimum seven and no maximum Both natural and juristic persons
Directors	Partnership: N/A LLP: as per private company	Private: minimum one and maximum subject to Articles of Association Public: minimum two and maximum subject to Articles of Association
Establishment	Partnership: by partnership agreement LLP: registration with the Registrar of Companies	Private and public: registration with the Registrar of Companies
Registration	Partnership: N/A LLP: registration with the Registrar of Companies	Registration with the Registrar of Companies
Minimum capital	N/A	R100
Liability	Partnership: no limited liability LLP: limited for partners other than the general partner	Both have limited liability
Governance	Partnership: partnership agreement LLP: per King II, Companies Act 1973, as amended, and the Memorandum and Articles of Association	Per King II, Companies Act 1973, as amended, and the Memorandum and Articles of Association
Audit requirements	Partnership: no audit required LLP: audit required	Both public and private are required to be audited
Taxation	Partnership: transparent LLP: 35%; transparent	35%

II CORPORATION TAX

Legal form / Description	Resident corporation	Permanent establishment (PE)
General description	Levied on taxable income	
Taxable entities	Entities incorporated in Namibia	PEs of foreign entities
Taxable income	Worldwide income subject to certain exemptions for activities undertaken outside Namibia	Namibian source income
Calculation of taxable profits	Gross receipts minus exemptions and allowable deductions	
Interest payments	Deductible, subject to thin capitalisation rules	
Related party transactions	Transactions not carried out at arm's length may be brought within the ambit of the anti-avoidance legislation	
Tax year, return and payment	Any financial year of the company ending during the calendar year in question. Taxes paid based on an estimated value with two instalments and a final top-up	
Capital Gains	No Capital Gains Tax	
Losses	Losses may be carried forward indefinitely provided entity is trading	
Tax group	N/A	
Tax rate	• Standard rate 35% • Special incentives for manufacturers • Export Processing Zone (EPZ) companies are exempt from all taxes • Mining companies, except diamond, oil and gas companies, are taxed at 37.5% • Diamond mines are taxed at a rate of 50% plus surcharge of 10% of the 50% (5%), totalling thus 55%	

III   TAXES FOR INDIVIDUALS

		Residents	Non-residents
Income Tax	General description	Taxed on worldwide income	Taxed on income from Namibian sources of income or deemed Namibian sources
	Taxable entities and taxable income	A natural person ordinarily resident in Namibia or anyone who spends in the country more than 91 days per tax year in the current year and in the previous 5 years and in aggregate more than 915 days during the previous 5 tax years	
	Types of taxable income	• Employment income • Business income • Interest • Rentals • Royalties • Pensions	
	Calculation of income	Aggregate of gross income less exempt income	
	Tax year, tax assessment and tax payment	Tax year – 1 March to the last day of February *No return is required for persons whose sole income is derived from remuneration and does not exceed N$36,000 per annum.* Exemption for submission of returns where other income is beyond the threshold may be granted upon application Remuneration subject to monthly PAYE deductions but taxpayers obliged to also become provisional taxpayers if income from other sources exceeds certain levels Provisional taxes payable based on an estimated value with two instalments and a final top-up (if required)	
	Losses	May be carried forward indefinitely	
	Tax rates	Progressive block rates Maximum marginal rate of 35%	
Capital Gains Tax (CGT)	General description	N/A	
	Taxable entities and chargeable assets	N/A	N/A
	Calculation of gain	N/A	
	Tax year, tax assessment and tax payment	N/A	
	Losses	N/A	
	Tax Rates	N/A	N/A

		Domiciled	Non-domiciled
Inheritance Tax (IHT)	General description	N/A	
	Taxable entities and chargeable assets	N/A	N/A
	Calculation of charge	N/A	
	Taxable events	N/A	N/A
	Allowances	N/A	N/A
	Tax rates	N/A	

IV WITHHOLDING TAXES

	Payments to non-residents
Dividends	10%
Interest	Nil
Royalties	Nil
On payments to artists and sportsmen	Nil

V   INDIRECT TAXES

		Residents	Non-residents
Value Added Tax (VAT)	General description		
	Entities being obliged to levy VAT	Any entity whose taxable supplies exceed R200,000 per annum	
	Taxable activities	Any supply of goods or services in the course or furtherance of a taxable activity, other than exempt supplies	
	Taxable activities – zero rated (examples)	• Supplies made by charitable similar organisations • Exports of goods and services • Supply of an enterprise or part of as a going concern • Supplies of telecommunication services to residential telephone accounts • Supply of electricity, water, refuse removal and sewerage of residential accounts • Supply of petrol, diesel and paraffin • Supply of basic certain foodstuffs • Supply of land and buildings for residential purpose and the erection, improvement or extension to residential buildings.	
	Exemptions (examples)	• Residential leases and fringe benefit accommodation • Public passenger transport • Property rates levied by local authorities • Educational services • Medical services and services provided by hospitals • Fringe benefits to employees	
	Refund of VAT	Upon assessment and after Receiver of Revenue Audit	At customs upon departure
	Tax liability	Settlement by due date of return (every 2 months)	
	Tax rates	Standard rate of 15%	
	Administrative obligations	Submission of returns	Keep proof of purchases and sales invoices
Stamp Duty Land Tax		• Natural persons – sliding scale of 0–8% • Other – 8%	
Stamp Duty		Is payable as set out in the Stamp Duty Act	

The Netherlands

(Ton Krol, Amsterdam, tkrol@hbh.nl)

I MAIN LEGAL FORMS

Legal form / Characteristics	Partnership (VOF) and Limited Liability Partnership (CV)	BV (private corporation) and NV (public corporation)
Partners/shareholders • Number • Restrictions	• Two or more • None[1]	• One or more • None
Directors	Management by partners	Management by director(s)[2]
Establishment	No formal requirements[3]	Notarial deed of incorporation
Registration	Chamber of Commerce and tax authorities[4]	
Minimum capital	None	€18,000 for BV[5] and €45,000 for NV
Liability	Unlimited[6]	Limited to capital[7]
Governance	Partners, general meeting, works council[8]	Managing Director/Board of Directors, supervisory board, shareholders' meeting, works council[8]
Audit requirements	No audit requirements for partnerships	No audit requirement if for 2 consecutive years at least two of the three conditions below were not exceeded: • Turnover does not exceed €8.8m • Total assets do not exceed €4.4m • Number of employees does not exceed 50

---

1 The limited partner should not legally represent the CV in external relations.
2 A private and public company must have at least one director.
3 Partnership agreement in writing is advisable.
4 Not every partnership has to register with Chamber of Commerce.
5 As of 2009 to be reduced to €1, according to a bill recently sent to parliament.
6 For CV unlimited liability will apply to at least one partner. Other partners' liability may be limited to their capital.
7 Management can be liable in case of misconduct.
8 Works council is required if 50 employees or more.

Legal form / Characteristics	Partnership (VOF) and Limited Liability Partnership (CV)	BV (private corporation) and NV (public corporation)
Taxation	Partners are subject to Dutch income tax on their share of profits[9]	Dutch resident companies are subject to corporation tax on their profits derived anywhere in the world
Usage	Professional and financial organisations, joint ventures of small, medium-sized and large companies	BV used for small and medium-sized enterprises. NV used for larger companies and companies seeking listing on any market

---

9   Capital gains are not taxed separately but included in the profit share/taxable income.

II CORPORATION TAX

Legal form / Description	Dutch-resident corporation	Permanent establishment (PE)
General description	Tax levied on the taxable profit of a chargeable company for a year of assessment[10]	
Taxable entities	Companies incorporated in the Netherlands and/or foreign companies with central management and control located in the Netherlands	PE located in the Netherlands
Taxable income	Worldwide profits	Profits derived by PE in the Netherlands
Calculation of taxable profits	Accounting profit is adjusted for various tax add-backs, allowances and exemptions to arrive at the taxable profit Dividends from qualifying participations are exempt	
Interest payments	• Transfer pricing rules are in place that require funding arrangements to be at arm's length for interest payment to remain tax deductible • Thin capitalisation rules of 1:3 apply with a threshold of €500,000 • Anti-abuse provisions can deny interest deduction in certain cases • Anti-abuse provisions and case law can recategorise loans as capital	
Related party transactions	All related party transactions must take place on arm's length basis	
Tax year, return and payment	Tax period normally coincides with accounting period Tax return must be submitted to tax authorities within 5 months from the end of the accounting period[11] Tax payment should be made monthly during the accounting period[12]	
Capital gains	Capital gains are subject to corporation tax at normal rates Capital gains on qualifying participations are exempt	
Losses	Within a year losses can be offset against other current year profits A current year loss can be carried back one year and carried forward 9 years	
Tax group	A fiscal unity can be formed by a parent company and its 95% subsidiaries[13]	Foreign entities with Dutch PEs can unite the Dutch PEs in a fiscal unity[14]
Tax rate	Between 20% and 25.5% *Profits (€)* *Rate* Up to 40,000 20% 40,000–200,000 23% 200,000+ 25.5%	

10 Capital gains are not taxed separately but treated/taxed as taxable profit.

11 The tax authorities grant tax advice firms an extension for their clients which enables them to file the returns proportionally over a period of 14 months after the end of the accounting period.

12 For over- or underpayment interest is received respectively due.

13 Fiscal unity means that the group is taxed and treated as one company for corporation tax purposes.

14 As long as the 95% ownership condition is met.

III TAXES FOR INDIVIDUALS

		Residents[15]	Non-residents
Income Tax	General description	Tax levied on the chargeable income of a chargeable person for a year of assessment[16]	
	Taxable entities and taxable income	Individuals who are resident in the Netherlands are liable to tax on their worldwide income	Individuals who are not resident in the Netherlands are liable to tax on income arising in the Netherlands, subject to provisions in double taxation agreements
	Types of taxable income	• Worldwide trading income of a trade, profession or vocation (box 1) • Worldwide employment income (box 1) • Worldwide income from substantial shareholding (box 2) • Worldwide property income (box 1 or 3) • Worldwide savings and investment income (box 3) • Worldwide income from trusts or estates (box 3)	• Dutch-sourced trading income of a trade, profession or vocation (box 1) • Dutch employment income (box 1) • Dutch-sourced income from substantial shareholding (box 2) • Dutch property income (box 1 or 3)
	Calculation of income	• Box 1 – accrual basis, income/benefit received • Box 2 – actual income received • Box 3 – income is a fixed yield of 4% on average value[17]	
	Tax year, tax assessment and tax payment	Tax year – calendar year Tax assessment – after submitting individual tax return Tax payment due – during the tax year[18]	
	Losses	• Box 1 – 3 year carry back, 9 years carry forward • Box 2 – 1 year carry back, 9 years carry forward • There are restrictions for loss compensation between the boxes	
	Tax rates	• Box 1 – progressive (from 33.6% up to 52%) • Box 2 – 25% • Box 3 – 30%	
Capital Gains Tax (CGT)	General description	Capital gains are not taxed separately but treated/taxed as chargeable income	

---

15 Double taxation will be prevented by double tax treaty or the Dutch Unilateral Decree to prevent double taxation.

16 Capital gains are not taxed separately but treated/taxed as chargeable income.

17 Capital gains are 'included' in the fixed yield and thus not taxed separately.

18 For over- or underpayment interest is received respectively due.

		Dutch residents	**Non-residents**
Inheritance Tax (IHT)	General description	Tax charged on a chargeable transfer of value made by a lifetime gift or estate on death[19]	
	Taxable entities and chargeable assets	Estate or lifetime gifts received from a Dutch[20] deceased or donor	Estate or lifetime gifts, which are not specifically excluded, situated in the Netherlands
	Calculation of charge	Value of the estate or lifetime gift	
	Taxable events	• Lifetime gifts • Estates on death and gifts made 180 days prior to death of donor	• Lifetime gifts • Estate on death of assets situated in the Netherlands
	Allowances	There are various exemptions for estate and lifetime gifts under various conditions Charities are exempted from paying tax on estate and lifetime gifts	
	Tax rates	• 0–27% for children and spouses • 26%–53% for parents, brothers and sisters • 41%–68% others	

19 Inheritance tax treaties can override the right of the Netherlands to tax a taxable estate or lifetime gift.
20 Dutch refers to Dutch residents, which includes foreign citizens residing in the Netherlands. Dutch citizens who were Dutch residents 10 years prior to the taxable event are treated as Dutch residents for inheritance tax purposes.

IV   WITHHOLDING TAXES

	Payments to non-residents[21]
Dividends	15%
Interest	None
Royalties	None
On payments to artists and sportsmen	0%[22]

---

21 Reduced rates of withholding tax may apply in the case of double tax treaty and under the EU Parent Subsidiary Directive.
22 The 0% is applicable if the artist or sportsman is from a country which has a tax treaty with the Netherlands. Without a tax treaty the withholding rate amounts 20%.

V INDIRECT TAXES

		Residents	Non-residents
Value Added Tax (VAT)	General description	Tax on the supply of goods and services	
	Entities being obliged to levy VAT	• Any individual, partnership, corporation or other body, which carries out taxable activities in the Netherlands • If supplies are made outside the Netherlands. The supplies must be outside the scope of Netherlands VAT with the right to recover related input tax • Other situations may also arise, eg distance selling, sale of assets, acquisitions from other EC member states	
	Taxable activities	• Supply of goods and services, import of goods, intra-Community acquisition of goods, etc • Place of supply of goods and services must be in the Netherlands (following Article 9 of the EC Directive)	
	Taxable activities – zero rated (examples)	Supply of goods or services to companies residing in another EU member state Export of goods and certain services to everybody outside the EU	
	Exemptions (examples)	• Transactions related to the sale of any Dutch property used for more than 2 years and the lease of any Dutch property (option to tax for VAT available for commercial property) • Banking and insurance services • Educational supplies • Certain welfare services including hospital and medical care services	
	Refund of VAT	• VAT paid on supplies and services is deductible as input tax, if incurred in the course or furtherance of the business and for the purpose of making taxable supplies (including zero-rated supplies) • There is no credit for input tax incurred which relates to the provision of exempt supplies • Where mixed supplies occur (taxable and exempt supplies), subject to anti-abuse provisions, input tax must be apportioned and recovered according to a partial exemption method	• EC 8th Directive refund system for non-resident businesses established within the EU, providing its business is not otherwise required to be registered in the Netherlands • EC 13th Directive refund system for non-resident businesses established outside the EU, providing its business is not otherwise required to be registered in the Netherlands • Strict time limits apply to claims[23]
	Tax liability	• Normally the supplier of goods and services is responsible for charging VAT • Reverse charge for certain supplies of goods and services (eg consultancy services provided by non-resident businesses to Dutch businesses) • With a licence Dutch residents can defer the VAT payable upon import of goods into the EU to their Dutch VAT return[24]	

---

23 Filing the claim after the deadline will be rewarded but any denial cannot be disputed in court.
24 No cash flow because the reported import VAT is recovered as input VAT on the same return.

		Residents	Non-residents
Value Added Tax (VAT)	Tax rates	• Standard rate = 19% • Reduced rate = 6% (eg food) • Zero rate = 0%	
	Administrative obligations	• Formal requirements concerning business records and invoices • Monthly or quarterly self-assessment VAT returns plus payment of any VAT liability to tax authorities • VAT groups are allowed subject to certain requirements • VAT identification number must be shown on all invoices issued • EU invoicing directive must be adhered to	• Registration for VAT purposes, if making supplies of goods and services in the Netherlands • Appointment of fiscal tax representative possible but not obligatory
Property Transfer Tax		• Transactions related to the transfer of Dutch property with the purchaser liable • Tax rate 6% on value of transaction and in some cases exemptions	
Insurance Tax		• Transactions related to the sale of insurances • 7.5% on insurance premiums with a range of exemptions	

New Zealand

(Barry Tuck, Partner, btuck@cstnexia.co.nz)

I MAIN LEGAL FORMS

Legal form / Characteristics	Partnership	Limited Liability Partnership (LLP)[1]	Limited liability company	Trust
Partners/shareholders • Number • Restrictions	Two or more	Two or more (minimum one general, one limited)	One or more No restriction	Minimum: one trustee
Directors	Management by partners	Management by general partner	Management by directors	One or more trustees
Establishment	Deed	Deed	Constitution	Trust deed
Registration	General partnerships: none	Limited partnerships: companies office register	Companies: register with companies office (Ministry of Economic Development)	None
Minimum Capital	$0	$0	$1	$1
Liability	Unlimited	Ltd partner: limited to capital General partner: joint and several	Limited to capital	Trust property
Governance	Partners	Partners	Management/ Directors	Trustees meeting
Audit requirements	None	None	Required if issuer or where 25% or more overseas shareholding	None

---

1 NZ currently has general and special partnerships, and have recently introduced limited liability partnerships effective 1 April 2008

Legal form / Characteristics	Partnership	Limited Liability Partnership (LLP)[1]	Limited liability company	Trust
Taxation	Taxed in partners hands per their share at their marginal rates	Flow-through of aggregated result at marginal rates	NZ resident company taxed on worldwide income	Income retained in trust taxed at company tax rates, income passed out taxed at beneficiaries marginal tax rate
Usage	No restriction	No restriction	No restriction	No restriction

II CORPORATION TAX

Legal form / Description	New Zealand resident corporation	Permanent establishment (PE)
General description	Company tax	Profits attributable to PE in New Zealand
Taxable entities	Incorporated in New Zealand, head office in New Zealand or central management and control is exercised from New Zealand	Taxed as a branch in New Zealand
Taxable income	Worldwide income from all sources is taxable	Income derived from New Zealand
Calculation of taxable profits	Accounting profit adjusted by various add-backs/deductions – including timing adjustments	Profits attributable to New Zealand
Interest payments	Deductible subject to thin capitalisation	
Related party transactions	Transfer pricing rules apply (arm's length principle)	
Tax year, return and payment	Generally 31 March although companies may have alternative dates with approval from the authorities Tax returns must be filed by 7 July but extended to 31 March if filed by a tax agent Companies must pay provisional tax in three instalments – commencing 4 months after balance date Terminal tax payable 7 Feb or 7 April if returns are filed by a tax agent	
Capital Gains	No CGT in New Zealand. However certain gains from land and foreign investment transactions may be taxable[2] – subject to specific Controlled Foreign Company/ Foreign Investment Fund regimes	No CGT in New Zealand. However certain gains from land and foreign investment transactions may be taxable
Losses	Most losses are allowable and may be carried forward where 49% shareholder continuity maintained, or offset or subvented amongst group companies where 66% continuity maintained	
Tax group	Consolidated group may file returns where 100% commonly owned	
Tax rate	Flat rate of 33%	33% unless limited under specific DTA article

---

2 New legislation has been enacted with effect from the 2008 income year which changes the way income from financial investments is taxed where shares are held in countries outside New Zealand and Australia (generally applies to direct shareholdings of less than 10%) – introduction of Fair Dividend Rate, de minimis exemptions apply to individuals. Different rules apply to indirect investments through Portfolio Investment Entities (PIEs) – investors will pay tax at marginal rates capped at 33%.

III   TAXES FOR INDIVIDUALS

		Residents		**Non-residents**
Income Tax	General description	Tax levied on a persons income for the year (worldwide for residents) Non-residents are liable to tax on New Zealand sourced income		
	Taxable entities and taxable income	Persons with a permanent place of abode in New Zealand Personally present in New Zealand for longer than a total of 183 days in any 12-month period		Absent from New Zealand for more than 325 days in any 12-month period Does not maintain a permanent place of abode
	Types of taxable income	• Employment income • Business income • Interest • Rentals • Dividends • Foreign investment		
	Calculation of income	• Employment income – income when received • Business income – derived on accrual basis • Interest – individuals: income cash or accrual, expenditure on accrual basis • Rentals – generally income derived on cash basis, expenditure on accrual basis • Dividends – income derived on a cash basis • Foreign investment – see note under companies CGT		
	Tax Year, tax assessment and tax payment	The tax year runs to 31 March. Residents are generally required to file a tax return where income has been received from sources with no tax deducted (ie other than New Zealand employment income/interest and dividends). Returns must be filed by 7 July if no agent or 31 March if taxpayer has an agent		Non-resident returns required if New Zealand sourced income or profits attributable to New Zealand – same dates as residents
		Provisional tax is payable in three equal instalments Due 28th day of 5th, 9th and 13th months except for GST registered persons using ratio method or who are 6 monthly filers – payments due in December or April will be due 15 January and 7 May respectively Terminal tax due 7 February no agent or 7 April if agent Temporary tax exemption on foreign income for new migrants and returning New Zealanders applies from 1 April 2006 to exempt most sources of foreign income from tax in New Zealand for 4 years. Returning New Zealanders must have been away for more than 10 years to qualify		
	Losses	May be utilised and carried forward indefinitely		
	Tax rates	Tax is levied on a graduated scale depending upon the level of taxable income 19.5%–39% (note personal tax cuts are being phased in from October 2009)		19.5%–39% (see also note for residents)

		Residents	**Non-residents**
Capital Gains Tax (CGT)	General description	No CGT in New Zealand. However certain gains from land and foreign investment transactions may be taxable	
	Taxable entities and chargeable assets	N/A	
	Calculation of gain	N/A	
	Tax year, tax assessment and tax payment	N/A	
	Losses	Not deductible	
	Tax rates	N/A	
		Domiciled	**Non-domiciled**
Inheritance Tax (IHT)	General description	Estate duty was abolished in 1993 Gift duty applies subject to certain exemptions where dutiable gifts exceeding $27,000 are made in a 12-month period	
	Taxable entities and chargeable assets	Dutiable gifts are gifts of property situated in New Zealand and gifts of property situated outside New Zealand where the donor is domiciled in New Zealand or is a body corporate incorporated in New Zealand	N/A
	Calculation of Charge	Level of gift	N/A
	Taxable Events	Dutiable gift	N/A
	Allowances	Exemptions apply to small gifts in good faith made to same donor of less than $2,000	N/A
	Tax Rates	*Gift ($)* *Gift duty* 1–27,000 nil 27,001–36,000 5% of amt > $27,000 36,001–54,000 $450 + 10% of amt > $36,000 54,001–72,000 $2,250 + 20% of amt > $54,000 72,000+ $5,850 + 25% of amt > $72,000	N/A

IV   WITHHOLDING TAXES

	Payments to non-residents
Dividends	15%
Interest	15% Approved Issuer Levy 2% on interest not paid to associated person
Royalties	15%
On payments to artists and sportsmen	20% non-resident entertainers 15% non-resident contractors

V INDIRECT TAXES

		Residents	Non-residents
Value Added Tax (GST)	General description	Goods and Services Tax (GST)	
	Entities being obliged to levy GST	Where operating a taxable activity in New Zealand and turnover exceeds $40,000 per annum	
	Taxable activities	Any activity which is carried on continuously or regularly by any person, whether or not for a pecuniary profit, and involves or is intended to involve, in whole or in part, the supply of goods and services to any other person for a consideration; and includes any such activity carried on in the form of a business, trade, manufacture, profession, vocation, association, or club	
	Taxable activities – zero rated (examples)	Exports	
	Exemptions (examples)	• Financial services • Residential rents • Donated goods and services	
	Refund of GST	• Input tax claimable upon purchase of goods and services acquired for the principal purpose of making taxable supplies • No input claim available for certain financial services • Claim can be made on apportionment basis where supplies are mixed – apportionment rules apply	• Non-residents can be registered and make input claims where carrying on a taxable activity in NZ
	Tax liability	• Obligation is on supplier to charge GST where appropriate • Reverse charge (self assessed) applies to some imported services where a non-resident supplies a resident recipient who makes more than 5% of non-taxable supplies	
	Tax rates	Standard rate = 12.5% Zero rate = 0%	
	Administrative obligations	• Prescribed record keeping and tax invoice requirements • Returns filed monthly, 2 monthly or 6 monthly depending on turnover and choice • Grouping allowed where requirements met	• Non-residents can be registered and make input claims where carrying on a taxable activity in New Zealand
Stamp Duty Land Tax		N/A	
Stamp Duty		N/A	

Nigeria

(Yinka Olapade, olapade@sulaimonandco.com)

I   MAIN LEGAL FORMS

Legal form / Characteristics	Partnership and Limited Liability Partnership (LLP)	Ltd (private corporation) and Plc (public corporation)
Partners/shareholders • Number • Restrictions	• Minimum of two • Maximum of 20	• Minimum of two members for Ltd and Plc • Maximum of 50 for Ltd, no restriction for Plc
Directors	N/A	At least two
Establishment	Deed	Memorandum and Articles
Registration	The Corporate Affairs Commission is responsible for the registration of all partnerships and companies	
Minimum capital	N/A	Minimum of NGN 10,000 for private and NGN 500,000 for public companies
Liability	Unlimited and lies with the partners (no LLP status)	Limited
Governance	Board of Partners	Board of Directors
Audit requirements	None	Not later than 6 months after the accounting year end
Taxation	Partners are assessed as individuals under Personal Income Tax Act	Resident companies are subject to corporation tax on their profits derived anywhere in the world

II COMPANIES INCOME TAX

Legal form / Description	Resident corporation	Permanent establishment (PE)
General description	Income tax	
Taxable entities	Corporations incorporated in Nigeria	PE located in Nigeria
Taxable income	Worldwide profits	Profits received or brought into Nigeria. Shipping, airline and telecommunications are taxed on the proportion of profits which turnover in Nigeria bears on worldwide turnover (minimum 2%)
Calculation of taxable profits	Accounting profit is adjusted for various tax add-backs and allowances to arrive to profits chargeable to corporation tax (PCTCT)	
Interest payments	Interest on foreign loans is exempt from withholding tax on a sliding scale basis. 100% exemption if repayment period exceeds 7 years	
Related party transactions	All related party transactions must take place on arm's length basis	
Tax year, return and payment	The tax year is the calendar year, but company can choose accounting year The tax return must be filed within 6 months after the end of the tax year Provisional tax equal to the prior year liability is paid within 3 months of the start of the year with the balance offset against the next year's liability	
Capital gains	Rate = 10%	
Losses	Net operating tax losses may be carried forward indefinitely and set off against taxable profits. Insurance companies can carry forward for 4 years only	
Tax group	No group taxation	
Tax rate	• 30%, or 20% for manufacturing, agricultural or mining companies with turnover less than NGN 500,000 • Companies with turnover of NGN 100m or more to pay 1% of PBT as IT tax • Companies with turnover of NGN 10m and more to pay 1% of PBT and IT tax	

III   TAXES FOR INDIVIDUALS

		Residents	**Non-residents**
Income Tax	General description	Tax levied on the chargeable income of a chargeable person for a year of assessment	
	Taxable entities and taxable income	Residents are taxed on their income derived in Nigeria	Non-residents are taxable on all income arising in Nigeria
	Types of taxable income	• Property income (usually rent) • Income from capital investment (interest, sale of goodwill, dividends, royalties, annuities) • Income from business activities • Income from employment, personal services or pensions	
	Calculation of income	The balance of gross income less total allowable relief is taxed as per the tax rates below	Basic personal allowance of NGN 5,000 plus 20% of earned income
	Tax year, tax assessment and tax payment	Tax year is the calendar year Taxpayers (with incomes over NGN 30,000) are required to file a return indicating income for previous year ended 31 December PAYE	
	Losses	0.05% of gross income	
	Tax rates	*NGN* *Rate (%)* 0–30,000 5 30,001–60,000 10 60,001–110,000 15 110,001–160,000 20 160,001 + 25	
Capital Gains Tax (CGT)	General description	Gains on disposal of assets other than in the normal course of business	
	Taxable entities and chargeable assets	Individual and companies Chargeable on assets except shares and other capital market instruments	
	Calculation of gain	Proceeds of sale less cost, improvements and incidental expenses	
	Tax year, tax assessment and tax payment	Normally assessed along with income tax	
	Losses	No relief is granted	
	Tax rates	10%	
		Domiciled	**Non-domiciled**
Inheritance Tax (IHT)	General description	No inheritance taxes	

IV   WITHHOLDING TAXES

	Payments to non-residents[1]
Dividends	10%
Interest	10%
Royalties	10%
On payments to artists and sportsmen	10%

---

1   Reduced rates of withholding tax may apply where there is an appropriate double tax treaty.

V   INDIRECT TAXES

		Residents	Non-residents
Value Added Tax (VAT)	General description	Tax on the supply of goods and services (VAT)	
	Entities being obliged to levy VAT	All registered businesses	
	Taxable activities	Trade, manufacturing, services, etc	
	Taxable activities – zero rated (examples)	Zero-rated status, as from April 2007, for non-oil exports, goods and services purchased by diplomats and goods for use in humanitarian donor-funded projects	
	Exemptions (examples)	Medical supplies, educational materials, basic food items and services allied to these	
	Refund of VAT	A mechanism for claiming refunds is to be brought into operation by end of 2007	
	Tax liability	No effect on income tax liability except for zero-rated status companies	
	Tax rates	• Standard rate = 5% • Exports = 0%	
	Administrative obligations	Returns are filed by the 21st of the month following the month of transaction	
Stamp Duty Land Tax		3.5%	
Stamp Duty		Charged by government for individuals or federal government for companies	

Sultanate of Oman

(Usamah Tabbarah & Company, oman@utcnexia.com)

I MAIN LEGAL FORMS

Legal form / Characteristics	Partnership and Limited Liability Partnership (LLP)	Ltd (private corporation) and Plc (public corporation)
Partners/shareholders • Number • Restrictions	*General Partnership:* • minimum partners – two • all the partners have to be Omani nationals *Limited Partnership:* • minimum partners – two • one of the partners has to be a general partner and be an Omani national another partner has to be a limited partner	Two types of *joint stock* companies are permitted in Oman: *Closed Joint Stock Companies* whose shares are not publicly traded *Public Joint Stock Companies* whose shares are publicly traded *Limited Liability Companies (LLC)* • Must have at least two shareholders and no more than 30 shareholders
Directors	N/A	Minimum: three Maximum: 12
Establishment	*Partnership*: by the execution of the Articles of Partnership and/or the Memorandum of Association	Companies incorporated in accordance with provisions of the Oman Commercial Companies Law, Articles of Association and other incorporation documents must be filed with the Companies Registrar
Registration	Register with the Commercial Registrar and must have the prior approval of the Minister of Commerce and Industry for Companies	

Legal form / Characteristics	Partnership and Limited Liability Partnership (LLP)	Ltd (private corporation) and Plc (public corporation)
Minimum capital	N/A	• Closed joint stock companies: OMR 50,000 • Public joint stock companies: OMR 150,000 • The minimum capital is set at OMR 150,000 for both types of joint stock companies if there is foreign participation • Limited Liability Companies (LLC): share capital may not be less than OMR 10,000 when all partners are Omani and OMR 150,000 if there is foreign participation
Liability	General partners liable to full extent of the partnership liabilities	Limited: to the extent of the unpaid share (par) value
Governance	N/A	Board of Directors and Articles of Association
Audit requirements	Not mandatory	Closed joint stock companies and LLC: auditor appointment mandatory
Taxation	Transparent[1]	Corporation Tax

---

1 The Tax Law defines the words 'Entity with Permanent Presence' in Art 2(11) as: 'An entity that has a fixed place of activity in which the project conducts all or part of its business' and it includes in particular: 'a place for selling; a place for management; a branch; an office; a manufacturing facility; a mine, quarry, or any other place for natural resources; a construction site or place or an assembly plant'.

II CORPORATION TAX

Characteristics \ Legal form	Corporate Tax	Permanent establishment (PE)
General description	Tax is levied on the taxable income which has been realised or has arisen in Oman	
Taxable entities	Corporation and foreign entities which derive income from Oman	
Taxable income	Total income less deductible expenses	
Interest payments	Normally deductible. No thin capitalisation rules	
Related party transactions	Should be on arm's length basis	
Tax year, return and payment	• The tax year is the period of 12 months commencing from 1 January and ending on 31 December following • Provisional tax declaration to be submitted within 3 months from the relevant tax year-end date, together with settlement of the tax liability • Final declaration within 6 months from the tax year-end date, together with settlement of taxes due	
Capital gains	Capital gains are treated as part of taxable income	
Losses	A tax loss in any single year is set off against taxable income arising in the subsequent years, to a maximum period of 5 years after the year in which the tax loss was incurred	
Tax group	N/A	
Tax rates	The corporate income tax rate of 12% on taxable profits exceeding OMR 30,000 applies to: • all companies incorporated in Oman • branches and permanent establishments in Oman of companies incorporated in the other Gulf Co-operation Council (GCC) member states (Bahrain, Kuwait, Qatar, Saudi Arabia and United Arab Emirates) In permanent establishments in Oman of non-GCC companies the tax rate ranges from 0%–30%, depending upon amount of taxable profits. For these entities, the rate once determined will be applied to the total taxable profits	

III   TAXES FOR INDIVIDUALS

		Residents	Non-residents
Income Tax	General description	There are no personal income taxes	
Capital Gains Tax (CGT)	General description	Not taxable	
		Domiciled	**Non-domiciled**
Inheritance Tax (IHT)	General description	There are no inheritance taxes	

IV   WITHHOLDING TAXES

	Payments to non-residents
Dividends	Nil
Interest	Nil
Royalties, management contracts, leases of equipment and machinery, technical expertise and/or research and development	10% of total fees and or income received
On payments to artists and sportsmen	Nil

V   INDIRECT TAXES

		Residents	Non-residents
Value Added Tax (VAT)	General description	There is no VAT	
Stamp Duty Land Tax		There is no Stamp Duty Land Tax	
Stamp Duty		There is no Stamp Duty	

Pakistan

(Sheik Masood, smmco@nexlink.net.pk)

I   MAIN LEGAL FORMS

Legal form / Characteristics	Partnership and Limited Liability Partnership (LLP)	Ltd (private corporation) and Plc (public corporation)
Partners/shareholders • Number • Restrictions	• Minimum two members and a maximum of 20, except for professional firms • No concept of LLPs	• Single Member Company Private Limited (SMC-PVT) has only one shareholder • Other private companies have minimum two members and maximum 50 members • Public Limited Companies (Plc) which are not listed on Stock Exchange must have at least three members. No restriction on maximum number of members • Listed Public Limited Company (Plc) must have at least seven members. No restriction on maximum numbers
Directors	N/A	• SMC-PVT can only have one director • Other private limited companies must have minimum two directors • Public Limited Companies (Plc) which are not listed on Stock Exchange must have minimum three directors • Listed Public Limited Company (Plc) must have minimum seven directors. No restriction on maximum number of directors
Establishment	Partnership Deed	Companies are established under Companies Ordinance 1984
Registration	Registrar of firms	Both private and public companies are registered with SECP
Minimum capital	N/A	None

Legal form / Characteristics	Partnership and Limited Liability Partnership (LLP)	Ltd (private corporation) and Plc (public corporation)
Liability	Unlimited	The liability of members in limited companies is restricted to unpaid value of their shares, if any
Governance	N/A	The companies are governed by SECP in accordance with the Companies Ordinance 1984
Audit requirements	Not compulsory	• Public companies and private companies having share capital exceeding Rs 3m or more must appoint the auditor who is member of the Institute of Chartered Accountants of Pakistan (ICAP) • Public listed companies must appoint an auditor who has a satisfactory grade rating from ICAP • All private companies having share capital more than Rs 7.5m will also file relevant records with SECP
Taxation	Partnership profits assessed to tax. Share in hands of partner exempt	Resident companies are subject to corporation tax on their profits derived worldwide

II CORPORATION TAX

Legal form / Description	Resident corporation	Permanent establishment (PE)
Taxable entities	Corporations incorporated in Pakistan	PE located in Pakistan
Taxable income	Worldwide profits with consideration of double taxation treaties	Profits derived by PE in Pakistan
Calculation of taxable profits	Accounting profit is adjusted for various tax add-backs and allowances to arrive to profits chargeable to tax	
Interest payments	Interest payments can be claimed as expense in computing the taxable income Debt to equity ratio should not exceed 3:1	
Related party transactions	Arm's length basis	
Tax year, return and payment	Income years specified for different classes of income • Tax year is period from 1 July to 30 June • Tax is payable within 15 days of assessment by commissioner or at the time of filing of income tax return • Tax return is due on 31 December if income year-end falls between 1 January and 30 June, and due on 30 September otherwise	
Advance Tax	The estimate tax liability for the year is to be paid in four instalments as given below: *Quarter* *Due date of instalment* September on or before 15 September December on or before 15 December March on or before 15 March June on or before 15 June	
Capital gains	Gains on movable assets are treated as income, however, gains on assets held for more than one year are restricted to 75%	
Losses	• Net operating tax losses may be carried forward for 6 years and set off against taxable profits • Depreciation losses may be carried forward without any restriction of number of years	
Tax group	Wholly-owned subsidiaries and holding company can file a single return	
Tax rate	• Generally 35% • Small company 20%	

III   TAXES FOR INDIVIDUALS

		Residents	Non-residents
Income Tax	General description	Tax levied on the chargeable income of a chargeable person for a year of assessment	
	Taxable entities and taxable income	Residents are taxed on their worldwide income	Non-residents are taxed on income derived in Pakistan
	Types of taxable income	• Property income • Income from business activities • Employment from personal services or pensions • Income from capital investment (interest, sale of goodwill, dividends, royalty and annuities)	
	Tax year, tax assessment and tax payment	• Tax year is period of 12 months from 1 July to 30 June • Tax is payable within 15 days of date of assessment or at the time of filing of return • Tax return is due on 30 September	
	Losses	• Business losses are fully deductible from any other income, for the same year, and thereafter only against business income within the subsequent 6 years • Depreciation losses may be carried forward without any restriction of number of years	
	Tax rates	Individuals and AOP Income exceeding Rs 150,000 is subject to tax at graduated rates ranging from 0.5% to 25%	
Capital Gains Tax (CGT)	General description	Gains on disposal of capital assets	
	Taxable entities and chargeable assets	Taxable residents	
	Calculation of gain	Capital gains are computed by deducting cost of the asset from the consideration received on disposal of asset. In addition to above loss on disposal of other asset is deducted from the consideration. If the asset is held by more than one year the gain is reduced to 75%	
	Tax year, tax assessment and tax payment	Income years specified for different classes of income • Tax year is period of 12 months from 1 July to 30 June • Tax is payable within 15 days of assessment by commissioner or at the time of filing of income tax return • Tax return is due on 31 December if income year falls between 1 January and 30 June, and due on 30 September otherwise	
	Losses	Losses may be carried forward but can be offset against capital gains only	
	Tax rates	Same rates applicable as in case of income from other heads	
		Domiciled	Non-domiciled
Inheritance Tax (IHT)	General description	There is no IHT in Pakistan	

IV WITHHOLDING TAXES

	Payments to non-residents[1]
Dividends	10%
Interest	30%
Royalties	15%
On payments to artists and sportsmen	6%

---

1 Reduced rates of withholding tax may apply where there is an appropriate double tax treaty.

V   INDIRECT TAXES

		Residents	Non-residents
Value Added Tax (VAT)	General description	Tax on the supply of goods and services (VAT)	
	Entities being obliged to levy VAT	In Pakistan VAT is commonly known as Sales Tax and is leviable on importers, manufacturers, retailers and wholesalers	
	Taxable activities	Taxable activity involves supply of goods, rendering of services, business, trade or manufacture	
	Taxable activities – zero rated (examples)	Exports of goods, supply and repair of ships, aircrafts, spare parts, supply of equipment for navigation purpose	
	Exemptions (examples)	Supply of live animals, meat of bovine animals, fish, crustaceans, milk, etc, supply of provisions for consumption	
	Refund of VAT	Input tax exceeding output tax should be refunded. However, refund relating to zero-rated goods must be refunded within 30 days Refund must be claimed within one year	
	Tax liability	Output tax (tax on sales, supplies, etc) minus input tax on imports, purchase, etc	
	Tax rates	• Standard rate = 16% • Exports = 0% • Retail tax = 2%	
	Administrative obligations	Collectors and deputy collectors	
Stamp Duty Land Tax		N/A	
Stamp Duty		The following instruments are chargeable with stamp duty: • every bill of exchange otherwise payable on demand • promissory notes made or drawn outside Pakistan but presented for payment in Pakistan, etc	

Panama

(Bartolome Mafla, bmafla@nexiapanama.com)

I   MAIN LEGAL FORMS

Legal form / Characteristics	Corporations (1927 Law)	Limited Liability Companies
Partners/shareholders • Number • Restrictions	No limit	Only 25 shareholders are allowed
Directors	Three as a minimum	Two as a minimum
Establishment	Articles of Incorporation	
Registration	Before a Public Notary and registered at the Public Registry	
Minimum capital	US$10,000	US$5,000
Liability	Only limited to unpaid subscribed capital. In general shareholders are not liable for the company's debts. The only liability a shareholder may have is limited to the extent of any unpaid shares of stock if they were subscribed by the shareholder but never paid	Limited to capital
Governance	A legal representative needs to be appointed	
Audit requirements	Financial statements must be kept but no filing requirements	
Taxation	Transparent	Corporation tax
Usage	Widely used	Not very common

II CORPORATION TAX

Legal form / Description	Resident corporation	Permanent establishment (PE)
General description	Corporation tax	Income tax derived by PE in Panama
Taxable entities	Anyone deriving Panamanian sourced income	
Taxable income	Income from goods and services provided in Panama	
Calculation of taxable profits	Taxable profits are defined as the higher of: • Gross income minus deductions (traditional method) or • Gross income minus 95.33% (4.67%) (see Tax rate below)	
Interest payments	Normally deductible	
Related party transactions	No comprehensive transfer pricing policy exists	
Tax year, return and payment	31 March; an automatic extension is granted for 2 months	
Capital gains	Generally taxed as income	
Losses	May be carried forward for 5 years and up to 20% per year	
Tax group	No consolidation is possible	
Tax rate	30% on the higher of: • Net income or • Gross income minus 95.33% (approximately 1.4% of gross income)	

III   TAXES FOR INDIVIDUALS

		Residents	Non-residents
Income Tax	General description	No formal definition exists to distinguish residents from non-residents	
	Taxable entities and taxable income	Individuals and legal entities are taxable	
	Types of taxable income	Every kind of income derived from any source A very extensive definition of income has been traditionally taken by the Tax Authorities	
	Calculation of income	Aggregate income	
	Tax year, tax assessment and tax payment	31 March is the deadline to file tax returns An automatic extension (2 months) is granted if requested before such date	
	Losses	May be carried forward 5 years and used up to 20% in each of these years	
	Tax rates	0–27% for individuals	
Capital Gains Tax (CGT)	Taxable entities and chargeable assets	All assets other than inventory	
	Calculation of gain	Ordinary income if more than ten sales are made of a given asset per year When an asset other than inventory is sold the buyer withholds 5% of the purchase price The seller decides whether to be taxed either at 10% on the net capital gain realised or considers the 5% withholding at source as a final payment Should the 10% option be taken, a refund may be claimed due to losses and/or the 10% rate on the net capital gain being lower than the 5% withholding	
	Tax year, tax assessment and tax payment	Immediately upon sale for assets other than inventory	
	Losses	Should the 10% option be taken, a refund may be claimed due to losses and/or the 10% rate on the net capital gain being lower than the 5% withholding	

		Domiciled	Non-domiciled
Inheritance Tax (IHT)	General description	No inheritance taxes	

IV   WITHHOLDING TAXES

	Payments to non-residents[1]
Dividends	10%
Interest	15%
Royalties	15%
On payments to artists and sportsmen	15%

---

1   Reduced rates of withholding tax may apply where there is an appropriate double tax treaty.

V INDIRECT TAXES

		Residents	Non-residents
Value Added Tax (VAT)	General description	No formal definition exists	
	Entities being obliged to levy VAT	Any taxpayers with gross receipts in excess of US$36,000	
	Taxable activities	Services rendered in Panama and goods (other than intangibles and real property) whose passage of title occurs in Panama	
	Taxable activities – zero rated (examples)	No zero rate is applicable since refunds are given through coupons usable to pay VAT. This certificate is limited to: • taxpayers exclusively dedicated to the pharmaceutical industry • taxpayers whose only activity is the food industry	
	Exemptions (examples)	• Goods from nature • Food • Medicine • Intangibles and their use • Services whose final consumer is located abroad • Restaurants not selling alcohol	
	Refund of VAT	Not possible	
	Tax liability	Any consumer must pay VAT on goods purchased.	
	Tax rates	• 5% (general rate) • 10% alcohol • 15% cigarettes	
	Administrative obligations	Filing a monthly VAT return This obligation is fulfilled every 3 months by liberal professionals and by taxpayers whose gross receipts are below US$60,000	
Stamp Duty Land Tax		N/A	
Stamp Duty		US$1.00 for every US$1,000 invoiced in activities not covered by VAT	

Paraguay

(Angel Devaca Pavon, cyce@conexion.com.py)

I MAIN LEGAL FORMS

Legal form / Characteristics	Partnership and Limited Liability Partnership (LLC)	Ltd (private corporation) and Plc (public corporation)
Partners/shareholders • Number • Restrictions	• The number of partners shall not exceed 25, and they shall be solely liable for the amount of their contributions (Civil Code, Art 1160) • The company shall not be allowed to engage in banking, insurance, capitalisation and savings operations, and neither in those activities that, according to the laws, require other legal status of the company (Art 1162)	• The quota shares of the partners are represented by shares (Civil Code, Art 1048) • The partners authorising the transactions made on behalf of the company before its registration are limited and severally liable to third parties (Art 1052)
Directors	The management, conducting and representation of the company shall be performed by one or more managers, being partners or not, who shall have the same rights and duties of the directors of a corporation (Art 1174)	Non-shareholders may be directors, and they can be re-elected, and their designations are revocable (Art 1103)

Legal form / Characteristics	Partnership and Limited Liability Partnership (LLC)	Ltd (private corporation) and Plc (public corporation)
Establishment	Any agreements shall be in writing, and by a public deed in the cases ruled by the Civil Code (Art 967)	The company shall be organised by a public deed. The organisation deed shall state: • the name, nationality, civil status, profession and address of the partners, and the number of shares integrated by each of them • the name and address of the company, and of the eventual branches, within or out of the Republic • the social purpose • the amount of capital subscribed and paid in • the nominal value and the number of shares, and if these are nominative or payable to the holder • the value of the assets contributed in kind • the rules by which profits shall be distributed • the participation in profits eventually assigned to promoters or founding partners • the number of managers and their powers, stating who has the representation of the company and • the term of duration of the company (Art 1050)
Registration	The companies acquire a legal status since their relevant filing with the relevant authorities (Art 967)	Corporations acquire legal status and start their existence after being duly registered with the Registry of Companies and Associations created by Art 345 of Law No 879/81. Such registration of the relevant public deed shall state the organisation deed, by-laws, and the designation of the first board of directors, and of the first comptrollers (Art 1050)
Minimum Capital	In a LLC, the capital is divided in equal quotas with a value of PYG 1,000 or multiples (Art 1160, there is no minimum capital specified)	No minimum capital specified
Liability	The liability of the partners shall be up to the value of their contributions (Art 1165) The managers are severally liable to the company for the compliance of the duties established by the law (Art 974)	The partners authorising the transactions made on behalf of the company before its registration are limited and severally liable to third parties (Art 1052)

Legal form / Characteristics	Partnership and Limited Liability Partnership (LLC)	Ltd (private corporation) and Plc (public corporation)
Governance	The management, conducting and representation of the company shall be performed by one or more managers, being partners or not, who shall have the same rights and duties of the directors	One or more directors shall be in charge of the management of the company, duly designated by an ordinary meeting of shareholders, when not designated by the organisation act
Auditing requirements	Taxpayers with an annual gross income equal or in excess of PYG 6,000m shall obtain a tax opinion of an external audit (Art 33, Law 2421/04)	If and when required by the customer. Taxpayers with an annual gross income equal to PYG 6,000m or more shall obtain a tax opinion by an independent auditing company (Art 33, Law 2421/04)
Taxation	Subject to Value Added Tax (VAT), corporate income tax, advanced payment of income tax	Subject to VAT, corporate income tax, and advanced payment of income tax

II CORPORATION TAX

Legal form / Description	Resident company	Permanent establishment (PE)
General description	Corporate income tax on territorial basis	*Corporate income tax*: tax applied to Paraguayan source income arising from commercial, industrial and non-personal service activities
Taxable entities	Resident and non-resident companies which derive income from business conducted in Paraguay	
Taxable income	Income derived in Paraguay	
Calculation of taxable profits	Taxable income less deductible expenses	
Interest payments	Normally deductible, no thin capitalisation rules	
Related party transactions	No formal transfer pricing legislation	
Tax year, return and payment	Calendar year Tax payments made in 4 instalments Tax returns should be filed by 30 April	
Losses	N/A	
Tax group	N/A	
Tax rates	10%	

III TAXES FOR INDIVIDUALS

		Residents	**Non-residents**
Income Tax	General description	Applied to Paraguayan source income coming from activities generating personal income	Not applied to non-residents. Except for individuals that generate occasional income within the Paraguayan territory.
	Taxable entities and taxable income	• Residents • An individual is resident in Paraguay if present in the country for more than 120 days in a 12-month period	
	Types of taxable income	• Trading income, employment, professional income, income derived from real estate and capital gains	
	Tax year, tax assessment and tax payment	Taxes are applied on an annual basis: 1 January to 31 December Tax returns to be filed by 30 June and tax is payable on the same date	
	Losses	N/A	
	Tax rates	• 10% if incomes are in excess of PYG 120 minimum annual wages • 8% if incomes are less than PYG 10 minimum annual wages	
Capital Gains Tax (CGT)	General description	Taxed as income	
Inheritance Tax (IHT)	General description	N/A	
	Taxable entities and chargeable assets		
	Calculation of charge		
	Taxable events		
	Allowances		
	Tax rates		

IV   WITHHOLDING TAXES

	Payments to non-residents[1]
Dividends	15%
Interest	15%
Royalties	15%
On payments to artists and sportsmen	20%

---

1   Reduced rates of withholding tax may apply where there is an appropriate double tax treaty.

V INDIRECT TAXES

		Residents	Non-residents
Value Added Tax (VAT)	General description	Tax on the supply of goods and services, imports etc.	
	Taxable activities	Supply of goods and services	
	Taxable activities – zero rate (examples)	The following items are exempted: • Alienation of: – agriculture and livestock products in raw condition – foreign currencies, public and private assets, as well as securities, including stock shares – tickets, vouchers and other documents related to gambling and wagers – magazines of educational, cultural and scientific interest, as well as books and newspapers – export activities • Certain financial services	
	Refund of VAT	Exporters VAT on purchases	
	Tax Liabilities	Input VAT is credited against output VAT so that the value added to taxable supplies is taxed	
	Tax rates	• The usual rate of 10% • A reduced rate of 5% applies in some cases	
	Administrative obligations		

Peru

(Florentino Urbizagástegui Pacheco, ura@nexiaperu.com.pe)

I MAIN LEGAL FORMS

Legal form / Characteristics	Partnership and Limited Liability Partnership (LLP)	Ltd (private corporation) and Plc (public corporation)
Partners/shareholders • Number • Restrictions	• Two or more • None	• Two or more • None
Directors	Two or more	Two or more
Establishment	Partnership deed	Articles of Incorporation
Registration	Recorded at the Public Registry	
Minimum capital	None	No minimum requirements
Liability	The liability of the contracting parties is determined by the General Corporations Law and Articles of Incorporation, depending on the type of entity	
Governance	The governing bodies are determined by the General Corporations Law and Articles of Incorporation, depending on the type of entity	
Audit requirements	These are determined by the Articles of Incorporation, given that the only legal obligation for auditing financial statements applies to those entities whose shares are quoted on stock exchanges	
Taxation	Corporate taxes on worldwide income	

II   CORPORATION TAX

Legal form / Description	Resident corporation	Permanent establishment (PE)
General description	Corporation tax	
Taxable entities	Corporations resident in Peru, branches of companies and banks	PE trading in Peru
Taxable income	Worldwide profits with considerations for double taxation treaties	Income arising in Peru
Calculation of taxable profits	Accounting profit is adjusted for various tax add-backs and allowances to arrive to profits chargeable to corporation tax (PCTCT)	
Interest payments	Interest payments to related parties are not deductable when the debt to equity ratio exceeds 3:1 threshold	
Related party transactions	All related party transactions must take place on an arm's length basis	
Tax year, return and payment	Mandatory 1 January–31 December tax year Return and payment within the 3 months following the end of the tax year	
Capital gains	Includes those gains produced by rent, sub-leasing, assignment of goods, interest on capital placements, royalties, etc	
Losses	Losses can be carried forward for 4 years, being used up whenever profit arises	
Tax group	None	
Tax rate	30%	

III TAXES FOR INDIVIDUALS

		Residents	Non-residents
Income Tax	General description	Tax levied on the chargeable income of a chargeable person for a year of assessment	
	Taxable entities and taxable income	Residents are taxed on their worldwide income	Certain types of income arising in Peru
	Types of taxable income	• Property income (usually rent) • Income from capital investment (interest, sale of goodwill, dividends, royalties, annuities) • Income from business activities • Employment from personal services or pensions	
	Calculation of income	Based on the consolidated income from capital, income as an independent professional and as an employee	
	Tax year, tax assessment and tax payment	Mandatory 1 January–31 December tax year Payments on account are made monthly. The final accounting and payment is made within the 3 months following the end of each tax year	
	Losses	Losses on real estate are offset against future income during the 4 years following occurrence	
	Tax rates	Net capital income (gross income less 20% for first and second category income) is taxed at 6.25%	
		Net income from work (for fourth and fifth category income), according to the following scale: • Up to 27 UIT = 15% • 27–54 UIT = 21% • More than 54 UIT = 30%	
Capital Gains Tax (CGT)	General description	Normally taxed as income	

		Domiciled	Non-domiciled
Inheritance Tax (IHT)	General description	No inheritance taxes	

IV   WITHHOLDING TAXES

	Payments to non-residents[1]
Dividends	4.1%
Interest	30% 4.99% to non-related parties
Technical assistance	15%, after certification of the effective provision of international technical assistance by an audit firm of prestige
Royalties	30%
On payments to artists and sportsmen	In the case of live shows with the participation of non-resident artists and performers, 15% In the case of sportsmen, they are included in the regime of Section III
Other income	This includes the interest derived from foreign loans that does not meet the requirements established in Art 56 of the Income Tax Law. The interest paid abroad by private companies in Peru for loans granted by a foreign company with which it is economically related is 30%

---

1   Reduced rates of withholding tax may apply where there is an appropriate double tax treaty.

V   INDIRECT TAXES

		Residents	Non-residents
Value Added Tax (VAT)	General description	Tax on the supply of goods and services	
	Entities being obliged to levy VAT	• Central government • Ministry of Economy and Finance • National Superintendent of Tax Administration	
	Taxable activities	• Sales of real estate • Providing services within the country • Construction contracts • First sale of real estate made by builder • Import of goods	
	Exemptions (examples)	• Export of goods • Export of services indicated in the law • Transfer of goods resulting from business reorganisations	
	Refund of VAT	• Advance recovery regimen • Credits in favour of exporter • Drawbacks	• Advance recovery regimen • Credits in favour of exporter • Drawbacks
	Tax liability	Those corporations and individuals that carry out taxable activities	
	Tax rates	Standard rate = 19%	
	Administrative obligations	Monthly payments of a definitive nature	
Stamp Duty Land Tax		Land sales are not subject to tax	
Stamp Duty		Value Added Tax has replaced this tax	

Poland

(Miroslaw Kosmider, mkosmider@proaudit.pl)

I MAIN LEGAL FORMS

Characteristics \ Legal form	Registered Partnership (RP) (spółka jawna) and Limited Partnership (LP) (spółka komandytowa)	Ltd (private corporation) and Plc (public corporation)
Partners/shareholders • Number • Restrictions	• A minimum of two individuals or legal persons	• One or more individuals or legal persons • The only restriction states that a Limited Liability Company (LLC) and Plc can not be established solely by another single-member LLC
Directors	RP: partners LP: general partner and limited partner	Ltd: Board of Directors Plc: Board of Directors and supervisory board (no less than three people)
Establishment	• A deed of partnership (must be executed in writing) • Contributions of partners • Registration in National Court Register • Additionally the agreement of limited partnership must be notarised • The partnership is established upon its registration. After this one must obtain a statistical number, register with the Social Security Institute (ZUS) and with the tax office (after opening a bank account)	• The Articles of Association or the Statute have to be drafted in the form of a notarial deed • Contributions to the company's share capital. In LLCs the initial capital should be contributed in full before registration. There are some exceptions in a joint stock company, where it is admissible that only a certain part of the capital is paid • Appointing of the management board and in the case of Plc, supervisory board • A supervisory board or an auditor's committee must be established in LLCs if the share capital exceeds PLN 500,000 and there are more than 25 shareholders • Registration in the National Court Register

Characteristics \ Legal form	Registered Partnership (RP) (spółka jawna) and Limited Partnership (LP) (spółka komandytowa)	Ltd (private corporation) and Plc (public corporation)
		• Registration within the Central Statistics Office (GUS) • Opening of a bank account • Registration within the Tax Office • Registration within Social Security Office
Registration	Every company must be registered in the National Court Register	
Minimum capital	No restrictions	Ltd: PLN 50,000 (the value of one share at least PLN 50) Plc: PLN 500,000 (the value of one share at least PLN 0.01)
Liability	RP: Unlimited liability LP: Limited to capital except for the general partner	Limited to capital
Governance	RP: Every partner has the right to represent the partnership Every partner has the right and obligation to manage the partnership's affairs LP: General partner represents partnership and manages its affairs Limited partner can represent partnership only as a plenipotentiary and has no right to manage partnership affairs unless the Articles of Association provide otherwise	Board of Directors conducts the company's affairs and is authorised to represent the company
Audit requirements	If in the prior financial year for which the financial statement was prepared at least two of the following conditions are met the audit and the publication of the financial statement is obligatory: • the total assets as at the end of the financial year were at least the Polish zloty equivalent of €2.5m • the net revenue from the sales of goods for resale and finished goods and the financial transactions for the financial year, was at least the Polish zloty equivalent of €5m • the annual average number of employees in full-time equivalents amounted to at least 50 people	Ltd: The same requirements as for registered and limited partnerships Plc: The financial statement is required to be audited and published every year
Taxation	Personal income tax or corporate income tax – each partner pays tax separately	Corporate income tax

Legal form / Characteristics	Registered Partnership (RP) (spółka jawna) and Limited Partnership (LP) (spółka komandytowa)	Ltd (private corporation) and Plc (public corporation)
Usage	Suited for small-scale service provision or production Limited partnership is a form of organisation that is used by professionals who want to limit their liability for partnership debts	Ltd: Suited for small- and medium-scale ventures that do not need to pool capital from a large group of investors Plc: Mainly intended for large-scale ventures

II   CORPORATION TAX

Legal form / Description	Resident corporation	Permanent establishment (PE)
General description	All legal persons and organisational units having a legal personality are subject to corporate income tax. Corporate income tax does not apply to: • revenue earned on agricultural activity, with the exception of income from special branches of agricultural production • revenue earned on forestry activities within the limits of the Forestry Act • revenue earned on activities, which cannot constitute the subject of a legally effective contract	
Taxable entities	Companies Partnerships	
Taxable income	Resident companies	Income derived by a PE in Poland
Calculation of taxable profits	Accounting profits as adjusted by disallowable expenses and non-taxable incomes	
Interest payments	Interest where the debt to equity ratio exceeds 3:1 will be subject to restrictions for deductibility	
Related party transactions	With regard to transactions between related parties, the duty to prepare tax documentation arises if the joint contract price (or its equivalent) or the amount for services actually paid in the tax year exceeds the Polish zloty equivalent of: • €100,000 – if the transaction value does not exceed 20% of the share capital • €30,000 – in case of rendering services and sale of intangibles • €50,000 – in other cases Tax havens are excluded from this exemption	
Tax year, return and payment	Tax year – calendar year Annual return filed within 3 months Tax payments made monthly	
Capital gains	Assessed as part of income	
Losses	Losses may be carried forward for 5 years, up to 50% of the loss may be set off in each year. Loss carry back is not allowed	
Tax group	Resident companies with an average share capital of at least PLN 1m may form a tax group. A tax group must be formed for a period of 3 years	
Tax rate	19%	

III TAXES FOR INDIVIDUALS

<table>
<tr><td rowspan="9">Income Tax</td><td></td><td colspan="2" style="text-align:center">Residents</td><td style="text-align:center">Non-residents</td></tr>
</table>

		Residents	Non-residents
Income Tax	General description	The tax is assessed on the income of natural persons, independently of the source of origin	
	Taxable entities and taxable income	Under the Polish Personal Income Tax Act, individuals who are residents of Poland (persons whose place of residence is in Poland), with the exception of diplomats and certain other limited categories, including persons benefiting from international privileges are liable to tax on their worldwide income (unlimited income tax liability)	Individuals earning income in Poland whose stay is temporary and who do not have the status of Polish residents, are subject to taxation on income arising in Poland or because of their work performed in Poland, irrespective of the place of salary payment unless otherwise stated by treaty (limited tax liability)
	Types of taxable income	The tax applies to the following sources of income: • income from employment, including benefits-in-kind • income from self-employment in recognised professions • income from other self-employment, other than agriculture • income from certain non-mainstream types (known as special sectors) of agriculture, such as heated greenhouses, beekeeping, fur farming, battery farming of poultry, etc • income from real estate, including assigning and granting leases and subleases • capital gains and income from other property rights • income from personal investments in bonds, shares, deposits	
	Calculation of income	Income may be reduced by the taxpayer by the amount of social security premiums paid during the tax year The tax may be reduced by the taxpayer by the part of the national health insurance premium If the taxpayer receives income from more than one source a sum of the income from all sources is subject to taxation. However, there are some exceptions to this rule that refer to the following: • revenue (income), which is subject to lump-sum taxation • income which is subject to flat-rate tax	In general, if following requirements are not met non-residents apply Polish tax regulations: • the employee is present in Poland for a period or period not exceeding in the aggregate 183 days in any 12-month period commencing or ending in the fiscal year concerned • the remuneration is paid by, or on behalf of, an employer who is not a resident of Poland • the remuneration is not borne by a permanent establishment which the employer has in Poland
	Tax year, tax assessment and tax payment	Tax year – calendar year During the tax year the taxpayers are obliged to make advance payments for their income tax (by the 20th day of the following month for the preceding month) and, after the end of the given tax year, pay the tax due in a final amount (ie not later than 30 April of the following year)	
	Losses	Losses may be carried forward for 5 years. Only 50% of the loss may be set off in each year. No carry back is allowed	

		Residents	**Non-residents**

Income Tax	Tax rates	• Contracts of employment – progressive scale from 19–40%
		• Business income – 19% or progressive rates to 40%
		• Rental income:
		  – progressive rates to 40% or
		  – lump-sum tax: 8.5% if annual income does not exceed €4,000, then the tax is 20% of the surplus of annual income over €4,000
		• Investment income – lump-sum tax 19%	

Capital Gains Tax (CGT)	General description	Assessed as part of income	
Inheritance Tax (IHT)	General description	Tax applies to the transfer by inheritance of wealth situated in Poland, or the transfer of wealth situated abroad to Polish citizens or persons whose usual place of residence is in Poland. In most cases, the tax obligation falls on the recipient	
	Taxable entities and chargeable assets	For Polish residents the tax liability is on assets both in Poland and outside	
	Calculation of charge	Tax is levied on the net market value of all assets received	
	Taxable events	Acquisition of inheritance	
	Allowances	Inheritance is free of charge where the value does not exceed the amount of PLN 4,902–9,637, depending on the character of relationship of the parties to the inheritance. There are three different kinds of relationship: • Class I includes transfers between spouses, parents and children (also adopted children), parents and children-in-law, grandparents, grandchildren, brothers and sisters and step-parents. Tax-free transfer – below PLN 9,637 • Class II includes transfers between nephews, nieces, aunts and uncles, spouses of adopted children and brothers and sisters-in-law. Tax-free transfer – no more than PLN 7,276 • Class III includes all other transfers. Tax-free transfer – below PLN 4,902	The transfer is not taxable if the transfer takes place in Poland but neither the transferor nor the transferee is a Polish citizen or resident of Poland
	Tax rates	The tax is calculated according to the progressive scale (from 3–20%) and its level depends on the character of relation between donor and recipient and on the value of the asset. In general the closer the relationship, the lower the rate of tax payable	N/A

IV   WITHHOLDING TAXES

	Payments to non-residents[1,2]
Dividends	19%
Interest	20%
Royalties	20%
On payments to artists and sportsmen	20%

---

1   Reduced rates of withholding tax may apply where there is an appropriate double tax treaty.
2   Payments of dividends to EU-resident companies are reduced to nil.

V   INDIRECT TAXES

		Residents	Non-residents
Value Added Tax (VAT)	General description	There are three indirect taxes in Poland: tax on goods and services (VAT), excise duty, game tax	
	Entities being obliged to levy VAT	Legal entities, individuals in business and organisational units without a legal entity who: • are required to pay customs duty • make intra-Community acquisitions of goods • are the recipients of the services supplied to the taxpayers whose registered office, residence or stay is located outside the territory of Poland • acquire goods, if the goods are supplied on the territory of Poland by a taxpayer who has no registered office, permanent business location or residence on the territory of Poland • are the purchasers of new vehicles The exception to this rule applies to the entities whose estimated annual turnover does not exceed €10,000	
	Taxable activities	Supplying goods for consideration on the territory of Poland defined as the transfer of the right to manage the goods as their owner Supplying of services for consideration on the territory of Poland The following activities are also taxable: • a commitment to refrain from performing activities, or to tolerate activities or situations • the transfer of rights to intangibles • the provision of services in accordance with an order issued, a public government organ or an organ acting on its behalf, or an order arising by virtue of the law • the free of charge supply of services for the taxpayer's personal needs or the personal needs of its current and former employees, partners, shareholders, etc	
	Taxable activities – zero rated (examples)	• Export of goods and services • Intra-Community supply transactions • Some international transportation services	
	Exemptions (examples)	• Financial services • Educational services • Development of technology	
	Refund of VAT	Usually in 60 days after deposit declaration (in some cases in 180 days)	
	Tax liability	Tax liability arises at the earlier of: • the moment the goods are delivered and services are performed • the moment of issuing invoice, not later however than the 7th day after the day of delivery of goods or service provision, if the transaction was to be confirmed by invoice • at the moment of receipt of payment, including partial one, before delivery of goods or performing the service • at the moment of elapse of term of payment, not later, however, than at the moment of receipt of whole or partial payment – in the case of the lease services or transactions of similar nature The taxpayer may reduce the amount of output VAT by the amount of input VAT to the extent to which the goods and services are used to perform taxable activities	

		Residents	Non-residents
Value Added Tax (VAT)		The surplus of output VAT over input VAT determines how much VAT is payable/repayable	
		Tax is paid monthly. Taxpayers with turnover in the previous year lower than €800,000 may choose to make quarterly settlements	
	Tax rates	The standard tax rate is 22%. There are three reduced rates applied as follows: • 7% rate refers mainly to some goods connected with healthcare, groceries, services connected with housing construction, hotel services • 3% rate is applied to the sale of certain unprocessed or semi-processed products of agriculture, forestry, hunting and fishery • 0% rate refers to export of goods and intra-Community supply of goods, international transport services	
	Administrative obligations	Monthly or quarterly declaration (for small entities)	For PE – monthly or quarterly declaration (for small entities)
Stamp Duty Land Tax		Annual tax rates are determined by resolutions of the local government and may be different in each administrative area	
		The following constitute the tax base: • for buildings and their parts – their usable area • for other types of constructions – their value • for land – its area	
		However, the tax charges in the year 2008 cannot be higher than: • PLN 0.62/square metre – for land • PLN 17.31/square metre – for buildings • 2% of its value – for other types of constructions	
Stamp Duty		Entrepreneurs are obliged to pay stamp duty due on activities associated with certain transactions with the authorities. The most common are applications, certificates, permits (licences), etc and other filings associated with registration of legal documents. There are many different charges, eg VAT registration – PLN 170	

Portugal

(Rui Guedes Henriques, ruighenriques@nexia.pt)

I MAIN LEGAL FORMS

Legal form / Characteristics	Partnership and Limited Liability Partnership (LLP)	Ltd (private corporation) and Plc (public corporation)
Partners/shareholders • Number • Restrictions	General partnership (*sociedade em nome colectivo*): • Minimum number of partners: two Limited partnership (*sociedade em comandita*): • Minimum number of partners: two, or five if capital is represented by shares	Single Person Private Limited Liability (*Sociedade Unipessoal por Quotas*): • Number of quotaholders: one Private Limited Liability (*Sociedade por Quotas*): • Minimum number of quotaholders: two Corporation (*Sociedade Anónima*) (SA): • Minimum number of shareholders: five
Directors	Management attributed to the partners or to entities appointed as directors, who may or may not be partners	• Director: management attributed to one or more directors, who may or may not be quotaholders General meeting takes the relevant decisions and the directors take day-to-day decisions • Unitary System: Board of Directors, or a single director overseen by an Audit Committee or an Individual Qualified Auditor (*Conselho Fiscal or Fiscal Único*) • Dual system: management powers shared between a single manager or a Board with a maximum number of five managers and an Advisory Board (*Conselho Geral*), overseen by an individual qualified auditor

Legal form / Characteristics	Partnership and Limited Liability Partnership (LLP)	Ltd (private corporation) and Plc (public corporation)
Registration	Companies have to register at: • Registry of Company Names (Registo Nacional de Pessoas Colectivas) • Commercial Company Registrar (Registo Comercial) • Tax authorities declaring the start of activity	
Minimum capital	No minimum share capital	€5,000 €50,000 (SA)
Liability	General partnership: unlimited Limited partnership: unlimited for individual partners and unlimited for partners that have the legal form of Private Limited Liability or Corporation	Limited to capital
Governance	Partners	Board of Directors
Audit requirements	Auditing is optional unless two of the following three limits are exceeded in 2 consecutive years: • total net assets: €1.5m • total net sales and other profits: €3m • number of employees: 50	Auditing is optional for limited liability companies unless two of the following three limits are exceeded in 2 consecutive years, companies are required to appoint a qualified auditor (Revisor Oficial de Contas): • total net assets: €1.5m • total net sales and other profits: €3m • number of employees: 50 Auditing is compulsory for corporations. Depending on the governance model adopted, audit requirements for corporations may differ
Taxation	Transparent	Corporation tax
Usage	Minimal	Mainly small and medium-sized companies adopt this legal form. SA larger/listed companies

II CORPORATION TAX

Legal form / Description	Resident corporation	Permanent establishment (PE)
General description	Corporation tax	
Taxable entities	Corporations incorporated or effectively managed in Portugal	PE located in Portuguese territory
Taxable income	Worldwide income	Income attributable to the Portuguese territory
Calculation of taxable profits	Accounting profit is adjusted for various tax add-backs and allowances to arrive at taxable income/tax losses	
Interest payments	In general, interest is deductible under general deduction rules	
	Exceptions may apply to pure holding companies under specific tax regime	
	Thin capitalisation rules:	
	• Interest related to loans granted to Portuguese entities by related entities which are not resident in Portugal or in another EU member state are deductible if that entity maintains a debt to equity ratio of 2:1 • If the debt to equity ratio is exceeded, the related interest can still be deductible if the taxpayer proves that the higher ratio is still adequate under market conditions	
	Thin capitalisation rules also apply to loans granted by non-resident entities (which are not resident in another EU member state) that are guaranteed by related parties	
Related party transactions	All related party transactions must take place on arm's length basis	
Tax year, return and payment	Tax follows the calendar year but companies may ask for a different annual period	
	Tax returns are filed up to the fifth month following the tax year	
	Three payments on account are made during the year based on previous year assessment, the balance being paid when filing the tax return	
	A special payment on account (that may be due in two instalments) based on previous year's turnover with a cap, deducted from previous year payments on account	
Capital gains	Included in the computation of the taxable income	
	Capital gains arising from the disposal of fixed and specific financial assets complying with certain requirements may be reduced to 50% provided the sale proceeds are reinvested in the acquisition of qualifying assets in the year prior to the disposal, in the year of the disposal, or in the 2 following years	
	Under specific conditions, capital gains computed by pure holding companies, from the disposal of shareholdings interest in other companies are exempted (participation exemption)	
Losses	Tax losses may be carried forward for a period of 6 years, excepting for the tax years, during that period, which taxable income was calculated under indirect methods	
Tax group	The tax group is applicable for groups of Portuguese companies held by a parent company, directly or indirectly, at least in 90% of the share capital and more than 50% of the voting rights of the subsidiary. Other requirements apply	

Legal form / Description	Resident corporation	Permanent establishment (PE)
Tax rate	25% standard rate (to which is added, in most municipalities, a municipal surcharge (Derrama) resulting in a maximum combined rate of 26.5%)	

III TAXES FOR INDIVIDUALS

		Residents	Non-residents
Income Tax	General description	Tax levied on the chargeable income of a chargeable person for a year of assessment	
	Taxable entities and taxable income	Residents are taxed on their worldwide income	Non-residents are taxable on all income arising in Portugal
	Types of taxable income	• Real estate income (usually rental income) • Income from capital investment (interest, capital gains, dividends, royalties) • Income from business activities • Employment income or pensions	
	Calculation of income	Taxpayer is entitled to make deductions to the sum of the different natures of income (eg employment income, business income, property income, dividends, etc) resulting in the taxable income which is subject to progressive tax rates	
	Tax year, tax assessment and tax payment	Tax year – calendar year Individual taxpayers must file annual returns between March and May of the following year, the timing depending on the combination of income sources The computation of taxable business and self-employment income is based: (a) on the rules of the so-called 'simplified regime'; (b) on the rules applicable to isolated acts of business and self-employment services; or (c) on organised accounting records Individuals with business and self-employment income may have to make advance payments in July, September and December Employment and pensions income is subject to withholding tax at the time of payment, as prepayment of the ultimate tax liability On the other hand, under some conditions, self-employment, real estate, and specific capital investment income are also subjected to withholding taxes Non-residents must appoint a tax representative under certain conditions	
	Losses	Losses computed in the context of business and self-employment activities (based on accounting records) can be offset against income in the subsequent 6 years Capital losses computed in the context of disposal of real estate can be offset against positive income of same nature in the subsequent 5 years	
	Tax rates	*Taxable Income*	

Taxable Income (€)	Marginal tax rate (%)	Deduction (€)
0–4,639	10.5	0
4,640–7,017	13	115.98
7,018–17,401	23.5	852.76
17,402–40,020	34	2,679.86
40,021–58,000	36.5	3,680.36
58,001–62,546	40	5,710.39
62,546+	42	6,961.31

		Residents	Non-residents
Capital Gains Tax (CGT)	General description	The positive annual balance between capital gains and capital losses is subject to taxation (eg disposal of real estate, shares, bonds)	
	Taxable entities and chargeable assets	Worldwide income qualified as capital gains under Portuguese tax legislation obtained by individuals	Income attributable to Portuguese territory obtained by individuals (eg sale of real estate located in the Portuguese territory, disposal of shares in Portuguese companies)
	Calculation of gain	Examples: • Gains on real estate used as permanent residence are not taxable if sale proceeds are reinvested within 2 years, or in the previous 12 months, in real estate with the same purpose • Gains on securities acquired before 1989 are not taxed • Only 50% of gains from real estate and related rights are taxable	
	Tax year, tax assessment and tax payment	Tax year corresponds to calendar year Income included in annual tax return to determine tax liability	
	Tax rates	• Shares held for more than 12 months – no taxation • Shares held for 12 months or less – taxation at a flat 10% rate • Bonds and other debt certificates – no taxation • 'Quotas' and securities other than those mentioned above – taxation at a flat 10% rate • Capital gains not attributable to a PE in Portugal obtained by non-residents are taxed at a flat 10% (shares and other securities, warrants and certificates) or 25% rate Other capital gains, obtained by individuals qualifying as tax residents, are subjected to the progressive tax rates	
		Domiciled	**Non-domiciled**
Inheritance Tax (IHT)	General description	The inheritance tax was abolished. Nonetheless, inheritances received by individuals are subject to a 10% Stamp Tax rate Inheritances received from spouses, parents and children are exempt from Stamp Tax	

IV   WITHHOLDING TAXES

	Payments to non-residents[1]
Dividends	20%
Interest	20%
Royalties	15%
On payments to artists and sportsmen	25%

---

1   Reduced rates of withholding tax may apply where there is an appropriate double tax treaty.

V   INDIRECT TAXES

		Residents	Non-residents
Value Added Tax (VAT)	General description	Tax on the supply of goods and services	
	Entities being obliged to levy VAT	• Individuals, companies, collective bodies who independently and regularly engage in the production/commerce of goods or in the supply of services • Persons who engage in occasional transactions which qualify as commercial transactions according to the law • Importers	
	Taxable activities	Supply of goods and services and importation of goods	
	Taxable activities – zero rated (examples)	Exports	
	Exemptions (examples)	Financial transactions, real estate rental, transactions subject to Property Transfer Tax	
	Refund of VAT	As a general rule, when VAT credit exceeds approximately €10,000 Payment within 3 months	
	Tax liability	In general, 5 days after the delivery of goods or the rendering of services or, if advance payments are made, by the moment the payment is received	
	Tax rates	• Standard rate = 20% • Intermediate rate = 12% • Reduced rate = 5% • Madeira and Azores = 4%, 8% or 14%	
	Administrative obligations	Tax returns due on a monthly basis if annual turnover is equal or higher than €650,000 or on a quarterly basis if turnover is lower than that amount Annual tax return summarising the annual activities, including the identification of clients and suppliers with annual transactions exceeding €25,000	
Stamp Duty Land Tax		Stamp tax is due on the acquisition of ownership or other rights on real estate – 0.8% Property Transfer Tax is levied on the transfer of real estate: • urban property not exclusively for residential purposes – 6.5% • urban property exclusively for residential purposes (acquisition value higher than €521,700) – 6%. Lower progressive tax rates apply to smaller amounts • urban property exclusively for permanent residential purposes (acquisition value higher than €543,900) – 6%. Lower progressive tax rates apply to smaller amounts • rural property – 5% • property acquired by residents in tax havens – 8% Municipal Property Tax is levied on an annual basis, due by the property owner: • urban property – 0.2%–0.5% • rural property – 0.8% • property owned by residents in tax havens – 1%	
Stamp Duty		Levied on deeds, documents, books, papers, acts and other situations specified in the Code, including gifts and donations, as mentioned above under IHT Specific tax rates depending on the taxable event	

Qatar

(Usamah Tabbarah & Company, qatar@utcnexia.com)

I MAIN LEGAL FORMS

Legal form / Characteristics	Partnership and Limited Liability Partnership (LLP)	Ltd (private corporation) and Plc (public corporation)
Partners/Shareholders • Number • Restrictions	*Simple Partnership Company*: minimum partners – two. All the Partners have to be natural persons *Joint Partnership Company*: minimum partners – two. One of the partners has to be a joint partner who is personally responsible for the company's liabilities, and another has to be a trustee partner whose liability is limited to the value of his share in the capital *Limited Shares Partnership Company*: • minimum joint partners – one who shall be a natural person • minimum trustee partners – four Joint partners are personally responsible for the debts of the company. Trustee partners' liability is limited to the value of shares held in the capital *Joint Venture Company*: minimum venturers – two. If non-Qataris are participant(s) only business activities stipulated by law for non-Qataris are allowed	*Public Shareholding Company*: minimum shareholders – five A public shareholding company shall have a definite term which can be extended by an extraordinary resolution of the shareholders *Closed Public Shareholding Company*: minimum shareholders – five The entire shares of the company are held by at least five persons and the shares cannot be offered for public subscription *Limited Liability Company*: • minimum shareholders – two • maximum shareholders – 50 A limited liability company shall not engage in the business of insurance, or in the investment of funds, whether as a principal or an agent *One Person Company* is where every economic activity and its full share capital is held by one natural person or corporate entity *Holding Company* is a joint stock, limited liability or one person company financially and administratively controlling one or more other companies by holding at least 51% of the shares of such companies

Legal form / Characteristics	Partnership and Limited Liability Partnership (LLP)	Ltd (private corporation) and Plc (public corporation)
Directors	N/A	*Public Shareholding Company:* • minimum – five • maximum – 11 Tenure: 3 years – can be re-elected once unless otherwise stated in the Articles of Association
Establishment	*Partnership*: by the execution of the Articles of Partnership and/or the Memorandum of Association *Joint Venture*: unincorporated entity without validity against third parties and not subject to registration procedures in the Commercial Register. A Memorandum of Joint Venture may be provided by all evidential means	Companies' incorporation in accordance with provisions of the State of Qatar Commercial Companies Law (CCL), No 5 of 2002, and CCL No 16 of 2006, Memorandum of Association and Articles of Association and other incorporation documents must be filed in the Commercial Register
Registration	Register with the Commercial Register and must have the prior approval of the Minister of Economy and Commerce	
Minimum Capital	*Limited Shares Partnership Company:* Qatari Riyals (QR) 1m	*Public Shareholding Company:* QR 10m. The minimum par value per share is QR 10 *Closed Public Shareholding Company:* QR 2m *Limited Liability Company:* QR 200,000. The minimum par value per share is QR 10 *One Person Company:* QR 200,000 *Holding Company:* QR 10m
Liability	• General partners: unlimited liability • Trustee partners: limited liability	Limited to the extent of the share capital
Governance	General partners per Articles of Partnership and/or Memorandum of Association	Board of Directors and ultimately the equity shareholders in General Meeting
Audit requirements	Not mandatory	Every shareholding company – auditor appointment mandatory
Taxation	Tax is not levied on Qatari-owned business enterprises. Nationals of Gulf Cooperation Council states are treated as Qatari citizens for income tax purposes	
Usage	Unlimited	

II CORPORATION TAX

Legal form / Characteristics	Partnership and Limited Liability Partnership (LLP)	Ltd (private corporation) and Plc (public corporation)
General description	Tax is levied on the taxable income for every tax year which has been realised or has arisen in Qatar	
Taxable entities	Income tax is levied on partly or wholly foreign-owned business entities (foreign companies, partnerships and individuals) operating in Qatar. Tax is not levied on Qatari-owned or pro rata on partly Qatari-owned businesses	
Taxable income	Accounting profit is adjusted for various tax add-backs and allowances to arrive at the profits assessable to tax	
Calculation of taxable profits	Income chargeable to tax less allowable deductions (eg upkeep and maintenance of fixed assets, depreciation, bad debts, superannuation and staff welfare, donations, and direct expenses)	
Interest payments	Interest on borrowings to earn taxable income is deductible	
Related party transactions	Related party transactions should be on an arm's length basis	
Tax year, return and payment	The tax year is the period of 12 months commencing from 1 January and ending on 31 December following, however a taxpayer may apply to prepare his financial statements for a 12-month period ending on a day other than 31 December. The taxpayer must maintain his accounting records in Qatari Riyals	
	Tax declaration to be submitted within 4 months of the end of the financial period.	
	Tax shown in the tax declaration is payable on the due date of filing the tax return	
Capital Gains	Capital gains are treated as part of taxable income	
Losses	A tax loss in any single year is set off against taxable income arising in the subsequent years, to a maximum period of 3 years after the year in which the tax loss was incurred	
Tax group	Businesses are taxed as separate entities. There are no provisions for group taxation or relief	
Tax rates	The first QR 100,000 is exempt from tax. The subsequent amounts are taxed at rates varying for different assessable income bands, with the top rate of 35% on income exceeding QR 5m	

III　TAXES FOR INDIVIDUALS

		Residents	Non-Residents
Income Tax	General description	There are no personal income taxes	
Capital Gains Tax (CGT)	General description	Capital gains are treated as part of taxable income	
	Losses	Deductible	
		Domiciled	**Non-Domiciled**
Inheritance Tax (IHT)	General description	There is no inheritance tax	

IV WITHHOLDING TAXES

	Payments to non-residents
Dividends	There are no withholding taxes in Qatar
Interest	
Royalties, management contracts, leases of equipment and machinery, technical expertise and/or research and development	
On payments to artists and sportsmen	

V   INDIRECT TAXES

		Residents	Non residents
Value Added Tax (VAT)	General description	Qatar does not impose a VAT or sales tax	
Stamp Duty Land Tax		There is no Stamp Duty Land Tax	
Stamp Duty		There is no Stamp Duty	

Romania

(Luminita Ristea, Luminita.ristea@consultingr.ro)

I MAIN LEGAL FORMS

Characteristics / Legal form	Partnership and Limited Liability Partnership (LLP)	Ltd (private corporation) and Plc (public corporation)
Partners/shareholders • Number • Restrictions	A limited partnership consists of one or more general partners who manage the business of a partnership and one or more limited partners who contribute to capital	Ltd: from 1–50 partners Plc: at least two shareholders
Directors	The general partner provides the professional management of the partnership	Ltd: directors/managers are appointed in the Articles of Association or by the General Assembly Plc: directors are appointed by the General Assembly of shareholders, which establishes their empowerment and accountability, for a maximum period of 4 years
Establishment	Various documents submitted to the Local Trade Registry The procedure for setting up a company usually takes 3 days, from the date the whole requested documentation is submitted	
Registration	The company is a legal entity from the date of its registration with the Trade Register and therefore each legal entity has the obligation to apply for registration with the Trade Register where the entity is located (their head office). Every change of shareholders' structure, locations, object of activity, directors, auditors, etc must be filled in on the basis of entity's application registration forms	
Minimum capital	No legal provisions	Ltd: at least Lei 200 Plc: at least Lei 90,000
Liability	Unlimited liability for partnerships LLP – limited to partnership capital	Limited to the company's capital

Legal form / Characteristics	Partnership and Limited Liability Partnership (LLP)	Ltd (private corporation) and Plc (public corporation)
Governance	General partners ensure the administration of the company	• Ltd and Plc: the management is assumed by a Board of Directors • If the company is audited according to the law then it must have at least three administrators • The administrators cannot be employed on the basis of the labour contract as an employee • Plc can be managed by a dual system: Board of Directors and a Supervision Council as well

Audit requirements	Generally not required	Required in some circumstances:
		
		• Plc only in case of dual system
		• listed (quoted) companies
		• companies (Plc, Ltd) meeting two of three criteria:
		  − total assets over €3.65m
		  − net turnover over €7.3m
		  − number of employees more than 50

Taxation	Transparent	Corporation tax
Usage	Rarely used	Commonly used

II CORPORATION TAX

Legal form / Description	Resident corporation	Permanent establishment (PE)
General description	Corporation tax	
Taxable entities	Corporations incorporated and managed in Romania	PE located in Romania
Taxable income	Worldwide taxable profits with considerations for double taxation treaties for Romanian companies	Taxable profits assigned to the PE derived in Romania
Calculation of taxable profits	Accounting profit is adjusted for various tax add-backs and allowances to arrive to profits chargeable to corporation tax (PCTCT)	
Interest payments	For long-term loan agreements interest expenses are fully deductible in the case where the debt to equity ratio is less than three; exceeding amount may be carried forward	
Related party transactions	All related party transactions must be taken into consideration on arm's length basis	
Tax year, return and payment	Tax year – calendar year	
	Payments are due on the 25th of the month following each quarter	
	Final date for submitting the annual tax return is 15 April in the following year	
	Returns must be filed with the accounts on a quarterly basis	
	Starting with 2010 a new system of quarterly payments in advance taking into consideration the corporation tax calculated for the previous year is applied for companies	
Capital gains	Treated as income	
Losses[1]	Only fiscal losses may be carried forward 5 years	
	Starting from 1 January 2009 fiscal losses may be carried forward 7 years	
Tax group	None	
Tax rate	16%	

---

1   There are special rules allowing the company to utilise other losses such as capital losses and loan relationship deficits.

III TAXES FOR INDIVIDUALS

		Residents	Non-residents
Income Tax	General description	Tax levied on the chargeable income of a chargeable person for a fiscal year	
	Taxable entities and taxable income	Residents are taxed on their worldwide income	Non-residents are taxed on the income derived in Romania
	Types of taxable income	• Property income (usually rent) and real estate transactions income • Intellectual property rights • Income from capital investments (interest, stocks, bonds, dividends, annuities, income from company's liquidation) • Income from business activities • Wage and salary • Pensions • Income from agriculture • Other incomes	
	Calculation of income (examples)	• Property income (usually rent): 75% of the gross income from rental • Property income from real estate transactions: different quota applied to the transaction value taking into consideration the ageing of property held and the transaction value (less than Lei 200,000 or more then Lei 200,000) • Intellectual property income: 50%–60% of the gross income from intellectual property income minus social contributions • Income from capital investment (interest, stocks, bonds, dividends, annuities, income from company's liquidation) after deducting the support expenses • Income from business activities: gross income minus deductible expenses • Wages and salary: gross income minus social contributions minus personal allowance minus certain other items	
	Tax year, tax assessment and tax payment	Tax year – calendar year Tax return must be filed by 15 May in the following year Payments are made in advance on a quarterly or half-yearly basis according to the income	
	Losses	Losses can be offset against income of the same source in the subsequent 5 years	
	Tax rates	16% applied on taxable income for all income, except: • *Real estate transaction* – the quota is 1%–3% applied on the transaction's value taking into consideration the ageing of property held and the transaction value (less than Lei 200,000 or more than Lei 200,000) • *Stocks sold held for more than 365 days* – the quota applied is 1% During the year 2009 the capital gains from stocks sold are non-taxable incomes • *Gambling income* – the quota is 20%, respectively 25% for net income from gambling	

		Residents	**Non-residents**
Capital Gains Tax (CGT)	General description	No capital taxes	
Inheritance Tax (IHT)	General description	Successional asset	
	Taxable entities and chargeable assets	Individuals for real estate	
	Calculation of charge	If the successional asset is finalised within 2 years no tax is applied If the successional asset is not debated within 2 years, the due tax is 1% applied on the real estate value	
	Taxable events	Individuals for the real estate properties heritable, *if the successional asset is not debated in the 2-year period*	
	Allowances	If the successional asset is debated within 2 years no tax is due	
	Tax rates	1%	

IV   WITHHOLDING TAXES

	Payments to non-residents
Dividends	16%
Interest	16% 10% to EU residents
Royalties	16% 10% to EU residents
On payments to artists and sportsmen	16% and the double treaty agreements applicable

V INDIRECT TAXES

		Residents	Non-residents
Value Added Tax (VAT)	General description	Tax on the supply of goods and services	
	Entities being obliged to levy VAT	All legal entities performing an economic activity in the production, commerce and services department, or persons practising freelance activities are subject to VAT	
	Taxable activities	All supply of goods and services	
	Taxable activities – zero rated (examples)	No zero-rated activities	
	Exemptions (examples)	There are three categories: • exempt operations without credit (deduction): public interest activities, such as hospitals, education, mailing; and also other activities, such as financial and banking services, gambling, insurance, rental and sale of real estate properties (with the possibility of option for taxation) • exempt operations with credit (deduction), such as export of goods, services in connection with the export, international transportation of persons, intra-Community delivery (under certain conditions) • exempt import operations, such as the import of goods whose delivery in Romania is exempted	
	Refund of VAT	Romanian VAT-registered entities are entitled to reclaim VAT	
	Tax liability	• Taxable entities who perform taxable activities whose place is, or is considered to be in Romania • The beneficiary of the intangible services (chargeable persons) provided by another chargeable entity established abroad • Non-resident EU entities liable to pay VAT can appoint a fiscal representative • Non-resident non-EU entities must appoint a fiscal representative	
	Tax rates	Standard rate = 19% Reduced rate = 9%	
	Administrative obligations	• Registration • VAT identification code	• Registration • Appoint a fiscal representative
Stamp Duty Land Tax		Notarial fees are applied	
Stamp Duty		Notarial fees are applied	

Russia

(Natalia Malofeeva, Moscow, malofeeva@mkpcn.ru)

I MAIN LEGAL FORMS

Legal form / Characteristics	Partnerships		Companies		
				Joint stock company (JSC)	
	Full partnership	Partnership in commendam	Limited liability company	Closed JSC	Open JSC
Partners/shareholders • Number • Restrictions	Consists of full partners. Only individual entrepreneurs and (or) commercial organisations may be participants of full partnership. No restrictions as to the number of partners	Consists of full partners and partners in commendam. Only individual entrepreneurs and (or) commercial organisations may be full partners. Natural persons and legal entities may be partners in commendam	May contain from 1–50 participants. Legal entities and natural persons may be participants	May contain from 1–50 participants. Legal entities and natural persons may be participants	No restrictions as to the number of shareholders. Legal entities and natural persons may be participants. May contain one participant
	A person may participate as a full partner in only one partnership		A company may not have as its sole participant another company with a sole individual participant		
Directors	Management by mutual agreement of all partners	Management by full partners	Managed by executive body which may be collective (governing board, directorate) and/or consist of one person (eg general director)		
Establishment	Established on the basis of a foundation contract signed by all partners	Established on the basis of a foundation contract signed by all full partners	Established by the foundation meeting of participants, where a charter of a company must be approved and a constitutive treaty signed. A one-man company is established by the decision of the sole participant	Established by the foundation meeting of participants, where a charter of a company must be approved. At the meeting founders must conclude a treaty, which is not a foundation contract but an agreement on cooperation. A one-man company is established by the decision of the sole participant	

| Legal form | Partnerships | | Companies | | |
Characteristics	Full partnership	Partnership in commendam	Limited liability company	Joint stock company (JSC) Closed JSC	Open JSC
Registration	In order to be registered an entity should submit to tax authorities the following documents: • application according to the form • foundation documents (Charter, foundation contract if any) • decision on establishment of an entity (minutes, contract, etc) • document certifying payment of state duty In case one of the founders is a foreign legal entity: • extract from companies' register of the country of origin					
Minimum capital	No requirements as to the minimum capital though there should be some joint capital		100 minimum wages (10,000 rubles)	1,000 minimum wages (100,000 rubles)	
Liability	Partners bear all the liability with their property for the obligations of the partnership	Full partners bear all the liability with their property for the obligations of the partnership. Partners in commendam only bear the risk of losses associated with the activities of the partnership within the limits of the sums of their investments	Limited to share capital		

Legal form / Characteristics	Partnerships		Companies		
	Full partnership	Partnership in commendam	Limited liability company	Joint stock company (JSC)	
				Closed JSC	Open JSC
Governance	Management by mutual agreement of all partners	Management by full partners	• General meeting of participants (the highest body) • Board of Directors (if provided for in a charter) • Executive body (may be collective and/or consist of one person)	• General meeting of shareholders (the highest body) • Board of Directors (obligatory body in a company with more than 50 shareholders) • Executive body (may be collective and/or consist of one person)	
Audit requirements	In some cases may be subject to obligatory audit				Obligatory audit is prescribed by law
Taxation	Common order of taxation for all legal forms				
Usage	Used seldom		Used in small and medium-sized businesses		Used in large businesses

II CORPORATION TAX

Legal form / Description	Resident corporation	Permanent establishment	Foreign entity not doing business through a representative office	
General description	Corporate profit tax			
Taxable entities	Legal entities established under the legislation of the Russian Federation (RF)	Foreign entities doing business through permanent representative office	Foreign entities not doing business through a representative office, but drawing income from sources in the RF	
Taxable income	Worldwide income	Income drawn from activities exercised in the RF	Income drawn from sources in the RF, including dividends, interests, income received from sale of real estate, income received from lease, income received from international transportations, etc	
Calculation of taxable profits	Enterprises registered under Russian legislation are liable to tax on their worldwide profits		Foreign enterprises are subject to tax only on profits derived from business activities of a permanent representative office within the Russian Federation	Profits derived from sources in the Russian Federation are taxable at source. International agreement on double-tax avoidance may provide for another scheme of taxation
	All types of income are included in gross income. Generally, taxable profit is computed by lessening the sum of total profit (which includes profit from the sale of goods, works or services and revenues from non-sales transactions) on the sum of incurred expenses and allocations to the reserve funds, listed in the Tax Code (assets repair reserve, reserve for warranty repair and maintenance, vacation pay reserve, reserve for doubtful debts). Some expenses are limited for purposes of taxation. There are some differences between financial and fiscal accounting rules			

Legal form / Description	Resident corporation	Permanent establishment	Foreign entity not doing business through a representative office
Interest payments	Interest payments are taken into account when determining tax base in the following limits: interest charged on borrowings of any kind – average interest on borrowing issued under comparable conditions or Central Bank of Russia refinancing rate increased by 1.1 (for borrowing in foreign currency up to 15%)		
Related party transactions	In transactions with related parties a deviation from the market price of more than 20% may prompt the tax authorities to recalculate the payments for tax purposes taking into account market prices		
Tax year, return and payment	Calendar year – reporting periods are: • for taxpayers that compute their monthly tax advances proceeding from profit received – one month, 2 months, 3 months and so on until the end of the calendar year • for other taxpayers – first quarter, half a year and 9 months of the calendar year Advance payments of tax are made at the end of each reporting period Advance payments are set off as a result of reporting (tax) period		Declaring, deduction and payment of taxes is effected by entity being the source of income. Tax normally deducted at source
Capital gains	There is no special tax for capital gains in the Russian legislation Dividends are taxed as a part of profit but at a lower tax rate		
Losses	Current losses may reduce current profits for the current tax year Losses can be carried forward for 10 years following the year in which the loss was made		
Tax group	None		

Legal form / Description	Resident corporation	Permanent establishment	Foreign entity not doing business through a representative office

Tax rate	Basic rate of 24% is allocated as follows:
	
	 • federal budget – 6.5%
	 • regional budget – 17.5%.
	
	 The regional part may be lower in accordance with the regional law, but not lower than 13.5%
	
	 Dividends are taxed at the following rates:
	
	 • 0% – for dividends received from Russian legal entities on conditions that:
	
	   – by the day of income receiving a receiver posseses of more than 50% share in a payer's charter capital for a period of time longer than 365 days
	
	   – the size of share is not less than 500,000 rubles
	
	 • 9% – for dividends received from Russian and foreign legal entities
	 • 15% – for profit in the form of interests received from state and municipal securities
			• 10% – for profits from lease of vehicles used in international transportation
			 • 15% – for profits in the form of dividends received from Russian entities
			 • 20% – for other profits

III   TAXES FOR INDIVIDUALS

		Residents	Non-residents
Income Tax	General description	Income tax	
	Taxable entities and taxable income	• Natural persons who have been living in the RF not less than 183 days during 12 consecutive months • Worldwide income	• Natural persons who have been living in the RF less than 183 days during 12 consecutive months • Income from sources in the RF
	Types of taxable income	• Employment income • Dividends and interest • Rental income • Insurance payments • Royalties	
	Calculation of income	Every taxpayer has a right to certain deductions in their tax computation. There are several types of tax deduction: • standard deduction (includes deduction for every taxpayer and for taxpayers who have children) • social deduction – expenses on charity, medical treatment, and education may be deducted from the sum of income in determined limits • property deduction – income from property sales, sums spent on purchasing and construction of houses may be deducted (in determined limits) • professional deduction – such categories of taxpayers as individual entrepreneurs, individuals receiving author's emoluments and some other may deduct expenses on profit gaining from income	No tax deductions
	Tax year, tax assessment and tax payment	Taxable period is the calendar year Tax return (declaration) is due on 30 April of the following year. Tax is paid not later than 15 July the following year Legal entities and individual entrepreneurs paying income to natural persons are obliged to withhold tax at source	
	Losses	Are not taken into account when determining tax base	
	Rates	• Basic rate of 13% for residents • 35% is applicable to certain incomes, ie interest yields, winnings, prizes. • 9% in respect of income in the form of dividends	30% from all kinds of taxable income except dividends which are taxable at rate 15%

		Residents	**Non-residents**
Personal property tax			
The tax is local and concerns the owners of the real estate. The following kinds of real estate are subject to individual property tax: dwelling houses, flats, country cottages, garages and other buildings and premises			
Tax rates are established by the Law of the RF within the limit of 2% from the inventory cost of the property and differ depending on the cost of the property. Specific rates are determined by local authorities			
Capital Gains Tax (CGT)	General description	No capital taxes	

		Domiciled	**Non-domiciled**
Inheritance Tax (IHT)	General description	No IHT in Russia, but reward paid to heirs (successors) of authors of scientific works, literature and artists, as well as makers of discoveries, inventions and designs is liable to income tax	

IV WITHHOLDING TAXES

	Payments to non-residents[1]
Dividends	• 15% for individuals • 15% for legal entities
Interest	• 30% for individuals • 15% for legal entities
Royalties	• 30% for individuals • 20% for legal entities
On payments to artists and sportsmen	30% for individuals

1 Reduced rates of withholding tax may apply where there is an appropriate double tax treaty.

V   INDIRECT TAXES

		Residents	Non-residents
Value Added Tax (VAT)	Entities being obliged to levy VAT	Legal entities and individual entrepreneurs	
	Taxable activities	• Sales of goods, works, services and property rights in the RF • Import of goods	
	Taxable activities – zero rated (examples)	• Goods placed under customs export regime • Works (services) directly related to the production and sale of goods exported • Works (services) directly related to cross-border transportation of goods placed under customs transit regime	
	Refund of VAT	Where input VAT exceeds output VAT a refund is due	
	Tax liability	Amount of tax due to payment is calculated as the difference between output and input VAT. Input VAT may be admitted under observing the following rules: • goods, works, services and property rights were purchased in order to conduct operations subject to VAT • the mentioned goods have been entered into books • the taxpayer keeps the VAT invoice	Is calculated and paid by tax agent based on the profit from sale
	Tax rates	• 10% tax rate is levied on goods of basic necessity to society: major foodstuffs, goods for children, medical goods produced in Russia and imported, print periodicals (except erotic and advertising) and services related to their production • 18% tax rate is imposed on other goods (work, services) not mentioned above	
	Administrative obligations	There is a special order of VAT accounting in Russia • All taxpayers are obliged to draw up invoices, keep record books of received and issued invoices, keep purchase books and sale books • Tax period is one quarter. Payment should be made no later than the 20th day of the month following the past tax period • Tax return is submitted not later than the 20th day of the month following the past tax period	• Accounting, declaring and payment is made by tax agent • Payment of tax is made by the tax agent together with transfer of funds • Tax return is submitted by tax agent not later than the 20th day of the month following the past tax period
Land Tax		Taxpayers are individuals and entities – owners of land. Objects of taxation are lands situated within the borders of the territory in which this tax is established. The rates are fixed by local authorities within the limits set by the Tax Code. Maximum rate is 1.5%. Tax base is defined as cadastral cost of land	

	Residents	Non-residents
Stamp Duty	Russian tax legislation provides for state duty which is collected for execution of legal actions by state bodies, including for registration of rights when purchasing real estate, registration of issue of securities, etc	

Note: Starting from 2008 a quarter tax period is established for all taxpayers.

Saudi Arabia

(Usamah Ali Tabbarah & Co, rho@utcnexia.com)

I MAIN LEGAL FORMS[1]

Legal form / Characteristics	Partnership and Limited Liability Partnership (LLP) (personal companies)	Ltd (private corporation) and Plc (public corporation) (capital companies)
Partners/Shareholders • Number • Restrictions	General partnerships: minimum number of partners – two Limited partnerships: one general partner and at least one limited partner Partnerships limited by shares: one general partner and at least one limited partner	Corporations: minimum number of shareholders – five Par value of each share not less than SAR 50 LLP: minimum number of partners – two; maximum – 50
Directors	N/A	Each director should hold shares to the par value of SAR 10,000 or more Duly elected by shareholders
Establishment	In accordance with provisions in the Regulations for Companies	
Registration	Any company incorporated in accordance with the Saudi Arabia Companies Regulations is deemed to have Saudi nationality. Registration is mandatory in (a) the Companies Register and (b) the Commercial Register, for partnerships and for companies	
Minimum capital	• Partnership limited by shares: SAR 1m • Limited liability Partnership: SAR 500,000 • Personal companies licensed under the Foreign Investment Act: the amount of capital invested shall not be less than SAR 25m for agricultural projects, SAR 5m for industrial projects, and SAR 2m for other projects	• Private corporation: SAR 2m • Public corporation: SAR 10m • Corporate entities licensed under the Foreign Investment Act: the amount of capital invested shall not be less than SAR 25m for agricultural projects, SAR 5m for industrial projects, and SAR 2m for other projects

---

1 Article 1 of the New Income Tax Law – Definitions:
   • Capital company: a corporation, a limited liability company, or a company limited by shares. For the purpose of this Law, investment funds are considered capital companies.
   • Personal company: a general partnership, a silent partnership, or a limited partnership.

Legal form / Characteristics	Partnership and Limited Liability Partnership (LLP) (personal companies)	Ltd (private corporation) and Plc (public corporation) (capital companies)
Liability	General Partners liable to full extent of the partnership liabilities.	Limited: to share capital
Governance	General partners per Articles of Partnership	Board of Directors and ultimately the equity shareholders in General Meeting
Audit requirements	Provisions in the Articles of Partnership/Memorandum of Association will apply. Generally a Report of the Independent External Auditor to the partners plus an 'Attestation Report' in accordance with the Regulations	Report of the Independent External Auditor to the shareholders plus an 'Attestation Report' in accordance with the Regulations
Taxation: Zakat and income tax	Partners in personal companies are subject to Zakat or income tax rather than the personal companies themselves. Saudi partners are subject to Zakat and non-Saudi partners are subject to income tax For income tax purposes, non-Saudis[2] do not include citizens (nationals) of Gulf Cooperation Council (GCC) member states. Member states of the GCC are Bahrain, Kuwait, Oman, Qatar, Saudi Arabia and United Arab Emirates The share of equity attributable to interests owned by Saudi and GCC nationals in a company is subject to Zakat. The share of profits attributable to interests owned by non-Saudi and non-GCC nationals in that company is subject to income tax	Zakat and income tax: Saudi shareholders are liable to Zakat on their share of attributable net equity of the company. Non-Saudi nationals and non-GCC citizens are liable to income tax on their share of net profit Saudi wholly-owned companies are subject to Zakat, an Islamic tax on net worth. In joint ventures, Saudi shareholders' and GCC shareholders' attributable equity is subject to Zakat, whilst the foreigners' share of taxable income is subject to income tax Zakat is a religious wealth tax levied on Saudis and GCC nationals, and businesses operating in Saudi Arabia that they own outright or in proportion to their shareholding. It is levied on the Zakat payers' capital resources that are not invested in fixed assets, investments, and intangible assets. Such resources include an entity's capital, net profits, retained earnings, reserves, and provisions. The rate of Zakat is 2.5% A taxpayer should register with ZITD,[3] before the end of his first financial year

---

2   Article 1 of the New Income Tax Law – Definitions:
  • Saudi Citizen: a person who holds the nationality of Saudi Arabia or who is treated as a Saudi citizen, ('for instance, citizens or nationals of Gulf Cooperation Council (GCC) member-states are treated as Saudi citizens for Zakat purposes'.
3   Zakat and Income Tax Department (ZITD), which is the taxation authority in Saudi Arabia, is a department of the Ministry of Finance.

Legal form / Characteristics	Partnership and Limited Liability Partnership (LLP) (personal companies)	Ltd (private corporation) and Plc (public corporation) (capital companies)
		A yearly Zakat and Income Tax Clearance Certificate is required in order for the taxpayer to continue to carry out business activities in Saudi Arabia

II   CORPORATION TAX

Legal form / Description	Partnership and Limited Liability Partnership (LLP) (personal companies)	Ltd (private corporation) and Plc (public corporation) (capital companies)
General description	Zakat or income tax	
Taxable entities	Partners subject to Zakat or income tax The share of equity attributable to interests owned by GCC nationals in a company is subject to Zakat. The share of profits attributable to interests owned by non-Saudi and non-GCC nationals in that company is subject to income tax	Shareholders in capital companies are subject to Zakat or income tax rather than the capital companies themselves The share of equity attributable to interests owned by GCC nationals in a company is subject to Zakat. The share of profits attributable to interests owned by non-Saudi and non-GCC nationals in that company is subject to income tax
Taxable income and Zakat base	Zakat base – Saudi partners' and GCC nationals' share of net equity Non-Saudi and non-GCC nationals' share of profit accruing to foreign individuals or entities that have foreign shareholders	
Calculation of taxable profits and Zakat base	Accounting profit is adjusted for various tax add-backs and allowances to arrive at the profits chargeable to income tax Zakat base constitutes the Saudi partners' share of an entity's capital, net profits, retained earnings, reserves, and provisions less the aggregate of fixed assets and investments	
Interest payments	Interest is allowed on an accrual basis	
Related party transactions	Transactions between related companies or persons are deemed to take place at market value	
Tax year, return and payment	Partnerships choose their financial year. All persons carrying on business in Saudi Arabia must file annual Zakat and tax returns with ZITD. For personal companies the time for filing tax returns expires 60 days after the end of the financial year Payment of the Zakat and tax dues must be made with the return Estimated income tax: in order to enforce compliance with the statutory requirements of the Income Tax Law, ZITD may use estimated taxation on a taxpayer's relevant facts and circumstances Estimated Zakat: in order to enforce compliance with the statutory requirements of the Zakat Law, ZITD may use an estimated basis such as deemed profit of 15% on the estimated annual business turnover to give the Zakat base	Capital companies choose their financial year. All corporate entities carrying on business in Saudi Arabia must file annual Zakat and tax returns with ZITD. The time for filing tax returns expires 120 days after the end of the financial year. Payment of the Zakat and tax dues must be made with the return Estimated income tax: In order to enforce compliance with the statutory requirements of the Income Tax Law, ZITD may use estimated taxation on a taxpayer's relevant facts and circumstances Estimated Zakat: in order to enforce compliance with the statutory requirements of the Zakat Law, ZITD may use an estimated basis such as deemed profit of 15% on the estimated annual business turnover to give the Zakat base
Capital gains	Capital gains of non-Saudi nationals are treated as ordinary income and taxed at the regular income tax rates	

Legal form / Description	Partnership and Limited Liability Partnership (LLP) (personal companies)	Ltd (private corporation) and Plc (public corporation) (capital companies)
Losses (after adjustments for tax)	Losses after tax adjustments can be carried forward indefinitely. However, the maximum loss that can be offset against a year's profit is 25% of the tax adjusted profits for that year. Saudi tax regulations do not provide for the carry back of losses	
Tax/Zakat group	Entities are assessed for Zakat and income tax individually	Entities are assessed for Zakat and income tax individually
Tax rates	Overall: • Income tax @ 20% on income adjusted for tax • Zakat @ 2.5% of the Zakat base	

III   TAXES FOR INDIVIDUALS

		Residents	**Non-residents**
Income Tax	General description	Tax levied on the chargeable income of a chargeable person for a year of assessment. Gulf Cooperation Council (GCC) member state nationals are subject to Zakat, and not to income tax	
	Taxable entities and taxable income	Income is assessed on profits of the following: • non-Saudi shareholders of a resident company • a resident non-Saudi natural person who does business in Saudi Arabia • a non-resident who does business in Saudi Arabia through a permanent establishment • a non-resident who derives income subject to tax from sources within Saudi Arabia • a person engaged in the field of natural gas investment • a person engaged in the production of oil and hydrocarbon materials Partners in personal companies are subject to Zakat or income tax rather than the personal companies themselves For income tax purposes, non-Saudis do not include citizens (nationals) of GCC member states. Member states of the GCC are Bahrain, Kuwait, Oman, Qatar, Saudi Arabia, and United Arab Emirates The share of equity attributable to the interests owned by GCC nationals in a personal company is subject to Zakat. The share of profits attributable to interests owned by non-GCC nationals in that company is subject to income tax Saudi nationals and expatriate employees are not subject to tax on their employment income	All income arising in Saudi Arabia of non-residents is subject to withholding tax

Income Tax	Types of taxable income	• Property income (usually rent) • Income from capital investment (interest, sale of goodwill, dividends, royalties, annuities) • Income from business activities Professional income does not include income arising from sales of real estate and personal assets *Payroll and social security taxes:* Employers are required to contribute 9% of Saudi employees' salaries for insurance relating to old age, disability and death, with another 9% contributed by the employee. The employer also pays 2% for all workers, to cover occupational hazards. The upper limit of monthly salaries subject to social insurance is SAR 45,000
	Tax year, tax assessment and tax payment	All foreign natural persons/entities carrying on business in Saudi Arabia must file annual tax returns with ZITD
	Losses	Losses adjusted for tax can be carried forward indefinitely. However, the maximum loss that can be offset against a year's profit is 25% of the profits adjusted for tax for that year. Saudi tax regulations do not provide for the carry back of losses
	Tax rates: individuals	• Income tax @ 20% on income adjusted for tax • Zakat @ 2.5% of the Zakat base
Capital Gains Tax (CGT)	General description	Capital gains on sales by non-Saudi shareholders of shares in Saudi joint stock company traded on the Saudi stock exchange are exempt from tax if the shares (investments) were acquired after the effective date of the new tax regulations (30 July 2004). Gains on the disposal of property in a business activity are also exempt from capital gains tax
	Taxable entities and chargeable assets	Foreign persons and the chargeable assets comprise investments in stocks and shares
	Calculation of gain	The gain is calculated on the basis of the realisation value less the actual historical cost adjusted by a 3-year averaged profit
	Tax year, tax assessment and tax payment	N/A
	Losses	No relief for capital losses
	Tax rates	Capital gains realised by non-Saudi nationals are treated as ordinary income and taxed at the regular income tax rates
		Domiciled	**Non-domiciled**
Inheritance Tax (IHT)	General description	There are no inheritance taxes	

IV   WITHHOLDING TAXES[4]

	Payments to non-residents[5]
Dividends	5%
Interest	5%
Management fees	20%
Royalties and payments for services to Head Office or related company	15%
On payments to artists and sportsmen	15%
Any other type of payment	15%

---

4 Penalties for failure to file withholding tax are imposed on the party whose obligation it is to withhold, at 1% per month.
5 Reduced rates of withholding tax may apply where there is an appropriate double tax treaty.

V INDIRECT TAXES

		Residents	Non-residents
Value Added Tax (VAT)	General description	No indirect taxes	

Singapore

(Henry Tan, henrytan@nexiats.com.sg)

I MAIN LEGAL FORMS

Legal form / Characteristics	Partnership and Limited Liability Partnership (LLP)	Pte Ltd (private corporation) and Limited (public corporation)
Partners/shareholders • Number • Restrictions	Partnership: • Between two and 20 partners • Restriction on transferability of ownership • Non-perpetual existence LLP: • Minimum two partners	Pte Ltd: • Minimum one shareholder and not more than 50 shareholders • Restriction on rights to transfer shares Limited: • Minimum one shareholder
Directors	LLP: • At least one manager who is ordinarily resident in Singapore	Pte Ltd and Limited: • At least one director who is ordinarily resident in Singapore
Establishment	One working day. If the application needs to be referred to another authority, it may take another 14 days to 2 months	
Registration	Accounting and Corporate Regulatory Authority (ACRA)	
Minimum capital	N/A	S$1.00
Liability	Partnership: • Unlimited LLP: • Limited to capital	Pte Ltd and Limited: • Limited
Governance	Partnership: • Business Registration Act • Partnership Agreement LLP: • Limited Liability Partnerships Act • Limited Liability Partnership Agreement	Pte Ltd and Limited: • Memorandum and Articles of Association • Companies Act, Cap 50

Legal form / Characteristics	Partnership and Limited Liability Partnership (LLP)	Pte Ltd (private corporation) and Limited (public corporation)
Audit requirements	Partnership and LLP: • Not required. LLP is required to keep accounting and other records for 7 years	Pte Ltd: • Audit exemption for small private exempt company (EPC) and dormant company. A small EPC is a private company of which no beneficial interest in its shares is held, directly or indirectly, by any corporation and having not more than 20 members, and has annual revenues of S$5m or less Limited: • Statutory requirement
Taxation	Transparent	Pte Ltd and Limited: • Corporate tax on profits
Usage	Professional practices	Small and medium-sized enterprises (SMEs) and listed companies

II CORPORATION TAX

Legal form / Description	Resident corporation[1]	Permanent establishment (PE)
General description	Corporate income tax	
Taxable entities	Corporations incorporated or effectively managed in Singapore	PE located in Singapore
Taxable income	Profits derived from or accrued in Singapore and foreign sourced income if received in Singapore Foreign-sourced dividends, foreign branch profits and foreign-sourced service income received in Singapore are exempt from tax if conditions are met	Profits derived from or accrued in Singapore
Calculation of taxable profits	Accounting profits reported in the financial statements prepared under generally accepted accounting principles are adjusted in accordance with specific rules in the Singapore Income Tax Act to arrive at the taxable profits	
Interest payments	Deductible if wholly incurred in the production of income	
Related party transactions	Arm's length principle applies	
Tax year, return and payment	The basis period of any Year of Assessment (YA) generally refers to the financial year ending in the year preceding the YA The YA2008 tax return must be filed by 30 November 2008. From YA2009 onwards, the filing deadline is 31 October of each year Income tax payment is due within one month after the date of issue of the notice of assessment	
Capital gains	No capital gains tax	
Losses	May be carried forward, subject to conditions Up to S$100,000 may be carried back to the YA immediately preceding the current YA, subject to conditions	
Tax group	Group relief available for Singapore incorporated companies, subject to conditions	
Tax rate	Currently: 18% Partial tax exemption is given on normal chargeable income (excluding Singapore franked dividends) of up to S$300,000 as follows: • 75% of the first S$10,000 • 50% of the next S$290,000	

---

1 A company is resident in Singapore if the management and control of its business is exercised in Singapore.

III TAXES FOR INDIVIDUALS

		Residents	Non-residents
Income Tax	General description	Income tax levied on a territorial basis	
	Taxable entities and taxable income	Individuals who have worked or were physically present in Singapore for 183 days or more in the calendar year immediately preceding the YA concerned (excludes director of a company) or who have established a permanent home in Singapore Income derived from or accrued in Singapore	Income derived from or accrued in Singapore
		All income derived from or accrued in Singapore unless specifically exempted	
	Tax year, tax assessment and tax payment	The basis period of any YA is the calendar year ending in the year preceding the YA. For business income, the basis period is the financial year ending in the year preceding the YA Returns should be filed by 15 April following the year-end Income tax payment is due within one month after the date of issue of the notice of assessment	
	Losses	Business losses may be carried forward, subject to conditions Business losses of up to S$100,000 may be carried back to the YA immediately preceding the current YA, subject to conditions	
	Tax rates	Tax rates between 0% and 20%	Employment income – higher of 15% or the amount of tax payable on such income by a resident in the same circumstances All income other than employment income – 20%
Capital Gains Tax (CGT)	General description	No CGT, although gains on the disposal of property may be subject to income tax	

		Domiciled	Non-domiciled
Inheritance Tax (IHT)	General description	Estate duty has been removed for deaths occurring on or after 15 February 2008	

IV   WITHHOLDING TAXES

	Payments to non-residents[2]
Dividends	No withholding tax on dividend payment
Interest	15%
Royalties	10%
On payments to artists and sportsmen	• 15% of the gross income/fees payable to the foreign non-resident professional or • The non-resident rate of 20% if the foreign non-resident professional elects to be taxed on net income

---

2   Reduced rates of withholding tax may apply where there is an appropriate double tax treaty.

V   INDIRECT TAXES

<table>
<tr><th></th><th></th><th>Residents</th><th>Non-residents</th></tr>
<tr><td rowspan="7">Value Added Tax (VAT)</td><td>Entities being obliged to levy VAT</td><td colspan="2">Taxable persons</td></tr>
<tr><td>Taxable activities</td><td colspan="2">Levied on the supply of goods and services</td></tr>
<tr><td>Taxable activities – zero rated (examples)</td><td colspan="2">Goods exported overseas</td></tr>
<tr><td>Exemptions (examples)</td><td colspan="2">Sale and lease of residential properties and certain financial services</td></tr>
<tr><td>Tax rates</td><td colspan="2">With effect from 1 July 2007 – 7%</td></tr>
<tr><td>Administrative obligations</td><td>GST returns generally filed quarterly</td><td></td></tr>
<tr><td colspan="2">Stamp Duty Land Tax</td><td colspan="2" rowspan="2">Stamp duty is applicable on executed documents relating to properties or interest in properties and shares or interest in shares</td></tr>
<tr><td colspan="2">Stamp Duty</td></tr>
</table>

Slovak Republic

(RECTE AUDÍT sro, Bratislava, office@recte.sk)

I MAIN LEGAL FORMS

Legal form / Characteristics	Partnership and Limited Liability Partnership (LLP)	Ltd (private corporation) and Plc (public corporation)
Partners/shareholders • Number • Restrictions	Partnership – at least two persons/ shareholders LLP – at least one unlimited partner and at least one limited partner	Ltd – at least one, maximum 50 partners Plc – at least one, if the shareholder is a corporation or at least two
Directors	Partnership – all shareholders LLP – unlimited partner	Ltd – at least one executive Plc – Board of Directors
Establishment	Partnership agreement	Establishment contract (Plc) and Articles of Association (Ltd), both notarised
Registration	The request for registration to the Commercial Register must be placed within 90 days of the establishment of the company	
Minimum capital	Partnership – no requirements LLP – no requirements regarding the minimum capital, but the input (deposit) of the partner with limited liability must be at least €250	Ltd – €5,000, each shareholder minimum €750 Plc – €25,000
Liability	Partnership – unlimited liability of partners and company LLP – at least one partner with unlimited and at least one with limited liability who is liable up to the amount of unpaid capital	Shareholders (Plc) – no liability Ltd – limited up to the amount of unpaid capital
Governance	No specific rules	Ltd – partnership agreement/by general meeting Plc – partnership agreement, Board of Directors, Supervisory Board, General Meeting

Legal form / Characteristics	Partnership and Limited Liability Partnership (LLP)	Ltd (private corporation) and Plc (public corporation)

Audit requirements	Audit is obligatory, when the accounting entity:
	
	• is a corporation, which has fulfilled in the last year at least two of these criteria:
	  – an (adjusted) average number of employers of over 20
	  – a balance sheet total of over SKK 20m
	  – a net turnover overreach SKK 40m
	• is a public corporation (Plc)
	• is subject to special rules	

Taxation	Corporate tax: 19%	

II CORPORATION TAX

Legal form / Description	Resident corporation	Permanent establishment (PE)
General description	Corporate tax	
Taxable entities	Corporations incorporated in Slovak Republic and/or overseas companies with central management and control located in the Slovak Republic	PE located in the Slovak Republic
Taxable income	Income from worldwide sources	Income arising in the Slovak Republic
Calculation of taxable profits	Taxable profit is based on accounting profit adjusted under the tax law	Same, or on negotiation basis with tax authority
Interest payments	All interest payments are considered to be business expenses and are deductible (Valid as of 1 January 2009 – Thin Capitalisation Rule: • applies to credits and loans provided between related parties (domestic or foreign) • related party exists if the creditor has at least 25% direct or indirect participation in the share capital of the debtor or reversed • interest paid on the amount by which the average balance of credits and loans provided by the related parties during the taxable period exceeds six times the equity reported at the end of the preceding taxable period will not be treated as tax deductible item • applies only if the average balance of credits and loans exceeds the amount of SKK 100m per year; the average balance is to be calculated on a monthly or on a quarterly basis)	
Related party transactions	All related party transactions must take place on arm's length basis	
Tax year, return and payment	Tax year is the calendar year or a financial year agreed with the authorities Returns must be filed within 3 months of the year or a financial year-end and the income tax due is to be paid in this term. Advance payment must be made monthly or quarterly in advance	
Capital gains	Treated as income	
Losses	Tax losses may be carried forward 5 years	
Tax group	None	
Tax rate	19%	

III TAXES FOR INDIVIDUALS

		Residents	**Non-residents**
Income Tax	General description	Tax levied on the chargeable income of a chargeable person for a year of assessment	
	Taxable entities and taxable income	Residents are taxed on their worldwide income	Non-resident individuals are subject to income tax
	Types of taxable income	• Property income (usually rent) • Income from capital investment (interest, sale of goodwill, royalties, annuities) • Income from business activities • Employment income	
	Calculation of income	Employment income – all payments in cash, most benefits. Only a limited number of benefits are not taxable From the income you have to deduct: • health insurance: 4% • permanent health insurance: 1.4% • old age insurance: 4% • disability insurance: 3% • unemployment insurance: 1% Individuals have the right to deduct a non-taxable sum of tax base (monthly: SKK 8,208) from their income, to pay tax from a lower sum – deduction of a non-taxable sum can be used in one month only by one employer (subject to restrictions)	
	Tax year, tax assessment and tax payment	Tax year is the calendar year Tax return must be filed by 31 March the following year and the due income tax also paid in this term	
	Losses	Losses can be offset against income in the subsequent 5 years	
	Tax rates	19%	
Capital Gains Tax (CGT)	Taxable entities and chargeable assets	No CGT	

		Domiciled	**Non-domiciled**
Inheritance Tax (IHT)	Taxable entities and chargeable assets	No IHT	

IV WITHHOLDING TAXES

	Payments to non-residents[1]
Dividends	Nil
Interest	19%
Royalties	19%
On payments to artists and sportsmen	Income to artists and sportsmen is treated as income for tax purposes

1 Reduced rates of withholding tax may apply where there is an appropriate double tax treaty.

V INDIRECT TAXES

		Residents	Non-residents
Value Added Tax (VAT)	General description	Tax on the supply of goods and services	
	Entities being obliged to levy VAT	19% on the entities that are VAT registered	
	Taxable activities	Supplies of goods and services in Slovakia by a taxable subject, imports of goods, acquisition of goods for consideration within the territory of Slovakia from another Member State of the EU etc	
	Taxable activities – zero rated (examples)	Postal and financial services, healthcare, social help services, education, services related to sport, culture, export of goods and services, insurance services, etc	
	Exemptions (examples)	None	
	Refund of VAT	Possible only to VAT-registered subjects, after request submission	
	Tax liability	VAT-registered subjects. The registration is due when the subject's turnover exceeds SKK 1.5m in the preceding 12 months (valid as of 1 January 2009: €35,000 in the preceding 12 months)	
	Tax rates	• Standard rate = 19% • Reduced rate: 10% for pharmaceuticals, books • Zero rate = 0% (export of goods and services)	
	Administrative obligations	Registration (see Tax liability above)	
Stamp Duty Land Tax		None	
Stamp Duty		None	

South Africa

(Keith du Preez, Keith@nexiasa,com)

I MAIN LEGAL FORMS

Legal form / Characteristics	Partnership and Limited Liability Partnership (LLP)	(Pty) Ltd (private corporation) and Ltd (public corporation)
Partners /shareholders • Number • Restrictions	Partnership: maximum 20 LLP: maximum 50 Partnership: both natural and juristic persons LLP: only natural persons	Private: minimum one and maximum 50 Public: minimum seven and no maximum Both natural and juristic persons
Directors	Partnership: N/A. LLP: as per private company	Private: minimum one and maximum subject to Articles of Association Public: minimum two and maximum subject to Articles of Association
Establishment	Partnership: by partnership agreement LLP: registration with Companies and Intellectual Property Registration Office (CIPRO)	Private and public: registration with Companies and Intellectual Property Registration Office (CIPRO)
Registration	Partnership: N/A LLP: registration with CIPRO	Registration with CIPRO
Minimum capital	N/A	R1.00
Liability	Partnership: no limited liability LLP: limited for partners other than the general partner	Both have limited liability
Governance	Partnership: partnership agreement LLP: per King II, Companies Act 1973, as amended, and the Memorandum and Articles of Association	Per King II, Companies Act 1973, as amended, and the Memorandum and Articles of Association
Audit requirements	Partnership: no audit required LLP: audit required	Both public and private are required to be audited

Characteristics / Legal form	Partnership and Limited Liability Partnership (LLP)	(Pty) Ltd (private corporation) and Ltd (public corporation)
Taxation	Partnership: at individual rates LLP: at corporate rates	At corporate rates
Usage	Partnership: auditors, attorneys, doctors and other professionals, and small unregistered businesses LLP: auditors, attorneys, doctors and other professionals wanting business continuation	Private: small businesses, investment holding Public: all types of businesses including listed entities

II   CORPORATION TAX

Legal form / Description	Resident corporation	Permanent establishment (PE)
General description	Levied on taxable income	
Taxable entities	Entities incorporated in South Africa	Branches or agencies of foreign entities
Taxable income	Worldwide income subject to certain exemptions for activities undertaken outside South Africa	South African source income
Calculation of taxable profits	Gross receipts minus exemptions and allowable deductions	
Interest payments	Deductible, subject to thin capitalisation rules	
Related party transactions	Transactions not carried out at arm's length may be brought within the ambit of the anti-avoidance legislation	
Tax year, return and payment	Any financial year of the company ending during the calendar year in question. Taxes paid based on an estimated value with two instalments and a final top-up	
Capital gains	50% of worldwide gains taxed at corporate tax rate	
Losses	Losses may be carried forward indefinitely provided entity is trading	
Tax group	Asset transfers only. No tax consolidation of profits	
Tax rate	• Standard rate 28% • Allowances for small business • 33% for businesses engaged in certain activities and branches of overseas companies	

III   TAXES FOR INDIVIDUALS

		Residents	**Non-residents**
Income Tax	General description	Taxed on worldwide income	Taxed on income from South African sources or deemed South African sources
	Taxable entities and taxable income	A natural person ordinarily resident in South Africa or anyone who spends in the country more than 91 days per tax year in the current year and in the previous 5 years and in aggregate more than 915 days during the previous 5 tax years	A natural person ceases to be a resident on the day he leaves South Africa if he remains outside South Africa for a continuous period for at least 330 days
	Types of taxable income	• Employment income • Business income • Interest • Rentals • Royalties • Pensions	• Pensions • Rentals • Royalties
	Calculation of income	Aggregate of gross income less exempt income	
	Tax year, tax assessment and tax payment	1 March to the last day of February No return is required for persons whose sole income is derived from remuneration and does not exceed R120,000 per annum. Exemption for submission of returns where other income is beyond the threshold may be granted upon application Remuneration subject to monthly PAYE deductions but taxpayers obliged to also become provisional taxpayers if income from other sources exceeds certain levels. Provisional taxes payable based on an estimated value with two instalments and a final top up	
	Losses	May be carried forward indefinitely	
	Tax rates	Progressive block rates Maximum marginal rate of 40%	
Capital Gains Tax (CGT)	General description	Receipts and accruals of a capital nature subject to CGT with effect from 1 October 2001	
	Taxable entities and chargeable assets	Capital gains made on disposal of assets owned anywhere in the world	Capital gains made on disposal of fixed property situated in South Africa, including any interest in fixed property
	Calculation of gain	Aggregate gain set off against assessed capital gain losses brought forward. Net gain is multiplied by inclusion rate and then included in income	
	Tax year, tax assessment and tax payment	Individuals – 1 March to last day of February Taxpayers obliged to become provisional taxpayers if capital gain exceeds certain levels. Taxes payable on final top up 7 months after year-end	
	Losses	Carried forward indefinitely	
	Tax rates	Natural persons and special trusts – 25% of gain included in income and taxed at progressive block rates	

		Domiciled	Non-domiciled
Inheritance Tax (IHT)	General description	Estate duty and donations taxes are levied	
	Taxable entities and chargeable assets	Estate duty: all assets of deceased estates, as well as amounts regarded as property of the estate Donations tax payable by donor on any gratuitous disposal subject to exemptions	Only applicable to South African assets Exempt from donations tax
	Calculation of charge	Estate duty: total value of estate, after various deductions Donations tax – market value of asset	All non-South African assets are ignored
	Taxable events	Duty payable on a deceased estate Donations tax payable when donation is made	Duty payable on a deceased estate Exempt from donations tax
	Allowances	Estate duty: abatement of R3.5m and certain other deductions Donations tax: certain entities are exempt Different levels of allowances exist	Estate duty: abatement of R3.5m and certain other deductions Donation tax: unlimited
	Tax rates	20%	Estate duty – 20% Donations tax – 0%

IV   WITHHOLDING TAXES

	Payments to non-residents[1]
Dividends	Nil
Interest	Nil
Royalties	12%
On payments to artists and sportsmen	15%

---

1   Reduced rates of withholding tax may apply where there is an appropriate double tax treaty.

V   INDIRECT TAXES

		Residents	Non-residents
Value Added Tax (VAT)	Entities being obliged to levy VAT	Any vendor whose taxable supplies exceed R300,000 per annum	
	Taxable activities	Any activity carried on in South Africa in the furtherance of an enterprise, other than exempt supplies	
	Taxable activities – zero rated (examples)	• Exports of goods and services • Supply of an enterprise or part of as a going concern • Petrol and distillate fuel oil • Certain foodstuffs	
	Exemptions (examples)	• Supply of accommodation in any dwelling by letting • Supply of transport by road or rail to fare-paying passengers • Educational services	
	Refund of VAT	Upon assessment	At Customs upon departure
	Tax liability	Settlement by due date of return	
	Tax rates	Standard rate of 14%	
	Administrative obligations	Submission of returns	Keep proof of purchases
Transfer Duty		Natural persons – sliding scale 0–8% Other – 8%	
Stamp Duty		Levied on long-term leases at a fixed rate of 0.5% on the quantifiable amount of the lease. No stamp duty on transactions subject to VAT	

Spain

(David Jiménez, Pedrosa-Lagos, davidjimenez@pedrosalagos.com)

I MAIN LEGAL FORMS

Legal form / Characteristics	Partnership-like entities (Sociedad Colectiva, Sociedad Comanditaria Simple, Sociedad Comanditaria por Acciones, Contratos de Cuentas en Participación)	Limited Liability Company (Sociedad de Responsabilidad Limitada) and Joint Stock Company (Sociedad Anónima)
	There are three forms of commercial partnership-like entities: a *sociedad colectiva* (SC), which is similar to a general partnership; a *sociedad comanditaria* (SCm), which is similar to a limited partnership; and a *sociedad comanditaria por acciones* (SCmpa), which is similar to a limited partnership in which the participation of the limited partners is represented by shares	A *sociedad de responsabilidad limitada* (SRL) is a limited liability company, suited for family business and wholly owned subsidiaries of foreign companies. The capital of a SRL is divided into quotas that cannot be represented by security instruments and may be transferred only by notarial deed. A *sociedad anónima* (SA) is a corporation in which the shareholders' liability is the amount of their contributions to capital. The capital of an SA is represented by securities that can be easily transferred. The SA is the corporate form used by most private and all public companies. An SA's financial statements must be published in the Trade Registry and must also be audited if the company reaches a certain size

Legal form / Characteristics	Partnership-like entities (Sociedad Colectiva, Sociedad Comanditaria Simple, Sociedad Comanditaria por Acciones, Contratos de Cuentas en Participación)	Limited Liability Company (Sociedad de Responsabilidad Limitada) and Joint Stock Company (Sociedad Anónima)
Partners/shareholders • Number • Restrictions	A SC must be incorporated by a minimum of two partners A SCm is an association with two kinds of partners: (i) general partners, having the same status, rights and obligations as partners in a SC (ie joint and several liability); and (ii) limited partners, whose liability is limited to the amount of their contributions A SCmpa is similar to a SCm except that the capital contributed by the limited partners is divided into shares that can be represented by security instruments	SA and SL may vary from one shareholder to an unlimited number
Directors	All the partners are allowed to manage a SC Only general partners may manage a SCm A SCmpa must be managed by the general partners	Both SA and SL may be managed by: • a sole director • several directors acting individually • two directors acting jointly or • a Board of Directors. The Board of Directors may delegate most of its functions to one or more general managers
Establishment	Articles of Incorporation or Partnership deed	
Registration	N/A	Both SA and SL must be registered in the Trade Registry of the province where the company is domiciled
Minimum capital	N/A	SA: €60,101.21 SL: €3,005.06
Liability	Partners in a SC are exposed to unlimited liability for the payment of business debts, as are the general partners in a SCm or a SCmpa. The general partners of both SCms and SCmpas may be limited liability companies	SA and SL: the shareholders' liability is the amount of their contributions to capital
Governance	Partners	SA: all decisions outside the management's authority are made by the general shareholders' meetings SL: all decisions outside the management's authority must be adopted by the quota holders at a quota holders' meeting

Legal form / Characteristics	Partnership-like entities (Sociedad Colectiva, Sociedad Comanditaria Simple, Sociedad Comanditaria por Acciones, Contratos de Cuentas en Participación)	Limited Liability Company (Sociedad de Responsabilidad Limitada) and Joint Stock Company (Sociedad Anónima)
Audit requirements	N/A	Financial statements must be audited by independent auditors. Small corporations are exempt from this obligation
		Small companies are corporations that meet at least two of the following three criteria in 2 consecutive years:
		• their assets do not exceed €2.85m
		• their annual sales are less than €5.7m
		• the average number of employees is less than 50
Taxation	Subject to corporate income tax	
Usage	SC, SCm and SCmpa are rarely used as business entities	SA and SL are the most common forms of business entities

II   CORPORATION TAX

Legal form / Description	Resident corporation	Permanent establishment (PE)
General description	Corporation tax	Non-residents income tax
Taxable entities	Corporations incorporated and managed in Spain	PE located in Spain
Taxable income	Worldwide profits with considerations for double taxation treaties	Profits earned in Spain
Calculation of taxable profits	Accounting profit is adjusted for various tax add-backs and allowances to arrive to profits chargeable to corporation tax (PCTCT)	
Interest payments	• Deductible • Thin capitalisation rule equal to 3:1[1]	
Related party transactions	All related party transactions must take place on arm's length basis	
Tax year, return and payment	• Companies may choose their own tax years • Returns must be filed within 25 calendar days after a period of 6 months following the end of the taxable year • Tax liability must be paid at the time of filing	
Capital gains	Treated as income	
Losses[2]	Net operating tax losses may be carried forward 15 years	
Tax group	Group relief allowed within a Spanish group	
Tax rate	• 30% standard rate • Small companies have specific rates, 25% for the first €120,202.41 of the benefit and 30% for the rest	

---

1   Not applicable to EU-resident entities.
2   There are special rules allowing the company to utilise other losses such as capital losses and loan relationship deficits.

III TAXES FOR INDIVIDUALS

		Residents	Non-residents
Income Tax	General description	Tax levied on the chargeable income of a chargeable person for a year of assessment	
	Taxable entities and taxable income	Residents are taxed on their worldwide income	Non-residents are taxable on all income arising in Spain
	Types of taxable income	General taxable income: • employment from personal services or pensions • income from business activities • income from real estate Savings taxable income: • income from capital investments (interest, sale of goodwill, dividends, royalties, annuities) except from related entities • capital gains	
	Tax year, tax assessment and tax payment	• Tax year is the calendar year • Entrepreneurs and professionals must file returns and make advance payments quarterly, otherwise residents prepare an annual return • Return must be filed in May/June each year • Tax liability must be paid at the time of filing, also you could pay 60% at the time of filing and 40% in November	
	Losses	Losses can be offset against income in the subsequent 4 years	

	Tax rates	• General incomes (depends on the autonomous regions):
		  – Up to €17,707 24%
		  – €17,707–33,007 28%
		  – €33,007–53,407 37%
		  – €53,407 and above 43%
		
		• Savings incomes:
		  – Unique rate 18%	

Capital Gains Tax (CGT)	General description	There is no specific capital gains tax. Capital gains are included as part of either the personal income tax or the non-residents income tax	

		Spanish resident	Non-Spanish resident
Inheritance and Gift Tax (IGT)	General description	The inheritance and gift tax (IGT) applies to transfers of property on death or by inter vivos gift, including amounts received from certain life insurance policies when the beneficiary is not the contracting party. IGT is imposed on the recipient of the transfer. The tax is levied only if the recipient is an individual	
	Taxable entities and chargeable assets	If the beneficiary is a corporation, such transfers will be deemed to give rise to capital gains subject to corporate income tax (CIT)	
	Calculation of charge	The taxable amount is equal to the real value of the assets received minus deductible debts, liens, and encumbrances corresponding to each heir, legatee, donee or beneficiary	
	Taxable events	• Transfers of property on death • Transfers of property by inter vivos gift	

		Spanish resident	Non-Spanish resident
Inheritance and Gift Tax (IGT)	Allowances	The law provides for a system of general allowances, dependent on circumstances. The autonomous regions may establish different systems provided these do not result in a reduction of the total tax burden for IGT purposes	
	Tax rates	The tax rates depend on: the amount received by the heir, legatee, donee or beneficiary; his/her relationship with the deceased, donor or contracting party and the net worth of the recipient prior to the acquisition. The tax rate also depends on the competent Autonomous Region concerned	

IV   WITHHOLDING TAXES

	Payments to non-residents[3]
Dividends	18%
Interest	18%
Royalties	24%[4]
On payments to artists and sportsmen	24%

3   Reduced rates of withholding tax may apply where there is an appropriate double tax treaty.
4   Withholding tax rate is 10% if royalties are paid by a Spanish resident entity or a PE located in Spain.

V   INDIRECT TAXES

		Residents	**Non-residents**
Value Added Tax (VAT)	General description	Tax on the supply of goods and services (VAT)	
	Entities being obliged to levy VAT	VAT chargeable on the supply of goods and services by entrepreneurs and professionals	
	Taxable activities	Supply of goods and services	
	Taxable activities – zero rated (examples)	N/A	
	Exemptions (examples)	• Exports from EU and other transactions related to international goods traffic • Intra-EU supplies of goods • Certain public interest activities (it covers certain medical and sanitary supplies, the supply of services for the benefit of the community, educational services, athletic or cultural services, and the supply of certain waste products for recycling) • Financial and insurance transactions • Certain real property transactions. The general principle regarding transfers of ownership of land is that it will be taxable only when it is possible to use it for building purposes • Other exemptions: public lotteries, postal services, or services rendered by temporary unions of entrepreneurs (UTEs), Economic Interest Groups (EIGs), or European Economic Interest Groups (EEIGs) to their members provided, among other requirements, the services rendered by the members are also exempt	
	Refund of VAT	Taxpayers with excess input VAT may carry forward the excess and deduct it on subsequent tax returns. In the tax return corresponding to the last assessment period of the year, a taxpayer may choose between claiming a refund of the excess VAT paid or carrying the excess forward to subsequent periods. The tax authorities must pay refunds within 6 months. After this period, the tax authorities must pay delayed interests. In most cases, refunds are subject to substantial delays A taxpayer that, during the current or the previous taxable year, made exports, intra-EU supplies of goods or transactions deemed to be the equivalent of such supplies, with a total value of more than €120,202.42 may ask for a refund of excess VAT paid in each monthly filing period. Pursuant to regulations, the same rule applies in the case of certain specific activities	
	Tax rates	• Standard rate = 16% • Reduced rate = 7% • Exports = 0% • Necessities = 4%	
Tax on real property		A local tax levied by municipalities	
Transfer tax and stamp duty		The transfer tax and stamp duty governs three different taxes: • property transfer tax which is designed to tax all non-business transfers of property • tax on corporate events • tax on documented legal acts which is levied as a consequence of the issuance of certain kinds of documents to execute a transaction	

Sri Lanka

(Sanjanya Bandara, sbbr@sltnet.lk)

I   MAIN LEGAL FORMS

Legal form / Characteristics	Partnership and Limited Liability Partnership (LLP)	Ltd (private corporation) and Plc (public corporation)
Partners/shareholders • Number • Restrictions	• Minimum two • Maximum 20 No concept of LLPs	• Minimum two • Maximum – no limit
Directors	N/A	Minimum two
Establishment	Partnership Ordinance	Companies Act No 07 of 2007
Registration	With local authority	With Registrar of Companies
Minimum capital	Not specified	
Liability	Unlimited	Limited to share capital
Governance	• Partnership Ordinance • Local authority law	Companies Act No 07 of 2007
Audit requirements	Not compulsory	Compulsory
Taxation	Transparent, partners are taxed on the share of income	Compulsory at the rates specified in the Inland Revenue Act
Usage	Unlimited	Unlimited but generally used by large and listed businesses

II   CORPORATION TAX

Legal form / Description	Resident corporation	Permanent establishment (PE)
General description	Incorporated in Sri Lanka. Control or management of business exercised from Sri Lanka	Controlled from abroad
Taxable entities	Company and body of person	PE in Sri Lanka
Taxable income	All income arising in Sri Lanka or income deemed to arise under the statutes is subject to tax	Income arising or derived from Sri Lanka
Calculation of taxable profits	Certain expenditure incurred for the production of income can be deducted	
Interest payments	Business interest can be deducted, subject to thin capitalisation rules	
Related party transactions	Must be at arm's length value	
Tax year, return and payment	• Tax payable on account is estimated using the tax liability of the previous year • Final liability must be paid within 6 months of the end of the year of assessment • Return of income shall be submitted by 30 September	
Capital gains	Exempt from income tax	
Losses	Losses can be set off against the total statutory income up to 35% of total statutory income. Balance can be carried forward	
Tax group	No group taxation	
Tax rate	• Listed companies 33 1/3%, companies engaged in tourism and construction 15%, exporters 15% and other companies 35% • Dividend tax is 10% on gross dividend • Deemed dividend tax rate is 15%	

III   TAXES FOR INDIVIDUALS

		Residents	Non-residents
Income Tax	Taxable entities and taxable income	Persons present in Sri Lanka for 183 days or more during any year of assessment Residents taxed on worldwide income	Non-residents are taxed on income arising in Sri Lanka
	Types of taxable income	• Employment income • Business income • Interest income • Net annual value • Dividend income	
	Calculation of income	Certain expenditure incurred for the production of business income can be deducted	
	Tax year, tax assessment and tax payment	• Tax paid on PAYE basis with the employer liable for any shortfall in remittance • Tax payable in four quarterly instalments	
	Losses	May be carried forward and set off	
	Tax rates	Income tax – progressive rates from 5%–35%	
Capital Gains Tax (CGT)	Taxable entities and chargeable assets	No capital gains tax	

		Domiciled	Non-domiciled
Inheritance Tax (IHT)	General description	There is no IHT in Sri Lanka	

IV   WITHHOLDING TAXES

	Payments to non-residents[1]
Dividends	10%
Interest	15%
Royalties	10%

---

1   Reduced rates of withholding tax may apply where there is an appropriate double tax treaty.

V INDIRECT TAXES

		Residents	**Non-residents**
Value Added Tax (VAT)	General description	Goods and services tax and turnover tax	
	Entities being obliged to levy VAT	Individual, partnership, company and body of person	
	Taxable activities	Any activity carried on as business, trade, profession and vocation	
	Taxable activities – zero rated (examples)	Exports, repair of foreign ships or aircraft, international transportation of goods and passengers	
	Exemptions (examples)	Pharmaceutical products and drugs, rice, rice flour, green leaf	
	Refund of VAT	Refunds are entitled only for zero-rates suppliers	
	Tax liability	On value of supply at the time of supply	
	Tax rates	0%, 5%, 15%, 20%	
		Proposed to remove 5% with effect from 1 January 2009	
	Administrative obligations	Submit VAT returns on monthly/quarterly basis	
Stamp Duty Land Tax		N/A	
Stamp Duty		On receipt and discharge	
Nation Building Levy		Proposed to introduce 1% turnover subject to certain exemptions with effect from 1 January 2009 for 2 years	

Sweden

(Per Åke Bois, perake.bois@nexia.se)

I   MAIN LEGAL FORMS

Legal form / Characteristics	Partnership and Limited Liability Partnership (LLP)	Ltd (private corporation) and Plc (public corporation)
Partners/shareholders • Number • Restrictions	• Two or more • None	• One or more • None
Directors	Management by partners	Management by directors[1]
Establishment	Registration with Swedish Companies Registration Office	
Registration	Swedish Companies Registration Office (*Bolagsverket*) and the Swedish Tax Agency (*Skatteverket*)	
Minimum capital	None	Ltd: SEK 100,000 Plc: SEK 500,000
Liability	Unlimited Limited for LLPs	There is no personal liability, unless half of the share capital is used
Governance	None	Ltd: Board of Directors can appoint a CEO, but it is not mandatory Plc: Board of Directors must appoint a CEO
Audit requirements	None	Audit required: • Ltd: by approved public accountant • Plc: by authorised public accountant
Taxation	Partners are subject to taxation on their net income	Subject to corporation tax on their net income
Usage	Smaller businesses and start-ups	Ltd: usually large businesses Plc: only large businesses

---

1   Private company must have at least one director. Public company must have at least three directors.

II CORPORATION TAX

Legal form / Description	Swedish resident corporation	Permanent establishment (PE)
General description	Federal tax on income of corporations	
Taxable entities	Corporations registered with the Swedish Companies Registration Office	PE located in Sweden
Taxable income	Worldwide profits	Profits arising from the Swedish PE
Calculation of taxable profits	Accounting profit is adjusted for various tax add-backs and allowances to arrive to profits chargeable to corporation tax (PCTCT)	
Interest payments	Deductible. No thin capitalisation rules	
Related party transactions	All related party transactions must take place on an arm's length basis	
Tax year, return and payment	Financial year must end 31 December, 30 April, 30 June or 31 August Returns are due on 2 May of the assessment year Preliminary tax payments are due monthly with the balancing amount payable 90 days after the assessment is issued in December	
Capital gains	Capital gains on business shares are exempt from taxation There is no deduction on capital losses on business related shares Treated as income	
Losses[2]	Net operating losses may be carried forward indefinitely but must be offset against the next available profits	
Tax group	A group comprises a parent company and its 90% subsidiaries	PE:[3] N/A
Tax rate	28%	

2 There are special rules allowing the company to utilise other losses such as capital losses and loan relationship deficits.
3 For group relief purposes.

III   TAXES FOR INDIVIDUALS

		Residents	Non-residents
Income Tax	General description	Tax levied on the chargeable income of a chargeable person for a year of assessment	
	Taxable entities and taxable income	Residents are taxed on their worldwide income	Income arising in Sweden
	Types of taxable income	• Income from capital investment (interest, sale of goodwill, dividends, royalties, annuities), property income • Income from business activities • Employment from personal services or pensions	
	Calculation of income	Partly on cash basis, partly on account basis Certain limitations on the deduction of costs	
	Tax year, tax assessment and tax payment	Tax year is the calendar year with assessments made in the following year Tax return must be filed by 2 May following the year of assessment Income not subject to withholding tax is pre-assessed and tax is paid in instalments. Preliminary tax payable is 110% of the amount in the previous year, or 105% if the final tax in the previous year was less than the preliminary tax paid Date of tax payment: 12 February of each year, final payment in autumn	
	Losses	Losses can be offset against income of the same source in subsequent years	
	Tax rates	Up to SEK 340,900 = 33% SEK 340,901–501,100 = 53% Over SEK 501,101 = 58%	25%
Capital Gains Tax (CGT)	General description	Tax on increase in the value of asset between acquisition and disposal	
	Taxable entities and chargeable assets	Residents who disposed: • shares • investments • immovable property	Non-residents who disposed immovable property in Sweden
	Calculation of gain	• 100% of gain on personal related immovable property is taxable • 90% of gain on business related immovable property is taxable • 100% of gain of shares	
	Tax year, tax assessment and tax payment	Tax year is the calendar year with assessments made in the following year Tax return must be filed by 2 May the following year Tax payment on 12 February, final payment in autumn	
	Losses	70% of the losses are deductible	
	Tax rates	• 30% • 22% personal related immovable property	
		Domiciled	**Non-domiciled**
Inheritance Tax (IHT)	General description	No IHTs levied	

IV   WITHHOLDING TAXES

	Payments to non-residents[4]
Dividends	30%
Interest	0%
Royalties	30%
On payments to artists and sportsmen	15%

---

4   Reduced rates of withholding tax may apply where there is an appropriate double tax treaty.

V INDIRECT TAXES

		Residents	Non-residents
Value Added Tax (VAT)	General description	Tax on the supply of goods and services	
	Entities being obliged to levy VAT	Entities making a supply of goods and services over a threshold of SEK 30,000	
	Taxable activities	• Importation of goods • Supply of taxable goods and services by an entrepreneur • Intra-Community acquisition of goods	
	Taxable activities – zero rated (examples)	Exports	
	Exemptions (examples)	Leasing and transfer of immovable property	
	Refund of VAT	Deductible as input tax and a refund to the tax account after filing of the return	Goods bought for business outside Sweden
	Tax liability	Normally suppliers of goods and services; reverse charge for certain suppliers of goods and services (eg construction premises)	
	Tax rates	• Standard rate = 25% • Food and tourism = 12% • Newspapers, transport and entertainment = 6% • Medicines, gold for investment purposes, a number of financial services including insurance and reinsurance = 0%	
	Administrative obligations	Application to the Swedish Tax Agency for VAT registration PAYE must usually be filed monthly	Application to the Swedish Tax Agency for VAT registration or refund
Stamp Duty Land Tax		Standard rate 1.5%, legal activity 3% (eg transfer of immovable property)	
Stamp Duty		Standard rate = 1% (eg loans against movable property; mortgage loans)	

Switzerland

(Andreas Baumann, Andreas.Baumann@abt.ch)

I MAIN LEGAL FORMS

Legal form / Characteristics	Partnership and Limited Liability Partnership (LLP)	Sarl/GmbH (private corporation) and SA/AG (public corporation)
Partners/shareholders • Number • Restrictions	*General partnership:* • must be formed by at least two individuals • general partnership can only be set up by individuals and not by corporations *LLP:* • unlimited number of partners (at least one partner with unlimited liability) • LLP has two kinds of partners – one must be liable for the business without any limitation, while the other's accountability can be restricted to his investment • unlimited liability partners can only be individuals, whereas those with limited liability may be corporations	Must be formed by one or more individuals or legal entities, ie companies
Directors	No legal provisions	At least one person with legal domicile in Switzerland must be registered in the register of commerce. This person must not be a managing officer, but must be capable of acting for the company
Establishment	*General or LLP*: conclusion of the partnership contract	Adoption of the Articles of Incorporation, and by appointing the necessary management
Registration	Commercial Register	The company must be entered in the Company Register of its domicile

Legal form / Characteristics	Partnership and Limited Liability Partnership (LLP)	Sarl/GmbH (private corporation) and SA/AG (public corporation)
Minimum capital	None	*Sarl/GmbH*: minimum fixed and fully paid capital of CHF 20,000 which each partner invests a minimum of CHF 100 *SA/AG*: minimum fixed capital of CHF 100,000. At least 20%, but no less than CHF 50,000, has to be paid in prior to its incorporation if registered shares are issued. Bearer shares must be fully paid in
Liability	*General partnership*: no limitation of liability *LLP*: the general partner is liable for the business without any limitation, while the limited partner's accountability can be restricted to his investment	Limited to the company's assets
Governance	No rules Governance rule for LLP for collective investments	Strong governance rules for listed companies
Audit requirements	No audit requirement, except for the LLP for collective investments	Obliged to appoint independent auditors under certain preconditions (value of assets, turnover and number of employees exceeding ten). Special requirements for listed companies.
Taxation	The partnership is not subject to a separate income tax. Income and capital is assigned to the partners Foreign partnerships (cantonal practices differ between the foreign domicile of a partnership or foreign domicile of ownership) can be taxed as corporation	Resident companies are subject to corporation tax on their profits derived anywhere in the world, except income of permanent establishment or real estate located outside Switzerland
Usage	Small and medium-sized businesses	Corporations (especially Ltd) are the most common type of companies in Switzerland

II CORPORATION TAX

Legal form / Description	Resident corporation	Permanent establishment (PE)
General description	Resident companies and PEs are subject to: • federal income tax • cantonal/municipal income tax • cantonal/municipal net worth taxes	
Taxable entities	• Companies registered in Switzerland • Central management located in Switzerland	PE in Switzerland
Taxable income	Resident companies are subject to worldwide taxation, excluding PEs and real estate abroad	At least income derived from Switzerland (foreign losses not allowable against Swiss gains)
Calculation of taxable profits	Income shown in commercial financial statements according to Swiss civil law serves as the basis for taxation. It may be adjusted by the tax authorities according to specific provisions in the tax laws (eg depreciation, accruals, contributions to reserves, open or hidden profit distributions and unbusinesslike benefits to third parties etc) The corporate net worth tax is based on the value of a corporate entity's net assets, normally equal to shareholders' net equity	
Interest payments	Subject to the debt-to-equity rules, interest payments are deductible. Interest rates may not exceed arm's length rates.	
Related party transactions	Switzerland does not have statutory transfer pricing rules. Intercompany charges should follow the arm's length principle and be justified and documented. The tax authorities accept the transfer-pricing methods by the OECD (Organisation for Economic Co-operation and Development)	
Tax year, return and payment	• The basis for income tax in respect of taxable income is the financial year • Tax returns must be filled in once a year. Deadline and payment varies between the cantons	
Capital gains	Capital gains realised on the disposal of movable business assets as well as capital gains realised on financial transactions are generally included in taxable income at the federal and cantonal levels. Special rules may apply for capital gains on real estate assets and on participations	
Losses	Tax losses may be carried forward 7 years. All kinds of losses incurred in the normal course of business are deductible	
Tax group	None	
Tax rate	• Federal direct tax levied at a flat rate of 7.8% (on gain before taxes). Rates at cantonal level vary considerably • A varying rate of 0.01% to 0.5% of the company's net equity is levied annually by the canton. No federal capital tax is levied	

III TAXES FOR INDIVIDUALS

<table>
<tr><td rowspan="10">Income Tax</td><td></td><td>Residents</td><td>Non-residents</td></tr>
<tr>
<td>General description</td>
<td>Individuals are unlimited tax liable, if they has their fiscal domicile or fiscal residence in Switzerland

Fiscal domicile: a person has the intention of permanently staying in Switzerland

Fiscal residence: a person works in Switzerland for a period of at least 30 days or stays in Switzerland (without working) for a period of at least 90 days</td>
<td>All non-residents are only limited tax liable based on an economic affiliation, eg member of partnership, holder of PE, owner of real estate, broker of real estate, foreign workers, etc</td>
</tr>
<tr>
<td>Taxable entities and taxable income</td>
<td>• Normally the individual is directly liable to taxes and has to fulfil the tax obligations

Exception: tax liability of the employer for taxes on working income of foreign individuals without working permit C

• Resident individuals are subject to personal income and net wealth taxes
• Income taxes are levied by the confederation and also by the 26 cantons and their municipalities</td>
<td>Non-resident taxpayers are subject only to Swiss taxes on certain source income (limited tax liability to Swiss derived income)</td>
</tr>
<tr>
<td>Types of taxable income</td>
<td>• Investment income
• Employment income
• Pensions
• Income from real estate
• Business and professional income
• Participation income</td>
<td></td>
</tr>
<tr>
<td>Calculation of income</td>
<td colspan="2">Addition of income and deductions of expenses. Some special rules apply</td>
</tr>
<tr>
<td>Tax year, tax assessment and tax payment</td>
<td colspan="2">• Taxes are assessed for the calendar year
• All taxpayers must file a tax return after the end of each tax period, normally the end of March (possible to extend)
• Each canton applies its own rule regarding payments</td>
</tr>
<tr>
<td>Losses</td>
<td colspan="2">Losses related to a business activity may be carried forward 7 years. In cases of restructuring there is no time limit for the consideration of losses. Special rules may apply for capital losses on real estate assets

Losses on private equity may not be carried forward as gains – with a few exceptions – these are not taxable</td>
</tr>
<tr>
<td>Tax rates</td>
<td colspan="2">• In general, Swiss income tax rates are progressive. Different rates apply for married and single taxpayers, as income of husband and wife is aggregated and taxed as one
• The maximum federal income tax rate is 11.5%
• The cantonal and municipal tax rate varies considerably. The maximum cantonal and municipal income tax rate lies, depending on the canton, between approximately 15% and 32%
• Income from participations are taxed on a reduced tax rate depending on the canton of the taxpayers domicile</td>
</tr>
</table>

		Residents	**Non-residents**
Capital Gains Tax (CGT)	General description	Capital gains are tax exempt except for gains on real estate and some special rules for gains on participation	
	Taxable entities and chargeable assets	An individual is always tax liable Private assets: • capital gains realised on the disposal of immovable assets are subject to real estate gains tax. Real estate gains tax is levied on the transfer of ownership of real estate (land or land and building) with some exemptions • capital gains realised on some special taxable participation transactions are taxed together with the ordinary income Business assets: • capital gains realised on the disposal of movable business assets are generally included in taxable income at the federal and cantonal levels • capital gains realised on the disposal of immovable assets are subject to income tax. Some cantonal regimes, however, apply a real estate gains tax	
	Calculation of gain	Special rules apply to define the real estate gains tax. For capital gains on business assets the difference between the sales price and book value of an asset is taxed	
	Tax year, tax assessment and tax payment	• Tax year: see notes for income tax • For gains realised on the disposal of immovable assets, a special tax declaration may be filed • The tax is owed according to the federal and cantonal rules	
	Losses	Losses on gains realised on the disposal of movable business property may be carried forward (see notes for income tax)	
	Tax rates	• See rates on income tax of residents • Tax rates for real estate gains depend on the amount of the gain and the period of ownership and vary considerably from canton to canton	

		Domiciled	**Non-domiciled**
Inheritance Tax (IHT)	General description	The tax is applied on net asset transfers by inheritance and donation	
	Taxable entities and chargeable assets	• Heirs – domiciled or non-domiciled – are tax liable on the domicile (canton) in which the testator resided at the time of his death • IHT on real estate property is levied on the location of the real estate in consideration of the net worth of the whole inheritance • There are no such federal taxes	
	Calculation of charge	The tax is levied on the accretion of wealth by virtue of the statutory right of inheritance or by virtue of dispositions mortis causa	
	Taxable events	Transfers by inheritance or donation	
	Allowances	Many cantons do not levy this tax on net asset transfers to spouses or children or provide special deductions	
	Tax rates	• Tax rates vary, according to the value of the inheritance and the degree of relationship between the deceased and the heir (the closer the blood relationship the lower the inheritance tax) • There is no tax on federal level • On cantonal level the rates vary from canton to canton, eg one canton does not even levy any IHT. Usually the cantons provide for progressive rates between 0% and 54%	

IV   WITHHOLDING TAXES

	Payments to non-residents[1]
Dividends	Dividends are subject to withholding tax of 35%
Interest	Interests from banks and similar institutes are subject to a withholding tax of 35% Other interests are not subject to a withholding tax
Royalties	Nil
On payments to artists and sportsmen	Payments to artists and sportsmen are subject to a federal and cantonal withholding tax. The tax rates vary from canton to canton

1   Reduced rates of withholding tax may apply where there is an appropriate double tax treaty. Dividends to corporate shareholders domiciled in the EU could benefit from the EU Parent/ Subsidiary Directive.

V   INDIRECT TAXES

		Residents	Non-residents
Value Added Tax (VAT)	General description	Provisions basically follow, with some exemptions, the rules of the 6th EU Directive	
	Entities being obliged to levy VAT	A person is liable to tax if he/she independently carries out a business or professional activity for gain, even if there is no intention to achieve profit, insofar as that person's supplies of goods, services and self-supply within Swiss territory exceed CHF 75,000 in total per annum Certain exemptions apply	
	Taxable activities	Subject to VAT are turnovers of taxable persons on: • supplies of goods and services within Swiss territory • self-supply within Swiss territory • the receipt of services from enterprises with their domicile outside Swiss territory • importation of goods	
	Taxable activities – zero rated (examples)	• Export of goods • Export of services according to art 14 al 3 of the Swiss VAT Law	
	Exemptions (examples)	Similar to Art 13 of the 6th EU Directive: • supply of postal services • hospital and medical care • education (school, courses, etc) • cultural activities (theatre, museum, libraries, etc) • insurance and reinsurance transactions • granting and negotiation of credits • transactions in shares and other securities • real estate transfers • letting and leasing of real estate	
	Refund of VAT	Recovery through VAT declaration provided that they use the VAT charged expenses for taxable services. Exceptions according to the VAT Law	Non-resident enterprises can recover Swiss VAT in two ways: • through VAT declaration (see residents) or • if certain conditions are met by yearly VAT-refund request. The request must be filed annually using standard forms, by 30 June, following the end of the related calendar year
	Tax liability	• Taxable persons • Liquidators • Directors • Companies in respect of group taxation • Liability limitation until the amount due	
	Tax rates	• 7.6% standard rate • 2.4% reduced rate for certain essential goods of daily consumption • 3.6% accommodation services • A zero rate applies to the export of goods and services. Certain goods and services are tax exempt	

		Residents	**Non-residents**
Value Added Tax (VAT)	Administrative obligations	• File in the quarterly tax declarations • Payment of tax within the legal terms	Ordinary declaration: • fiscal representative • bank account with a Swiss based bank • file in the quarterly tax declarations • payment of tax within the legal terms • declaration by yearly request (see refund of VAT): special conditions apply
Stamp Duty Land Tax		• Subject to tax is the transfer of ownership of real estate (land or land and building) as well as the economic transfer of ownership (eg sale of majority of shares of a real estate company) with some exemptions • The tax is levied from the cantons or the municipalities where the property is situated • The rate varies from canton to canton and can range from 0% to 3.3% of the consideration or estimated worth of property transferred	
Stamp Duty		• Generally levied on legal documents of various kinds (eg subscription of shares, trading of securities and conclusion of certain insurance contract) • The confederation has the exclusive right to levy this tax • The rate varies from 0.06%–5% • Certain transactions, especially in the case of reorganisation are exempt from tax. Tax free is the subscription of share capital to an amount of CHF 1m	

Taiwan

(Cathy Wu, cathycpa@ms72.hinet.net)

I MAIN LEGAL FORMS

Legal form / Characteristics	Partnership	Ltd, Ltd by shares (private corporation) and Plc (Public Limited Company)
Partners/shareholders • Number • Restrictions	• Two • None	One shareholder for Ltd and two individual shareholders or one corporate shareholder for Ltd by shares and Plc
Directors	None	One director for Ltd and three directors and one supervisor for Ltd by shares and Plc
Establishment	Partnership deed	Articles of Incorporation
Registration	Ministry of Economic Affairs or City Government	
Minimum capital	None	NTD 250,000 for Ltd and NTD 500,000 for Ltd by shares
Liability	Unlimited	Limited
Audit requirements	None	• Capital over NTD 30m financial audit required and • Annual sale over NTD 100m tax return audit required
Taxation	Assessed directly on partners	Corporation tax on worldwide profits

II   CORPORATION TAX

Legal form / Description	Resident corporation	Permanent establishment (PE)
General description	Corporation tax	
Taxable entities	Corporations with a head office in Taiwan	PE located in Taiwan
Taxable income	Worldwide profits with considerations for double taxation treaties	Income arising in Taiwan
Calculation of taxable profits	Accounting profit is adjusted for various tax add-backs and allowances to arrive to profits chargeable to corporation tax (PCTCT)	
Interest payments	Interest on loans is deductible, no thin capitalisation restrictions	
Related party transactions	All related party transactions must take place on arm's length basis	
Tax year, return and payment	Tax year is the calendar year	
Capital gains	• Capital gain from sale of listed company stocks is tax-free • Capital gain from sale of property is taxable	
Losses	Net operating losses may be carried forward for 5 years if proper procedures are followed	
Tax group	Consolidated returns permissible for 90% subsidiaries of the parent	N/A
Tax rate	• NTD 0–50,000 = 0% • NTD 50,001–100,000 = 15% not exceeding 50% of taxable income over NTD 50,000 • NTD 100,001 and above = 25%	

III TAXES FOR INDIVIDUALS

		Residents	Non-residents
Income Tax	General description	Tax levied on the chargeable income of a chargeable person for a year of assessment	
	Taxable entities and taxable income	Residents are taxed on their worldwide income	Income arising in Taiwan
	Types of taxable income	• Property income (usually rent) • Income from capital investment (interest, sale of goodwill, dividends, royalties, annuities) • Income from business activities • Employment from personal services or pensions	
	Calculation of income	Gross consolidated income less standard deductions or itemised deductions and personal exemptions	
	Tax year, tax assessment and tax payment	Tax year is the calendar year	Tax is withheld at source
	Losses	Losses from sale of property can be offset against income of the same source in the subsequent 3 years	
	Tax rates	*Income (NTD)*　　　　　　　　*Tax rate* Up to 370,000　　　　　　　6% 370,001–990,000　　　　　22,200 + 13% 990,001–1,980,000　　　　102,800 + 21% 1,980,001–3,720,000　　　310,700 + 30% 3,720,001 and above　　　832,700 + 40% = 6%	
Capital Gains Tax (CGT)	General description	Gains realised from the difference between the acquisition and disposal price of an asset	
	Taxable entities and chargeable assets	Real estate, intangible assets	Tax is withheld at source
	Calculation of gain	Sale price less the related cost	
	Tax year, tax assessment and tax payment	Treated as income	
	Losses	Losses from sale of property can be offset against income of the same source in the subsequent 3 years	
	Tax rates	Capital gain is consolidated with personal income when filing individual income tax return	
		Domiciled	**Non-domiciled**
Inheritance Tax (IHT)	General description	No IHT in Taiwan	

IV   WITHHOLDING TAXES

	Payments to non-residents[1]
Dividends	20%
Interest	20%
Royalties	20%

V   INDIRECT TAXES

		Residents	Non-residents
Value Added Tax (VAT)	General description	Tax on the supply of goods and services	
	Entities being obliged to levy VAT	• Business entities which sell goods or services • The receivers or holders of imported goods • Those who receive services provided by foreign enterprises	
	Taxable activities	Any transaction involving goods or services within the territory of the Republic of China (ROC) including importation of goods is subject to VAT	
	Taxable activities – zero rated (examples)	• Exports • Services related to exports or services supplied within the ROC but used in foreign countries • International transportation	
	Exemptions (examples)	• Sale of land • Medical services • Nursing services • Education services • Textbooks • Newspapers, magazines, etc • Raw agricultural, forestry, fishing, etc • Services rendered by post and telecommunication offices	
	Refund of VAT	Tax overpaid: • on goods or services subject to 0% • on purchase of fixed assets • due to merger or consolidation, business transfer, dissolution or cessation of business	
	Tax rates	• Financial businesses = 5% • Reinsurance = 1% • Exports = 0% • Nightclubs and restaurants = 15% • Other bars and coffee shops = 25% • Agricultural businesses = 0.1% • Small and other specific businesses = 1% • Other entities = 5%–10%	
Land Tax		Ranges from 1%–5.5%, with some privileged rates from 0.2%–1% for land used in residential, public or approved projects	
Stamp Duty		Rate depends on the contract and provider	

Tanzania

(Paul Mushi, pclem@intafrica.com)

I MAIN LEGAL FORMS

Legal form / Characteristics	Partnership and Limited Liability Partnership (LLP)	Ltd (private corporation) and Plc (public corporation)
Partners/shareholders • Number • Restrictions	Partnerships must register their partnership name and usually have a partnership agreement No concept of LLPs	Company's membership regulation: • Plc not less than 50 members • Private Ltd not more than 50 shareholders
Directors	N/A	• Directors' maximum age is 70 years unless exemption is given • Loans to Directors are prohibited • Directors contracts of service must be disclosed • Directors are responsible for producing the accounts of the company
Establishment	Established by registering a partnership name and its owner-partners under the Business Names (Registration) Cap 213 of the laws	Under the Companies Act 2002 companies are established as: • Public liability company (Plc) • Private limited companies • Companies limited by guarantee or • Companies with un-limited liability
Registration	Partnership name registration	Registration requires filing of a Memorandum and Articles of Association. List of Directors/ Secretary and their addresses in case of a company
Minimum capital	There is no minimum capital requirement	
Liability	Unlimited	Limited to share capital

Legal form / Characteristics	Partnership and Limited Liability Partnership (LLP)	Ltd (private corporation) and Plc (public corporation)
Governance	Based on the principles of 'Uberrimae Fidei' among the partners	The following are mandatory: • shareholders'/directors' meetings • filing of resolutions • shareholder register • annual filling of returns • annual audit and tax reporting • compliance with companies A/C mandatory • best governance practices
Audit requirements	Audit requirements start from turnovers of Tshs 20m	Audit requirements start from turnovers of Tshs 20m
Taxation	Partnerships are taxed through the partner's share of partnership income. The partnership as such is not taxed	Corporation tax
Usage	None in particular	None in particular

II   CORPORATION TAX

Legal form / Description	Resident corporation	Permanent establishment (PE)
General description	Corporation tax	Corporation tax
Taxable entities	Corporations incorporated and managed in Tanzania	PE located in Tanzania
Taxable income	Worldwide profits with considerations for double taxation treaties	Profits earned in Tanzania
Calculation of taxable profits	Accounting profit is adjusted for various tax add-backs and allowances to arrive to profits chargeable to corporation tax (PCTCT)	
Interest payments	Deductible if connected with the production of income	
Related party transactions	These can subjected to transfer pricing adjustment	
Tax year, return and payment	Return and payment due 6 months after year-end If paying by instalments then return is due after the end of the first quarter following the year-end and subsequent payments are due at the end of each quarter	
Capital gains	Capital gain is calculated as part of the total income and taxed accordingly For corporate entities the rate is 30%	
Losses	Losses can be carried forward indefinitely, but effective from 2008 there is Alternative Minimum Tax (AMT) at 0.3% on turnover if losses are reported for more than 2 years	
Tax group	The tax group concept does not exist	
Tax rate	• Standard rate = 30% • Newly listed companies with at least 30% of its shareholding listed on the DSE = 25% • Repatriated profits = 10%	

III TAXES FOR INDIVIDUALS

		Residents	Non-residents
Income Tax	General description	Tax levied on the chargeable income of a chargeable person for a year of assessment	
	Taxable entities and taxable income	Residents are taxed on their worldwide income	Non-residents are taxable on all income arising in Tanzania
	Types of taxable income	• Property income (usually rent) • Income from capital investment (interest, sale of goodwill, dividends, royalties, annuities) • Income from business activities • Employment from personal services and pensions • Capital gains	
	Calculation of income	Income is calculated on the basis of gross total income net of expenditure wholly and exclusively incurred in producing the gross income Tax depreciations, incentive deductions and other specific deductions are given	
	Tax year, tax assessment and tax payment	The tax year is 31 December but this can be varied on application to the Tax Commissioner Tax assessments are in the form of self-assessments both provisional and final and tax is payable by five instalments, four during the accounting year and the last before the end of 6 months after the accounting year	
	Losses	Losses are available for carry forward indefinitely	
	Tax Rates	*Income (Tshs)* *Tax rate (%)* 0–100,000 0 Next 260,000 18.5 Next 180,000 20 Next 180,000 25 720,000+ 30	
Capital Gains Tax (CGT)	General description	Gains realised from the difference between the acquisition and disposal price of an asset	
	Taxable entities and chargeable assets	Any entity making a disposition of any asset	
	Calculation of gain	Difference of cost and realised amount. Gain not exceeding Tshs 15m for sale of a private residential house is exempt	
	Tax year, tax assessment and tax payment	Residents – 10% on registration of the title transfer and the balance at the applicable marginal rate	Non-residents – the rate is 20%
	Losses	Losses can be carried forward to be set off against corresponding future capital gains	
	Tax rates	10% first instalment for residents individuals	20% first instalment for non-resident individuals

		Domiciled	**Non-domiciled**
Inheritance Tax (IHT)	General description	Voluntary and involuntary dispositions	
	Taxable entities and chargeable assets	All entities and persons effecting transfers as above	When the asset is situated in Tanzania
	Calculation of charge	Difference between cost and realised amount/market value	
	Taxable events	On sale, exchange, transfer, death, dissolution or ownership ceases	
	Allowances	No allowance or reliefs	
	Tax rates	• If an individual at personal tax rate • For individuals transfer of agricultural land is exempted if the transfer value does not exceed Tshs 10m	

IV   WITHHOLDING TAXES

	Payments to non-residents
Dividends to companies controlling 25% of shares or more	10%
Dividends from DSE listed companies	5%
Dividend from other companies	10%
Rents	15%
Interest	10%
Insurance Premium	5%
Management/Consultancy Fees	15%
Royalties	15%
On payments to artists and sportsmen	15%

V   INDIRECT TAXES

		Residents	Non-residents
Value Added Tax (VAT)	General description	Tax on the supply of goods and services (VAT)	
	Entities being obliged to levy VAT	All entities supplying goods and services for consideration	
	Taxable activities	All supplies of goods and services by any entity	
	Taxable activities – zero rated (examples)	Exports of goods and services Generally and specifically services to: • ships • aircrafts • agricultural equipment • fertiliser and insecticides • veterinary medicine • human medicine	
	Exemptions (examples)	• Foodstuffs • Fertilisers and pesticides • Health and education supplies • Books and newspapers • Financial and tourism services • Agricultural implements • Aircrafts • Computers	
	Refund of VAT	Claims certified by a registered tax consultant are refundable	
	Tax liability	Must be paid by the end of month following the month of collection	
	Tax rates	Standard rate = 20% Exports = 0%	
	Administrative obligations	Compliance threshold is Tshs 40m	
Stamp Duty Land Tax		Land tax is nominal	
Stamp Duty		1% on shares and land transfers	

Thailand

(Suree Kamolnarumeth, vatc@ksc.th.com)

I MAIN LEGAL FORMS

Legal form / Characteristics	Partnership and Limited Liability Partnership (LLP)	Ltd (private corporation) and Plc (public corporation)
Partners/shareholders • Number • Restrictions	Thailand provides for three types of partnerships: • Unregistered ordinary partnerships, in which all partners are jointly and wholly liable for all obligations of the partnership • Registered ordinary partnerships. If registered, the partnership becomes a legal entity, separate and distinct from an individual partner. The ordinary partnership is the kind of partnership in which all the partners have joint and several liability • Limited partnerships. Individual partner liability is restricted to the amount of capital contributed to the partnership. Limited partnerships must be registered	Ltd: at least three people to be subscribers to the Memorandum of Association Plc: at least 15 shareholders subscribing to at least 5% of the shares
Directors	N/A	Board of Directors
Establishment	Partnerships Deed	The private company is governed by the Civil and Commercial Code, the public company by the Public Company Act
Registration	Registration with the Commerce Department	
Minimum capital	No minimum requirements	15 Baht for private companies 75 Baht for Plc
Liability	Unlimited	Limited to share capital
Governance	Partners	Board meetings

Legal form / Characteristics	Partnership and Limited Liability Partnership (LLP)	Ltd (private corporation) and Plc (public corporation)
Audit requirements	N/A	Financial statements must be certified by an authorised auditor and filed with the Ministry of Commerce within 5 months of the end of the fiscal year
Taxation	Transparent	Corporate income tax is calculated in accordance with generally accepted accounting principles as adjusted by the specific rules of income tax law

II CORPORATION TAX

Legal form / Description	Resident corporation	Permanent establishment (PE)
General description	Corporation tax	
Taxable entities	Corporations incorporated in Thailand	PE trading in Thailand
Taxable income	Worldwide profits	Income arising in Thailand
Calculation of taxable profits	Accounting profit is adjusted for various tax add-backs and allowances to arrive to profits chargeable to corporation tax (PCTCT)	
Interest payments	Interest should be calculated at the market value on the lending date	
Related party transactions	All related party transactions must take place on arm's length basis	
Tax year, return and payment	Companies may choose their year-end	
	Semi-annual income tax returns are filed together with payment within 2 months from the end of the first 6 months of the period, and annual income tax returns within 150 days of the year-end	
Capital gains	Included as part of taxable income	
Losses	Net operating losses may be carried forward for up to 5 consecutive years	
Tax group	None	
Tax rate	30%	
	For small companies (paid up capital not more than 5m Baht)	
	Net taxable profit (baht) *Tax rate*	
	0–150,000 exempt 150,001–1,000,000 15% 1,000,001–3,000,000 25% 3,000,001+ 30%	

III   TAXES FOR INDIVIDUALS

		Residents	Non-residents
Income Tax	General description	Tax levied on the chargeable income of a chargeable person for a year of assessment	
	Taxable entities and taxable income	Every person, resident or non-resident, who derives income from employment or business in Thailand, or assets located in Thailand is subject to personal income tax, whether such income is paid in or outside of Thailand Individuals residing for 180 days or more in Thailand in any calendar year are also subject to income tax on income from foreign sources if that income is brought into Thailand during the same taxable year that they are a resident	Income arising in Thailand
	Types of taxable income	• Property income • Income from capital investment (interest, sale of goodwill, dividends, royalties, annuities) • Income from business activities • Employment from personal services or pensions	
	Calculation of income	Taxable income arising in the year	
	Tax year, tax assessment and tax payment	Tax year is the calendar year Returns must be filed before 31 March the following year	
	Losses	Generally deductible against tax due income	
	Tax rates	*Progressive rates* *Baht*　　　　　　　　*%* 0–150,000　　　　　　0 150,001–500,000　　　10 500,001–1,000,000　　20 1,000,001–4,000,000　30 4,000,001+　　　　　　37	
Capital Gains Tax (CGT)	General description	Gains realised from the difference between the acquisition and disposal price of an asset	
	Taxable entities and chargeable assets	Capital gains derived from non-listed securities are taxable	
	Calculation of gain	Proceeds less allowable costs	
	Tax year, tax assessment and tax payment	Calendar year	
	Losses	No tax allowance from losses	

		Residents	Non-residents
Capital Gains Tax (CGT)	Tax rates	Progressive tax rates to be applied for capital gains from sale of securities outside Stock Exchange of Thailand For individual person, gains from sale of securities in stock exchange of Thailand, not including income from sale of debentures and bonds are exempted from personal income tax	15% for capital gains
		Domiciled	**Non-domiciled**
Inheritance Tax (IHT)	General description	No IHT in Thailand	

IV   WITHHOLDING TAXES

	Payments to non-residents[1]
Dividends	10%
Interest	15%
Royalties	15%
On payments to artists and sportsmen	Deduct at income tax rates

---

1   Reduced rates of withholding tax may apply where there is an appropriate double tax treaty.

V INDIRECT TAXES

		Residents	**Non-residents**
Value Added Tax (VAT)	General description	Tax on the supply of goods and services	
	Entities being obliged to levy VAT	Businesses with revenue above 1.8m Baht per annum	
	Taxable activities	VAT is collected from the sale of goods and services	
	Taxable activities – zero rated (examples)	Export of goods and services	
	Exemptions (examples)	• Operators earning yearly income less than 1.8m Baht • Sale or import of agricultural products, live stock fertiliser and feed • Sale or import of published material and books • Educational services Exemption rate which is equivalent to zero rate but the operator is not entitled to claim purchase tax	
	Refund of VAT	The registered operator can obtain a tax refund by cash or as tax credit to the following month	
	Tax liability	Sale tax – purchase tax = tax liability or tax credit/refund	
	Tax rates	• Sale of goods and services = 7% (7% is the current rate, maximum rate is 10%) • Exports = 0%	
	Administrative obligations	A monthly tax return must be filed with the revenue department by the 15th day of the following month	
Stamp Duty Land Tax		N/A	
Stamp Duty		Rate depends on the contract and provider	

Tunisia

(AFINCO, afinco@afinco.net)

I   MAIN LEGAL FORMS

Legal form / Characteristics	Partnerships	Ltd (private corporation) and Plc (public corporation)
Partners/shareholders • Number • Restrictions	• Minimum: one partner • Maximum: 50 partners	• Minimum: seven shareholders
Directors	One or more general manager(s) named by assembly or in Articles of Association	• Board of Directors named by shareholders' assembly • President Chief Executive Officer of Board of Directors (President may be separately named)
Establishment	• Signature of Articles of Association and partners' meeting minutes • Obtaining an investment declaration • Obtaining a fiscal ID • Obtaining a trade register matriculation • Advertising formalities • Obtaining a custom ID	• Signature of Articles of Association and shareholders' meeting minutes • Obtaining an investment declaration • Obtaining a fiscal ID • Obtaining a trade register matriculation • Advertising formalities • Obtaining a custom ID
Registration	The registration is completed ahead of the trade register of the tribunal	The registration is completed ahead of the trade register of the tribunal
Minimum capital	• TND 1,000 • TND 1 (under some conditions) In all cases, and if company is established under part exporting regime, share capital shall be at least equal to 30% of total investment	• Private: TND 5,000 • Listed: TND 50,000 In all cases, and if company is established under part exporting regime, share capital shall be at least equal to 30% of total investment
Liability	Unlimited	Limited to shareholder's participation in share capital
Governance	N/A	Possibility to designate a supervision council (Conseil de surveillance)

Legal form / Characteristics	Partnerships	Ltd (private corporation) and Plc (public corporation)
Audit requirements	Designation of a statutory auditor is mandatory when two of the following three conditions are reached: • Balance sheet total: TND 100,000 • Total sales: TND 300,000 • Employees average number: 10	Designation of a statutory auditor is mandatory
Taxation	Transparent	Corporate income tax

II CORPORATION TAX

Legal form / Description	Resident corporation	Permanent Establishment (PE)
General description	Corporation income tax	
Taxable entities	Companies established in Tunisia	PE established in Tunisia
Taxable income	Profits realised in Tunisia and abroad	Profits realised in Tunisia
Calculation of taxable profits	Taxable profits = accounting profits + add-backs – deductions	
Interest payments	Interests are submitted to a withholding tax of 20% (except interests on foreign currency investment which are exempted)	
Related party transactions	Arm's length principle	
Tax year, return and payment	Tax year: from 1 January to 31 December. However, company may choose a different accounting year-end date	
	Tax return must be filed by day 25 of third month following the end of the accounting year	
	Tax is payable in quarterly instalments based on prior year income tax	
	Balance of tax is payable on the tax return filing date	
Capital gains	Included in the taxable profit	Included in the taxable profit
Losses	Tax losses may be carried forward for 4 years and deducted from future taxable profits	
	The loss arising from assets depreciation can be carried forward indefinitely	
Tax group	Specific regime	N/A
Tax rate	• Common rate is 30% • Some companies are submitted to a rate of 35% or more (banks, insurance, oil and gas companies, telecommunication, etc) • Totally exporting companies are exempted from corporate tax for a period of 10 years	

III TAXES FOR INDIVIDUALS

<table>
<tr><th></th><th></th><th>Residents</th><th>Non-residents</th></tr>
<tr><td rowspan="7">Income Tax</td><td>General description</td><td>Residing in Tunisia more than 183 days or having a home residence</td><td>Residing less than 183 days in Tunisia or not having a home residence</td></tr>
<tr><td>Taxable entities and taxable income</td><td>Residents are taxed on their worldwide income (under provision of particular specifications provided in double tax treaty)</td><td>Non-residents are taxed on all income arising in Tunisia (under provision of particular specifications provided in double tax treaty)</td></tr>
<tr><td>Types of taxable income</td><td colspan="2"><ul><li>Industrial and commercial profits</li><li>Non-commercial benefits (fees)</li><li>Agriculture and fishing profits</li><li>Salaries and wages</li><li>Property (real estate) revenues</li><li>Capital gains</li></ul></td></tr>
<tr><td>Calculation of income</td><td colspan="2">The total of the different categories above, taking into account the withholding taxes operated

Different deductions and add-backs are operated (mainly for industrial and commercial profits and non-commercial benefits)

Double tax treaties may provide particular provisions</td></tr>
<tr><td>Tax year, tax assessment and tax payment</td><td colspan="2">Tax year is the calendar year

Tax return must be filed the year after the concerned one, and before:<ul><li>25 February for capital gains and property revenues</li><li>25 April for commerce revenues</li><li>25 May for non-commercial revenues or for individuals realising different kind of revenues</li><li>25 July for handcraft revenues</li><li>25 August for agricultural or fishing revenues</li><li>5 December for salaries</li></ul>Tax on commercial profits is payable in three quarterly instalments based on prior year tax

Balance of tax is payable on the tax return filing date (after deducting tax instalments and/or withholding taxes)

For salaries and wages, tax is payable through the withholding operated by the employer</td></tr>
<tr><td>Losses</td><td>Losses are carried forward for 4 years

Losses originated from depreciation are carried forward indefinitely</td><td>Losses are carried forward for 4 years

Losses originated from depreciation are carried forward indefinitely</td></tr>
</table>

		Residents	**Non-residents**
Income Tax	Tax rates	On the basis of the individual income tax scale with progressive rates: *Income (TND)* *Tax rate (%)* 0–1,500 0 1,501–5,000 15 5,001–10,000 20 10,001–20,000 25 20,001–50,000 25 50,001+ 35 Income gain from shares sale are subject to a 10% rate	Non-residents receiving salaries from total exporting companies or hydrocarbons companies may choose the lump tax rate of 20% Otherwise, their salaries are subject to the progressive scale rates as applied for residents
Capital Gains Tax (CGT)	General description	• Interests on debts • Interests on finance investments • Interests on current accounts • Added value on shares' sale • Rentals from real estate • Added value on real estate sale	
	Taxable entities and chargeable assets	Entities paying interests shall apply withholding tax	Entities paying interests shall apply withholding tax
	Calculation of gain	Real estate rental: • from revenues are deducted 30% of revenues and expenses necessary to maintain the real estate in good state Real estate sale: • from sale revenue is deducted the acquisition cost majored of 10% by each year of acquisition	
	Tax year, tax assessment and tax payment	Tax year is the calendar year Tax return must be filed before 25 February of the year following the calendar year	
	Losses	Loss on shares' sale is deducted from business profit	
	Tax rates	On the basis of the individual income tax scale, except: • shares' sale profit: 10% (exempted however up to TND 10,000) • real estate sale profit: 10% (up to 10 years' possession) and 5% (more than 10 years' possession)	
		Domiciled	**Non-domiciled**
Inheritance Tax (IHT)	General description	The registration duties on inheritance (inheritance tax) is applied on a variable tax scale	
	Taxable entities and chargeable assets	Inheritance tax is based on properties and goods located in Tunisia, for resident person Inheritance tax is based on properties and goods located in Tunisia or abroad, if the died person is resident in Tunisia However, properties and goods located abroad which already bore the inheritance tax is exempted in Tunisia	Inheritance tax is based on properties and goods located in Tunisia, for non-resident person

		Domiciled	**Non-domiciled**
Inheritance Tax (IHT)	Calculation of charge	For the tax calculation basis, debts duly proved are admitted in deduction	
	Taxable events	N/A	N/A
	Allowances	Tax is applied on the established capital, no matter the price for the depreciation	Tax is applied on the established capital, no matter the price for the depreciation
	Tax rates	• 2.5% between ascendant – descendant and between spouses • 5% between brothers and sisters • 25% between uncles and aunts; between nephews and nieces, between cousins • 35% between relatives at fourth degree or non-relative persons	Same rates applied as those for residents

IV   WITHHOLDING TAXES

	Payments to non-residents (subject to double taxation treaties)
Dividends	0%
Interest	• 20% • 2.5% on interests paid to non-resident banks
Royalties	15%
On payments to artists and sportsmen	15%

V   INDIRECT TAXES

		Residents	**Non-residents**
Value Added Tax (VAT)	General description	VAT paid on acquisitions is deducted from the one imposed on sales/revenues. The difference is paid to tax authorities VAT on sales/revenues rendered to public client (state or public company) is withheld by latter for 50%	VAT invoiced by non-residents is 100% withheld by local client
	Entities being obliged to levy VAT	Companies and individuals exerting commercial activity, except those complying with certain conditions (revenues less than TND 30,000; retailers)	Non-resident companies operating commercial activity in Tunisia
	Taxable activities	Supply of goods and services	Services/works rendered in Tunisia by non-residents
	Taxable activities – zero rated (examples)	• Education services • Agriculture products	Public bids executed by non-residents and financed by international donation
	Exemptions (examples)	• Export of goods and services • Oil and gas activity	N/A
	Refund of VAT	Refund of VAT is mainly applied in case of: • VAT credit remaining for a minimum of 6 months • VAT credit due to export operations • VAT credit due to withheld tax operated by the state or public company	
	Tax liability	VAT to be paid before day 28 of the month following the concerned one	
	Tax rates	• Standard rate: 18% • Other rates: 0%, 6%, 12%	
	Administrative obligations	Obligation to mention on invoice: • VAT rate • VAT amount • Tax ID	
Stamp Duty Land Tax		N/A	
Stamp Duty		Duties varying from TND 0.300 to TND 100, depending on the type of document or authorisation	

Turkey

(Tugrul Ozsut, tozsut@nexiaturkey.com.tr)

I MAIN LEGAL FORMS

Legal form / Characteristics	Limited Liability Partnership (LTD)	AŞ (Private corporation) and Plc (Public corporation)
Partners/shareholders • Number • Restrictions	• Minimum: two • Maximum: 50	• Minimum: five • No restriction
Directors	Partners or a manager who may not be partner	Management by board
Establishment	Notarisation of Articles of Association and submitting it to Trade Registry Office	Establishment of public corporation is subject to approval. But other private entities except banks, holding companies are not subject to an approval
Registration	Trade Registry Offices	
Minimum Capital	5,000 TRY	50,000 TRY
Liability	Limited to capital share for partners	Limited to capital amount of partners
Governance	Board of shareholders	General Meeting and Board of Management
Audit requirements	Audit is not obligatory but advantageous for big companies	Audit is not obligatory but advantageous for big companies Auditing is required by Capital Markets Board and obligatory for public corporations
Taxation	• 20% corporate tax • 15% distributed profit shares • The sales of shares of real entity is subject to income tax	• 20% corporate tax • 15% distributed profit shares • The sales of real entity shares which are held for at least 2 years are not subject to income tax

II CORPORATION TAX

Legal form / Description	Resident corporation	Permanent establishment (PE)
General description	Corporation tax on profit	
Taxable entities	The worldwide profits of resident companies in Turkey are subject to tax	The profits in Turkey are subject to tax
Taxable income	Worldwide profits	Profits derived in Turkey
Calculation of taxable profits	Sales and other income minus costs of generating the income which are allowed under the commercial code	
Interest payments	Generally deductible as a business expense	
Related party transactions	Transactions between related parties which are not under arm's length principles are considered as profit distributions and subject to tax	
Tax year, return and payment	Tax year – calendar year The tax rate is 20% Tax payments are due quarterly in advance in March, June, September and December All taxes paid within the calendar year are deductible from the final liability, the tax return for which has to be submitted in the April following 31 December	
Capital Gains	• No tax for capital gains distributed to partners (legal entities) of a resident corporate • 15% tax on capital gains distributed to real entity partners • 15% tax on capital gains distributed to foreign corporate and real entity partners • The provisions of the relevant Double Taxation Agreements (DTA) should be taken into consideration	
Losses	Losses can be carried forward for 5 years	None
Tax rate	20% corporate tax	

III TAXES FOR INDIVIDUALS

		Residents	**Non-residents**
Income Tax	General description	Tax levied on the chargeable income of a chargeable person for a year of assessment	
	Taxable entities	Individuals resident in Turkey are subject to income tax for all of their worldwide income	Income in Turkey is subject to tax
	Types of taxable income	• Business income • Agricultural income • Self-employment income • Returns on stocks and bonds • Property income • Increase/appreciation in value of income	
	Calculation of income	The calculation of taxable income of business profits is based on results found by deducting the expenses specified by law from profit gained within a calendar year Taxable income for self-employment is difference between collected cash and cash equivalents, and related expenses and costs (profits are taxable on cash basis, not accrual basis)	
	Tax year, tax assessment and tax payment	Tax year – calendar year Business and self-employment income returns are quarterly basis Tax returns are due by March of the year succeeding the tax year and paid in two instalments in March and July	
	Losses	Losses related with business and self-employment profit, may be carried forward 5 years	None
	Tax rates	*Income (TRY)* *Rate (%)* Up to 7,800 15 7,800–19,800 20 19,800–44,700 27 44,700+ 35	Self-employment income: 20% Salaries and business income are subject to same rate as residents
Capital Gains Tax (CGT)	General description	Tax on gains derived from disposal of movable and immovable properties	
	Taxable entities and chargeable assets	Gains derived from disposal of securities within 2 years, immovable property within 5 years and from sales of partnership rights	
	Calculation of gain	Revenue from the sale or transfer of goods or rights minus costs of the goods or rights and other expenses paid by the supplier	
	Tax year, tax assessment and tax payment	Tax year – calendar year Tax returns are due to be filed by 31 March each year following the calendar year Tax is payable in two instalments in March and July	
	Losses	No relief is available	None
	Tax rates	15%–35% progressive tax	

		Residents	**Non-residents**
Inheritance Tax (IHT)	General description	Tax charged on a chargeable transfer of value made by a lifetime gift or estate on death	
	Taxable entities and chargeable assets	Inheritance tax is levied on the individual receiving the *inheritance* of properties of Turkish Republic citizens and properties in Turkey. The properties inherited abroad by a Turkish citizen are also subject to tax	Tax is levied on the Turkish resident who receives an inheritance of Turkish situs assets of a foreign deceased
	Calculation of charge	Tax is computed on the value of the inherited asset less any debts attached to such assets	
	Taxable events	• Land and buildings, money, movable properties, rights and receivables on death • Every kind of lifetime gifts (estates, money, etc)	
	Allowances	• On death spouse and each of children: 96,075 TRY • Lifetime gifts: 2,216 TRY	
	Tax rates	*Tax Base (TRY)*　　*Rate on death (%)*　　*Rate on lifetime gifts (%)* 150,000　　　　　1　　　　　　10 Next 320,000　　　3　　　　　　15 Next 680,000　　　5　　　　　　20 Next 1,380,000　　7　　　　　　25 2,530,000　　　　10　　　　　　30	

IV WITHHOLDING TAXES

	Payments to non-residents
Dividends	15% (DTA conditions taken into consideration)
Interest	Deposit rate: 15% Treasury Bill: 0%
Royalties	17%
On payments to artists and sportsmen	Payments to artists: 20% Payments to sportsmen: 15%

V INDIRECT TAXES

		Residents	Non-residents
Value Added Tax (VAT)	General description	Value added tax is levied on all goods and services supplied within the scope of commercial industrial, agricultural and independent professional activities and on the import of goods and services	
	Entities being obliged to levy VAT	Any individual, partnership, corporation, association and foundation which carries out taxable activities	
	Taxable activities	• Supply of goods and services • Import of goods • Post, telephone, radio and TV services • Organising and participating in gambling	
	Taxable activities – zero rated (examples)	Export of goods and supply of services to abroad	
	Exemptions (examples)	• Export of goods and services • Forwarding services from Turkey to abroad • Export of goods to free zones and services performed in free zones • Delivery of naval, air and road vehicles and goods and services to be used in manufacturing these vehicles	
	Refund of VAT	There is a VAT refund mechanism in transactions: • which are exempt from VAT (export sales) and • where there are rate differences in output and inputs (output rate is 1% or 8%, input rate is 18%)	• Non-residents in forwarding business can recover VAT issued for fuel, spare parts, maintenance and repair expenses • Companies in all sectors that participated in fairs can recover VAT under some conditions
	Tax liability	The supplier (company, partnership) of goods and services is responsible for charging VAT	
	Tax rates	• Standard rate = 18% • Goods that are subject to VAT at 1% such as: vegetable and animal products, newspapers, magazines • Employed at college = 8% • Textile and apparel products = 8% • Accommodation services provided at hotel, motel, holiday village, etc = 8% • Health services, pharmaceuticals and medical devices = 8%	
Stamp Duty		Any agreement that is written and signed is subject to stamp tax based on the value stated in the agreement	
		Different tax rates apply	
		Papers prepared abroad are subject to stamp duty if they are declared to official authorities	

Ukraine

(Andriy Kostyuk, ak@pso.com.ua)

I MAIN LEGAL FORMS

Legal form / Characteristics	Ltd (private corporation)	Plc (public corporation)
Partners/shareholders • Number • Restrictions	Up to 10 (no minimum)	• No minimum or maximum • No company with single partner can establish another single-partner company
Directors	No restrictions	
Establishment	By the decision of founders. Anti-trust committee consent in specific cases	
Registration	State registration and incorporation, registration with tax authority, pension and three social security funds Formal procedures take 2–3 weeks	
Minimum capital	Around €7,170	Around €89,600
Liability	Limited to capital	
Governance	• General assembly • Director of Board of Directors • Auditor	
Audit requirements	None	Annual
Taxation	Taxable on worldwide profits	
Usage	Small businesses	Major establishments, that plan to attract external financing

II   CORPORATION TAX

Legal form / Description	Resident corporation	Permanent establishment (PE)
General description	Corporation tax	
Taxable entities	Corporations incorporated in the Ukraine	PE in the Ukraine
Taxable income	Worldwide income	Income arising in the Ukraine
Calculation of taxable profits	Calculated on rules of tax accounting, which do not always correspond to general accounting rules and restrict expenditure	
Interest payments	Deductible, no thin capitalisation restrictions	
Related party transactions	Related party transactions must be made on an arm's length basis	
Tax year, return and payment	Tax year – calendar year Returns must be filed 40 days after the end of each quarter Quarterly payments are made within 10 days of the filing deadline	
Capital gains	Treated as income	
Losses	Losses may be carried forward indefinitely	
Tax group	None	
Tax rate	• Standard rate = 25% • Reduced rate available for agriculture and insurance companies	

III TAXES FOR INDIVIDUALS

		Residents	Non-residents
Income Tax	General description	Tax levied on the chargeable income of a chargeable person for a year of assessment	
	Taxable entities and taxable income	Residents are taxed on their worldwide income	Income arising in the Ukraine
	Types of taxable income	• Property income (usually rent) • Income from capital investment (interest, sale of goodwill, dividends, royalties, annuities) • Income from business activities • Employment from personal services or pensions	
	Calculation of income	Gross income reduced by deductible expenses and allowances	
	Tax year, tax assessment and tax payment	Tax year – calendar year Payer is liable for tax assessment, unless income is taxed at source Taxpayers who have income not taxed at source must file a return by 1 April the following year, and make payments of 25% of the total liability on 15 March, May, August and November	
	Losses	Losses may not be carried forward	
	Tax rates	15%	30%
Capital Gains Tax (CGT)	General description	Treated as part of income	

		Domiciled	Non-domiciled
Inheritance Tax (IHT)	General description	No IHT in the Ukraine	

IV   WITHHOLDING TAXES

	Payments to non-residents[1]
Dividends	15%
Interest	15%
Royalties	15%
On payments to artists and sportsmen	15%

---

1   Reduced rates of withholding tax may apply where there is an appropriate double tax treaty.

V   INDIRECT TAXES

		Residents	**Non-residents**
Value Added Tax (VAT)	General description	Tax on the supply of goods and services	
	Entities being obliged to levy VAT	Each entity carrying out taxable operations for more than €40,000 per annum	
	Taxable activities	Supply of goods and services	
	Taxable activities – zero rated (examples)	Export	
	Exemptions (examples)	Certain medicines and healthcare, domestically produced baby food, banking, insurance, sale of land	
	Refund of VAT	Applicable, very sophisticated bureaucratically	No refund
	Tax rates	Standard rate = 20%	
Stamp Duty Land Tax		N/A	
Stamp Duty		N/A	

United Arab Emirates

(Usamah Tabbarah & Company, dxbho@utcnexia.com)

I   MAIN LEGAL FORMS[1]

Legal form / Characteristics	Partnership and Limited Liability Partnership (LLP)	Ltd (private corporation) and Plc (public corporation)
Partners/Holders • Number • Restrictions	*General partnership:* minimum number of partners: two. All the partners have to be UAE nationals *Limited Partnership:* general partners: one or more *and* limited partners – one or more. Only UAE nationals may be general partners; limited partners may be non-UAE nationals. There is no minimum capital equipment	*Public Joint Stock Company:* shares freely transferable but 51% must be held by UAE nationals; for insurance, banking, or the investment of funds on behalf of third parties, the establishment of a public joint stock company is a legal requirement – no other type of company may be established for such activities

---

1   United Arab Emirates (UAE) Federation consists of seven emirates that came together in 1971, namely Abu Dhabi, Dubai, Sharjah, Ajman, Umm al Qaiwan, Fujairah and Ras Al Khaimah with each enjoying a large degree of autonomy. Only entities permitted under the UAE Commercial Companies Law (Law No 8 of 1984 (CCL)) are legally recognised. Exceptions apply only for companies located in a Free Trade Zone.

Besides the companies permitted under the CCL, the UAE Civil Transactions Law (Federal Law No 5 of 1985) provides for the formation of civil companies for any object that is not considered to be commercial, namely the exploitation of the personal expertise or skills of the proprietor. Companies in the free zones are outside the ambit of the CCL and are expressly excluded from its operation. The only form of business entities that can be established, under a licence issued by the respective free zone, are (a) the Free Zone Establishment (FZE) and (b) branches of foreign companies (without local sponsor or partner) – except for the Saadiyat Free Zone. Companies in free zones benefit from a tax exemption of both corporate and income tax for a guaranteed number of years (normally 15 years) with a renewable option for an additional 15 years. The licence from a free zone authority mainly relates to four kinds: trading licence; service licence; manufacturing licence; or national industries licence. An FZE's minimum capital is AED 1m to be fully paid up at time of incorporation: at all times an FZE must have at least one director and one secretary, and also an office within the free zone.

Legal form / Characteristics	Partnership and Limited Liability Partnership (LLP)	Ltd (private corporation) and Plc (public corporation)
	Partnership Limited by Shares: only UAE nationals can be general partners; other partners participating (with liability limited by their shares) may be non-UAE nationals *Joint Venture (JV):* can be carried out only in the private name of one of the UAE national JV partners	*Private Joint Stock Company:* founding members, minimum three, must fully subscribe to the company's capital themselves; shares cannot be offered for public subscription. Public subscription excepted, all other provisions in the CCL applicable to the public joint stock companies are applicable to private joint stock companies. CCL provides for the conversion of a private joint stock company to public joint stock company *Limited Liability Company (LLC):* minimum of two and maximum of 50 shareholders. Not permitted to raise capital by public subscription, accept deposits or take loans from the public. Minimum par value of share AED 1,000. Value of all shares must be paid at time of incorporation
Directors	N/A	*Public Joint Stock Company:* minimum three and maximum 15 Chairman must be a UAE national Majority of directors must be UAE nationals
Establishment	Partnership Deed	*Public Joint Stock Company:* minimum of ten founding members
Registration	Each entity must be registered and licensed with the UAE Federal Ministry of Economy and Commerce and with the appropriate authority in the Emirate in which its office will be located, as a condition precedent to the commencement of business Some formalities regarding the incorporation for a joint stock company are also applicable to a partnership limited by shares	
Minimum Capital	*Limited partnership:* minimum – nil *Partnership Limited Shares:* minimum – AED 500,000	*Public Joint Stock Company:* AED 10m of which minimum 20% (maximum 45%) to be settled on subscription *Private Joint Stock Company:* AED 2m *Limited Liability Company:* • in Abu Dhabi – AED 150,000 • in Dubai – AED 300,000
Liability	Unlimited: general partners liable to full extent of the partnership liabilities	Limited: to the extent of share capital

Legal form / Characteristics	Partnership and Limited Liability Partnership (LLP)	Ltd (private corporation) and Plc (public corporation)
Governance	*General Partners:* Articles/Deed of Partnership and or Memorandum of Association *Partnership Limited by Shares:* Board of Supervisors: at least three participating partners to be appointed by the General Assembly	Board of Directors and ultimately the equity shareholders in general meeting
Audit requirements	Provisions in the Articles/Deed of Partnership/Memorandum of Association will apply	*Public Joint Stock Company and LLC:* auditor appointment mandatory
Taxation	No taxation	In practice only the profits of oil companies and those branches of foreign banks are taxed

II   CORPORATION TAX

Legal form / Description	Resident corporation	Non-resident corporation
Taxation entities	No taxation except for oil companies	Oil Companies and branches of foreign bank are taxable All other enterprises are not subject to taxation
Taxable income	Net profit adjusted for tax	
Tax rate	Oil companies (which include any chargeable person that deals in oil or right to oil, both offshore and onshore) pay flat rate of 55% on their taxable income in Dubai, and 50% in the other Emirates. In addition they pay royalties on production	Foreign banks are taxed at 20% of their taxable income in the Emirates of Abu Dhabi, Dubai, and Sharjah Oil companies pay a flat rate of 55% on their taxable income in Dubai, and 50% in the other Emirates. In addition they pay royalties on production

III   TAXES FOR INDIVIDUALS

		Residents	**Non-residents**
Income Tax	General description	There are no personal taxes	
Capital Gains Tax (CGT)	General description	There is no CGT	
Inheritance Tax (IHT)	General description	There is no IHT or gift tax	

IV   WITHHOLDING TAXES

	Payment to non-residents
Dividends	N/A
Interest	N/A
Royalties	N/A
On payments to artists and sportsmen	N/A

V INDIRECT TAXES

		Residents	Non-residents
Value Added Tax (VAT)	General description	There are no consumption taxes or VAT, however, individual Emirates may charge levies on certain products such as liquor and cigarettes and on some services such as those in the hospitality industry	
Stamp Duty Land Tax		No stamp duty is payable on the purchase of real estate within the UAE market	
		1.5% land registration fee which is payable on the purchase consideration upon completion of the purchase transaction	
Stamp Duty		There is no stamp duty	
Customs Duties		Customs duties are levied on the CIF value or ad valorem or value specific to the goods concerned	
		Some goods, including air transit cargo, are exempt from duty (eg foodstuffs, medicines and public sector imports)	
		The duty is 5% for all other goods except foodstuffs and government and oil company-destined goods	

United Kingdom

(Rajesh Sharma, rajesh.sharma@smith.williamson.co.uk)

I MAIN LEGAL FORMS

Legal form / Characteristics	Partnership and Limited Liability Partnership (LLP)	Ltd (private corporation) and Plc (public corporation)
Partners/shareholders • Number • Restrictions	• Two or more • None	• One or more • None
Directors	Management by partners	Management by directors[1]
Establishment	Registration with Companies House	Registration with Companies House or purchase of shelf companies
Registration	Companies House and HM Revenue and Customs (HMRC)[2]	
Minimum capital	None	£1 for Ltd and £50,000 for Plc[3]
Liability	Unlimited[4]	Limited to capital
Governance	Partners, general meeting	Managing Director/Board of Directors, secretary, shareholders' meeting
Audit requirements	No audit requirements for partnership[5] No audit requirements for LLP provided: • turnover does not exceed £5.6m • total assets do not exceed £2.8m	No audit requirements for Ltd provided: • turnover does not exceed £5.6m • total assets do not exceed £2.8m Audit is required for Plc

1 Private company must have at least one director and one secretary. From 1 October 2008, every company must have at least one director who is a natural person, ie not a corporate body. There will be a grace period until October 2010 for any company that did not have a natural person as a director on the date the Companies Act 2006 received Royal Assent (8 November 2006). Public company must have at least two directors and one secretary.
2 Ordinary partnerships do not have to register with Companies House and individual partners remain responsible for their personal tax compliance including registration with HMRC.
3 Ltd can have any share capital of at least £1, which does not have to be paid up. Plc must have allotted shares to the value of at least £50,000 and a quarter, £12,500, must be paid up.
4 For LLP unlimited liability will apply to a least one partner. Other partners' liability may be limited to their capital.
5 There is no requirement for partnerships to be audited unless they are regulated.

Legal form / Characteristics	Partnership and Limited Liability Partnership (LLP)	Ltd (private corporation) and Plc (public corporation)
Taxation	Transparent	UK resident companies are subject to corporation tax on their profits derived anywhere in the world
Usage	Professional and financial organisations	Small and medium-sized enterprises and Plcs used for larger companies seeking listing on AIM or main market

II CORPORATION TAX

Legal form / Description	UK resident corporation	Permanent establishment (PE)
General description	UK corporation tax	
Taxable entities	Companies incorporated in the UK and/or overseas companies with central management and control located in the UK	PE located in the UK
Taxable income	Worldwide profits	Profits derived by PE in the UK
Calculation of taxable profits	Accounting profit is adjusted for various tax add-backs and allowances to arrive to profits chargeable to corporation tax (PCTCT)	
Interest payments	Transfer pricing rules are in place that require funding arrangements to be at arm's length for interest payment to remain tax deductible	
Related party transactions	All related party transactions must take place on arm's length basis	
Tax year, return and payment	Tax period normally coincides with accounting period Tax return must be submitted to HMRC within 12 months from the end of the accounting period Tax payment should be made 9 months and one day after the accounting period end while large companies pay tax in quarterly instalments	
Capital gains	Capital gains are subject to corporation tax at normal rates	Capital gains arising on assets used for UK trading are subject to corporation tax at normal rates
Losses[6]	Current year trading losses can be offset against other current year profits After a current period claim, a further claim can be made to carry back the trading losses and offset them against profits of the previous 12 months Alternatively, trading losses can be carried forward without time limit and offset against future profits arising from the same trade[7] Trading losses can also be relieved against profits of other UK group subsidiaries provided certain conditions are satisfied	All rules mentioned for the UK resident corporation will also apply to PE but only to the profits and losses of the UK trade
Tax group	A group comprises a parent company and its 75% subsidiaries[8]	Overseas entities with UK PE can also be included in the group
Tax rate	Between 21% or 22% and 28%[9]	Between 21% or 22% and 28%

6 There are special rules allowing the company to utilise other losses such as capital losses and loan relationship deficits.
7 There are certain restrictions on the utilisation of trading losses where there is a change in the nature of the trade and a change in the ownership of the company.
8 For group relief purposes.
9 The rate of corporation tax depends on the level of company's profits. Small companies' rate of 21% (2008/09) or 22% (2009 onwards) is applied where taxable profits are below £300,000 but this benefit is phased out for taxable profits between £300,000 and £1.5m where marginal relief operates. The standard rate of 28% is applied where taxable profits are equal to or exceed £1.5m. Trading income, capital gains, interest income and overseas dividend income are taxed at the appropriate rate of corporation tax. Dividends received from other UK companies are exempt.

III   TAXES FOR INDIVIDUALS

		Residents	**Non-residents**
Income Tax	General description	Tax levied on the chargeable income of a chargeable person for a year of assessment	
	Taxable entities and taxable income	• Individuals, trustees and estates that are resident in the UK are liable to tax on their worldwide income • Special rules for non-domiciled residents	Non-residents are liable to tax on income arising in the UK, subject to provisions in double taxation agreements
	Types of taxable income	• Property income • Trading income of a trade, profession or vocation • Savings and investment income • Employment income • Income from trusts or estates • Miscellaneous income – annual profits or gains not taxed elsewhere	
	Calculation of income	• Property – accrual basis • Trading – current year basis • Savings – actual income received • Employment – income/benefit received	
	Tax year, tax assessment and tax payment	Tax year – fiscal year – 6 April to following 5 April Tax assessment – individual self-assessment returns for each taxpayer to be filed by 31 October (31 January if filed electronically) Tax payment due – 31 January following the tax year	
	Losses	Number of reliefs available where a trading loss arises	
	Tax rates	• Personal allowance (tax-free earnings) £5,435. From September 2008 – £6,035 • Higher allowances and reliefs available for over 65s • Progressive tax rate • 20% for income up to £36,000. From September 2008 – £34,800[10,11] • 40% (32.5% for dividends) for income over £36,000. From September 2008 – £34,800	Personal allowance can only be claimed by British subjects, EEA citizens and Commonwealth citizens
Capital Gains Tax (CGT)	General description	Tax on increase in the value of asset between acquisition and disposal, not chargeable to income or corporation tax	
	Taxable entities and chargeable assets	Any person resident in the UK during the tax year in which the gain arises. Worldwide assets are chargeable for CGT	No charge unless ordinarily resident in the UK. Temporary non-UK residents may still be charged to gains in the year they return to the UK

---

10 Dividend income may be taxed at 10% and 32.5%. Rates of income for discretionary trusts and accumulation and maintenance trusts are 32.5% for dividend income and 40% for non-dividend income.

11 Starting rate of 10% remained for savings income up to £2,320. It is removed for earned income and pension income.

		Residents	**Non-residents**
Capital Gains Tax (CGT)	Calculation of gain	• Disposal proceeds less allowable expenditure • Indexation allowance and taper relief available to reduce gain • Amount of relief dependent on whether a business asset and length of ownership	
	Tax year, tax assessment and tax payment	Tax year – fiscal year – 6 April to following 5 April	
		Tax assessment – reportable on same individual self-assessment as income tax	
		Tax payment due – 31 January following the tax year	
	Losses	• Losses utilised against gains in year • Excess carried forward and set against future gains • Indexation allowance and taper relief cannot create a loss	
	Tax rates	Annual exemption – £9,600	
		Chargeable gain is treated as top slice of income taxed at 18%	

		UK domiciled	**Non-UK domiciled**
Inheritance Tax (IHT)	General description	Tax charged on a chargeable transfer of value made by a lifetime gift or estate on death	
	Taxable entities and chargeable assets	Estate or lifetime gifts, which are not specifically excluded, situated worldwide	Estate or lifetime gifts, which are not specifically excluded, situated in the UK
	Calculation of charge	Loss in value of the donor's estate after gift has been made or value of estate on death	
	Taxable events	• Certain lifetime gifts • Estates on death and gifts made in prior 7 years on death of donor	• Lifetime gifts and estate and gifts on death of assets situated in the UK
	Allowances	• Spouse exemption on all gifts • Annual exemption – £3,000 • Nil rate band – £312,000	If recipient spouse is foreign domiciled transfers exempted up to £55,000
	Tax rates	• 20% on lifetime transfers • 40% on estates and gifts made in prior 7 years on death of donor • Taper relief available to gifts becoming chargeable on death	

IV   WITHHOLDING TAXES

	Payments to non-residents[12]
Dividends	0%
Interest	20%
Royalties	20%[13]
On payments to artists and sportsmen	20%

---

12 Reduced rates of withholding tax may apply where there is an appropriate double tax treaty.

13 Payments of interest and royalties between EU associated companies (ie at least 25% interest in the share capital is required) can be made gross if the payer believes that payee is entitled to the exemption under the EU Directive.

V   INDIRECT TAXES

		Residents	Non-residents
Value Added Tax (VAT)	General description	Tax on the supply of goods and services	
	Entities being obliged to levy VAT	• Any individual, partnership, corporation or other body, which carries out taxable activities in the UK, subject to turnover limit of £67,000 • On request, if turnover from taxable activities is below £65,000 • On request, if supplies are made outside the UK. The supplies must be outside the scope of UK VAT with the right to recover related input tax • Other situations may also arise, eg distance selling, sale of assets, requisitions from other EC member states	
	Taxable activities	• Supply of goods and services, import of goods, intra-Community acquisition of goods, etc • Place of supply of goods and services must be in the UK (following Art 9 EC Directive)	
	Taxable activities – zero rated (examples)	• Export of goods and supply of services with another EU member state • First sale or long lease (over 21 years) of new residential accommodation by developer • Sale of books and printing of leaflets, children's clothing, transport, etc	
	Exemptions (examples)	• Transactions related to the sale or lease of any property located in UK (option to tax for VAT available for commercial property) • Banking and insurance services • Educational supplies • Certain welfare services including hospital and medical care services	
	Refund of VAT	• VAT paid on supplies and services is deductible as input tax, if incurred in the course or furtherance of the business and for the purpose of making taxable supplies (including zero-rated supplies) • There is no credit for input tax incurred which relates to the provision of exempt supplies • Where mixed supplies occur (taxable and exempt supplies), subject to de minimis provisions, input tax must be apportioned and recovered according to a partial exemption method. Agreement with HMRC is required for non-standard partial exemption methods	• EC 8th Directive refund system for non-resident businesses established within the EU, providing its business is not otherwise required to be registered in the UK • EC 13th Directive refund system for non-resident businesses established outside the EU, providing its business is not otherwise required to be registered in the UK • Strict time limits apply to claims
	Tax liability	• Normally the supplier of goods and services is responsible for charging VAT • Reverse charge for certain supplies of goods and services (eg consultancy services received from businesses established outside the UK)	

		Residents	Non-residents
Value Added Tax (VAT)	Tax rates	• Standard rate = 17.5% (decreased to a temporary rate of 15% from 1 December 2008) • Reduced rate = 5% (eg certain residential conversions) • Zero rate = 0%	
	Administrative obligations	• Formal requirements concerning business records and invoices • Quarterly self-assessment VAT return plus quarterly payment of any VAT liability to HMRC (special arrangements and schemes available for smaller businesses and repayment traders where monthly returns are possible) • VAT groups are allowed subject to certain requirements • Certain arrangements may need to be disclosed • VAT identification number must be shown on all invoices issued • EU Invoicing Directive must be adhered to	• Registration for VAT purposes, if making supplies of goods and services in the UK • Appointment of fiscal tax representative possible but not obligatory
Stamp Duty Land Tax		Transactions related to the sale or lease of property located in the UK, with the purchaser liable	
		Tax rate between 1%–4% depending on value of transaction, and some limited exemptions	
Stamp Duty		Transactions related to purchase and sale of securities	
		0.5% with a range of exemptions and reliefs	

United States

(Len Wolf, l.wolf@thewolfgroup.com)

I   MAIN LEGAL FORMS

Legal form / Characteristics	Partnership and Limited Liability Partnership (LLP)	Ltd (private corporation) and Plc (public corporation)
Partners/shareholders • Number • Restrictions	• No limit on the number of partners • Foreign persons may be partner/members, subject to special withholding rules	• No limit on number of corporate shareholders • Foreign persons may own shares of a US corporation
Directors	N/A	No limitation
Establishment	Partnership agreement Articles of Organisation	Articles of Incorporation
Registration	Registration with local state	
Minimum capital	No minimum capital requirements	No minimum capital requirements
Liability	LLP: limited liability General Partnership: general partner has unlimited liability	Limited to capital
Governance	By state law	
Audit requirements	No statutory audit requirements imposed	No statutory audit requirements imposed upon private companies (only public companies)
Taxation	Transparent	Taxable on worldwide income

II   CORPORATION TAX

Legal form / Description	Resident corporation	Permanent establishment (PE)
General description	Corporation tax	
Taxable entities	Corporations incorporated in United States	PE trading in United States
Taxable income	Worldwide profits with considerations for double taxation treaties	Income arising in United States
Calculation of taxable profits	Accounting profit is adjusted for various tax add-backs and allowances to arrive to profits chargeable to corporation tax (PCTCT)	
Interest payments	Deductible subject to thin capitalisation restrictions	
Related party transactions	All related party transactions should take place on arm's length basis	
Tax year, return and payment	Companies may use calendar or fiscal year Returns are filed on the 15th day of the third month after the year-end Payment is on or before the due date for the tax return	
Capital gains	Treated as income	
Losses[1]	Net operating losses can be carried back 2 years and then forward 20 years (you may elect to waive the entire carry back period by the return due date including extensions)	
Tax group	Tax consolidation permissible for 80% owned subsidiaries	
Tax rate	$ *Tax rate* Up to 50,000 15% 50,001–75,000 25% 75,001–100,000 34% 100,001–335,000 39% 335,001–10,000,000 34% 10,000,001–15,000,000 35% 15,000,001–18,333,333 38% 18,333,334 and above 35%	

---

1   There are special rules allowing the company to utilise other losses such as capital losses and loan relationship deficits.

III TAXES FOR INDIVIDUALS

		Residents	Non-residents
Income Tax	General description	Tax levied on the chargeable income of a chargeable person for a year of assessment	
	Taxable entities and taxable income	Residents are taxed on their worldwide income	Certain types of income arising in United States
	Types of taxable income	• Property income (usually rent) • Income from capital investment (interest, sale of goodwill, dividends, royalties, annuities) • Income from business activities • Employment from personal services or pensions	
	Calculation of income	Gross income as reduced by deductible items and allowances	
	Tax year, tax assessment and tax payment	Tax year is the calendar or fiscal year Individual Income Tax returns must be filed by 15th day of the fourth month of the following year The full amount is due on or before the return filing date	
	Losses	Losses can be carried back 2 years or carried forward 20 years (you may elect to waive the entire carry back period by the return due date including extensions).	
	2008 Tax rates	Filing status: Single *Income ($)* *Tax rate* Up to 8,025 10% 8,025–32,550 15% 32,550–78,850 25% 78,850–164,550 28% 164,550–357,700 33% 357,700 and above 35% Filing status: Married filing jointly or qualifying widow(er) *Income ($)* *Tax rate* Up to 16,050 10% 16,050–65,100 15% 65,100–131,450 25% 131,450–200,300 28% 200,300–357,700 33% 357,700 and above 35% Filing status: Married filing separately *Income ($)* *Tax rate* Up to 8,025 10% 8,025–32,550 15% 32,550–65,725 25% 65,725–100,150 28% 100,150–178,850 33% 178,850 and above 35% Filing status: Head of household *Income ($)* *Tax rate* Up to 11,450 10% 11,450–43,650 15% 43,650–112,650 25% 112,650–182,400 28% 182,400–357,700 33% 357,700 and above 35%	

		Residents	**Non-residents**
Capital Gains Tax (CGT)	General description	Gains realised from the difference between the acquisition and disposal price of an asset	
	Taxable entities and chargeable assets	Assessed as part of business income	
	Calculation of gain	Gross proceeds less adjusted tax basis and selling expenses = capital gain	
	Tax year, tax assessment and tax payment	Reported with Individual Income Tax Return (see Taxes for individuals).	
	Losses	Capital losses may be deducted from capital gains or carried forward indefinitely Losses of up to $3,000 may be deducted from ordinary income	
	Tax rates	Short-term capital gains (assets held less than a year) are taxed as ordinary income subject to normal tax rates Long-term (assets held one year or more) capital gains are taxed at 15%	

		US domiciled	**Non-US domiciled**
Inheritance Tax (IHT)	General description	Tax on the transfer of property	
	Taxable entities and chargeable assets	All worldwide assets included	US assets
	Calculation of charge	Gross estate less allowances	
	Taxable events	Transfer by gift or by bequeath at death	
	Allowances	$2m for 2008 $3.5m for 2009 Special rules for non-citizen surviving spouse	$60,000
	Tax rates	$ *Tax rate* Up to 2,150 15% 2,150–5,000 25% 5,000–7,650 28% 7,650–10,450 33% 10,450 and above 35%	

IV WITHHOLDING TAXES

	Payments to non-residents[2]
Dividends	30%
Interest	30%
Royalties	30%
On payments to artists and sportsmen	30%

V   INDIRECT TAXES

		Residents	**Non-residents**
Value Added Tax (VAT)	General description	Tax on the supply of goods and services	
	Entities being obliged to levy VAT	The United States does not impose a VAT tax. Rather, each state (and many localities) typically imposes a sales tax on taxable sales (as defined in each state). Tax is imposed upon the sale to the ultimate consumer	
	Tax rates	Each state defines its own tax rate: from 4%–9%	
Stamp Duty Land Tax		Varies by state	
Stamp Duty		Varies by state	

Uruguay

(Luis Rafael Normey, rnormey@npyas-nexia.com.uy)

I MAIN LEGAL FORMS

Legal form / Characteristics	Partnership and Limited Liability Partnership (LLP)	Ltd (private corporation) and Plc (public corporation)
Partners/shareholders • Number • Restrictions	• Two or more • None	• One or more • None
Directors	Management by partners	Management by directors
Establishment	Notarial Deed	Articles of Incorporation
Registration	Commercial Register	
Minimum capital	Partnership: none LLP: U$800	U$10,000
Liability	Partnership: unlimited for all partners LLP: limited for all partners	Limited for all shareholders
Governance	Managing partners General partners' meeting	Board of Directors Shareholders' meetings
Audit requirements	Only for large enterprises and for those with loans greater than U$1.3m	
Taxation	Transparent	Corporation tax

II CORPORATION TAX

Legal form / Description	Resident corporation	Permanent establishment (PE)
General description	Tax on earnings derived from industrial, commercial and rural activities or services	
Taxable entities	Resident corporations or non-resident with PE in Uruguay	
Taxable income	Income received in Uruguay	
Calculation of taxable profits	Accounting profit is adjusted for various tax add-backs and allowances to arrive at taxable profits	
Interest payments	No thin capitalisation rules	
Related party transactions	Transfer pricing rules apply to cross-border transactions	
Tax year, return and payment	Tax year = business year (calendar year-end or any other year-end)	
	Payment and tax return = 4 months	
	Monthly prepayments, final payment or refund after tax assessment	
Capital gains	Capital gains on disposal of shares and listed shares are exempt	
	Other gains included with taxable income	
Losses	5-year loss carry back possible	
Tax group	None but dividends from subsidiaries are exempt	
Tax rate	25%	

III   TAXES FOR INDIVIDUALS

<table>
<tr><th></th><th></th><th>Residents</th><th>Non-residents</th></tr>
<tr><td rowspan="7">Income Tax</td><td>General description</td><td colspan="2">Income tax levied on the chargeable income of a chargeable person for a year of assessment</td></tr>
<tr><td>Taxable entities and taxable income</td><td>Individuals with habitual residence in the country deriving income in Uruguay</td><td>Individuals without habitual residence in the country but deriving income in Uruguay</td></tr>
<tr><td>Types of taxable income</td><td colspan="2"><ul><li>Property income</li><li>Income from capital investment (interest, sale of goodwill, dividends, royalties, annuities)</li><li>Income from personal services or pensions</li><li>Income derived from professional services or employment income</li><li>Gains on disposal of capital assets</li></ul></td></tr>
<tr><td>Tax year, tax assessment and tax payment</td><td colspan="2">Tax returns are filed on a fiscal basis and tax liabilities paid on a monthly basis</td></tr>
<tr><td>Losses</td><td colspan="2">Loss can be carried back for 2 years and offset against similar source of income</td></tr>
<tr><td>Tax rates</td><td><ul><li>Standard rate = none</li><li>Employment income: progressive rates from 0–25%</li><li>Capital gains or rental income: 12%</li><li>Profits: 7%</li><li>Social security:
– employers 19%
– employees 24%</li></ul></td><td><ul><li>General rate = 12%</li><li>Profits: 7%</li></ul></td></tr>
<tr><td>Inheritance Tax (IHT)</td><td>General description</td><td colspan="2">No IHT in Uruguay</td></tr>
</table>

IV   WITHHOLDING TAXES

	Payments to non-residents
Dividends	7%
Interest	10%
Royalties	12%
On payments to artists and sportsmen	12%

V INDIRECT TAXES

		Residents	Non-residents
Value Added Tax (VAT)	General description	Tax on the supply of goods, services and imports	
	Entities being obliged to levy VAT	All corporations and individuals involved in economic activities	
	Taxable activities	Supply of goods and services in Uruguay, and import of goods	
	Taxable activities – zero rated (examples)	Export of goods and services	
	Exemptions (examples)	• Agriculture goods and agriculture machines • Educational material • Milk • Oil • Exports	
	Refund of VAT	VAT on supplies may be refunded when a corporation has more income from exports than from supplies in Uruguay	
	Tax rates	10%–22% depending on the nature of goods and services	
	Administrative obligations	Monthly returns and payments	
Stamp Duty Land Tax		None	
Stamp Duty		None	

Vietnam

(Hoang Khoi, hoang.khoi@nexiaacpa.com)

I MAIN LEGAL FORMS

Legal form / Characteristics	Limited Liability Company (LLC)	Joint Stock Company	Partnership	Private Company
Partners/ shareholders • Number • Restrictions	• Single member LLC: one member • Multi-members: 2–50 members	• At least three shareholders • No restriction of maximum number of shareholders	• At least two co-owners of the partnership with jointly common business name • Partner must be individual	One individual
Directors	• Single member LLC: one or more • Multi-member LLC: Members' Council	Board of Management	Managed by partners	Managed by the owner
Establishment	Formed by individual(s) and/or organisation(s)		Formed by individuals	Formed by individual
Registration	Business Registration Office of Department of Planning and Investment (district level and above)			
Minimum capital	Not required except for business lines related to finance, banking, real estate, tourism and employment services			
Liability	Limited to capital for member(s)	Limited to capital for all shareholders	Unlimited to all partners	Unlimited to the owner
Governance	Members' Council meeting	Shareholders' meeting	Partners' Council	Owner
Audit requirements	Financial statements of the following enterprises must be audited: • companies listed on the securities market • state-owned enterprises • foreign-invested enterprises • organisations carrying on credit or banking activities and Development Assistance Fund • financial institutions and enterprises carrying out insurance business • reports on the finalisation of capital for construction of group A projects • other entities as specified by the laws, ordinances, decrees and decisions of the Prime Minister			
Taxation	Complying with the law on corporate income tax			

II   CORPORATION TAX (CORPORATE INCOME TAX, CIT)

	Resident corporation	Non-resident corporations	Permanent establishment (PE)
General description	Enterprises incorporated under foreign law with resident location in Vietnam	Enterprises incorporated under foreign law without resident location in Vietnam	Enterprises incorporated under Vietnamese law
Taxable entities	Income arising in or outside of Vietnam that is related to its operation in Vietnam	Income sourced from Vietnam	Income arising from Vietnam and foreign sources
Taxable income	<ul><li>Income from producing and trading goods or services</li><li>Other income from ownership rights, right to use assets, profit made from assignment, leases, liquidation of assets, deposit, loans, sales of foreign currency</li></ul>		
Calculation of taxable profit	Total revenue X *Minus* Deductible expenses Y *Plus* Other taxable incomes Z Taxable profit T		
Interest payments	Interest payments that exceed 150% of the prime rate of the State Bank of Vietnam are excluded from deductible expenses (Y)		
Related party transactions	Adherence to the arm's length principle Detailed transfer pricing methodologies, procedures and requirements		
Tax year, return and payment	Tax year = Fiscal year Quarterly CIT Declaration and Annual CIT Finalisation Tax payment must be made within 30 days for Quarterly CIT Declaration and 90 days for Annual CIT Finalisation		
Capital Gains	<ul><li>Before 1 January 2009: CIT rate: 28%</li><li>From 1 January 2009: CIT rate: 25%</li></ul>		
Losses	<ul><li>No carry back allowed</li><li>Losses may be carried forward for a maximum period of 5 years from the year following the year in which the loss arose</li></ul>		
Tax group	No tax applicable for group of companies		

Tax rate		*Before 1 January 2009*	*From 1 January 2009*
	Standard tax rate	28%	25%
	Oil and gas companies and companies involved in exploitation of precious minerals	28%–50%	32%–50%

III   TAXES FOR INDIVIDUALS

			Residents	**Non-residents**
Income Tax (PIT)	General description		Levy on income arising inside and outside Vietnam	Levy on income arising inside Vietnam
	Taxable entities	Before 2009	• All Vietnamese citizens living in Vietnam or overseas • Foreigners present in Vietnam at least 183 days within 12 consecutive months	Foreigners present in Vietnam less than 183 days within 12 consecutive months
		After 2009	• Vietnamese citizens and foreigners present in Vietnam at least 183 days within 12 consecutive months and • Have a permanent address, or engaged in a house leasing contract	Those who do not meet either of the resident conditions
	Taxable income and types of taxable income	Before 2009	*Regular income* • Salary and wages (including remuneration of members of the board of companies) • Income from copyrights for use of patents, brands, author's remuneration • Income earned by individuals who are not subject to CIT such as income from technological services, consultancy services, design services • Other income *Irregular income* • Income from transfer of technology, right to use industrial properties • Income from winnings and prizes	
		After 2009	• Salary and wages (including remuneration of members of the board of companies) • Income from royalties activity • Income from winnings and prizes • Income from business activity • Income from investment activity • Income from franchising activity • Gains from transfer of an equity interest or securities • Gains from transfer of immovable property rights • Receipt of an inheritance of equity interest/securities, immovable property rights or other registered assets and • Receipt of a gift of securities or an equity interest, immovable property rights or other registered assets	
	Calculation of income	Before 2009	Taxable income = income – compulsory deductions *Note*: Compulsory deductions are in a variety of forms such as compulsory social and health insurance, severance allowance, allowance stipulated by laws	Taxable income = total income arising from Vietnam
		After 2009	• Taxable income to be determined in variety of formula based on the type of income • Income for each activity shall be calculated for tax separately and add up to total tax payable	Taxable income = total income arising from Vietnam

			Residents	Non-residents
Income Tax (PIT)	Tax year	Before 2009	• Regular income: calendar year • Irregular income: as it arises	As it arises
		After 2009	• Income from business and salary and wages activities: calendar year • Others: as they arise	As it arises
	Tax assessment		Self-declaration regime. Tax assessment shall be done upon request by the Tax Authority There are penalties for incompliance in declaration and payment of PIT	
	Tax payment		• Regular income: within 20 days of the succeeding month • Irregular income: within 10 days of tax obligation arising • Tax Finalisation at the calendar year-end: within 90 days of the succeeding year	Within 10 days of tax obligation arising
	Losses		N/A	N/A

	Tax Rates	Before 2009	• Regular income:
			  – To Vietnamese citizens and others that settle in Vietnam
			
			Monthly income (million VND) *Rate (%)*
			
			Up to 5 0
			5–15 10
			15–25 20
			25–40 30
			40+ 40
			
			  – To foreigners who reside in Vietnam and Vietnamese citizens working overseas
			
			Monthly income (million VND) *Rate (%)*
			
			Up to 8 0
			8–20 10
			20–50 20
			50–80 30
			80+ 40
			
			• Irregular Income:
			  – Technology transfer: 5%
			  – Lottery winning in any form: 10%
				• Flat rate of 25% on Vietnamese-sourced income
				• There is opportunity for Double Taxation Avoidance (DTA) Application in respect of an expatriate that is resident of a country that signed the DTA Treaty with Vietnam and the expatriate satisfies the condition for DTA Application

			Residents		Non-residents	
Income Tax (PIT)	Tax Rates	After 2009	• Progressive rates (Vietnamese and foreigners)		*Type of Income*	*Tax rate (%)*
			Monthly income (million VND)	*Rate (%)*	Income from business activity:	
			Up to 5	5	– goods	1
			5–10	10	– services	5
			10–18	15	– production, construction, transport and others	2
			18–32	20		
			32–52	25		
			52–80	30	Salary, wages	20
			80+	35	Interest and dividends	5
			• Fixed rates		Gains on equity interest or securities	0.1
			Assessable Income	*Rate (%)*	Gains on immovable property rights	2
			Interest (except bank interest)	5	Royalties and franchise	5
			Dividend	5	Prizes, inheritance and gift	10
			Income from franchises/ royalties	5	There is opportunity for DTA Application in respect of an expatriate that is resident of a country that signed DTA Treaty with Vietnam and the expatriate satisfies condition for DTA Application	
			Income from winnings/ prizes	10		
			Income from inheritances/gifts (>VND 10m)	10		
			Income from sales of shares (gains or proceeds)	20 or 0.1		
			Income from transfer of real estate/land use rights	20 or 2		
Capital Gains Tax (CGT)	General description		• Before 1 January 2009: covered under Corporate Income Tax Law re party in the transfer is organisation. No Capital Gains Tax applicable for individual • From 1 January 2009: covered under Personal Income Tax Law			
	Taxable entities and chargeable assets					
	Calculation of gain					
	Tax year, tax assessment and tax payment					
	Losses					
	Tax rates					
			Domiciled		**Non-domiciled**	
Inheritance Tax (IHT) (After 2009)	General description		• Before 1 January 2009: N/A • From 1 January 2009: covered under Personal Income Tax Law			
	Taxable entities and chargeable assets					
	Calculation of charge					
	Taxable events					
	Allowances					
	Tax rates					

IV   WITHHOLDING TAXES

	Payments to non-residents
Dividends	N/A
Interest	• 10% applies to any loans agreements signed after 31 December 1998 • Exempted or reduced from interest withholding tax where a relevant DTA or Inter-Governmental Agreement is applied
Royalties	Before 1 January 2009: • 10% applies in the case of payments made to a foreign party for transfers of intellectual property and technology and for the leasing of machinery and equipment • exempted or reduced from interest withholding tax where a relevant DTA or Inter-Governmental Agreement is applied From 1 January 2009: not yet released
On payments to artists and sportsmen	N/A

V   INDIRECT TAXES

<table>
<tr><td colspan="2"></td><th>Residents</th><th>Non-residents</th></tr>
<tr><td rowspan="11">Value Added Tax (VAT)</td><td>General description</td><td colspan="2">VAT applies to goods and services used for production, trading and consumption in Vietnam (including goods and services purchased from abroad)</td></tr>
<tr><td>Entities being obliged to levy VAT</td><td colspan="2">All organisations and individuals producing, trading or importing goods and rendering services</td></tr>
<tr><td>Taxable activities</td><td colspan="2">All goods or services used for production, trading and consumption in Vietnam</td></tr>
<tr><td>Taxable activities – zero rated (examples)</td><td colspan="2">• Exported goods and services
• From 1 January 2009, international transportation service enjoys VAT rate of 0%</td></tr>
<tr><td>Exemptions (examples)</td><td colspan="2">• Certain agricultural products, including those imported
• Transfer of technology and software services, except exported software which is entitled to 0% rate</td></tr>
<tr><td>Refund of VAT</td><td colspan="2">Applicable for application of VAT under deduction method: by way of tax credit in the chain of company activity or to be refunded in cash or via bank transfer after tax assessment upon request and satisfies certain VAT refund condition</td></tr>
<tr><td>Tax liability</td><td colspan="2">Filing monthly before 20th of the succeeding month</td></tr>
<tr><td>Tax rates</td><td colspan="2">0%, 5%, and 10% are varied depending on type of goods, services</td></tr>
<tr><td>Administrative obligations</td><td colspan="2">• Vietnamese Accounting System to be applied
• Good conduct of tax compliance</td></tr>
<tr><td colspan="2">Stamp Duty Land Tax</td><td colspan="2">Stated in details by the Government</td></tr>
<tr><td colspan="2">Stamp Duty</td><td colspan="2">Stated in details by the Government</td></tr>
</table>

Nexia contacts by country

Argentina   Roberto Murmis   *Telephone:* + 54 11 4312 8525
                Abelovich, Polano & Asociados S.R.L.   *Facsimile:* + 54 11 4312 8525
                                                             Email: Rmurmis@estabe.com.ar

                Alejandra Capriotti   *Telephone:* + (54-11) 4343-6099
                Brihet & Asociados   *Facsimile:* + (54-11) 4343-6099
                                                             Email: acapriotti@brihetyasociados.com

                Ethel St Mary   *Telephone:* + 54 (0341) 447 3247
                Chiarotti Consulting   *Facsimile:* + 54 (0341) 447-3247 int. 103
                                                             Email: pchiarotti@chiarotti.com.ar

                Graciela María Vallés   *Telephone:* + 54 11 4381 0416
                Estudio Giordano & Asociados   *Facsimile:* + 54 11 4381 0416
                                                             Email: gvalles@ega-nexia.com

                Viviana López   *Telephone:* + 54 (02293) 421 952
                Estudio Mora & Asociados   *Facsimile:* + 54 (02293) 423 500
                                                             Email: cmora@speedy.com.ar

                Hector Nervi   *Telephone:* + 54 (2944) 423 380
                Hector P. Nervi & Asociados –   *Facsimile:* + 54 (2944) 432 106
                Contadores Públicos   *Email:* hectornervi@speedy.com.ar

                Atilio J González   *Telephone:* + 54 11 4312 6330
                Kalkin Group Consulting   *Email:* agonzalez@kalkingroup.com.ar

                Jorge L Mladineo   *Telephone:* + (54-11) 4322-7227
                Mladineo & Asociados   *Facsimile:* + (54-11) 4322-7227
                                                             Email: mladineopatagonia@ciudad.com.ar

                Nora Tapia   *Telephone:* + 54 (0261) 420-0019
                Palumbo, Nieto & Asociados   *Email:* estudiocontable@pna-nexia.com.ar

                Veronica Sigillito   *Telephone:* + 54 11 4876 7000
                Piccardo & Cia   *Facsimile:* + 54 11 4876 7050
                                                             Email: vsigillito@piccardo.com.ar

Australia   Andrew Roscoe   *Telephone:* + 61 (03) 9867 1555
                Anderson Roscoe   *Facsimile:* + 61 (03) 9867 1550
                                                             Email: andrew@andersonroscoe.com.au

                Michael Bannon   *Telephone:* + 61 (02) 6279 5400
                Duesburys Nexia   *Facsimile:* + 61 (02) 6279 5444
                                                             Email: michael.bannon@dnexia.com.au

Australia – continued	Bill Tonkin Forsythes	*Telephone:* + 61 (02) 4926 2699 *Facsimile:* + 61 (02) 4929 1435 *Email:* btonkin@forsythes.com.au
	Stephen Liu *LWK*	*Telephone:* + 61 (02) 9290 1588 *Facsimile:* + 61 (02) 9290 2997 *Email:* stephen.liu@lwkca.com
	Rob Ashby *Nelson Wheeler Nexia*	*Telephone:* + 61 (08) 8177 5799 *Facsimile:* + 61 (08) 8223 3593 *Email:* r.ashby@nwnexia.com.au
	John La Rocca *Nexia ASR*	*Telephone:* + 61 (03) 9608 0100 *Facsimile:* + 61 (03) 9670 8325 *Email:* jlarocca@nexiaasr.com.au
	Stephen J Rogers *Nexia Court & Co*	*Telephone:* + 61 (02) 9251 4600 *Facsimile:* + 61 (02) 9251 7138 *Email:* srogers@nexiacourt.com.au
	Craig A Vivian *Ord Nexia*	*Telephone:* + 61 (08) 9321 3514 *Facsimile:* + 61 (08) 9321 3523 *Email:* cvivian@ordgroup.com.au
	Murray Howlett *Pilot Partners*	*Telephone:* + 61 (07) 3023 1300 *Facsimile:* + 61 (07) 3229 1227 *Email:* mhowlett@pilotpartners.com.au
Austria	Vinzenz Hamerle *Hamerle & Partner Wirtschaftstreuhand GmbH*	*Telephone:* + 43 (1) 712 4114 0 *Facsimile:* + 43 (1) 712 4114 20 *Email:* office@hamerle-partner.at
	Wolfgang Korp *K & E Wirtschaftstreuhand GmbH*	*Telephone:* + 43 (316) 384640 *Facsimile:* + 43 (316) 38464020 *Email:* wolfgang.korp@ketreuhand.at
	Cornelius Kodrnja *Libertas Intercount Revisions und Beratungs GmbH*	*Telephone:* + 43 1 533 94 16 0 *Facsimile:* + 43 1 533 94 16 20 *Email:* c.kodrnja@libertas.at
	Herbert Glotz *Profund Wirtschaftstreuhand Kitzbühel GmbH*	*Telephone:* + 43 (5356) 661 77 *Facsimile:* + 43 (5356) 661 77 – 10 *Email:* tax-glotz@nexia.at
	Harald Czajka *Treuhand – Union Wien*	*Telephone:* + 43 1 533 88 32 *Facsimile:* + 43 1 533 88 32 14 *Email:* harald.czajka@treuhand-union.com
Bahrain	Nabeel A Al Saie *Nabeel Al-Saie – Public Accountants*	*Telephone:* + 973 1722 4772 *Facsimile:* + 973 1722 4426 *Email:* nabilsai@batelco.com.bh
Belgium	Edwin Vervoort *VGD*	*Telephone:* + 32 3 247 43 00 *Facsimile:* + 32 3 247 43 02 *Email:* edwin.vervoort@vgd.eu
	Werner Van den Broeck *VMB*	*Telephone:* + 32 (0)3 237 65 60 *Facsimile:* + 32 (0)3 237 07 14 *Email:* werner.vandenbroeck@vmb.be
Bolivia	E Willy Tudela Cornejo *Tudela & TH Consulting Group S.R.L.*	*Telephone:* + 591 2 244 2188 *Facsimile:* + 591 2 244 4085 *Email:* tztudela@tztudela.com

Brazil	Edson Pereira de Carvalho *Directa Auditores*	*Telephone:* + 55 11 2141 6300 *Facsimile:* + 55 11 2141 6323 *Email:* epc@directa.com.br
	Ricardo J Rodil *Nexia Villas Rodil Auditores e* *Consultores*	*Telephone:* + 55 11 3078 7077 *Facsimile:* + 55 11 3167 0697 *Email:* rodil@nexia.com.br
	Domingos Xavier Teixeira *Teixeira & Associados*	*Telephone:* + 55 31 3282 9939 *Facsimile:* + 55 31 3282 0867 *Email:* teixeira.dx@teixeira-auditores.com. br
British **Virgin** **Islands**	Kenneth Morgan *Nexia Restructuring and Recovery* *Limited*	*Telephone:* + 1 284 494 5414 *Facsimile:* + 1 284 494 5417 *Email:* kenneth.morgan@rawlinson-hunter. vg
Bulgaria	Ivaylo Pazvanski *VSI-KO*	*Telephone:* + 359 73 88 59 29 *Facsimile:* + 359 73 88 59 29 *Email:* vsi_ko@abv.bg
Burkina **Faso**	Oumarou Gilbert Sinare *SOFIDEC – Audit & Conseil*	*Telephone:* + 226 50 30 53 90 *Facsimile:* + 226 50 30 53 91 *Email:* sinare@sofidec-nexia.com
Cameroon	Claude Simo *CLS Audit Conseil*	*Telephone:* + 237 33 43 32 74 *Facsimile:* + 237 33 42 10 15 *Email:* contact@clsauditconseil.com
Canada	Bradley Allen *Davidson & Company LLP*	*Telephone:* + 1 604 687 0947 *Facsimile:* + 1 604 687 6172 *Email:* ballen@Davidson-Co.com
	Paul Neilson *Hudson LLP*	*Telephone:* + 1 (403) 265 0340 *Facsimile:* + 1 (403) 265 3142 *Email:* generalinfo@hudsonllp.ca
	Graham J. Sweett *Lyle Tilley Davidson*	*Telephone:* + 1 (902) 543 1044 *Facsimile:* + 1 (902) 543 0925 *Email:* graham@ltdca.com
	Jonathan Bicher *Nexia Friedman LLP*	*Telephone:* + 1 514 731 7901 *Facsimile:* + 1 514 731 2923 *Email:* bicher@nexiafriedman.ca
	Mark Strohl *Perreault, Wolman, Grzywacz & Co*	*Telephone:* + 1 514 731 7987 *Facsimile:* + 1 514 731 8782 *Email:* mark.strohl@pwgca.com
	Brian T McGee *Zeifmans LLP*	*Telephone:* + 1 416 256 4000 *Facsimile:* + 1 416 256 4001 *Email:* bm@zeifman.ca
Cayman **Islands**	Alex S Bodden *Bodden Anglin & Associates Ltd*	*Telephone:* + 1 (345) 743 3000 *Facsimile:* + 1 (345) 743 3001 *Email:* alex.bodden@boddenanglin.com
	Charles (Chuck) Ludmer *J H Cohn LLP*	*Telephone:* + 1 345 949 6333 *Email:* cludmer@jhcohn.com

Cayman Islands – continued	Peter Anderson *Nexia Restructuring & Recovery (C.I.) Limited*	*Telephone:* + 1 (345) 949 7576 *Facsimile:* + 1 (345) 949 8295 *Email:* peter.anderson@rawlinson-hunter.com.ky
Channel Islands, Guernsey	Mark Le Ray *Saffery Champness*	*Telephone:* + 44 1481 721374 *Facsimile:* + 44 1481 722046 *Email:* mark.leray@saffery.gg
Channel Islands, Jersey	Mark Pesco *Langtry International Ltd*	*Telephone:* + 44 (1534) 750000 *Facsimile:* + 44 (1534) 750075 *Email:* mark.pesco@ifgint.com
Chile	Gerardo Vial *Humphreys & Cia*	*Telephone:* + 56 (2) 204 7315 *Facsimile:* + 56 (2) 223 4937 *Email:* Gerardo.Vial@humphreys.cl
China	K K Leung *Fan Chan & Co – Fan Chan Business Advisory (Shanghai) Limited*	*Telephone:* + (86) 21 5877 3952 *Facsimile:* + (86) 21 5877 3951 *Email:* kk@fanchan.com
	Hiltung Fong *Guangzhou Xin Zhong Nan CPAs Co Ltd.*	*Telephone:* + 86 20 8354 3498 *Facsimile:* + 86 20 8354 8834 *Email:* fanght@163.net
	Henry Tan *Nexia China Pte Ltd – Nexia TS (Shanghai) Co Ltd*	*Telephone:* + 65 6536 5466 *Facsimile:* + 65 6534 5766 *Email:* henrytan@nexiats.com.sg
	Ke Ren Sun *Nexia HDDY (Shanghai) CPAs Co Ltd*	*Telephone:* + 8621 6255 8738 *Facsimile:* + 8621 6253 1968 *Email:* seacpa@online.sh.cn
	Cherry Mao *Shanghai Fuxing Mingfang*	*Telephone:* + 86 21 6390 1881 *Facsimile:* + 86 21 6390 1882 *Email:* fuxingcpa@vip.citiz.net
	Shawn, Shouyuan Wu *Zhonglei Certified Public Accountants*	*Telephone:* + 86 10 5112 0372 *Facsimile:* + 86 10 5112 0377 *Email:* wushouyuan66@gmail.com
Colombia	Javier Fernando Gomez Estrada *Montes y Asociados S.A.*	*Telephone:* + 57 68 814666 *Facsimile:* + 57 68 857744 *Email:* impuestos@nexiamya.com.co
Costa Rica	Mitry Breedy *Mitry Breedy y Asociados CPA*	*Telephone:* + 506 2290 4050 *Facsimile:* + 506 2231 7752 *Email:* mbreedy@racsa.co.cr
Croatia	Hrvoje Zgombić *Nexia Croatia Ltd*	*Telephone:* + 385 1 4699 555 *Facsimile:* + 385 1 4699 500 *Email:* hrvoje.zgombic@zgombic.hr
Cyprus	Athos Kakofengitis *Bestservus Ltd*	*Telephone:* + 357 25 340 930 *Facsimile:* + 357 25 342 484 *Email:* athos@bestservus.eu

Cyprus – *continued*	Michael Kourtellas *Nexia Poyiadjis*	*Telephone:* + 357 22 456 111 *Facsimile:* + 357 22 666 276 *Email:* michael.kourtellas@nexia.com.cy
Czech Republic	Vladimir Králicek *AUDIT PLUS s.r.o.*	*Telephone:* + 420 221 584 301 *Facsimile:* + 420 221 584 319 *Email:* vladimir.kralicek@auditplus.cz
	Josef Zizala *VGD, s.r.o*	*Telephone:* + 420-261 222 516 *Facsimile:* + 420-261 222 517 *Email:* vgd.prague@vgd.eu
Denmark	Iver Haugsted *Christensen Kjaerulff*	*Telephone:* + 45 33 30 15 15 *Facsimile:* + 45 33 13 19 91 *Email:* ih@ck.dk
Dominican Republic	Carlos Daniel *Francisco y Asociados*	*Telephone:* + 1 809 689 3881 *Facsimile:* + 1 809 687 3883 *Email:* cdaniel@franciscoyasociados.com
Ecuador	Manuel Alvarado *AlvaradoSchaffer & Asociados*	*Telephone:* + 59 34 238 3491 *Facsimile:* + 59 34 2881 694 *Email:* enqugtas@gye.satnet.net
	Cristina Trujillo *Astrileg Cia, Ltda*	*Telephone:* + 593 2 2452 635 *Facsimile:* + 593 2 2452 636 *Email:* cristina.trujillo@astrileg.com.ec
Egypt	Sherif William *Adel Saad & Co*	*Telephone:* + (202) 2417 2045 *Facsimile:* + (202) 2417 4086 *Email:* sherif.william@adelsaadandco.com
El Salvador	Eddie Gamaliel Castellanos López *Castellanos, Gómez, Cabrera y* *Asociados, S.A. de C.V.*	*Telephone:* + 503 2226 2230 *Facsimile:* + 503 2226 2234 *Email:* ecastellanos@cgcauditores.com
Estonia	Evald Veldemann *Audiitorbüroo ELSS AS*	*Telephone:* + 372 7 301 345 *Facsimile:* + 372 7 301 333 *Email:* evald.veldemann@elss.ee
Finland	Karri Nieminen *Fiscales Ltd*	*Telephone:* + 358 9 6829 670 *Facsimile:* + 358 9 6829 6777 *Email:* karri.nieminen@nexia.fi
	Kare Kotiranta *Nexia Tilintarkastus Oy, KHT-auditors* *(APA)*	*Telephone:* + 358 207 419 270 *Facsimile:* + 358 207 419 289 *Email:* kare.kotiranta@nexia.fi
France	Alain Fitzgerald *Auditeurs & Conseils Associés*	*Telephone:* + 33 1 47 66 77 88 *Facsimile:* + 33 1 47 66 77 80 *Email:* a.fitzgerald@aca.nexia.fr
	Stéphane Marie *Corevise*	*Telephone:* + 33 1 53 70 19 70 *Facsimile:* + 33 1 53 70 19 71 *Email:* smarie@corevise.com
	Laurent Gilles *Novances*	*Telephone:* + 33 4 72 82 22 00 *Facsimile:* + 33 4 72 82 22 02 *Email:* lgilles@novances.fr

France – *continued*	Bernard Hinfray *SEFICO – JWA*	*Telephone:* + 33 1 44 34 08 00 *Facsimile:* + 33 1 44 34 08 32 *Email:* b.hinfray@sefico-jwa.com
	Yves Sevestre *Yves SEVESTRE – Tax Lawyer*	*Telephone:* + 33 (0) 1 70 80 98 80 *Facsimile:* + 33 (0) 1 40 70 09 65 *Email:* y.sevestre@cabinet-sevestre.com
French Polynesia	Veronique Morin *Edec Sarl*	*Telephone:* + 689 43 86 00 *Facsimile:* + 689 43 34 02 *Email:* veronique.morin@edec-compta.com
Germany	Frank Heinze *ATW Allgemeine Treuhand* *Wirtschaftsberatung GmbH*	*Telephone:* + 49 (0) 711 222 969 60 *Facsimile*: + 49 (0) 711 222 969 89 *Email:* stuttgart@nexia.de
	Rolf-Dieter Schmitz *BRM Themis GmbH*	*Telephone:* + 49 (0) 69 570 050 *Facsimile:* + 49 (0) 69 570 051 90 *Email:* brm-frankfurt@brm-online.de
	Dr. Helmut Weyer *BTR – DR. WELTE, HIEKE & PARTNER* *KG*	*Telephone:* + 49 (0) 761 70 30 30 *Facsimile:* + 49 (0) 761) 70 30 33 3 *Email:* freiburg@nexia.de
	Dr. Gregor Meurer *BTR MECKLENBURG & KOLLEGEN* *(Law – Group)*	*Telephone:* + 49 (0) 711 2229 200 *Facsimile:* + 49 (0) 711 2229 2020 *Email:* stgt@btr-mecklenburg.de
	Lutz v Majewsky *BTR SUMUS GMBH*	*Telephone:* + 49 (0) 451 480 020 *Facsimile:* + 49 (0) 451 472 807 *Email:* sumus@t-online.de
	Ralf Krüger *CORDES + PARTNER GMBH*	*Telephone:* + 49 (0) 40 37 47 44 0 *Facsimile:* + 49 (0) 40 37 47 44 666 *Email:* ralf.krueger@cfh-hamburg.de
	Dr. Heinrich Watermeyer *DHPG DR. HARZEM & PARTNER KG*	*Telephone:* + 49 (0) 228 81 00 00 *Facsimile:* + 49 (0) 228 81 00 020 *Email:* heinrich.watermeyer@dhpg.de
	Dr. Markus Emmrich *Ebner Stolz Mönning Bachem* *Partnerschaft*	*Telephone:* + 49 (0) 40 370 97 177 *Facsimile:* + 49 (0) 40 370 97 599 *Email:* markus.emmrich@ebnerstolz.de
	Stefan Sommerer *ETH Erlanger Treuhand GmbH*	*Telephone:* + 49 (0) 9131 6906 765 *Facsimile:* + 49 (0) 9131 6906 170 *Email:* info@eth-wpg.de
	Uwe Lehmann *LHP Lehmann Hahn & Partner*	*Telephone:* + 49 (0) 9841 90 90 *Facsimile:* + 49 (0) 9841 90 91 6 *Email:* bad.windsheim@lhp.de
	Josef Winkler *LTS Rechtsanwälte Wirtschaftsprüfer* *Steuerberater*	*Telephone:* + 49 (0) 5221 693 061 *Facsimile:* + 49 (0) 5221 693 069 2 *Email:* info@lts-rechtsanwaelte.com
	Klaus Senft *MÜNCHENER WIRTSCHAFTSPRÜ-* *FUNGSGESELLSCHAFT GMBH*	*Telephone:* + 49 (0) 89 124 880 1 *Facsimile:* + 49 (0) 89 124 881 00 *Email:* muenchen@nexia.de
	Alexander Schmidt *NEXIA BERLIN GMBH*	*Telephone:* + 49 (0) 30 203 015 0 *Facsimile:* + 49 (0) 30 203 015 20 *Email:* berlin@nexia.de

Germany – continued	Torsten Seidel *NEXIA HANNOVER GmbH*	*Telephone:* + 49 (0) 511 300 350 *Facsimile:* + 49 (0) 511 300 353 00 *Email:* t.seidel@nexia.de
	Paul-Bernhard Weiss *Paul-Bernhard Weiß, Dipl.-Kfm.*	*Telephone:* + 49 (0) 2871 21 19 0 *Facsimile:* + 49 (0) 2871 21 19 70 *Email:* bocholt@nexia.de
	Horst Mackenstedt *RTW Revisions-, Treuhand- und* *Wirtschaftsberatungs-KG*	*Telephone:* + 49 (0) 421 162 100 *Facsimile:* + 49 (0) 421 162 101 0 *Email:* wirtschaftspruefer@rtw-bremen.de
Ghana	Kwame Manu-Debrah *Nexia Debrah & Co*	*Telephone:* + (233-21) 228083 *Facsimile:* + (233-21) 228390 *Email:* debrah@nexiadebrah.com
Gibraltar	Moe Cohen *Benady Cohen & Co*	*Telephone:* + 350 (200) 74854 *Facsimile:* + 350 (200) 51477 *Email:* mcohen@benadycohen.com
Greece	Spyridon Michopoulos *Dinamiki EPE*	*Telephone:* + 30 210 612 4663 *Facsimile:* + 30 210 806 9239 *Email:* dinamiki@otenet.gr
	Eleni Kaprani *Nexia Eurostatus Certified Auditors S.A*	*Telephone:* + 30 210 900 8400 *Facsimile:* + 30 210 924 9568 *Email:* estatus@eurostatus-nexia.gr
Guatemala	Jorge Garcia *W Garcia y Asociados*	*Telephone:* + 502 2387 6100 *Facsimile:* + 502 2387 6105 *Email:* jgarcia@wgarciayasociados.com
Honduras	Milton Rodolfo Palao *Nexia Auditores & Consultores*	*Telephone:* + 504 557 6191 *Facsimile:* + 504 557 6313 *Email:* mpalao@nexiahonduras.com
Hong Kong **SAR**	Vickie Fan *Fan, Chan & Co*	*Telephone:* + 852 2572 4377 *Facsimile:* + 852 2891 5103 *Email:* vickiefan@fanchan.com
	Brenda Chan *Nexia Charles Mar Fan & Co*	*Telephone:* + (852) 2520 0333 *Facsimile:* + (852) 2529 4347 *Email:* bk@charles-marfan.com
Hungary	József Láng *ABT Hungária Ltd*	*Telephone:* + 36 1 430 3400 *Facsimile:* + 36 1 430 3402 *Email:* jozsef.lang@abt.hu
	Anita Páli *ITAG-OKOLEX Auditing Ltd*	*Telephone:* + 36 96 512 760 *Facsimile:* + 36 96 512 769 *Email:* anita.pali@itag-audit.hu
	Andrea Nagy *VGD Ferencz & Partner Kft.*	*Telephone:* + 36 1 225 7575 *Facsimile:* + 36 1 225 7574 *Email:* andrea.nagy@vgd.hu
India	Percy H Italia *Agarwal & Italia*	*Telephone:* + 91 40 2784 8700 *Facsimile:* + 91 40 2781 8165 *Email:* percy@agarwalanditalia.com

India – continued	Krupal Kanakia *Chaturvedi & Shah*	*Telephone:* + 91 22 3021 8500 *Facsimile:* + 91 22 2284 0892 *Email:* krupal@chaturvedi-and-shah.com
	Maulik Doshi *SKP Group*	*Telephone:* + 91 22 6617 8000 *Facsimile:* + 91 22 6617 8002 *Email:* maulik.doshi@skparekh.com
Indonesia	M Hardy *KAP Kanaka Puradiredja, Suhartono*	*Telephone:* + 62 21 831 3861 *Facsimile:* + 62 21 831 3871 *Email:* m.hardy@kanaka.co.id
Iran	Shirin Moshirfatemi *Behrad Moshar Certified Public Accountants*	*Telephone:* 98 21 8832 6527/8 *Facsimile:* 98 21 8830 9490 *Email:* s.m.fatemi@behradmoshar.com
Ireland	Stephen Brown *Hayden Brown*	*Telephone:* + 353 1 6771951 *Facsimile:* + 353 1 6771308 *Email:* stephen.brown@haydenbrown.ie
	Brian Egan *Smith & Williamson Freaney Limited*	*Telephone:* + 353 (1) 614 2500 *Facsimile:* + 353 (1) 614 2555 *Email:* brian.egan@swf.ie
Isle of Man	Craig Brown *Abacus Trust Company Limited*	*Telephone:* + 44 (0) 1624 689 600 *Facsimile:* + 44 (0) 1624 689 601 *Email:* craig.brown@abacusiom.com
Israel	Guy Faigenboim *I Strauss Lazer & Co*	*Telephone:* + 972 (3) 623 7743/5 *Facsimile:* + 972 (3) 561 3824 *Email:* guy@slcpa.co.il
	Jacob Kuperberg *Kuperberg & Co*	*Telephone:* + 972 3 613 1490 *Facsimile:* + 972 3 613 1492 *Email:* cpa@kuperberg.co.il
Italy	Gigliola Bertoglio *Audirevi S.r.l.*	*Telephone:* + 39 02 6733 8202 *Facsimile:* + 39 02 6733 8322 *Email:* gigliola.bertoglio@audirevi.it
	Luciano Leonello Godoli *Studio Maurizio Godoli*	*Telephone:* + 39 051 232450 *Facsimile:* + 39 051 232347 *Email:* lgodoli@studiogodoli.it
	Salvatore Tarsia *TCFCT – Studio Associato Consulenza Societaria e Tributaria*	*Telephone:* + 39 02 805 8011 *Facsimile:* + 39 02 805 80190 *Email:* s.tarsia@tcfct.it
Japan	*Sosuke Yasuda Gyosei & Co*	*Telephone:* + 81 (0) 3 5211 7878 *Facsimile:* + 81 (0) 3 5211 7879 *Email:* s-yasuda@gyosei-grp.or.jp
Jordan	Sinan S Ghosheh *Ghosheh & Co*	*Telephone:* + 962 6 5561204 *Facsimile:* + 962 6 5561204 *Email:* sinan@ghosheh.com
Kazakhstan	Vitaliy Sipakov *Kazakhconsulting Ltd*	*Telephone:* + 7 (727) 22-72-401 *Facsimile:* + 7 (727) 22-72-398 *Email:* sipakov@nexia.kz

Kenya	Charles Gitau *Carr Stanyer Gitau & Co Certified Public Accountants*	*Telephone:* + 254 (20) 2730 300 *Facsimile:* + 254 (20) 2730 298 *Email:* csg@carrstgitau.com
	Owen Koimburi *KOKA Koimburi & Co*	*Telephone:* + 254 20 2727 121 *Facsimile:* + 254 20 2727 160 *Email:* okoimburi@scikt.co.ke
Korea	Hyun-soo Kwon *Nexia Samduk*	*Telephone:* + 82 (2) 397 6700 *Facsimile:* + 82 (2) 730 9559 *Email:* cpakwon@chollian.net
Kuwait	Nayer Nazar *Nazar & Partners*	*Telephone:* + 965 242 4661 *Facsimile:* + 965 240 2690 *Email:* nazarnexia@hotmail.com
Latvia	Jelena Rakova *Audit Advice LLC*	*Telephone:* + 371 26 54 23 54 *Facsimile:* + 371 67 33 32 27 *Email:* ius@auditadvice.lv
Lebanon	Mosbah A Majzoub *Majzoub & Partners, CPAs*	*Telephone:* + 961 1 612224 *Facsimile:* + 961 1 612225 Ex 108 *Email:* mosbah@scmajzoub.com
	Dr Oussama Ali Tabbara *Usamah Tabbarah & Co*	*Telephone:* + 961 (1) 751 111 *Facsimile:* + 961 (1) 746 749 *Email:* otabbara@utcnexia.com
Liechtenstein	Louis Oehri *LOPAG Louis Oehri & Partner Trust reg*	*Telephone:* + 423 377 3617 *Facsimile:* + 423 373 2131 *Email:* lopag@lopag.li
	Roger Beggiato *ReviTrust Revision AG*	*Telephone:* + 423 237 42 42 *Facsimile:* + 423 237 42 92 *Email:* roger.beggiato@nexia.com
	Dr. Thomas Wilhelm *Wilhelm & Partner*	*Telephone:* + 423 399 48 50 *Facsimile:* + 423 399 48 51 *Email:* twilhelm@awp.li
Lithuania	Ruta Samuleviciute *Accounting and Control CJSC Auditas*	*Telephone:* + 370 5 261 9772 *Facsimile:* + 370 5 278 4843 *Email:* audito@takas.lt
Luxembourg	Pierre-François Wéry *a&c – audit & compliance s.à r.l.*	*Telephone:* + 352 27 621 345-1 *Facsimile:* + 352 27 621 346 *Email:* pfwery@audit-compliance.lu
	Marc Van Hoek *Luxfiducia*	*Telephone:* + 352 26 43 29 97 *Facsimile:* + 352 26 43 29 98 *Email:* mark.vanhoek@luxfiducia.lu
	Lut Laget *VGD*	*Telephone:* + 352 26 38 48 1 *Facsimile:* + 352 26 25 94 54 *Email:* lut.laget@vgd.eu
Malawi	Joseph Ndovi *Graham Carr*	*Telephone:* + 265 1 823 288 *Facsimile:* + 265 1 823 168 *Email:* josephndovi@grahamcarrmw.com

Malaysia	Jason Sia Sze Wan *SSY Partners / Noordin Jaafar / Sia & Co*	*Telephone:* + 60 3 4042 0611 *Facsimile:* + 60 3 4041 0704 *Email:* jasonsia@ssypartners.com
Malta	Karl Cini *Brian Tonna & Co*	*Telephone:* + 356 2163 7778 *Facsimile:* + 356 2163 4383 *Email:* karl@briantonna.com
Mauritius	Ouma Shankar Ochit *Nexia Baker & Arenson*	*Telephone:* + 230 207 0600 *Facsimile:* + 230 210 7878 *Email:* sochit@nexia.intnet.mu
	James Ho Fong *SCI Essell Associates*	*Telephone:* + 230 210 8588 *Facsimile:* + 230 210 8590 *Email:* eos@intnet.mu
Mexico	Ramiro Gonzalez F *Gonzalez Espinosa y Asociados S.C.*	*Telephone:* + 52 81 89 89 98 81 *Facsimile:* +52 81 81 14 66 06 *Email:* mgonzalezf@geasc.com.mx
	Héctor J García Martínez *Gossler, S.C.*	*Telephone:* + 52 (81) 8347 0072/ 3575 *Facsimile:* + 52 (81) 8348 9887 *Email:* hgarcia@gossler.com.mx
	Pedro Nunez Rosas *Nunez Rosas y Asociados*	*Telephone:* + 52 33 36 30 14 30 *Facsimile:* + 52 33 36 30 14 41 *Email:* nunezra@prodigy.net.mx
	Alfredo Solloa G *Solloa, Tello de Meneses y Cia., S.C.*	*Telephone:* + 52 55 2629 7232 *Facsimile:* + 52 55 2629 7239 *Email:* alfredo.solloa@solloacp.com.mx
Mongolia	Davaasuren Chimid *NIMM Audit Co, Ltd*	*Telephone:* + 976 11 463 313 *Facsimile:* + 976 11 463 882 *Email:* nimmaudit@mongol.net
Morocco	Mohamed Ouedghiri *Nexia Fiducia*	*Telephone:* + 212 22 36 45 88 *Facsimile:* + 212 22 36 48 25 *Email:* fidunex@casanet.net.ma
Namibia	Richard Theron *Grand Namibia*	*Telephone:* + 264 61 228423 *Facsimile:* + 264 61 227078 *Email:* rtheron@grandnam.net
Nepal	Kumud Tripathy *R. BAJRACHARYA & CO*	*Telephone:* + 977-1-442 1684 *Facsimile:* + 977-1-442 4247 *Email:* kumudt@mos.com.np
Netherlands, The	Cor van Marle *FACET Audit B.V.*	*Telephone:* + 31 10 4526 144 *Facsimile:* + 31 10 4525 187 *Email:* c.vanmarle@facet-accountants.nl
	Bas Opmeer *FSV Accountants + Adviseurs B.V.*	*Telephone:* + 31 20 301 2244 *Facsimile:* + 31 20 301 2202 *Email:* b.opmeer@fsv.nl
	Ton Krol *Horlings Belastingadviseurs (tax)*	*Telephone:* + 31 (0)20 570 0200 *Facsimile:* + 31 (0)20 676 4478 *Email:* tkrol@horlings.nl

Netherlands The – continued	Chris Leenders Koenen en Co	*Telephone:* + 31 (0)45 5723 350 *Facsimile:* + 31 (0)45 5724 975 *Email:* c.leenders@koenenenco.nl
	Hans Eppink KroeseWevers Accountants en Belastingadviseurs	*Telephone:* + 31 (0)53 850 4900 *Facsimile:* + 31 (0)53 850 4901 *Email:* enschede@kroesewevers.nl
Nevis	John Terry Dixcart Management Nevis Limited	*Telephone:* + 1 869 469 2829 *Facsimile:* + 1 869 469 6509 *Email:* john.terry@dixcartnevis.com
New Zealand	Barry Tuck CST NEXIA LTD	*Telephone:* + 64 (9) 262 2595 *Facsimile:* + 64 (9) 262 2606 *Email:* btuck@cstnexia.co.nz
	Murray Winder Marriotts Ltd	*Telephone:* + 64 3 379 0829 *Facsimile:* + 64 3 366 7144 *Email:* murray@marriotts.co.nz
Nigeria	David Olaleye Agbo Abel & Co	*Telephone:* + 234 9 671 3473 *Facsimile:* + 234 9 523 7476 *Email:* agboabels@yahoo.com
	Yinka Olapade Sulaimon & Co	*Telephone:* + 234 (062) 240 776 *Facsimile:* + 234 (062) 240 779 *Email:* olapade@sulaimonandco.com
Norway	Helge A Østvold Bakke Hjelmaas Larsen	*Telephone:* + 47 66 85 59 00 *Facsimile:* + 47 66 98 05 70 *Email:* hao@bhl.no
	Vidar Haugen Kjelstrup & Wiggen AS	*Telephone:* + 47 23 11 42 00 *Facsimile:* + 47 23 11 42 01 *Email:* vidar.haugen@k-w.no
	Tom-Bertil Smeby Nexia DA	*Telephone:* + 47 23 11 48 00 *Facsimile:* + 47 23 11 48 10 *Email:* smeby@nexia.no
Oman	Dr Oussama Ali Tabbara Usamah Tabbarah & Co – Certified Public Accountants	*Telephone:* + 968 24 567 251 *Facsimile:* + 968 24 567 480 *Email:* otabbara@utcnexia.com
Pakistan	Sarfraz Mahmood Riaz Ahmad and Company	*Telephone:* + 92 42 571 8137 *Facsimile:* + 92 42 571 8136 *Email:* sm@racopk.com
	S. M. Masood S. M. Masood & Co	*Telephone:* + 92 (42) 571 2554 *Facsimile:* + 92 (42) 571 2556 *Email:* smma@nexlinx.net.pk
Palestine	Salah Abu Watfeh El Wafa & Co	*Telephone:* + 970 (8) 282 4662 *Facsimile:* + 970 (8) 282 5477 *Email:* elwafaco@palnet.com
Panama	Bartolomé Mafla H. Nexia Auditores (Panama)	*Telephone:* + 507 302-7800 *Facsimile:* + 507 302-7405 *Email:* bmafla@nexiapanama.com

Paraguay	Angel Devaca Pavón *CYCE – Consultores y Contadores de* *Empresas*	*Telephone:* + 595 (021) 446 883 *Facsimile:* + 595 (021) 442 641 *Email:* devaca@cyce.com.py
Peru	Dr Luis Cayo *Urbano Ventocilla & Asociados S. Civ.*	*Telephone:* + 511 441 5041 *Facsimile:* + 511 441 4929 *Email:* lcayo@nexiauvperu.com
	Alfonso Pinedo Mirano *Urbizagástegui & Asociados S.Civ. R.* *Ltda.*	*Telephone:* + 51 (1) 440 1032 *Facsimile:* + 51 (1) 421 3759 *Email:* apinedom@nexiaperu.com
Poland	Maria Korycka *Korycka, Budziak* *& Audytorzy sp. z o.o.*	*Telephone:* + 48 22 522 23 90 *Facsimile:* + 48 22 522 23 91 *Email:* maria.korycka@kba.com.pl
	Miroslaw Kośmider *PRO AUDIT Kancelaria Biegłych* *Rewidentów Spółka z o.o.*	*Telephone:* + 48 12 632 80 32 *Facsimile:* + 48 12 632 80 64 *Email:* mkosmider@proaudit.pl
Portugal	Rui Guedes Henriques *Camacho Palma & Lisboa Afonso –* *SROC*	*Telephone:* + 351 21 413 55 00 *Facsimile:* + 351 21 413 55 09 *Email:* ruighenriques@nexia.pt
	Joao Araujo *SANTOS CARVALHO & ASSOCIADOS,* *SROC, S.A.*	*Telephone:* + 351 22 519 36 60 *Facsimile:* + 351 22 519 36 61 *Email:* info@santoscarvsroc.pt
Puerto Rico	Enrique Cardona *Nexia Cardona & Co, PSC*	*Telephone:* + 1 (787) 522-0300 *Facsimile:* + 1 (787) 522-0301 *Email:* emcardona@nexiacardona.com
Romania	Luminita Ristea *Consulting R Group*	*Telephone:* + 4031 402 2563 *Facsimile:* + 4031 402 2562 *Email:* luminita.ristea@consultingr.ro
	Alina Balaciu *Cunescu, Balaciu & Associates* *(Attorneys at Law)*	*Telephone:* + 4021 327 6633 *Facsimile:* + 4021 327 4310 *Email:* alina.balaciu@cbalaw.ro
	Anna Karina Nicolau *KG Audit & Accounting*	*Telephone:* + 4021 320 2014 *Facsimile:* + 4021 320 2089 *Email:* office@kgaudit.ro
Russia	Natalia Malofeeva *ICLC*	*Telephone:* + 7 495 621 10 15 *Facsimile:* + 7 495 621 56 87 *Email:* malofeeva@mkpcn.ru
	Olga Goryacheva *Nexia CIS*	*Telephone:* + 7 (495) 780-62-50 *Facsimile:* + 7 (495)) 785-94-61 *Email:* goryacheva@pacioli.ru
	Alexey Kruchkov *ROSCO Corporation*	*Telephone:* + 7 (495) 251 5392 *Facsimile:* + 7 (495) 250 8089 *Email:* kruchkov@ros-co.ru
Saudi **Arabia**	Abdulrazzaq Waly Sait *Abdulrazzaq & Ahmed Waly Sait Co*	*Telephone:* + 966 2 644 5045 *Facsimile:* + 966 2 644 1971 *Email:* walysaitcpa@awalnet.net.sa

Saudi Arabia – *continued*	Dr Oussama Ali Tabbara *Usamah Ali Tabbarah & Co*	*Telephone:* + 966 (1) 462 0682 *Facsimile:* + 966 (1) 462 1576 *Email:* oussamatabbara@utcnexia.com
Singapore	Sarah Geok Hong Koh *Nexia TS Public Accounting Corporation*	*Telephone:* + 65 6534 5700 *Facsimile:* + 65 6534 5766 *Email:* sarahkoh@nexiats.com.sg
	Shanker Iyer *Shanker Iyer & Co*	*Telephone:* + 65 6532 5746 *Facsimile:* + 65 6532 7680 *Email:* shanker@iyerpractice.com
Slovak Republic	Vladimír Kolenic *INTERAUDIT Group, s.r.o*	*Telephone:* + 421 2 555 658 96 *Facsimile:* + 421 2 555 658 96 *Email:* ia-group@iag.sk
	Erika Klarik *RECTE AUDIT s.r.o.*	*Telephone:* + 421 2 6720 2211 *Facsimile:* + 421 2 6241 0396 *Email:* erika.klarik@recte.sk
South Africa	Keith du Preez *Nexia Cape Town*	*Telephone:* + 27 (21) 527 3400 *Facsimile:* + 27 (21) 527 3434 *Email:* keith@nexiasa.com
	Petrus Roets *Nexia HBLT Chartered Accountants (East Rand) Incorporated*	*Telephone:* + 27 11 421 8374 *Facsimile:* + 27 11 421 5777 *Email:* petrus@nexia-er.biz
	Elza Prinsloo *Nexia Levitt Kirson*	*Telephone:* + 27 (11) 483 4000 *Facsimile:* + 27 (11) 483 1638 *Email:* elza@lkg.co.za
	Bashier Adam *SAB&T Incorporated*	*Telephone:* + 27 12 682 8800 *Facsimile:* + 27 12 682 8801 *Email:* bashier@sab-t.co.za
Spain	Javier Estellés *Laes Nexia*	*Telephone:* + 34 91 576 8432 *Facsimile:* + 34 91 577 7712 *Email:* j.estelles@laesnexia.com
	Xavier Echeverria *Laudis Consultor, S.L.*	*Telephone:* + 34 932 387 387 *Facsimile:* + 34 932 387 388 *Email:* xe@laudis.es
	Jaume Pigem *LAVINIA AUDITORIA & CONSULTORIA, S.L.*	*Telephone:* + 34 932 417 240 *Facsimile:* + 34 932 417 241 *Email:* jpigem@laviniaudit.com
	José Juan Andújar *Pedrosa Lagos*	*Telephone:* + 34 93 368 05 10 *Facsimile:* + 34 93 238 47 43 *Email:* jjandujar@pedrosalagos.com
Sri Lanka	Nihal De Silva *B. R. de Silva & Co*	*Telephone:* + 94 11 451 0268 *Facsimile:* + 94 11 451 2404 *Email:* brds@eureka.lk
Sweden	Per-Åke Bois *Nexia Revision Stockholm*	*Telephone:* + 46 (8) 562 561 00 *Facsimile:* + 46 (8) 562 561 99 *Email:* perake.bois@nexia.se
	Karin Rosén *Revidentia HB*	*Telephone:* + 46 8 674 63 30 *Facsimile:* + 46 8 674 63 39 *Email:* karin.rosen@revidentia.a.se

Sweden –   Thomas Jönsson
continued   *Revisorsgruppen i Malmö AB*

Telephone: + 46 (40) 664 63 80
Facsimile: + 46 (40) 664 63 89
Email: thomas@revisorsgruppen.nu

Leif Bohman
Synneby Revisionsbyrå KB

Telephone: + 46 (31) 719 1700
Facsimile: + 46 (31) 162 780
Email: leif.bohman@synnebyrevision.se

Switzerland   Peter Moorhouse
Abacus Fiduciary (Suisse) SA

Telephone: + 41(0) 22 560 61 54
Facsimile: + 41(0) 22 560 60 60
Email: peter.moorhouse@abacusiom.com

Andreas Baumann
*ABT Treuhandgesellschaft Andreas
Baumann & Co*

Telephone: + 41 44 711 90 90
Facsimile: + 41 44 711 90 99
Email: andreas.baumann@abt.ch

Michel Queloz
Controlgest SA

Telephone: + 41 26 347 14 99
Facsimile: + 41 26 322 29 35
Email: controlgest@bluewin.ch

Fabrizio Biaggi
FIDI BC SA

Telephone: + 41 91 910 63 63
Facsimile: + 41 91 910 63 93
Email: fabrizio.biaggi@fidibc.com

Patrick Tritten
Fiduciaire Patrick TRITTEN

Telephone: + 41 22 342 27 01
Facsimile: + 41 22 342 27 21
Email: trittenfid@bluewin.ch

Roland Schaer
Firex Audit & Consulting SA

Telephone: + 41 22 908 01 50
Facsimile: + 41 22 908 01 51
Email: rschaer@firexaudit.ch

Michael Bächli
Internationale Treuhand AG (ITAG)

Telephone: + 41 61 319 51 51
Facsimile: + 41 61 319 52 52
Email: michael.baechli@itag.ch

Louis Oehri
LOPAG Louis Oehri & Partner Trust reg

Telephone: + 423 377 36 17
Facsimile: + 423 373 21 31
Email: lopag@lopag.li

Xavier Mo Costabella
Mo Costabella Pirkl Avocats

Telephone: + 41 22 317 79 90
Facsimile: + 41 22 317 79 91
Email: ppxmc@iurlex.ch

Dr. Paul Peyrot
Peyrot & Schlegel Law Office

Telephone: + 41 500 55 70
Facsimile: + 41 500 55 71
Email: paul.peyrot@peyrot-schlegel.ch

Roger Beggiato
ReviTrust Revision + Treuhand AG

Telephone: + 41 81 750 68 68
Facsimile: + 41 81 750 68 78
Email: roger.beggiato@revitrust.com

Andrew Cleeton
Saffery Champness (Suisse) S.A.

Telephone: + 41(0) 22 319 0978
Facsimile: + 41(0) 22 319 0977
Email: andrew.cleeton@saffery.ch

Taiwan   Cathy Wu
Nexia Sun Rise CPAs & Co

Telephone: + 886 (2) 2751 0306
Facsimile: + 886 (2) 2740 1817
Email: cathycpa@ms72.hinet.net

Richard Hung
Trans-Asia & Co

Telephone: + 886 7 281 1388
Facsimile: + 886 7 241 2236
Email: Service@tacpa.com.tw

Tanzania	Ibrahim Ituja *Paul Clem & Associates*	*Telephone:* + 255 22 2112 250 *Facsimile:* + 255 22 2131 443 *Email:* pclem@intafrica.com
Thailand	Prawat Tirakotai *V. A. T. Accounting*	*Telephone:* + 66 (2) 890 5894-99 *Facsimile:* + 66 (2) 890 5893 *Email:* vataudit@ksc.th.com
Tunisia	Mourad Abdelmoula *AFINCO*	*Telephone:* + 216 71 354 451 *Facsimile:* + 216 71 354 676 *Email:* afinco@afinco.net
	Faycal Derbel *Finor*	*Telephone:* + 216 (70) 728 450 *Facsimile:* + 216 (70) 728 405 *Email:* faycal.derbel@planet.tn
Turkey	Hayrullah Doğan *DENETIM Y.M.M. LTD.ŞTI, ISTANBUL*	*Telephone:* + 90 212 465 88 33 *Facsimile:* + 90 212 465 88 38 *Email:* hdogan@nexiadenetimturkey.com
	Tugrul Ozsut *Nexia Turkey – AS CPA & Auditing Co*	*Telephone:* + 90 (212) 225 68 78 *Facsimile:* + 90 (212) 225 62 52 *Email:* tozsut@nexiaturkey.com.tr
Ukraine	Roman Bilyk *Audit and Consulting Group DK-Ukraine*	*Telephone:* + 38 (044) 537 70 10 *Facsimile:* + 38 (044) 537 70 90 *Email:* rbilyk@dku.com.ua
	Iryna Kosarieva *K.A.C. Limited*	*Telephone:* + 38 (044) 569 1060 *Facsimile:* + 38 (044) 569 1061 *Email:* audit@kac.relc.com
	Andriy Kostyuk *Pavlenko, Statsenko & Osinchuk*	*Telephone:* + 38 (032) 298 97 97 *Facsimile:* + 38 (032) 298 97 96 *Email:* ak@pso.com.ua
United Arab Emirates	Shahab Haider *Sajjad Haider & Co*	*Telephone:* + 971 42 222126 *Facsimile:* + 971 42 238881 *Email:* shahab@sajjadhaider.com
	Dr. Oussama Ali Tabbara *Usamah Tabbarah & Company*	*Telephone:* + 971 (4) 321 1005 *Facsimile:* + 971 (4) 321 1050 *Email:* otabbara@utcnexia.com
United Kingdom	Pat Murray *Jones Peters*	*Telephone:* + 44 (0) 28 4062 5 ,27 *Facsimile:* + 44 (0) 28 4062 5 02 *Email:* pat.murray@jonespet⟨ ⟩s.co.uk
	Alasdair Imray *Meston Reid & Co*	*Telephone:* + 44 (0) 1224 ⟨ 25 554 *Facsimile:* + 44 (0) 1224 ⟨ 26 089 *Email:* imraya@mestonr⟨ d.com
	Mike Beattie *Saffery Champness*	*Telephone:* + 44 (0) 2⟨ 7841 4000 *Facsimile:* + 44 (0) 2⟨ 7841 4100 *Email:* mike.beattie⟨ saffery.com
	Jason Fayers *Scrutton Bland*	*Telephone:* + 44 (⟨) 1473 259 201 *Facsimile:* + 44 (⟨) 1473 231 643 *Email:* jason.fa⟨ ⟨rs@scruttonbland.co.uk
	Rajesh Sharma *Smith & Williamson*	*Telephone:* + ⟨4 (0) 20 7131 4181 *Facsimile:* + ⟨4 (0) 20 7131 4021 *Email:* rajes'⟨.sharma@smith.williamson.co.uk

United States	Pete Graham *Catrakilis & Company*	*Telephone:* + 1 770 495 9077 *Facsimile:* + 1 770 495 9013 *Email:* peteg@cpaofgeorgia.com
	Teri M Kaye *Friedman Cohen Taubman & Company*	*Telephone:* + 1 954 315 7100 *Facsimile:* + 1 954 315 7101 *Email:* terik@fctcpa.com
	Maureen O'Gara-Adford *Gish Seiden LLP*	*Telephone:* + 1 818 854 6100 *Facsimile:* + 1 818 854 6103 *Email:* mogara@gishseiden.com
	Richard D Jergenson *Hansen, Jergenson, Nergaard & Co, LLP*	*Telephone:* + 1 952 893 6740 *Facsimile:* + 1 952 896 3649 *Email:* dickj@hjnandco.com
	George A Ashman *Harb, Levy & Weiland LLP*	*Telephone:* + 1 (415) 974 6000 *Facsimile:* + 1 (415) 974 5488 *Email:* gashman@hlwcpa.com
	James Wall *J H Cohn LLP*	*Telephone:* + 1 973 228 3500 *Facsimile:* + 1 973 228 0330 *Email:* jwall@jhcohn.com
	Larry J Soldinger *L J Soldinger Associates*	*Telephone:* + 1 847 726 8100 *Facsimile:* + 1 847 726 6770 *Email:* solly@soldinger.com
	Lawrence J Chastang *LarsonAllen LLP*	*Telephone:* + 1 (407) 802 1200 *Facsimile:* + 1 (407) 802 1250 *Email:* lchastang@larsonallen.com
	Arthur Louie *Louie & Wong LLP*	*Telephone:* + 1 415 981 9999 *Facsimile:* + 1 415 989 9999 *Email:* alouie@louiewongcpa.com
	John C MacAlpine *MacAlpine, Carll & Company LLC*	*Telephone:* + 1 215 923 1101 *Facsimile:* + 1 215 923 9188 *Email:* jcm@macalpinecarll.com
	Wesley Middleton *Malone & Bailey, PC*	*Telephone:* + 1 713 343 4200 *Facsimile:* + 1 713 266 1815 *Email:* wmiddleton@malone-bailey.com
	Peter J Chudyk *Maloney + Novotny LLC*	*Telephone:* + 1 216 363 0100 *Facsimile:* + 1 216 363 0500 *Email:* pchudyk@maloneynovotny.com
	Ricky Max *Miller, Cooper & Co*	*Telephone:* + 1 847 205 5000 *Facsimile:* + 1 847 205 1400 *Email:* rmax@millercooper.com
	Lauren Carnes *O'Connor & Drew, PC*	*Telephone:* + 1 617 471 1120 *Facsimile:* + 1 617 472 7560 *Email:* lcarnes@ocd.com
	Deborah C Fallucca *Rehmann*	*Telephone:* + 1 (248) 952-5000 *Facsimile:* + 1 (248) 952-5750 *Email:* debbie.fallucca@rehmann.com
	John Jabouri *Schowalter & Jabouri, PC*	*Telephone:* + 1 314 842 2929 *Facsimile:* + 1 314 842 3483 *Email:* jjabouri@sjcpa.com
	Dick Lackey *Shannon & Associates, LLP*	*Telephone:* + 1 253 852 8500 *Facsimile:* + 1 253 852 0512 *Email:* rlackey@shannon-cpas.com

United States – *continued*	Leonard S Wolf *The Wolf Group*	*Telephone:* + 1 703 502 9500 *Facsimile:* + 1 703 502 3970 *Email:* l.wolf@thewolfgroup.com
	Toni M Mayfield *Whitley Penn LLP*	*Telephone:* + 1 214 393 9300 *Facsimile:* + 1 214 393 9301 *Email:* toni.mayfield@wpcpa.com
Uruguay	Diego Bonomi *Estudio Bonomi*	*Telephone:* + 598 2 915 1353 *Facsimile:* + 598 2 915 6819 *Email:* dbonomi@estudiobonomi.com
	Luis Rafael Normey *Normey – Peruzzo & Asociados*	*Telephone:* + 598 (2) 408 0114 *Facsimile:* + 598 (2) 401 3523 *Email:* rnormey@npyas-nexia.com.uy
Venezuela	Luis Cardona R *Cardona Avila Blanco y Asociados*	*Telephone:* + 58 (212) 992 5833 *Facsimile:* + 58 (212) 992 5333 *Email:* luis.cardona@nexia.com.ve
Vietnam	Khoi Hoang *NEXIA ACPA Auditing & Consulting Co Ltd*	*Telephone:* + 84 4 3755 6080 *Facsimile:* + 84 4 3755 6081 *Email:* hoang.khoi@nexiaacpa.com